Fysikinstitutionen Frescati
Frescativägen 24
104 05 STOCKHOLM

Neurocomputers

CHAPMAN & HALL NEURAL COMPUTING SERIES

Series editors:
Igor Aleksander, Imperial College, London, UK
Richard Mammone, Rutgers University, New Jersey, USA

Since the beginning of the current revival of interest in Neural Networks, the subject is reaching considerable maturity, while at the same time becoming of interest to people working in an increasing number of disciplines. This series seeks to address some of the specializations that are developing through the contributions of authoritative writers in the field. This series will address both specializations and applications of neural computing techniques to particular areas.

1. **Delay Learning in Artificial Neural Networks**
   Catherine Myers
2. **Analogue Neural VLSI**
   A pulse stream approach
   Alan Murray and Lionel Tarassenko
3. **Neurons and Symbols**
   The stuff that mind is made of
   Igor Aleksander and Helen Morton
4. **Artificial Neural Networks for Speech and Vision**
   Edited by Richard J. Mammone
5. **Neurocomputers**
   An overview of neural networks in VLSI
   Manfred Glesner and Werner Pöchmüller
6. **Artificial Neural Networks for Speech Analysis/Synthesis**
   Mazin G. Rahim

Neurocomputers

An overview of neural networks in VLSI

Manfred Glesner
Head of Department for Microelectronics

and

Werner Pöchmüller
Research Assistant

Institute of Computer Engineering
Darmstadt University of Technology
Darmstadt, Germany

CHAPMAN & HALL
London · Glasgow · Weinheim · New York · Tokyo · Melbourne · Madras

Published by Chapman & Hall, 2-6 Boundary Row, London SE1 8HN, UK

Chapman & Hall, 2-6 Boundary Row, London SE1 8HN, UK

Blackie Academic & Professional, Wester Cleddens Road, Bishopbriggs, Glasgow G64 2NZ, UK

Chapman & Hall GmbH, Pappelallee 3, 69469 Weinheim, Germany

Chapman & Hall USA, One Penn Plaza, 41st Floor, New York, NY10119, USA

Chapman & Hall Japan, ITP-Japan, Kyowa Building, 3F, 2-2-1 Hirakawacho, Chiyoda-ku, Tokyo 102, Japan

Chapman & Hall Australia, Thomas Nelson Australia, 102 Dodds Street, South Melbourne, Victoria 3205, Australia

Chapman & Hall India, R. Seshadri, 32 Second Main Road, CIT East, Madras 600 035, India

First edition 1994

© 1994 Manfred Glesner and Werner Pöchmüller

Printed in Great Britain at the University Press, Cambridge

ISBN   0 412 56390 8

Apart from any fair dealing for the purposes of research or private study, or criticism or review, as permitted under the UK Copyright Designs and Patents Act, 1988, this publication may not be reproduced, stored, or transmitted, in any form or by any means, without the prior permission in writing of the publishers, or in the case of reprographic reproduction only in accordance with the terms of the licences issued by the Copyright Licensing Agency in the UK, or in accordance with the terms of licences issued by the appropriate Reproduction Rights Organization outside the UK. Enquiries concerning reproduction outside the terms stated here should be sent to the publishers at the London address printed on this page.
    The publisher makes no representation, express or implied, with regard to the accuracy of the information contained in this book and cannot accept any legal responsibility or liability for any errors or omissions that may be made.

A catalogue record for this book is available from the British Library

Library of Congress Cataloging-in-publication available

∞ Printed on permanent acid-free text paper, manufactured in accordance with ANSI/NISO Z39.48-1992 and ANSI/NISO Z39.48-1984 (Permanence of Paper).

Contents

Preface		ix
1 Introduction		**1**
1.1	Why Neural Information Processing?	1
1.2	Dedicated Neural Network Hardware	3
1.3	About this Book	4
1.4	Source of Material	6
2 Categorization of Neural Network Hardware		**11**
2.1	Neural Network Type	11
2.2	Biological Evidence	12
2.3	Implementation Technology	16
2.4	Chip Cascadability	23
2.5	Network Mapping on Processing Elements	27
2.6	Flexibility	31
2.7	Summary	34
3 Nervous Systems and their Simulation		**37**
3.1	Neural Network Basic Building Blocks	37
3.2	Artificial Neural Networks	39
3.3	Summary	54
4 Digital VLSI Building Blocks		**55**
4.1	Introduction	55
4.2	Summation	56
4.3	Multiplication	60
4.4	Nonlinearities	62
4.5	Storage Elements	64

4.6	Other Elements	65
4.7	Summary	66

5 Analog Building Blocks   67
   5.1   Introduction   67
   5.2   Summation   68
   5.3   Multiplication   73
   5.4   Analog Storage Elements   90
   5.5   Nonlinear Elements   100
   5.6   Other Elements   103
   5.7   Summary   107

6 Optoelectronic and Optical Building Blocks   109
   6.1   Introduction   109
   6.2   Summation   110
   6.3   Multiplication   110
   6.4   Nonlinearities   112
   6.5   Weight Storage and other Tasks   112
   6.6   Summary   113

7 Digital Neurocomputers   115
   7.1   Introduction   115
   7.2   Sequential Computers   117
   7.3   Digital Signal Processor Arrays   119
   7.4   Transputer Networks   125
   7.5   RISC Arrays   128
   7.6   SIMD Arrays and Systolic Arrays   134
   7.7   Slice Architectures   166
   7.8   Weightless Neural Networks   177
   7.9   Wafer Scale Implementations   180
   7.10 Summary   188

8 Analog and Mixed Analog/Digital Neurocomputers   191
   8.1   Introduction   191
   8.2   Artificial Networks near to Biology   192
   8.3   Cellular Neural Networks   210
   8.4   Early NMOS and CMOS Hopfield Network Implementations   213
   8.5   Network Implementations based on Amorphous Silicon   220
   8.6   CCD and Floating-Gate Implementations   225
   8.7   CMOS Networks with Programmable Weights   230
   8.8   Pulse Stream Networks   243
   8.9   Summary   247

9	**Optoelectronic and Optical Neurocomputers**	**249**
	9.1 Introduction	249
	9.2 Optoelectronic Implementations	249
	9.3 Optical Implementations	255
	9.4 Summary	257

References   **259**

Index   **275**

Preface

Objectives of the Book

Our primary objective in presenting this book is to give an introduction to and an overview of the hot topic of neurocomputers to the interested audience. We do not therefore intend to concentrate on certain aspects of electronic realizations, or on our own research topics pursued during the last few years. Electronic neural networks underwent such an impetuous development during the 1980s and early 1990s, caused by the simultaneous and speedy development of neural algorithms and microelectronics, that it was possible to follow new approaches only by reading large numbers of conference proceedings and journals. At that time, many partners in our national and international research projects who were not directly involved in research on dedicated neural network hardware asked us for information and assistance on that topic. This thirst for knowledge induced us to write a book which is easy to read but covers all important aspects of electronic neural network hardware. The book will also help neural network users with practical information on available hardware, and it therefore covers most commercial products and tries to give performance and cost indications whenever obtainable.

On the one hand, the target group of this book is neural network users interested in using neurocomputers for high speed performance. They will find a wide range of dedicated hardware that is used to simulate or emulate neural networks. All principal design styles and many architectures are described in detail, and considered for both their advantages and disadvantages. Readers will be able to decide whether their problem can be solved by existing hardware, and to find those approaches which are most suitable for his purposes. On the other hand, this book is suitable as an introduction for students who plan to do some work in the area of neural network hardware, or to anyone who has some knowledge of neural network algorithms and who is interested in their electronic realization. There is always a trade-off between depth and breadth in such a project, and for the sake of readability we decided on more breadth. To get more information on certain approaches, readers are recommended to deepen their studies by reading the referenced material, or a book from the neurocomputing series of Chapman & Hall and other publishers that concentrate on the relevant topic.

Contents

This book gives an overview on all major electronic design styles and architectures dedicated to the simulation or emulation of neural networks. We do not know of any book currently on the market that covers the topic of neurocomputers in such breadth. Basic neural algorithms are covered with a view towards their implementability, as well as basic digital and analog building blocks, up to neurocomputer concepts developed by universities, research labs and industry. This presentation is completed with a small view beyond pure electronic implementations to optoelectronic and optical neurocomputing.

The amount of documentation on each neurocomputer in this work is often dictated by the availability of information, and is therefore not related to the significance of their designers. Throughout the world many researchers are working on that area, so it was impossible for us to mention every relevant person in the book. What we tried to do was make a representative selection of as many design styles as possible. We cannot take any responsibility for the correctness of speed figures and costs given throughout the book; they are taken from publications publicly available, and could not be proved or are subject to significant changes over time. However, references to the sources are given, enabling interested readers to ask for more up-to-date information.

Material Origin

Many sources served to deliver the material needed to assemble a book on state-of-the-art neurocomputing. Most important were international conference proceedings and journals from the last few years. From many national and international research projects we saw the need for broad information on dedicated neural network hardware. Part of the material was taught in industrial seminars, tutorials and graduate education programs at Darmstadt University of Technology. For us this need for information culminated in preparing the study "Neurocomputers" within ESPRIT project 2092 "ANNIE" (Applications of Neural Networks for Industry in Europe). All that material and teaching experience went into this book. Much time and additional work has been spent on the topic since the publication of the ANNIE study. To make this work more readable for non-experts and students, we have restructured chapters and sections, and included important historical approaches which had been omitted as well as new approaches that emerged during 1992 and the beginning of 1993. Furthermore, we have added a chapter on neural algorithms.

Acknowledgements

We acknowledge the contribution of the CEC by its support within ESPRIT project 2092 "ANNIE". We would like to thank the reviewers of the ANNIE project, Dr. Simon Garth and Dr. Robert Linggard, who strongly encouraged us to move towards a book publication.

Since so much work had to be done in preparing all the necessary material available from many conference proceedings, books and magazines, we relied on the help of colleagues and students in our institute. We would like to thank Mr. Saman Kumara Halgamuge who prepared most of the material dealing with analog circuitry, and contributed to this work by writing parts on analog neurocomputers. Mr. Andreas König collected material for the parts on optoelectronic and optical realizations. A first selection of papers and categorization of material was done by Mr. Arnaud Laprevote. Our special thanks go to Mr. Andreas Pabst and Mrs. Ling Chen who prepared many of the drawings that will be found in the book.

Manfred Glesner   Werner Pöchmüller

Darmstadt University of Technology
Institute for Microelectronic Systems
Karlstrasse 15
D-64283 Darmstadt, Germany

1
Introduction

1.1 Why Neural Information Processing?

In many applications classical information processing systems are facing virtually insurmountable problems. Due to sequential data processing, even using modern technology in the form of fast and complex VLSI (Very Large Scale Integration) circuits, only a limited data processing speed can be achieved. For example, in many image processing tasks, there is usually such an amount of data to be processed that sequential systems will not be able to cope with it within the requested short time slots. Another example of an application area where sequential systems are showing insufficient performance is the supervision of fast and complex processes. In such processes, a large amount of data provided by many sensors has to be processed in a very short time.

Figure 1.1 depicts the expected future development of CMOS technology. One can see that the clock frequency of systems and the complexity of single chips may not increase unchecked, thus restricting the maximum performance of sequential computers. Sufficient computational power for time consuming tasks can only be provided by parallel systems, but parallel systems often cause the problem of job sharing and how to handle communication between concurrently working processors. Neural networks seem to provide a successful alternative approach to solve these problems [Cro92]. Such a network consists of a large number of tightly connected, but very simple "processors". As a result of massive parallelism, an enormous computational power may be realized. Compared with classical parallel structures, there is no need to create a special job sharing or communication control between processing elements. This is a very important prerequisite to exploit existing parallelism through dedicated hardware.

Another very interesting neural network property is the ability to learn from sample data. Thus, it is not necessary to develop complex software with all the inherent possibilities for the inclusion of "bugs". Neural networks allow us to create a data processing system by simply training it

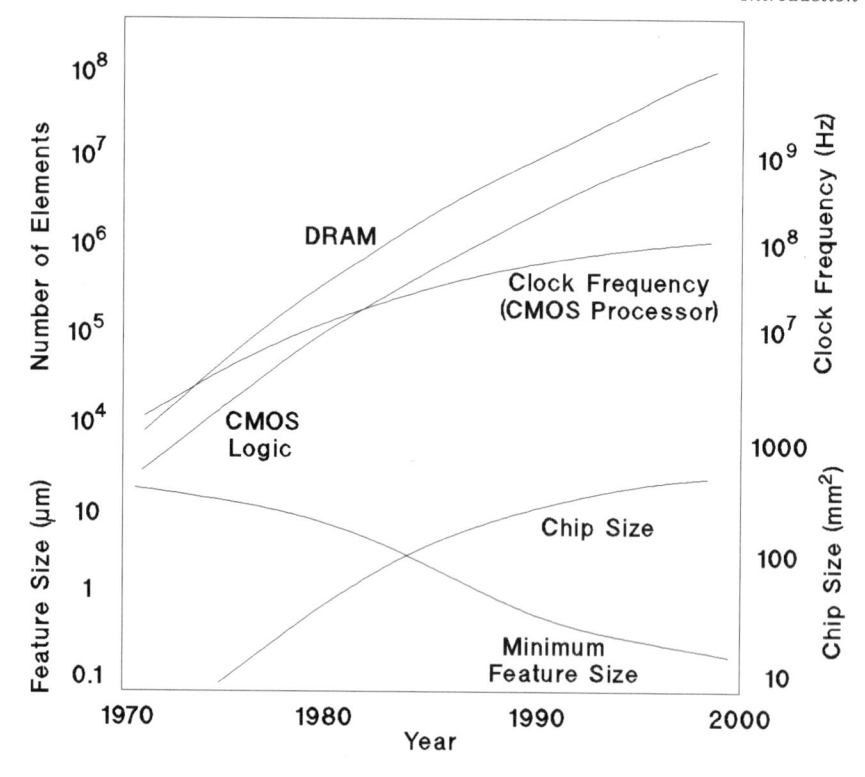

Figure 1.1 *CMOS technology trends (adapted from [Iwa90])*

with special training data. Furthermore, this property allows extremely fast prototyping.

However, there are not only advantages to neural network technology. Data processing is a crucial point in determining the performance of a neural network based system. It is naive to believe that using a network large enough with the right learning algorithm will be sufficient to solve any problem. Very often, dedicated data preprocessing with sufficient data reduction is absolutely necessary to enable a subsequent network block to give a reasonable performance. A disadvantage of network simulations on sequential computers is that, due to the large number of computations in particular during the learning phase, they are too slow for real-time applications and for extensive investigations during prototyping. Even with fast parallel hardware there are speed problems, now in the data preprocessing part. Thus it may also become necessary to parallelize preprocessing.

Furthermore, training vectors, presented to the system during learning, have a significant influence on later network performance. Therefore, choosing an appropriate set of training vectors is essential. One aspect of a "good" training set is that it must cover the whole event space. Frequently, this is a non-trivial task. For example, if data is taken from a running process the situation can occur where only one data type is available in sufficient supply (good specimen), whereas another type rarely occurs (bad specimen showing a rare, special type of fault). Training a network with such a data set may result in a modest performance.

Nevertheless, neural networks are demonstrating capabilities which make them very promising for application areas where conventional techniques do not perform well.

1.2 Dedicated Neural Network Hardware

Today, for investigation purposes and prototype development, neural networks are usually simulated on sequential computers. Unfortunately, even intrinsically parallel algorithms and systems may be simulated sequentially on a conventional computer by sequentializing parallel events. However, to benefit from the parallelism innate to neural systems, it is necessary to map them onto parallel hardware devices.

The roots of artificial neural network research go back to the 1940s and 1950s. Even at that early time, the hardware emulation of artificial neural networks was intriguing enough to warrant spending the effort on a realization using tubes and mechanical devices. Probably the first neural network emulation machine (neurocomputer) was built by Dean Edmonds and Marvin Minsky in 1951 [Ber81]. Edmonds and Minsky used 300 tubes and automatic electric clutches to adjust 40 control knobs (representing synaptic weights). During learning, the machine used the clutches to adjust its own knobs. This early neurocomputer actually worked. Even faults in the 300 tubes or thousands of manually soldered connections did not matter due to the fault tolerance inherent to neural systems.

Today, the semiconductor industry is able to provide technologies for the implementation of millions of transistors on a single chip. Thus, state-of-the-art VLSI technology and future ULSI (Ultra Large Scale Integration) technologies are, and will be, a good implementation medium for artificial neural circuits. This fact, together with the development of new important network types and learning algorithms especially during the mid-1980s, caused a breakthrough in artificial neural network technology. Since that time, a lot of research has been done world-wide, and the first commercial neural network products are now emerging. These products include various software packages as well as some dedicated artificial neural network simulation hardware. Also, the first neural network systems are being used in industrial applications. Modern VLSI technology can bring a speed factor of 100-1000 by using digital circuitry, and a speed factor of 10000 and more by using analog circuitry compared with simulations on a sequential computer. Even more computational power may be obtained by using optical technology or optoelectronic circuitry. Optical technologies are especially interesting for coping with the large number of network connections. This is because light beams can cross without affecting each other. The use of optoelectronics leads to some efficient and handsome small implementations, but holographic optical computers are still restricted to large devices in laboratories. In the near future, only optoelectronic realizations will become of commercial interest. Figure 1.2 shows a crude comparison of the computational potential of different neural network hardware technologies. The performance of some biological networks is compared against artificial realizations. Biological networks consist of neurons operating at a "switching" speed of about 100 Hertz. They obtain their computational power from an immense parallelism and sophisticated topology. Still, there is a large potential for future developments of artificial neural hardware.

1.3 About this Book

The topic of this book is neurocomputers. In the following, a neurocomputer will be defined as any piece of parallel hardware dedicated to simulating

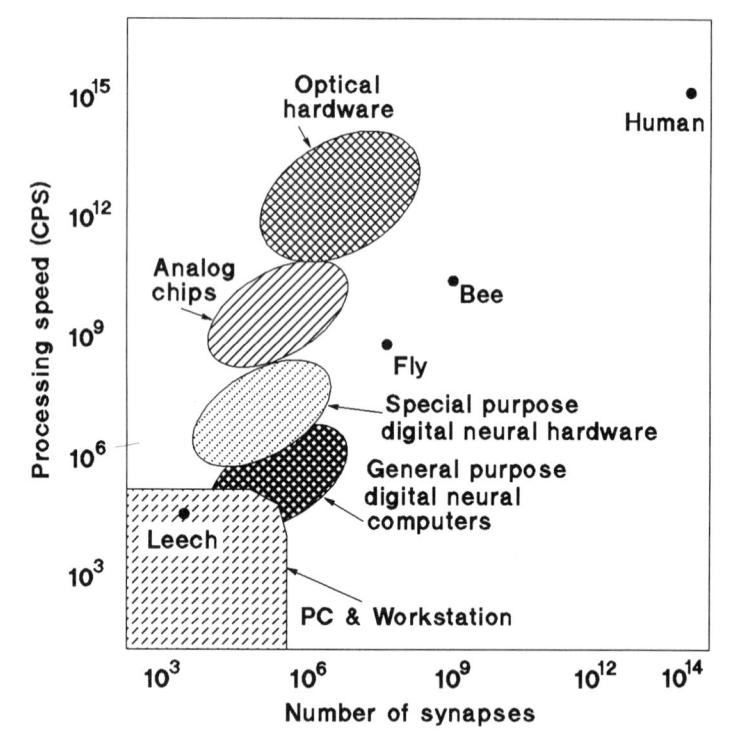

Figure 1.2 *Comparison of different neural network hardware technologies (adapted from [Iwa90])*

one or a variety of artificial neural algorithms. Hence, a neurocomputer does not necessarily have to be a copy of a completely understood biological nervous system. Even dedicated parallel hardware for simulating algorithms which are just inspired by biology to a certain degree will be termed "neurocomputers". Thus, parallel machines constructed to run a backpropagation algorithm or the Boltzmann machine algorithm, which are based on only a little or no biological evidence at all, because of the use of mathematical techniques such as gradient descent or simulated annealing, belong to the class of neurocomputers. During the last few years, a large variety of dedicated neural network hardware implementations have emerged in universities, research laboratories and industry. The approaches are very diverse, ranging from the first analog implementations of Hopfield type networks at the beginning of the 1980s through to more or less complex digital circuits, and up to state-of-the-art digital systolic and SIMD arrays or programmable analog architectures based on EEPROM or MNOS (Metal Nitride Oxide Semiconductor) and CCD (Charge Coupled Device) technology. Moreover, neurocomputing is not restricted to modern microelectronics as the implementation medium. Optoelectronics and purely optical circuitry show some interesting features for the implementation of highly parallel systems. All these hardware implementations have different properties with respect to their speed (degree of parallelism), accuracy of computation, learning support, cascadability, flexibility and cost. The aim of this book is to discuss several aspects of dedicated neural network hardware.

Chapter 2 serves to provide and explain some criteria which help to categorize neural network hardware approaches. Thus, the criteria of biological evidence, implementation technology, cascadability, mapping of network onto physical hardware and flexibility will be considered.

The basic idea of neurocomputing is to take advantage of existing knowledge on the operation of nervous systems. A large number of rather simple and slow processing elements show remarkable capabilities that emerge from a collective operation. Some basic elements of nervous systems and the formulation of abstract mathematical algorithms from this knowledge are discussed in Chapter 3.

Chapters 4, 5 and 6 provide the reader with some background knowledge on the realization of neural network building blocks. Building blocks are the basic computational entities that are necessary to form a neural network or to run artificial neural network algorithms. In this chapter, basic building blocks for summation (modification of neuron potential), multiplication (synaptic weighting), nonlinearities (nonlinear behavior of neuron output), information storage (synaptic weight storage) and some other elements which are specifically required by certain algorithms will be described. This description is separated into three parts: digital building blocks (Chapter 4); analog building blocks (Chapter 5); and optoelectronic/optical building blocks (Chapter 6).

An overview of existing hardware implementations and proposed architectures is given in Chapters 7, 8 and 9. Of course, it is not possible to mention every architecture or even every piece of silicon which has been developed to simulate neural algorithms, since too many architecture proposals and prototype implementations have been proposed, especially in recent years. However, the aim of these chapters is to cover commercial products as well as very powerful and important architectures and implementations. Most of the design styles and implementation technologies will be presented by mentioning at least one prototype implementation to give readers an impression of what is possible with state-of-the-art technology. Therefore, architectures are not just described but also assessed for their power, flexibility and cost. Digital architectures and implementations ranging from the simple sequential von Neumann machine (conventional computer) through to general purpose parallel computers and up to dedicated multi-processor neurocomputers are dealt with in Chapter 7. Chapter 8 is dedicated to analog and mixed digital/analog designs, whereas optoelectronic and optical solutions are considered in Chapter 9.

Readers with a profound background knowledge on neural networks and VLSI technology will concentrate more on the last three chapters, which give an overview on existing neurocomputer realizations, whereas the novice will first concentrate on Chapters 2, 3, 4, 5 and 6 to become familiar with some important basics.

1.4 Source of Material

As mentioned in the preface, neural network hardware has undergone a rapid development during the last few years. If a research area is still much in flux, conference proceedings and journals are the first source of information. As may be seen from the papers referenced, the contents of this book are based significantly on these sources. Those important conferences we relied on are:

International Conference on Neural Networks, San Diego, U.S.A., June 1987
Conference on Neural Information Processing Systems, Denver, U.S.A., November 1987
International Conference on Neural Networks, San Diego, U.S.A., June 1988
nNeuro'88, Paris, France, June 1988
Neuro Nimes 88, Nimes, France, November 1988
International Workshop on VLSI for Artificial Intelligence, Oxford, U.K., July 1988

Journée D'Électronique: Artificial Neural Networks, Lausanne, Switzerland, October 1989
Neuro Nimes 89, Nimes, France, November 1989
International Joint Conference on Neural Networks, Washington, U.S.A., January 1990
International Conference on Parallel Processing in Neural Systems and Computers, Düsseldorf, Germany, 1990
International Joint Conference on Neural Networks, San Diego, U.S.A., June 1990
First International Workshop on Microelectronics for Neural Networks, Dortmund, Germany, June 1990
International Neural Network Conference, Paris, France, July 1990
International Workshop on VLSI for Artificial Intelligence and Neural Networks, Oxford, U.K., September 1990
Neuro Nimes 90, Nimes, France, November 1990
International Conference on Artificial Neural Networks, Espoo, Finland, June 1991
International Joint Conference on Neural Networks, Seattle, U.S.A., July 1991
Second International Conference on Microelectronics for Neural Networks, Munich, Germany, October 1991
International Joint Conference on Neural Networks, Singapore, November 1991
Neuro Nimes 91, Nimes, France, November 1991
International Joint Conference on Neural Networks, Baltimore, U.S.A., June 1992
International Workshop on VLSI for Neural Networks and Artificial Intelligence, Oxford, U.K., September 1992
International Conference on Artificial Neural Networks, Brighton, U.K., September 1992
Neuro Nimes 92, Nimes, France, November 1992
International Joint Conference on Neural Networks, Beijing, China, November 1992
International Conference on Neural Networks, San Francisco, U.S.A., March and April 1993

Additional material was taken from numerous conferences on microelectronics which are not mentioned here. The important journals we used are:

Neural Networks, Pergamon Press
Neural Computation, MIT Press
IEEE Transactions on Neural Networks, Institute of Electrical and Electronics Engineers (IEEE)
Biological Cybernetics, Springer

One can find many different notations when reading publications on neural networks. In this book the following very common notations and abbreviations will be used:

Notation

α	learning rate
a_i	activation level of neuron i
β	weight decay rate
i_j, x_j	j-th network input
I_0	constant current
I_D	drain current
I_{Dsat}	MOS transistor saturation current
k	Boltzmann constant
o_i	output value of neuron i
q	elementary charge unit
Θ_i	threshold value of neuron i
T	temperature
T_{ij}	ternary weight from neuron j to neuron i
V_{CC}, V_{DD}, V_{ee}	constant supply voltages
V_{DS}	drain-to-source voltage
V_{GD}	gate-to-drain voltage
V_{GS}	gate-to-source voltage
V_T	MOS transistor cut-off voltage
V_{th}	thermal voltage $V_{th} = \frac{k \cdot T}{q}$
w_{ij}	synaptic connection from neuron j (emitter) to neuron i (receiver)
x_j	j-th network input

Abbreviations

ALU	Arithmetic Logic Unit
ASIC	Application Specific Integrated Circuit
CCD	Charge Coupled Device
CISC	Complex Instruction Set Computer
CMOS	Complementary Metal Oxide Semiconductor
CPG	Central Pattern Generator
CPS	Connections Per Second
CUPS	Connection Updates Per Second
DSP	Digital Signal Processor

ECL	Emitter Coupled Logic
EEPROM	Electrically Erasable Programmable Read Only Memory
EPROM	Electrically Programmable Read Only Memory
FAMOS	Floating Gate Avalanche Injection Metal Oxide Semiconductor
FIFO	First In First Out memory
LED	Light Emitting Diode
LVQ	Learning Vector Quantization
MIMD	Multiple Instruction Multiple Data
MNOS	Metal Nitride Oxide Semiconductor
MOS	Metal Oxide Semiconductor
MPX	Multiplexer
NMOS	N-Channel Metal Oxide Semiconductor
PD	Photo Detector
PE	Processing Element
PGC	Pulse Generating Circuit
PLN	Probabilistic Logic Node
PMOS	P-Channel Metal Oxide Semiconductor
PN	Processing Node
PNN	Probabilistic Neural Network
PU	Processing Unit
RAM	Random Access Memory
RBF	Radial Basis Function
RCE	Restricted Coulomb Energy
RISC	Reduced Instruction Set Computer
ROM	Read Only Memory
SIMD	Single Instruction Multiple Data
SLM	Spatial Light Modulator
SOFM	Self-Organizing Feature Map
ULSI	Ultra Large Scale Integration
UV	Ultra Violet
VLSI	Very Large Scale Integration

2

Categorization of Neural Network Hardware

During the last few years a large variety of very different approaches to neural network hardware have been developed. These approaches range from simple von Neumann machines without and with coprocessor and acceleration boards through parallel digital machines such as multi digital signal processor solutions, transputer networks, SIMD arrays, systolic arrays and dedicated analog hardware (special neurochips) to optical systems. Before describing such a vast range of different solutions, first it is necessary to find relevant criteria for a categorization. These criteria may be:

- type of network to be realized
- biological evidence of realization
- implementation technology
- cascadability
- mapping of network on processing elements
- flexibility.

In the following, each of the criteria will be discussed in terms of its suitability for the categorization of neural network hardware. Some suitable categorization schemes have been applied to structure network descriptions in subsequent parts of the book.

2.1 Neural Network Type

A large number of different neural networks and algorithms have been developed within the last decade. Some important and well known networks are:

- Hopfield networks
- multilayer Perceptron with backpropagation algorithm
- Kohonen feature map
- learning vector quantization (LVQ)

- associative memories
- ART networks
- counterpropagation networks
- Boltzmann machine.

More networks exist, as well as numerous derivatives of those mentioned above, which differ more or less in network topology, training schedule and parameters.

From the viewpoint of a neural network hardware designer or user, however, neural network types and algorithms are not particularly well suited for a classification of hardware platforms. This is especially applicable to flexible neurocomputer systems. Most of the digital VLSI implementations and nearly all commercial products are such flexible platforms, which permit the simulation of several varieties of a neural algorithm, or even completely different algorithms. Hence, they may not be categorized and distinguished by different types of network algorithm.

2.2 Biological Evidence

One possibility for categorizing neural network hardware is using biological evidence as the categorization criterion, as done by Przytula [Prz88]. He distinguishes between:

- neural networks mimicking biological neural systems
- neural networks on a somewhat higher level, e.g. early vision functions such as edge detection and others (these approaches also using an existing understanding of biological systems)
- neural networks inspired by biological evidence to a lesser degree.

Thus, the task a network is doing and its organization are considered, rather than its physical implementation and its basic building blocks. Pulse stream implementations do not belong to networks mimicking biological systems or performing biological functions on a higher level. Of course, pulse stream chips work with current and voltage pulses which seem to be similar to biological cells, but this is done to implement asynchronous analog circuits by means of a digital CMOS technology to combine their respective advantages [Mur89a]. Thus, pulse stream architectures are neither mimicking biological networks nor performing biological functions at a somewhat higher level.

2.2.1 Neural Networks Mimicking Biological Neural Systems

Without doubt, in this category one will find designs such as, for example, the silicon retina [Mead89] and electronic cochlea [Lyo88a] from

Biological Evidence

Carver Mead and his group. With that work they were systematically trying to design VLSI devices to act as sensory systems. It is characteristic of designs mimicking biological neural systems that the circuitry is modeled as closely as possible to the structures of mammalian sensory systems. Extensive knowledge of biological systems is necessary to carry out such designs. Since the organization of a mammalian brain, especially those regions responsible for complex functions, is still rather obscure compared with the receptive neural networks responsible for the perception of signals and early data preprocessing, designs are concentrating on receptive networks like the retina or cochlea (to be used as the first stage of an artificial auditory system). The task of these networks is to receive signals from the environment; however, they are also excellent information processing devices [Siv87]. In the retina of primates, most cells respond strongly to moving objects and weakly to stationary ones. Furthermore, there are lateral inhibitions which enhance contrast and provide gain control. There also exist horizontal cells providing lateral conductances to average signal values in the neighborhood. Figure 2.1 shows a receptor (R) array interconnected by a network consisting of resistors (RET30 design [Siv87]). Due to a sophisticated interconnection scheme of simple elements, such a network is not just a receptive system but also an important processing system for early data preprocessing. Another class of biological neural circuits are central pattern generators (CPGs) [Coh88]. Central pattern generators are relatively small, specialized circuits that contain only a few neurons. They generate rhythmic patterns of activity which drive motor behavior in animals. Such rhythmic patterns are generated by a CPG whenever it receives an action potential as its input. Figure 2.2 gives an example of a CPG generated pattern (output from PD and LP cells in the lobster stomatogastric ganglion [Mille85]).

In sum, it is characteristic of network designs mimicking biological systems to be direct implementations of biological neural networks. The designer is striving to implement each neural cell, each connection, by means of appropriate artificial elements.

2.2.2 Neural Networks on a Somewhat Higher Level

Networks of this type are designed to realize low-level neural functions. These implementations share their massive parallelism, high interconnectivity, fault tolerance, absence of a global clock and non-discrete analog computation with biological systems [Prz88]. Neural networks belonging to this group have (in common with artificial networks mimicking biological systems) no learning algorithms, and analog technology is used for their implementation in most cases. However, they are not an artificial hardware equivalent of a biological network. An example for such a network implementation is a motion detection system proposed by Hutchinson *et*

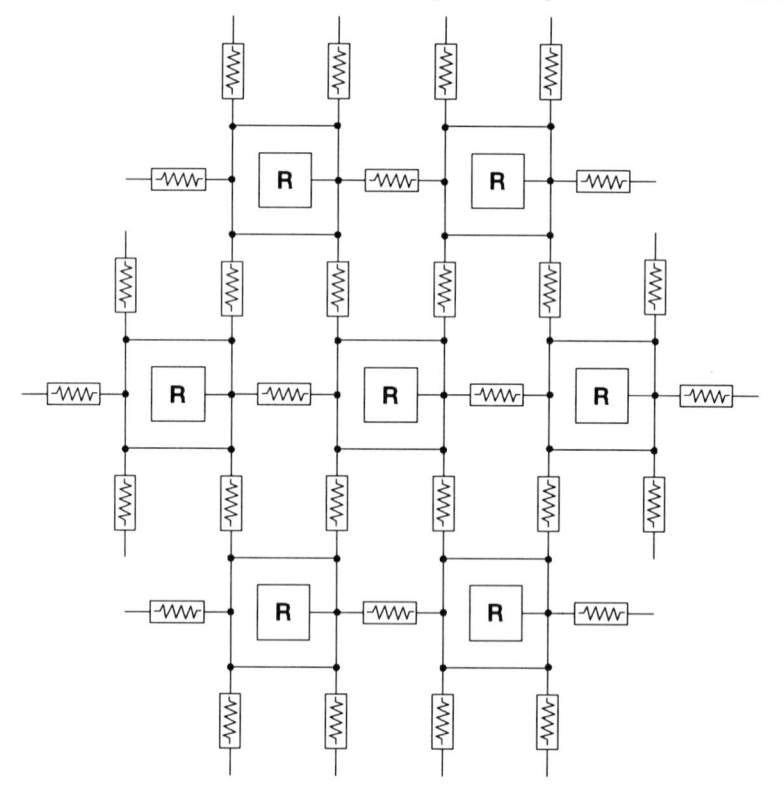

Figure 2.1 *Lateral conductances (adapted from [Siv87])*

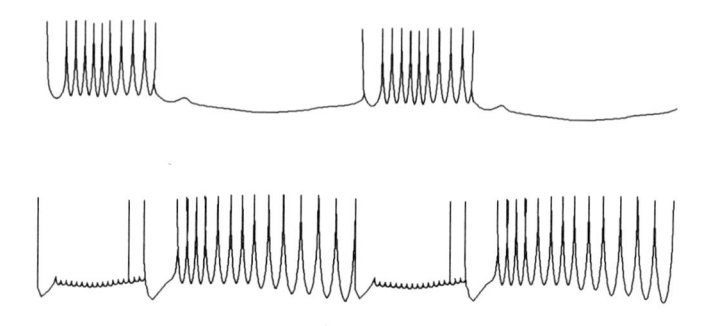

Figure 2.2 *Central pattern generator output (adapted from [Ryc89])*

al. [Hut88]. They designed a circuit as a CMOS resistive network with transistors operating in a subthreshold range to implement adjustable resistors. Other very interesting work was done by L.O. Chua and his group

[Chu88a, Chu88b]. Networks performing biological functions on a somewhat higher level are, for example:

- edge detection neural networks
- corner detection neural networks
- noise removal neural networks
- motion detection neural networks
- transform image coding neural networks.

A big problem in designing such networks is that, on the one hand, networks are on such a low level that programming or learning algorithms do not exist, and on the other hand, they are performing biological functions on a higher level, which makes it nearly impossible to benefit from biological examples since state-of-the-art knowledge on them is rather poor. The designer has full responsibility to find an appropriate network topology and synaptic weight values. However, some designs and chips do exist [Chu88a].

2.2.3 Networks Inspired by Biological Evidence to a Lesser Degree

This group includes all networks which share no more with biological neural networks than some basic principles. These principles are simple processing elements (which are usually summing weighted inputs and performing a nonlinear operation on that sum) and a tight interconnection between processing elements. However, techniques like the gradient descent method [Rum86] and simulated annealing [Aar89] are involved in the mathematics of these network models, which have no biological evidence at all. Networks are designed not to copy nervous systems but to form extremely fast, parallel signal processing systems. Characteristic of this group of networks is that more or less sophisticated programming and learning algorithms exist to find appropriate synaptic weights to solve a desired task. Recent research work has even led to algorithms that build up or change a network's topology. Networks usually applied to technical problems belong to this class of less biological but more mathematically oriented networks. Due to sophisticated learning algorithms, many of them may be applied to problems which request complex reasoning, whereas networks of the two previously described classes perform rather simple, early data preprocessing tasks. Well known representatives of more mathematically-oriented networks are, for example, the multilayer Perceptron with backpropagation algorithm [Rum86] and the Boltzmann machine [Hin84, Der84].

The three classes based on a distinction of biological evidence, as depicted in Figure 2.3, are well suited for a first classification of neural network hardware. However, this criterion (biological evidence) is not sufficient from the viewpoint of a neural network user. All the networks interesting for state-of-the-art technical application purposes belong to the third class. Networks

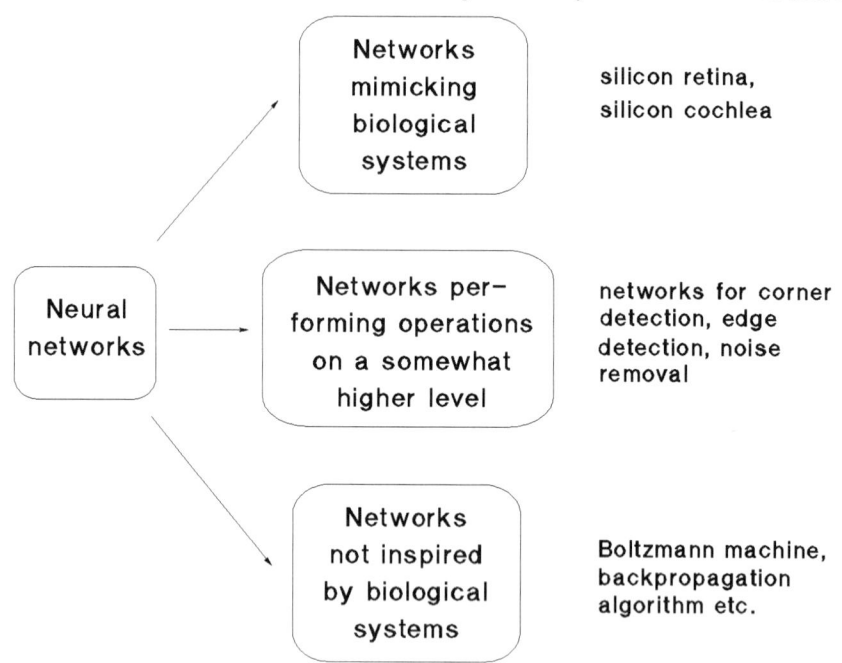

```
                    ┌─────────────┐
                    │  Networks   │
                    │  mimicking  │     silicon retina,
                    │  biological │     silicon cochlea
                    │   systems   │
                    └─────────────┘
                   ╱
                  ╱
┌──────────┐    ┌─────────────┐
│  Neural  │    │ Networks per-│    networks for corner
│ networks │───▶│forming operations│  detection, edge
│          │    │ on a somewhat│    detection, noise
└──────────┘    │ higher level │    removal
                └─────────────┘
                  ╲
                   ╲
                    ┌─────────────┐
                    │  Networks   │
                    │ not inspired│    Boltzmann machine,
                    │ by biological│   backpropagation
                    │   systems   │    algorithm etc.
                    └─────────────┘
```

Figure 2.3 *Classification of networks according to their biological evidence*

of the first two classes are usually fabricated on one chip, and are too small for industrial applications. The implementation medium for most of them is analog VLSI technology. They are used to investigate existing knowledge of biological systems. Therefore, additional classification criteria are necessary to classify the vast area of neural network realizations belonging to the latter class.

2.3 Implementation Technology

Neural networks consist of very simple elements, which are processing elements (neurons) and connecting elements (synapses). In general, the task of a processing element is to sum up arriving signals and to perform a non-linear threshold operation on the sum, whereas a connecting element has to weight an arriving signal with a simple multiplication. However, summations, multiplications and threshold operations may be performed with many different technical elements. For example, by exploiting Ohm's law, one may perform a weighting operation or multiplication with a simple resistor. Voltage V at the resistor is proportional to branch current I through the resistor branch, with resistance R as the proportionality factor. Using a potentiometer one may realize an adaptive synaptic weight. Amplifiers operating outside their linear range may serve as nonlinearities. Such a system was realized by D. Edmonds and M. Minsky [Ber81], as mentioned in Chapter 1.

However, a machine constructed from potentiometers, motors, amplifiers and clutches would never be able to simulate or emulate a network suitable for technical applications. Networks of a reasonable size comprise at least several tens or hundreds of neurons, together with thousands of synapses. The large number of synapses and connections in particular cause implementation problems. Two promising areas of technology for the implementation of rather large networks are VLSI and optical technology. Implementation with VLSI circuits is state-of-the-art, whereas usable optical implementations are not expected within the next years. A very attractive feature of optical implementations is the fact that an extremely dense storage of weights may be achieved. Furthermore, the interconnection problem may easily be solved by means of light beams which do not interfere with each other. Many problems still have to be solved, though, before a first competitive optical implementation of a neural network will become available.

2.3.1 VLSI Technology

Very Large Scale Integration (VLSI) is a technology which has been mature for many years, and allows us to implement a large number of electronic elements on a small area of silicon. State-of-the-art mask technology (optical lithography) allows the fabrication of structures of a size of less than 1μm, permitting the implementation of up to several million transistors per chip. With a further decrease of feature size by means of X-ray and E-beam lithography (feature size down to 0.1μm), ULSI (Ultra Large Scale Integration) chips will be made available. This trend is sketched in Figure 2.4 [McC91, McC90]. Problems which go along with such a trend from the viewpoint of the manufacturer are, first, the large number of faults which may occur in large circuits. This again is an aspect that makes neural networks a promising future technology due to their inherent fault tolerance. Unfortunately, silicon technology forces the designer to implement circuits on a two-dimensional plane with few available layers. However, in a brain, neurons (processing elements) are arranged in a three-dimensional space, offering many possibilities for interconnection. On a chip, neurons and synaptic interconnections have to be arranged on a two-dimensional area, which will be the most severe limitation for the implementation of large networks. Another strong limitation is the number of available pins to get information on and off the chip. Even if fully cascadable architectures are used, this will be a limitation (see the section on cascadability). Principally, two different styles of VLSI design (digital design and analog design) are possible, which will be commented on in subsequent sections.

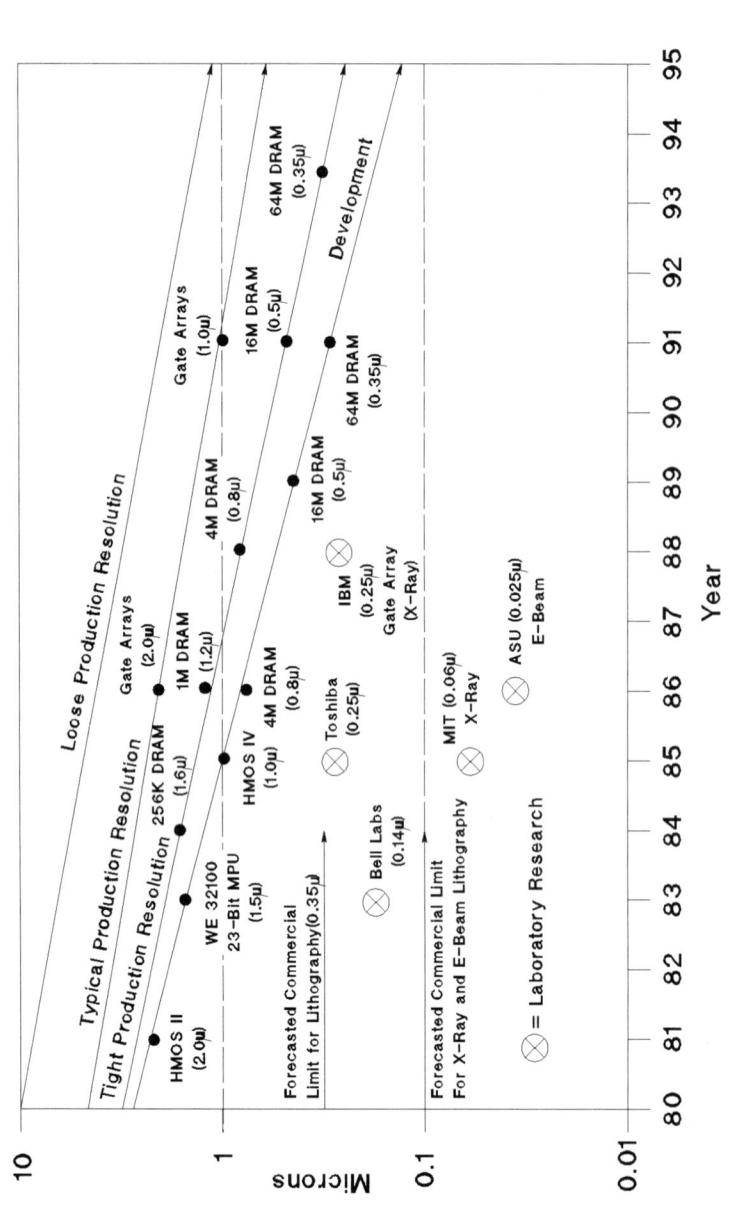

Figure 2.4 *IC feature size trends (adapted from [McC91])*

Implementation Technology 19

Digital VLSI Design

Today, for technical products digital design is the most important design style. Thereby, CMOS technology dominates. Its main features are small structures, extremely low power consumption, and high signal-to-noise ratio [Wes85]. Figure 2.5 shows that the importance of CMOS technology will even increase in future. In brief, important positive characteristics of digital VLSI design styles for neural network design are:

- simplicity
- high signal-to-noise ratio
- cascadability easy to achieve
- high flexibility
- cheap in fabrication
- rather few design experiences necessary.

Simplicity of design is a very important point for the designer. As a result of years of practical experience with many commercial digital designs, a large

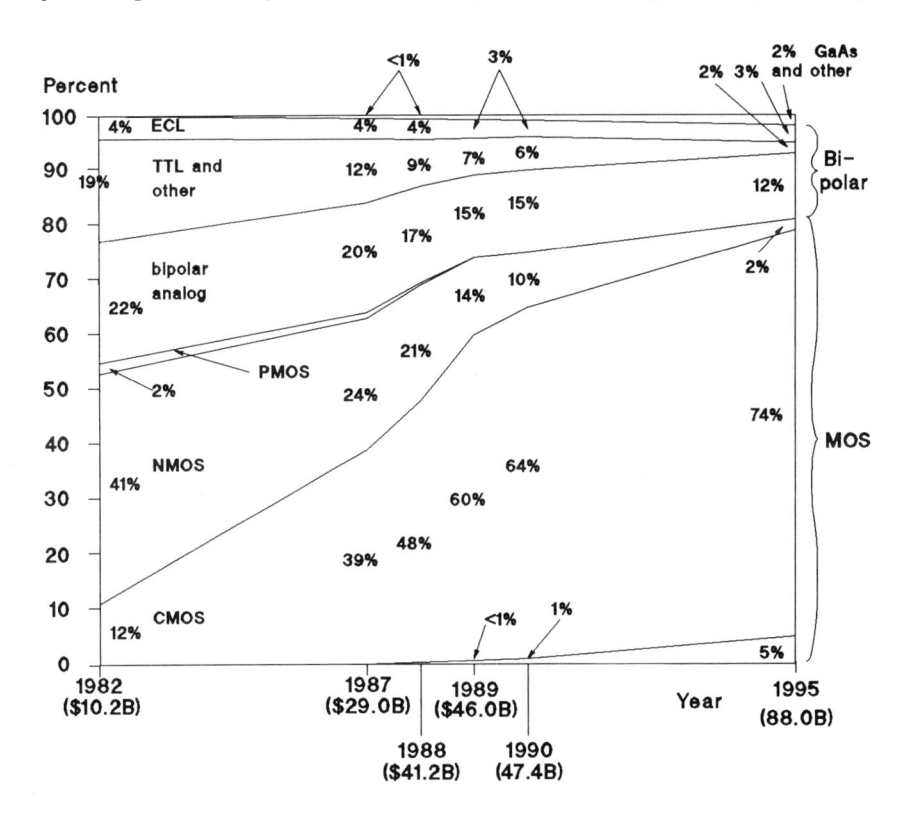

Figure 2.5 *IC technology trends (adapted from [McC91])*

variety of basic elements is available [Ann86, Gei90]. Basic elements are circuits for multipliers, adders, ALUs (Arithmetic Logic Unit), and more or less complex processing elements. An enormous advantage of digital circuits over analog designs is the high signal-to-noise ratio. Whereas voltages or currents are directly used to carry information in analog circuits, *i.e.* the value of the voltage or current directly represents information which may be at least partly lost if noise is added to the signals, this is not the case in digital circuits. Voltages and currents are either on or off, leaving a wide range in which a signal can be interpreted as being on or off. This range may be used to increase the signal-to-noise ratio. If the range is not exceeded by added noise, it will not be harmful to circuit performance. Therefore, noise does not influence the performance of digital circuitry. Furthermore, compared with the analog design, cascadability is easier to achieve. Due to parameter variations between different chips, absolute values of signals generated from equal analog circuits on different chips may differ from each other. Furthermore, it is possible that the same signals may be interpreted differently from corresponding circuits on different chips (see the section on cascadability). Digital signals, however, may be exchanged between chips, since small changes in an absolute signal value are of no significance if they do not exceed a specific range. Most of the digital designs are quite flexible. For example, a complex microprocessor can solve many tasks. Multiplications and summations are possible as well as logic operations. Last but not least, digital circuit fabrication is cheap, and many design systems are available to support a designer's work. Due to long experience with digital circuits, fabrication lines are reliable and stable. All the above mentioned arguments make digital VLSI design feasible even for a novice who has some knowledge of VLSI.

Analog VLSI Design

While designers now prefer to use digital methods, not all tasks can be solved by that technique optimally. The real world is analog, requiring analog interfacing circuits to be able to realize a complete system on one chip [Has88]. As mentioned in the previous section, analog circuits may also be apt for the implementation of neural network basic elements. For example, resistors may serve as synapses and operational amplifiers (nonlinearities) as neurons. From the viewpoint of neural network implementations, analog methods demonstrate the following features:

- extremely dense network implementations
- very fast circuits.

By exploiting physical laws one may implement extremely small "computational entities" (e.g. resistor used as a multiplier). Comparing the size of digital and analog solutions, however, does not lead to a clear statement. On the one hand, analog circuits for neural operations may be extremely small, which cannot be achieved by digital methods. But one also has to bear in mind calculation accuracy, which is rather poor in analog circuits, especially in simple and hence small circuits. If high precision in mathematical operations is required, specially designed analog circuits will become larger than digital circuits. A computational accuracy of 6-8 bits is probably the limit for analog computations. If more is required, digital circuits will be more efficient. A feature which will never be achieved by digital circuits is the enormous computational speed, which may be achieved by analog methods. Since thousands of computations in a feedback network are done within a short relaxation phase (no clock scheme involved), which needs nanoseconds or a few microseconds, such circuits have a large computational power [Jac87a]. Unfortunately, analog design has some severe disadvantages:

- tricky to design
- low signal-to-noise ratio
- influence of fabrication on performance (parameter variations)
- fabrication may be expensive (depending on implementation technology)
- cascadability difficult or impossible.

Everyone who has done an analog design knows how difficult this may be. Extensive simulations on the level of physical behavior have to be done (SPICE simulations), which is much more time consuming than a simple logic simulation of a digital circuit. In addition, there are many parameters to adjust (width and length of transistors) if a specific behavior of parts of the circuit is required. Furthermore, the signal-to-noise ratio is low, since even small disturbances of signals directly change calculated outputs. Another common problem in analog VLSI design is caused by the impact of fabrication parameters on final circuit performance, since parameters cannot be held constant during a fabrication process. For example, changes in doping influence the conductivity of transistors. Therefore, a difficult task for the designer is to take into account parameter variations, and to minimize their influence on circuit performance. An effect of parameter changes which may vary significantly between different chips is that signal values of separate chips are too unreliable for direct exchange, limiting the cascadability of such designs. In recent years, some designs were made using rather "exotic" technologies like bismuth resistors or MNOS technology. Some of these implementation technologies are mature for fabrication, but only a few manufacturers offer them as they are rather expensive compared with the widely available standard CMOS process.

2.3.2 Optical Technologies

Optical computing techniques are the result of a long evolution of research work, motivated largely by the intriguing fact that this form of information processing could outperform well-established electronic data handling methods.

There are three main properties of optics which make it an attractive candidate for numerical data handling and justify its use. First is the large time bandwidth of optical sources, which may approach a gigahertz for laser diodes. Second is the large space bandwidth product. Optical implementations, unlike electronic ones, exploit the third dimension for data processing, *i.e.* an extremely high number of resolvable elements, each of which can be considered as an individual communication channel or processing path, all working in parallel. In conjunction with the high speed of the individual processing element, a tremendous processing speed can be achieved. The third and most decisive characteristic feature of optical solutions for connectionist data processing approaches is the noninterfering nature of propagation, which means that "optical wires can cross". Two optical fields can propagate through each other without affecting one another. This property allows a degree of interconnectivity not achievable by electronic realizations.

Thus, concluding, optics provide those features that are of crucial importance for an efficient implementation of neural networks: massive parallelism, high processing power, high interconnectivity, and thereby large fan-in and fan-out. Some representatives of optical and optoelectronic neural network implementations will be described in Chapter 9 after an introduction of their basic building blocks in Chapter 6.

The authors do not intend to give a complete overview of optoelectronic and optical neural network implementations. Compared to digital and analog VLSI implementations, optical computers form a rather small part of this book. The topic was introduced for completeness, and to give the reader a small glimpse beyond the horizon of silicon implementations.

The principal structure of optoelectronic neural processing is displayed in Figure 2.6. The input, corresponding to an input vector, is optically interconnected with a two-dimensional medium that influences or weights trespassing light. This medium corresponds to the weight matrix of the neural calculus. Results achieved are passed through to an array of receptors, where they are accumulated and thresholded. This corresponds to the calculation of the neural activation and output. Feedback in such a system can be carried out by both optical or electronic means. A profound comparison between optical and electronic interconnects can be found in [Fel88]. The functions addressed are realized by light emitters and receptors and nonlinear optical elements like photorefractive materials, liquid crystals and semiconductors.

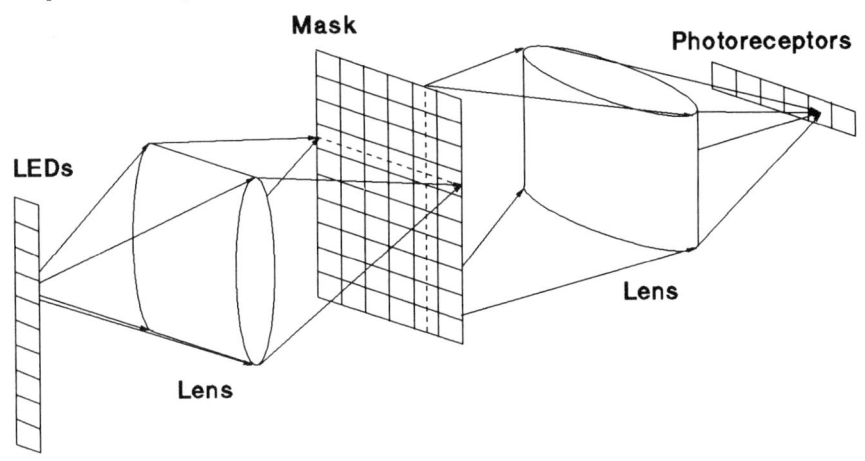

Figure 2.6 *Principle of optical neural network implementation (adapted from [Lal89])*

2.4 Chip Cascadability

From the architecture point of view, there are three different ways of using the customized silicon area to form parallel neural networks:

- the whole network on a single chip

- the network distributed on a whole wafer

- cascadable architectures

to be discussed in the following.

2.4.1 Single Chip Solutions

The first dedicated neural network chips, which emerged during the mid-1980s, belong to the first of the above-mentioned classes. These chips were hardware realizations of Hopfield type networks [Graf87a]. Operational amplifiers served to model the functionality of neurons, whereas resistors were used to store synaptic weight values and to perform synaptic multiplications (by benefitting from Ohm's law). The big disadvantage of single chip solutions is that even by using state-of-the-art VLSI technology, the integration complexity will not be sufficient for a reasonable network size. Furthermore, an insufficient silicon area does not allow the implementation of on-chip learning support. Single chip networks are used in the scientific area to implement prototypes for testing new technologies and implementation methodologies, but are of little commercial interest.

2.4.2 Wafer Scale Integration

A method providing sufficient silicon area is implementing a network not only on a single chip, but on a whole wafer. However, Wafer Scale Integration (WSI) is not a state-of-the-art technology [Jes86]. Problems associated with WSI are

- Yield:
  During chip fabrication a large number of defects are created as a result of material impurities and other causes. Different defect densities which may be expressed in terms of the number of defects per square centimeter are characteristic for different technologies and fabrication lines. The larger the silicon area used, the more defects will be included in circuits realized. One method to cope with defects is to fabricate redundant elements which may replace defective circuits [Moor88, Kar82]. This causes problems of how to find defective elements (an elaborate test of each wafer is necessary) and how to replace them (elements have to be connected via soft switches). Another method would be the implementation of circuits showing graceful performance degradation with an increasing number of defects. Neural networks are architectures with graceful degradation, which makes them promising candidates for WSI technology. However, for most of the networks and applications there exists no clear statement on how severely performance will be affected by defects (a missing or malfunctioning neuron or synapse).

- Packaging:
  Packaging of silicon wafers is still a topic of research. A large amount of information can be processed on a full wafer covered by ample processing elements. But how is it possible to transfer a large amount of information to be processed in a short time period onto the wafer or from it? Many pins may be necessary to do the job, causing packaging problems and extremely expensive packaging.

Despite these problems, the WSI realization of neural networks is a hot topic, and first results have been published [Yas90]. So far, no explicit benefit has been seen from the fault tolerance of neural networks with respect to WSI. Most of the work stops with architecture proposals for wafer scale integration. A lot of research work still has to be done in this area.

2.4.3 Cascadable Architectures

Most promising for today's dedicated neural network hardware are cascadable architectures. In such architectures, networks are distributed over the silicon area of several chips allowing then to benefit from quite a large area without causing problems concerning fabrication defects since, in contrast to wafer scale integration, malfunctioning chips may be separated and replaced by correctly functioning specimens. However, problems may be caused by the exchange of information necessary, especially if analog VLSI technology is involved. In the following, we distinguish between three different kinds of cascadability:

- no cascadability
- limited cascadability
- arbitrary cascadability.

Non-Cascadable Designs

This section refers to single-chip architectures, like Hopfield realizations of the mid-1980s. Figure 2.7 sketches the design principle. Input/output pins are used to send signals into the chip to set neurons to their initial state. The chip contains all the neurons and synapses with their interconnection scheme. From the initial state, the network is running freely to find a stable state (local minimum). Afterwards, in the final stable state, information about neuron states is read from the chip via input/output pins. Another example for chips of this type is the design of a six neuron Boltzmann machine with 15 synapses done by Joshua Alspector [Als88a] (chip architectures are described in Chapters 7 and 8).

Limited Cascadability

Figure 2.8 gives an example of what is called limited cascadability. Here, each chip carries a fixed number of neurons, with their respective fixed number of synapses. Chips are fully cascadable in the way that chip outputs may directly be fed into chip inputs. However, the number of synapses per neuron may never be changed, since special synapse chips providing only an array of synapses, do not exist. Hence, it is possible to form networks of a large size with an arbitrary number of layers and an arbitrary number of

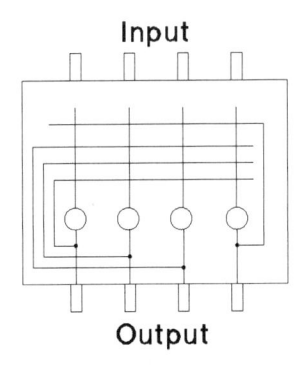

Figure 2.7 *Non-cascadable architecture*

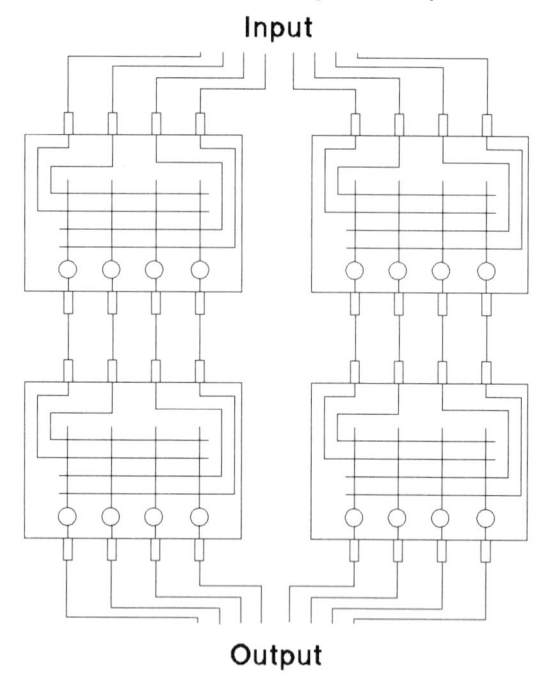

Figure 2.8 *Limited cascadability*

neurons per layer, but with a fixed number of receiving inputs per neuron which is limited by the chip architecture.

Arbitrary Cascadability

In the following, the notion of "arbitrary cascadability" will characterize a design's capability to form networks of an arbitrary size without limitation (at least theoretically). Figure 2.9 shows the design principle for arbitrary cascadability. Neurons and synapses are realized on different chips, which may be fitted together to form arbitrary networks. Often, neuron chips do not contain the equivalent of neurons, but a number of parallel computing facilities for performing multiplications (usually bit serial multiplication, which is done by several summations) and summations. Thus, synapse chips only store weight values which have to be transferred to the "neuron chips" and may be realized by standard RAM chips, which is a cheap and efficient solution (high storage density). Examples of this type of architecture are the Neural Bit Slice from Micro Devices [Mic89a] and the BACCHUS design from Darmstadt University of Technology [Gle89, Poe90]. Furthermore, flexible architectures like multiple digital signal processor solutions or transputer networks will be attributed to this class of cascadability, since

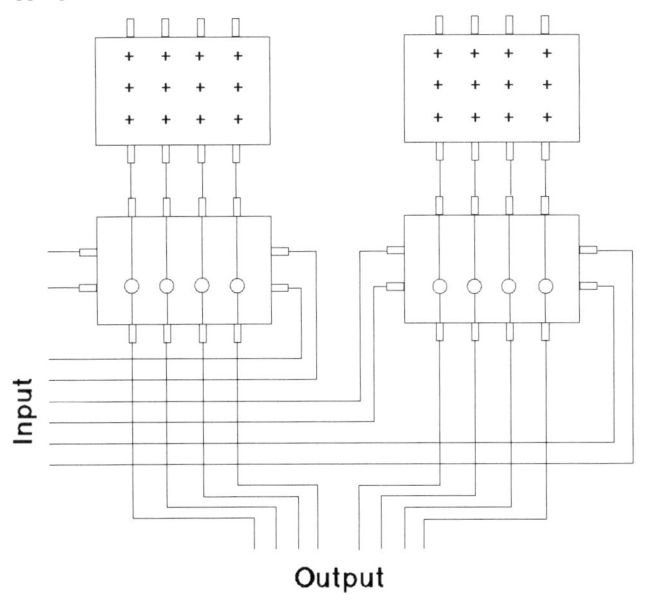

Figure 2.9 *Arbitrary cascadability*

an arbitrary number of computing chips and RAM chips may be used to simulate any kind of neural network even if there is no one-to-one correspondence between neurons and processing elements.

2.5 Network Mapping on Processing Elements

A classification may also be done by means of the mapping of neural networks onto hardware. A neural network to be simulated or emulated does not necessarily have to be mapped onto hardware in a one-to-one fashion. Therefore, it is necessary to distinguish strictly between a network and the underlying hardware on which the simulation is running. Dedicated hardware is comprised of some processing elements to perform a network's operations, but one processing element need not correspond to a specific neuron or synapse. Manifold correspondences between a number of neurons and synapses with a processing element are possible. In the following, we will distinguish between three classes of processing element correspondence with neural entities:

- network-oriented mapping
- neuron-oriented mapping
- synapse-oriented mapping.

Figure 2.10 sketches the principles of the three mapping classes, with

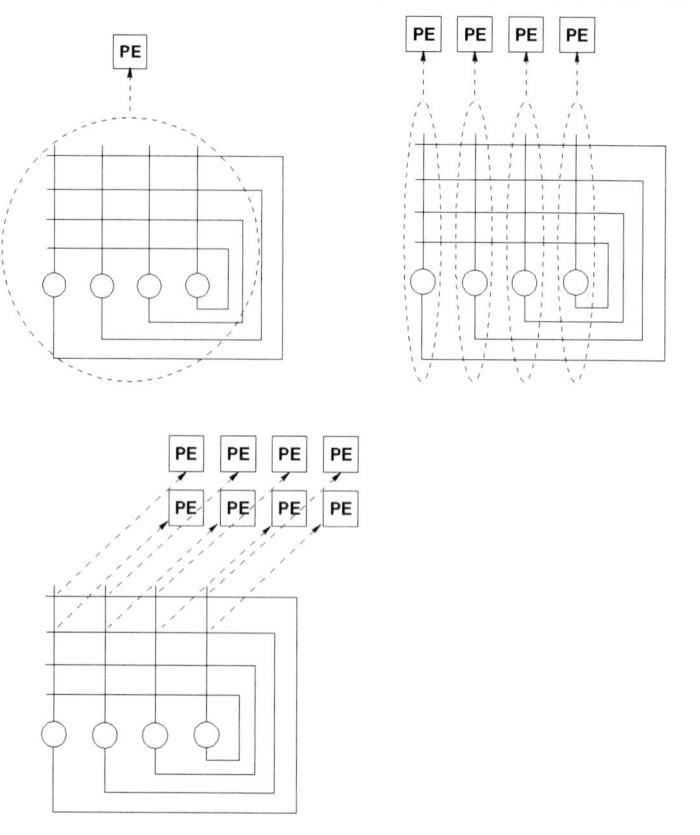

Figure 2.10 *Network mapping*

network-oriented mapping on the upper left, neuron-oriented mapping on the upper right, and synapse-oriented mapping on the lower left (neurons are represented by circles, synaptic connections by crossing lines).

2.5.1 Network-Oriented Mapping

An example of network-oriented mapping is given by the upper left sketch of Figure 2.10. There, the whole network with all necessary arithmetic computations is mapped onto one processing element. Information about the network state, *i.e.* the states of neurons as well as synaptic weights, is stored in a large memory block. This architecture generates all the problems associated with von Neumann machines (von Neumann bottleneck). On the one hand, all computations have to be done by one very complex processing element; on the other hand, information about the state of a synapse or neuron has to be taken from the memory block via the data bus. A sequential von

Neumann machine, which is still commonly used for neural network simulations, represents a network-oriented approach. No advantage is taken of a neural network's inherent parallelism; all operations are performed sequentially. A significant speed-up may be achieved by special hardware support in the form of extremely fast ALUs, floating point units and high speed memory. Dedicated neural network acceleration boards for PCs are available on the market [Wil89]. However, acceleration boards do not use the inherent neural network parallelism, either. Network-oriented architectures are extremely flexible since many algorithms may run on them, but they are slow due to the limited computational power of just a single processor.

2.5.2 Neuron-Oriented Mapping

The next step on the way towards increasing parallelism and computational power are neuron-oriented architectures. The term "neuron oriented" derives from the fact that now the entity to map onto a physical processing element is a neuron, with all its receiving synapses, or a group of neurons with their synapses. Figure 2.10 (upper right) shows the principle of neuron-oriented mapping. Thereby, one physical processing element sequentially performs multiplications and summations done in a neuron and all its receiving synapses. Several "neuron/synapse slices" (see Figure 2.10), however, may be mapped onto a processing element. Neuron-oriented architectures provide a low-to-medium degree of parallelism. Typical representatives are multi-signal processor architectures or transputer systems. Network mapping is very simple to recognize in bit slice architectures such as the BACCHUS architecture [Poe90] or the Neural Bit Slice (NBS) [Mic89a]. In both architectures, a physical processor exists for each neuron which has to perform the multiplication for each synapse belonging to the neuron, and to sum up signals arriving at the neuron. The same is valid for Fujitsu's digital signal processor (DSP) network [Kat90]. One signal processor is assigned to each neuron, and all the neuron's receiving synaptic weight values are stored in memory belonging to the DSP card. But mapping onto hardware may be more complicated than simply assigning a neuron with its receiving synapses onto one processor. A very efficient implementation of larger networks with a lot of training data was done on a linear systolic array by dividing training data and storing a small part of the training vectors on a processor [Pom88] (data partitioning method). The complete weight information on the network was stored in one separate cluster memory and pumped through the systolic array. However, this architecture is also assigned to neuron-oriented approaches, since operations belonging to several different synapses and several different neurons are performed by one physical processor.

2.5.3 Synapse-Oriented Mapping

Synapse-oriented designs provide the highest degree of parallelism. Processing elements are assigned to each synapse or group of synapses and each neuron (see lower left part of Figure 2.10). One-to-one mappings of networks onto hardware are the most extreme synapse-oriented designs, with a physical processing element for each synapse and each neuron. Thus, a physical processor may even be a simple element such as a resistor, which is the case in some early Hopfield type network implementations [Graf87a]. However, for synapse-oriented designs, it is not necessary to have a physical processing element for each synapse. It is also possible to map several synapses onto a single processing element.

Mapping of neural network entities onto physical processing elements is a well suited criterion for dedicated hardware categorization. All kinds of implementations of networks (biologically oriented as well as more mathematically-oriented networks) are covered by this criterion. A problem is posed by some architectures which cannot definitely be attributed to one of the three above-mentioned classes. For example, systolic arrays may serve as a neuron-oriented approach (small systolic array) as well as a synapse-oriented architecture (large systolic array). In that case, the available hardware has to be investigated in more detail in order to decide upon its affiliation. If a processing element of a large systolic array possesses only a little memory, it is impossible to use it for network simulations in the context of neuron-oriented mapping, since all synaptic weights belonging to at least one neuron have to be stored on one processor, including some additional memory which will be necessary to perform calculations. Furthermore, this categorization is not selective enough for synapse-oriented designs. Whereas the first two classes (network- and neuron-oriented) cover only digital hardware, a large variety of design styles exist in synapse-oriented designs. Digital solutions have been made (architecture proposals), as well as mixed digital/analog designs and many very different analog chips (including optic and optoelectronic circuits). In part, fully analog designs are based on rather "exotic" technologies (MNOS technology, bismuth resistors, optical solutions). Therefore, synapse-oriented approaches should be further categorized by another criterion such as implementation technology. Some examples of architectures belonging to the described classes are:

1. Network-oriented
   - conventional sequential computer (von Neumann machine)
   - conventional computer with acceleration board.

2. Neuron-oriented
   - multi-processor solutions with digital signal processors

Flexibility 31

- transputer networks
- RISC arrays (MIMD arrays)
- SIMD arrays
- linear systolic arrays (ring systolic arrays)
- small two-dimensional systolic arrays
- Neural Bit Slice (Micro Devices)
- BACCHUS: cascadable architecture for large binary networks.

3. Synapse-oriented

    - analog network solutions
    - optical network solutions
    - large two-dimensional systolic arrays
    - pulse stream implementations.

This enumeration is not complete; however, it gives an overview of the categorization of hardware for neural network implementations by means of network mapping.

2.6 Flexibility

Flexibility is an important feature for electronic systems. The more flexible a system is, the more cost effective it will be. This statement is also valid for neural network hardware. With respect to neural hardware, it is reasonable to distinguish three classes according to [Atl89], which are:

- general purpose computers for neural network simulations
- special purpose processors for neural network simulations
- dedicated artificial neural network hardware.

Flexibility offers many advantages to a neural network designer. The more flexibility that is available, the more freedom a designer has to change simulated algorithms for investigation purposes. But flexibility may also be important for a neural network user. One has to bear in mind that a neural network itself will not be sufficient to solve a technical problem. It is common to preprocess data with more or less complex algorithms to reduce the data flow and extract only "problem relevant" information. Thus, supposing that dedicated parallel neural network hardware is available, data preprocessing may become the bottleneck of the whole system. Therefore, a flexible parallel system (e.g. a SIMD array) which may also perform data preprocessing tasks could become valuable.

2.6.1 General Purpose Computers

This class comprises of the conventional sequential computer (von Neumann machine) as well as the large number of general purpose parallel computers. General purpose parallel computers consist of many, relatively independent and complex processors. Often, they are MIMD (Multiple Data Multiple Instructions) machines, since each processor has its own memory and its own data path and instructions. Today, several parallel computers are commercially available and used in research institutes. Hence, a large number of neural network simulations has been done on such machines. Most implementations reported in the literature have been made on transputer networks with a rather small network size of 4 to 64 transputers. Another approach is arrays of digital signal processors. Due to the very complex processing elements, these architectures are extremely flexible; however, large parallelism may be only achieved at the expense of a tremendous amount of hardware. Usually, these few complex processing elements are connected to each other via buses or special data channels. That may cause problems in large systems if the algorithms implemented need to exchange much information between processing elements. The next step towards increasing parallelism is the implementation of less complex and smaller processing elements (RISC processors) [Kat84, Goo89] and a more efficient interconnection grid. Clearly, this has to be paid for by a lesser degree of flexibility. Forrest *et al.* used a distributed array processor grid of 4096 processors for the simulation of a Hopfield network [For87]. The connection machine [Hil85] is a parallel computer with up to 65536 processing elements. Sixteen processors are integrated on a single chip, with a 4096 bit storing capacity each. Processors are interconnected in the form of a hypercube.

2.6.2 Special Purpose Computers

Many neural network simulation systems consist of commercially available VLSI chips (RAM circuits, digital signal processors, RISC processors, ALUs, transputers, *etc.*) which have been fitted together to form specific boards and systems dedicated to running neural algorithms. They offer the advantage that, due to the use of existing products, they are quite cheap, reliable and available to any interested and appropriately skilled user. However, the performance achieved is generally not that of highly parallel general purpose computers and special neural network VLSI implementations. Such special purpose processor systems may be divided into sequential and parallel "neurocomputers". Sequential systems try to benefit from very fast hardware circuits for neural network algorithm specific operations. Essentially, these operations are multiplication, summation and memory access. A typical example of a fast sequential system is the Delta

Flexibility

Floating Point Processor from Science Applications International Corporation (SAIC). The high speed in the SAIC board was not achieved by many parallel processing units, but by making use of very fast (35 nsec) static RAM memory, a floating point chip set implemented in extremely fast emitter coupled logic (ECL) technology, and a reduced instruction set computer (RISC) architecture [Wor88]. Sequential architectures have the advantage that very little hardware is necessary to integrate a system which allows complex floating point operations to be done, which is not the case in extremely parallel approaches that have to fit onto a small silicon area. Another example is the ANZA Plus card from Hecht-Nielsen Computers (HNC), which is a coprocessor compatible with PC-ATs. To accelerate neural network related operations, it is based on a 4-stage pipelined Harvard architecture. In Harvard architectures, instruction and data paths are kept separate from each other for more efficiency. In parallel systems several standard processors are used to share time consuming tasks. Neurocomputers (which are not built up from specially designed chips) consist of the same basic processors as general purpose parallel computers, *i.e.* digital signal processors (DSPs) (as TMS320C20/25, TMS320C30, or AT&T's DSP32C), transputers or RISC processors. However, they are put together to form systems with special features making them well suited for neural network simulations. One possibility is to tune processor boards with additional memory for weight storage, or extremely fast memory for fast information exchange. Special broadcast bus structures which are efficient in combination with neural algorithms can be found in many designs.

2.6.3 Dedicated Neural Network Hardware

In this class, neural network algorithms are mapped onto dedicated hardware designed for the simulation of a specific algorithm or a small class of algorithms. Thus, they offer limited flexibility. Often, such a dedicated piece of hardware can simulate only one specific network type. It may be possible that the architecture is not able to perform the training algorithm, only the recall phase. Some early implementations of the mid-1980s did not even allow a weight selection by the user. Networks had been personalized or programmed during the fabrication process. Afterwards, no further weight change was possible, thus fixing the network type, network size and network interconnections, leaving no flexibility at all for any changes. At present, all newly developed implementations allow user defined weight programming to configure networks according to a user's requirements. Otherwise, a dedicated neural network implementation will not be suitable for a user-specific application. However, many of the dedicated implementations are still not able to perform a learning algorithm supported by on-chip learning circuitry. But today, there is a strong trend towards the inclusion of learning into the hardware, at least in the form of "hardware in the loop learning", where parts of the learning procedure are supported by dedicated hardware and other parts are run on the host computer. In addition to low flexibility, the lack of on-chip learning in many designs is the second main disadvantage of specific implementations (either VLSI or optics) compared with general purpose or special purpose computers. The speed achieved in such systems, however, is unattainable by flexible hardware. The first representatives of specific neural network VLSI hardware were implementations of Hopfield type networks [Hop82] with fixed interconnectivity after fabrication. During the second half of the 1980s and early 1990s, a large variety of VLSI, optical and optoelectronic circuits have been realized. Many VLSI implementations were done using analog or hybrid analog/digital technology. Today, only a few products are commercially available (most of them implemented in digital CMOS technology).

Flexibility as a criterion to categorize neural network hardware is not as well suited as other criteria. First, one has to define what is meant by flexibility: the flexibility to choose between different calculation accuracies, the flexibility to simulate networks of a different size or even a different type, or the flexibility to run algorithms which have nothing in common with neural network algorithms (e.g. algorithms to preprocess data)? Furthermore, the distinction between general purpose and special purpose (neurocomputer) hardware is not very clear. Transputer solutions or multiple digital signal processor approaches essentially belong to both classes of computer system. Furthermore, this book will mainly concentrate on the latter class of hardware, which are dedicated VLSI circuits specially designed for neural network simulation.

2.7 Summary

Several criteria for the classification of dedicated neural network hardware have been described. None of the criteria is sufficient for such a classification if it is taken as the only criterion. Therefore, several different criteria to categorize architectures have to be applied. Appropriate criteria are:

- biological evidence
- mapping onto hardware
- implementation technology.

These criteria can be applied in a hierarchy, with biological evidence on the top level to distinguish between networks mimicking biological nets, networks performing biological functions on a higher level, and networks with very few or no biological evidence at all. Since the first two classes comprise only "academic" solutions with little or no impact on state-of-the-art neural network applications to real technical problems, they are not further categorized. Only a few realizations of such networks exist.

Summary

```
                    ┌─────────────────────────┐
                    │ Categorization according│
                    │  to biological evidence │
                    └─────────────────────────┘
```

                                                              no biological
                                                                evidence

archit. mimicking   networks on a
biological neural   somewhat higher
systems   level
                                                     ┌─────────────────┐
silicon retina;   noise removal networks;   │ Categorization │
silicon cochlea;   edge detection networks;   │   with mapping │
central pattern   corner detection networks; │   onto   │
generators   │   hardware   │
                              analog   └─────────────────┘
   analog

                                                             synapse-
                                                             oriented

network-oriented   neuron-oriented

conventional   classical parallel
computer   hardware   ┌─────────────────┐
(von Neumann);   (parallel computers);   │ Categorization │
computer with   linear systolic   │ according to   │
acceleration   arrays; ...   │ implementation │
board   │   technology   │
                              digital   └─────────────────┘
   digital

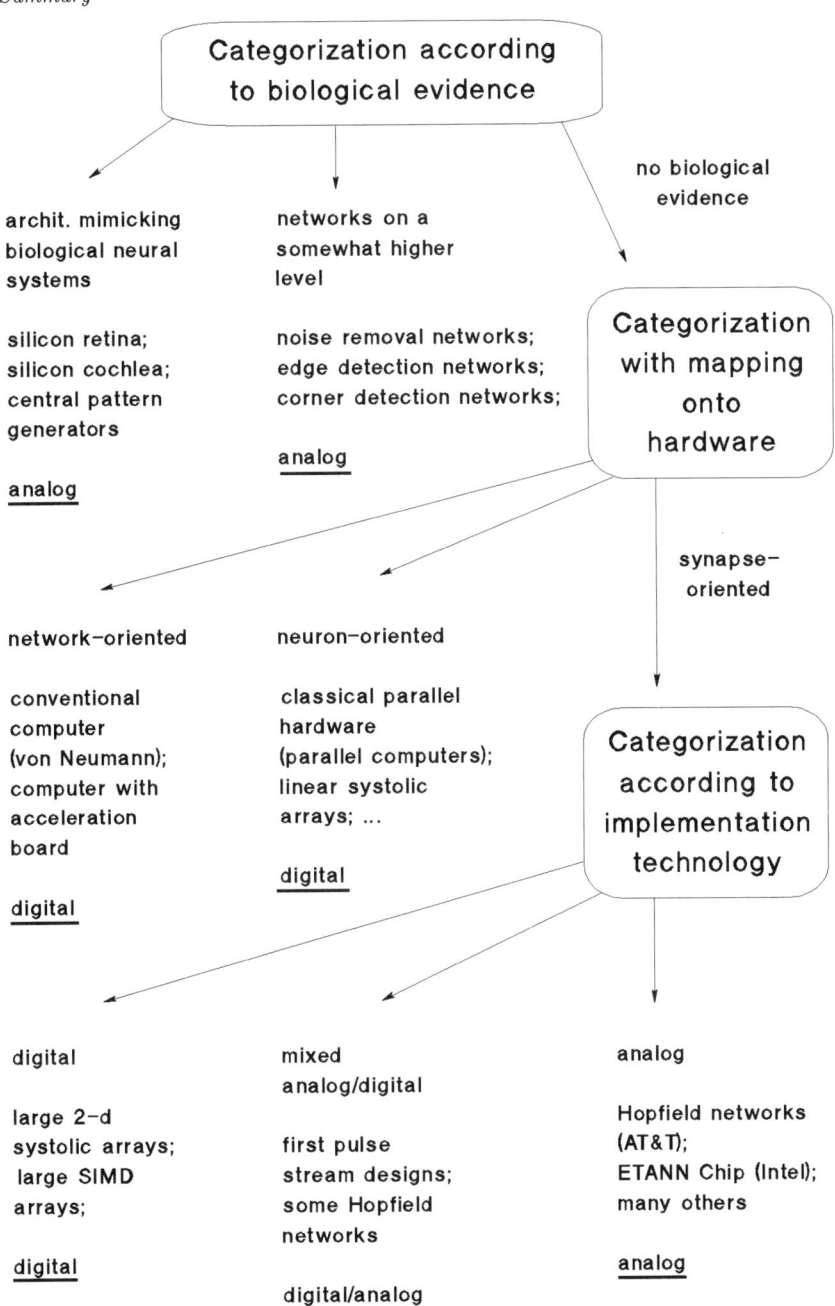

digital   mixed   analog
                         analog/digital
large 2-d   Hopfield networks
systolic arrays;   first pulse   (AT&T);
large SIMD   stream designs;   ETANN Chip (Intel);
arrays;   some Hopfield   many others
                         networks
   digital   analog
                            digital/analog

Figure 2.11 *Categorization of neural network implementations*

Most of the network algorithms and implementations belong to the class of no biological evidence. Due to the large variety of architectures implemented in different technologies, this class is further divided according to the mapping of the network onto the physical processing elements. Three classes exist: the network-oriented solutions, neuron-oriented architectures, and synapse-oriented approaches. Network-oriented architectures are several varieties of von Neumann machines. They all consist of one processor responsible for the mathematical computations and data transfer. To speed up simulations, the main processor can be supported by a coprocessor for floating point operations. For neuron-oriented architectures, it is characteristic that a neuron (or several neurons), with all its receiving synapses, is mapped onto a physical processing element. Due to more or less complex mapping of network functionality onto physical processing elements, where several neural entities (neurons, synapses) have to share a physical processor, only fully digital VLSI implementations are known. Therefore, no further division of hardware realizations seems to be necessary. The third class of synapse-oriented approaches, however, is comprised of a large number of very different implementations. Since each neural entity (synapse, neuron) receives its own "physical processor" (usually a very simple processor compared with processors of network- and neuron-oriented architectures), several implementation techniques are appropriate for a hardware solution. Therefore, on the lowest level of the categorization hierarchy, chips implemented in mixed digital/analog and analog VLSI technology and optical (optical and optoelectronic) implementations can be distinguished. Figure 2.11 shows the hierarchical categorization scheme pursued, which leads to a detailed separation of different neural network implementation approaches.

3
Nervous Systems and their Simulation

The aim of neural network hardware is to perform each information processing operation done in a neural network on a device implemented in a specific technology, which may be a piece of silicon (VLSI technology) or a crystal (optical implementations), for example. A neural network consists of very simple elements that only perform some basic operations. Computational power is not achieved by complex mathematical inferences or extremely complex and fast processing elements, but by a large number of slow and simple elements ordered in a sophisticated topology. So the cleverness of biological neural systems is not caused by sophisticated basic elements but an intelligent interconnection of quite simple devices. In this chapter, the basic building blocks of nervous systems will be described briefly, followed by a discussion of mathematical algorithms inspired by them. Only the most important and widespread algorithms will be considered. No deep mathematical analysis will be done, but only a crude description. The discussion is limited to hardware implementation aspects of different algorithms. For a more profound introduction to the mathematics of neural networks, the reader is recommended to read a book such as Hertz *et al.* [Her91].

3.1 Neural Network Basic Building Blocks

Neural networks consist of neurons and synapses. In biological networks a neuron possesses a dendritic tree which may receive and emit signals. However, in artificial networks the dendritic tree is usually the receiving part of a neuron. From a neuron's output, signals are emitted by the axon [Kat66]. Figures 3.1 and 3.2 sketch the principles of the neuron topology. Synapses serve as connectors between different neurons. Manifold synaptic connections between neurons are possible. There exist axodendritic (from axon to dendrite), dendrodentritic (from dendrite to dendrite) and reciprocal (from one dendrite to another dendrite, and *vice versa*) connections. If cur-

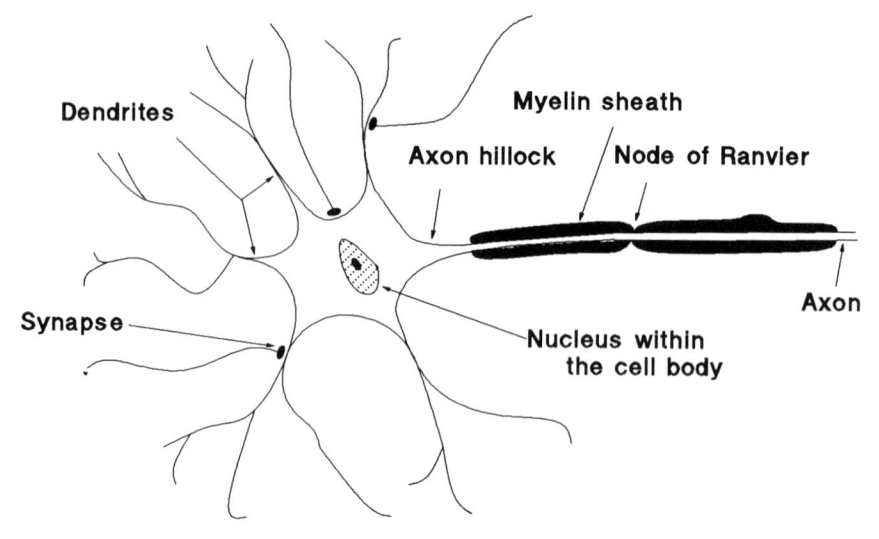

Figure 3.1 *Neuron consisting of dendritic tree, cell body, and axon (adapted from [Mead89])*

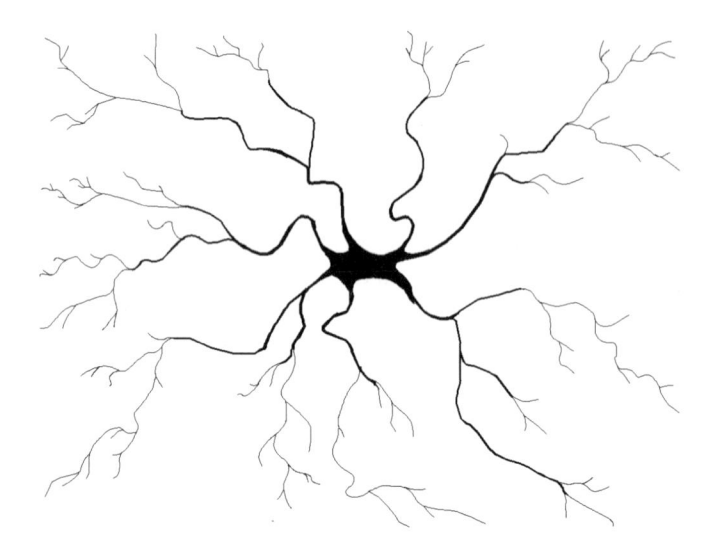

Figure 3.2 *Dendritic tree (adapted from [Mead89])*

rent pulses are injected into a neuron's cell membrane through a synaptic connection, it will respond at the axon as depicted in Figure 3.3. After raising the neuron's cytoplasm potential higher than -40 millivolts relative to the extracellular fluid, a strong potential is generated at the axon for a short moment. However, information processing is made possible through

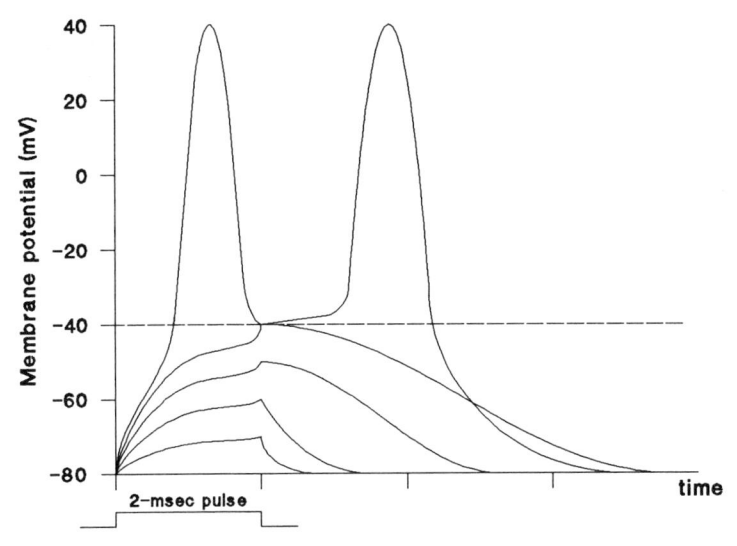

Figure 3.3 *Response of the axon to current stimuli (adapted from [Mead89])*

synapses that provide the ability to control conductance through another membrane. Therefore, synapses are key structures for information processing in neural systems. Figure 3.4 sketches a synaptic connection between two nerve fibres. Depolarization of the presynaptic membrane (change of membrane potential) results in a release of neurotransmitter [She79]. Neurotransmitter molecules emitted to the synaptic cleft diffuse to the postsynaptic membrane, where they cause events resulting in the opening of ion channels. The quantity of neurotransmitter released depends upon the presynaptic potential. Depending upon whether ion channels, which are opened by neurotransmitter, are sodium or potassium specific, the postsynaptic membrane will be depolarized or hyperpolarized, respectively. In the case of hyperpolarization, a synapse is inhibitory; otherwise (depolarization) it is excitatory. Hence, a single synapse shares some features of a transistor in electronic circuits, which is also able to control a current flow [Mead89].

3.2 Artificial Neural Networks

If observed from the level of chemical processes, synapses and neurons are highly nonlinear systems. However, artificial neural systems are constructed by doing some simplifications, as depicted in Figure 3.5 [Rum86]. One is no longer interested in the physical structure and behavior of a biological neuron. The whole dendritic tree is represented by a summing input of the neuron. In Figure 3.5 net_i is the net input to neuron i, *i.e.* the sum of all weighted inputs from preceding neurons. In a biological neuron this corresponds to the overall effect of excitatory and inhibitory postsynaptic activations. So net_i can be calculated as

$$net_i = \sum_j w_{ij} \cdot o_j. \qquad (3.1)$$

Thus o_j is an input signal receiving at neuron i which is emitted by neuron j, and w_{ij} is the respective synaptic weight (strength of connection) for the connection between neurons i and j. The functionality of a synapse is reduced to a simple multiplication (weighting operation). Furthermore,

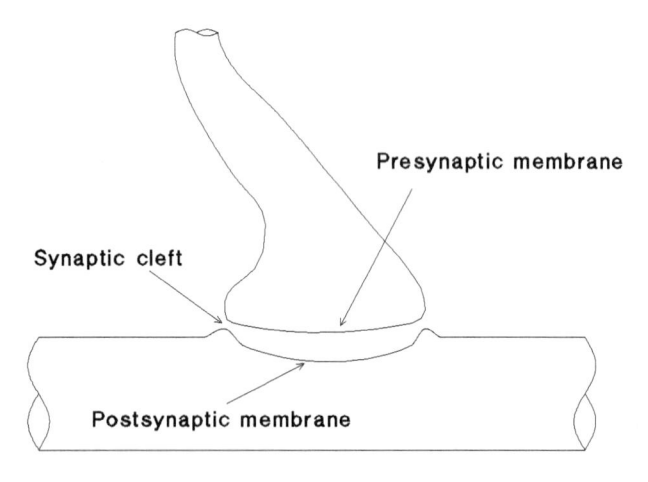

Figure 3.4 *Synaptic connection between nerve fibres (adapted from [Mead89])*

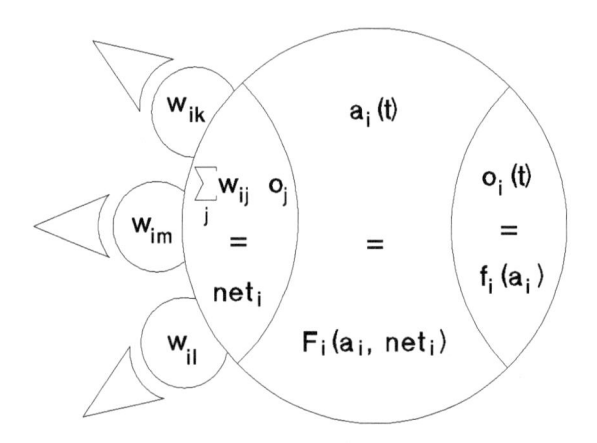

Figure 3.5 *Artificial neuron (adapted from [Rum86])*

some people are distinguishing between a neuron's activation $a_i(t)$, i.e.

$$a_i(t) = F_i(a_i, net_i) \tag{3.2}$$

and its output $f_i(a_i)$ [Rum86]. However, this distinction is not mathematically necessary, since the activation function $a_i(t)$ and output function $f_i(a_i)$ may be combined into one function. Then, $a_i(t)$ is identical to $o_i(t)$. Usually, this function is nonlinear and shifted by a threshold value Θ (a widespread function to model a neuron's nonlinearity is the sigmoid function). If there is a distinction between activation and output, the activation represents a neuron's state. If not stated otherwise, throughout this book we assume that $a_i(t) = o_i(t)$. Depending on the network model realized, the state may be a binary, integer or real value (bounded or not bounded), whereas the output is a value propagated to other neurons (which also may be a binary, integer or real value). For the simulation of such a generic neuron, it is sufficient to have hardware elements that may perform summations, multiplications and a thresholded nonlinearity. Furthermore, some elements will be required to store values such as a neuron's state or a synaptic weight. Some network algorithms such as those involved in Boltzmann machines, need additional circuitry. The Boltzmann machine is based on the simulated annealing algorithm, which is a stochastic algorithm. In some Hopfield type networks, simulated annealing is used to avoid local minima. Therefore, random number generators are required to support other circuits with randomly controlled events.

Equations 3.1 and 3.2 are common to all neural network paradigms. Neural network paradigms differ significantly, however, in both topology and learning.

3.2.1 Hopfield Networks

J.J. Hopfield boosted neural network research at the beginning of the 1980s with the publication of a famous paper on artificial neural networks, which he used for pattern completion and to solve optimization problems [Hop82]. These networks consist of one layer of neurons that are completely connected with each other (see Figure 3.6). Hopfield analysed the behavior of networks belonging to that type, and could prove mathematically that stable behavior may be achieved under certain conditions. The following two equations describe the dynamic changes of the state of neuron i:

$$T\frac{da_i(t)}{dt} = -a_i(t) + \sum_{j}^{N} w_{ij} o_j(t) - \Theta \tag{3.3}$$

$$o_i(t) = f(a_i(t)) \tag{3.4}$$

Thus, $a_i(t)$ is the activation of neuron i and $o_i(t)$ its output signal. The synaptic weight w_{ij} connects the output of neuron j with the input of

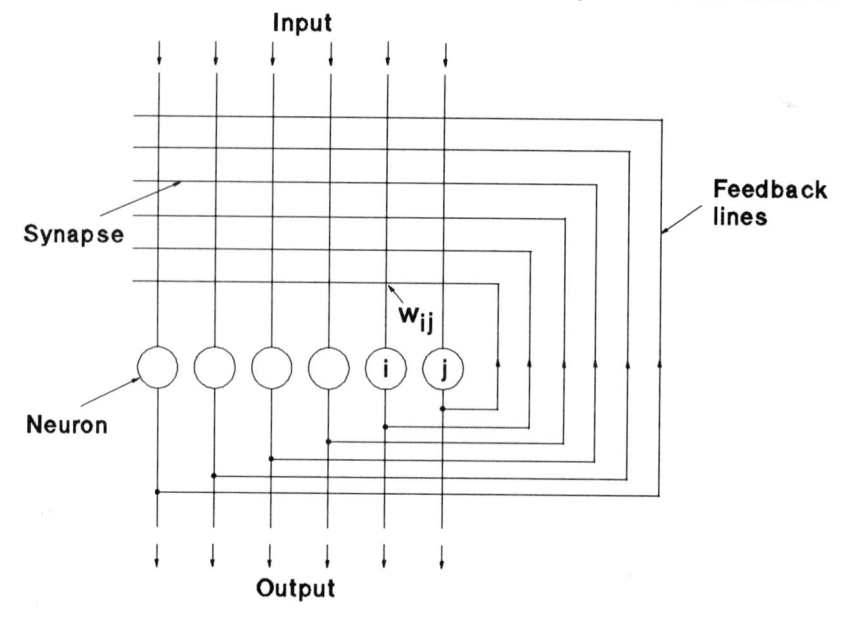

Figure 3.6 *Topology of a Hopfield type network*

neuron i, whereas Θ represents a certain threshold and T a time constant. Hopfield *et al.* proposed constructing electronic networks with neurons modelled by summing amplifiers and synaptic weights represented by resistors [Hop86]. Capacitors C and resistors R connecting amplifier inputs towards ground cause some losses. In this case the amplifier's output voltage may be described by Equations 3.3 and 3.4 with capacitances C and resistances R affecting time constant T and threshold Θ. If simulated on digital computers, through discretization (assuming $a_i(t) = o_i(t)$), Equation 3.3 may be expressed by

$$o_i(t) = \left(1 - \frac{\Delta t}{T}\right) o_i(t-1) + \frac{\Delta t}{T} \left(\sum_j^N w_{ij} o_j(t-1) - \Theta\right). \qquad (3.5)$$

This is a recursive equation typical for networks with feedback.

It can be shown that the dynamic behavior of Hopfield type networks is described by an energy surface. Each network state corresponds to a certain position on that surface. Through external clamping, neurons may be forced to certain states of activity, and thus the whole network may be forced to move to a well defined point on the energy surface. If the network is released, *i.e.* external clamping is removed, it will change its state in such a way that it moves on the energy surface towards new states of lower energy. Finally, neuron states will stop changing if a local minimum in the energy surface is reached. Through careful selection of weights, oscillations will be avoided.

Due to the energy minimizing behavior, an application area of Hopfield networks is optimization. In such an application an optimization problem is formulated as a neural network with well defined synaptic weights. In this way, a problem solution is coded as a network state vector (*i.e.* a vector describing the states of all network neurons). However, formulating optimization problems as neural networks is a difficult task. This task usually becomes impossible to solve if hard constraints are introduced into the optimization (this is the case in nearly all realistic optimization tasks). Aarts and Korst [Aar89] describe several optimization problems formulated as neural network topologies for Boltzmann machines.

Another application area is to use Hopfield networks as associative memories. The basic idea is to interpret each minimum in the energy surface or stable network state as a memory datum. If the network is in a stable local minimum energy state and one or very few neuron activities are changed from outside, the network will move out of its minimum a little. After removing the outside influence affecting the neuron activities, the network will immediately move into its local minimum. Hence, an application area for the network would be in solving pattern completion tasks. Some patterns are stored as local minima in the network energy (each minimum corresponding to a specific network activity pattern). If an unknown pattern is presented to the network by externally forcing neurons into a desired activation pattern, the network will move towards the most similar (*i.e.* the next local minimum in energy surface) stored pattern after the removal of external clamping.

If used as associative memory, the question arises as to how to chose a weight set generating minima at the desired positions in the energy surface. The simplest way is to use a Hebb type learning rule [Heb49, Hop82]. Vectors to be memorized are successively applied to the network, and weight updates Δw_{ij} are calculated according to

$$\Delta w_{ij}^k = \frac{o_i^k o_j^k}{N}, \qquad (3.6)$$

with o_i^k the state (output) of the i-th element of vektor k and N the total number of stored vectors.

Most neural network hardware implementations of the mid-1980s were those of Hopfield type networks. This is due to the simple and regular structure of these networks. One of the most significant aspects is that such a network may operate with a very limited weight range. Even ternary weights are sufficient to operate a simple network. Hence, hardware implementations may be simplified significantly, since with ternary synapses multiplication is reduced to gating signals. Furthermore, Hebbian learning can be realized with small on-chip circuitry. Only local information

(information in the near vicinity of the synapse) is required to update a weight reducing hardware expense.

A problem with Hebbian learning is caused by spurious memory states. These are local minima in the energy surface at positions which do not correspond to vectors that have to be learned. With simple learning algorithms like Hebbian learning it is impossible to avoid spurious states, especially if many of the training vectors are partially correlated with each other. The more spurious states that emerge, the less reliable a network will work. A rule of thumb is that a Hopfield network cannot store more vectors than 10-15% of its number of neurons. Other learning methods have been developed to better cope with partially correlated training vectors, such as the projection rule from Personnaz et al. [Per86], which are more or less complex to implement (some "hardware friendly" approximations were used by Weinfeld et al. [Wei89]).

Today, Hopfield type networks are rarely used. Problems associated with them include their low storage capacity through inefficient learning (spurious states) and limited applicability. Hopfield networks, both algorithms, as well as hardware implementations, are more of historical importance.

3.2.2 The Error-Backpropagation Algorithm

The error-backpropagation algorithm is one of the most important and well known learning algorithms for neural networks. Its importance results from the fact that multi-layer networks (multi-layer Perceptrons) can be adapted through supervised teaching with a training set of vectors. Figure 3.7 shows the topology of a network typically trained with the

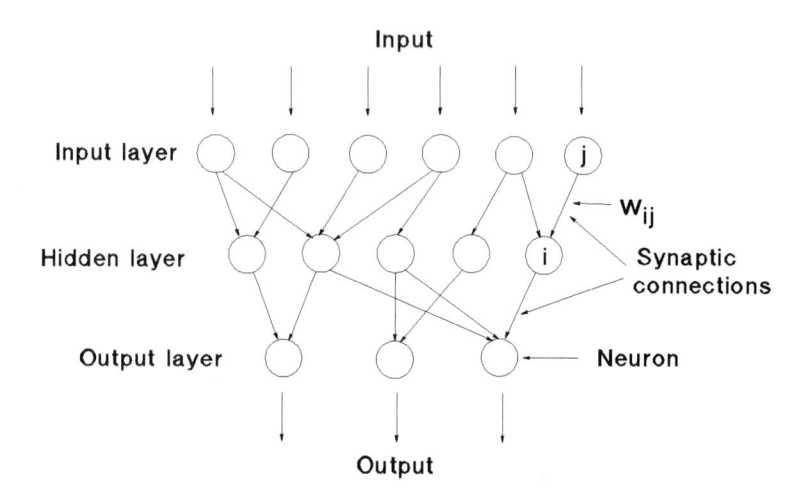

Figure 3.7 *Topology of a network trained by the backpropagation algorithm*

backpropagation algorithm. The basic algorithm idea is the generalized delta rule (see [Rum86]), which is formulated by

$$\Delta w_{ij}^k = \alpha(t_i^k - o_i^k)i_j^k \tag{3.7}$$

where α is a learning rate, t_i^k is the i-th component of the k-th (teaching) output vector, and o_i^k is the actual network output produced by applying the j-th component of k-th (teaching) input vector i_j^k to the j-th network input. This formula applies only to single layer networks (one layer of synaptic connections). Then, Δw_{ij}^k is the change of the weight between the i-th neuron and j-th input after presentation of the k-th teaching pattern. Rumelhart et al. [Rum86] give a proof that for linear neurons the generalized delta rule changes weights in such a way that the global squared error E with

$$E = \sum_k \frac{1}{2} \sum_i (t_i^k - o_i^k)^2 \tag{3.8}$$

is minimized through steepest descent ($\sum_i$ is a sum over all output neurons).

Rumelhart et al. extended this generalized delta rule to multilayered networks with nonlinear activation functions [Rum86]. Here, the problem is to generate an error signal for each network layer, since the direct network error may be determined at the network output only, through comparison of actual network outputs with desired outputs. Rumelhart et al. [Rum86] give three formulas for backpropagation learning. The first is the weight update rule

$$\Delta w_{ij}^k = \alpha \delta_i^k o_j^k, \tag{3.9}$$

which is the generalized delta rule from Equation 3.7 with output o_j^k from the preceding neuron layer replacing input i_j^k. Now, the difference between teaching output t_i^k and actual output o_i^k has been replaced by error signal δ_i^k. For a neuron in the output layer the error signal is straightforward to the generalized delta rule, given by

$$\delta_i^k = (t_i^k - o_i^k)f_i'(a_i^k). \tag{3.10}$$

The only difference is the introduction of the derivative of a neuron's activation function $f_i'(a_i^k)$ at activation level a_i^k. Error signals for hidden units are generated recursively from the errors of the following layers, starting from the output layer, according to

$$\delta_i^k = f_i'(a_i^k) \sum_m \delta_m^k w_{mi}. \tag{3.11}$$

This learning algorithm needs neurons with a continuously differentiable activation function. Furthermore, the activation function has to have zero slope at large and small inputs to guarantee the convergence of weight updates.

Error-backpropagation learning became important as it is a quite fast learning algorithm for multilayer networks, which are used in many real world applications. During the late 1980s and early 1990s, many varieties of the backpropagation algorithm emerged. Most of the developments were driven by the wish to obtain faster and more reliable convergence in learning. An early proposal was to introduce a momentum term to average weight updates according to

$$\Delta w_{ij}(t+1) = \alpha \delta_i^k o_j^k + \beta \Delta w_{ij}(t) \qquad (3.12)$$

where β is a second constant [Rum86]. Other varieties introduced network pruning components to make a network as small as possible during learning for better generalization and, again, faster convergence. However, the principles of all these varieties are the same, based on the generalized delta rule.

Due to many applications and the good performance of multilayer networks trained with the backpropagation algorithm, researchers tried to speed up computation intensive and therefore time consuming backpropagation learning with dedicated hardware. But this is a challenging task, for a number of reasons. One of the reasons is the sophisticated dataflow, since learning uses not only local information in a synapse's near vicinity. To obtain actual network outputs, first a complete feed-forward phase has to be performed by evaluating the following layers sequentially. Then, the dataflow has to be reversed to calculate the error signals, starting from the output layer, propagating back sequentially from layer to layer. Together with the error signal, the synaptic weights can be updated. Parallel operations occur only within a layer. A philosophy for introducing parallel hardware is to cut a network into slices along the network dataflow (from input to output). Each slice is mapped onto its own processor. This allocation of network parts onto processors causes problems in information exchange between processors. Kato *et al.* solved the information exchange problem by connecting processors via trays connected in a loop [Kat90]. Another approach is to separate training data into different sets. Then, a single processor updates the whole network, but only with part of the data. Other processors are operating concurrently with another training set. The calculated network updates from all processors are then averaged to update the network. Such an approach was chosen, for example, by Pomerleau *et al.* [Pom88]. However, it needs a large training set and a large epoch size, to work efficiently.

Another problem with the original backpropagation algorithm is that it needs continuously differentiable neuron activation functions and high precision computations. It is difficult to state what accuracy must be provided for successful learning since this is application dependent. Most networks are simulated on conventional computers with IEEE floating point format calculations. In the literature, minimum accuracies are given from 8

Artificial Neural Networks 47

bits for simple problems like a small XOR problem, up to a 32 bit floating point format for efficient learning. The authors have made some of their own experiments with the original backpropagation algorithm from Rumelhart *et al.* and obtained accuracy figures for several applications like the XOR problem and the control of an autonomous vehicle [Halg91]. A 16 bit fixed point format was sufficient to learn XOR but not to control the vehicle. Further simulations with 32 bit fixed point calculations showed good learning. Results were best if 21 bits were reserved for fractions. Asanovic *et al.* investigated the effect of modified learning on 16 bit fixed point format with real data from a phoneme classification task [Asa91]. They conclude that 16 bit fixed point accuracy is sufficient provided that numbers are rounded instead of truncated during computation (calculations are done with high precision and then rounded to fit onto the 16 bit fixed point format), and that weight and bias values are scaled separately. Hollis *et al.* [Holli90] and Montalvo *et al.* [Mon92] report that with modified backpropagation algorithms for analog VLSI circuitry, a minimum accuracy of 12 bits during learning and a minimum of 6 bits during recall may be sufficient. Montalvo *et al.* used a weight perturbation method to calculate weight updates by

$$w_{ij}(t) = w_{ij}(t-1) - \frac{\alpha \cdot \Delta E}{w_{pert}}. \quad (3.13)$$

The derivative used in the standard backpropagation algorithm is approximated by measuring the change of network error ΔE through a weight perturbation w_{pert}. Also, a neuron's gain is adjusted to use the full available weight range without clipping neuron outputs [Mon92].

3.2.3 Boltzmann Machines

The theory of Boltzmann machines is related to that of Hopfield networks. A Boltzmann machine consists of a set of neurons which are interconnected arbitrarily as sketched in Figure 3.8 (only some of the possible connections are drawn). In contrast to Hopfield networks and multi-layer Perceptrons, synapses in Boltzmann machines are bidirectional, *i.e.* information may flow through them in either direction. Any subset of neurons that are forced from the outer world to adopt certain input states can be defined as input neurons, whereas another arbitrary subset of neurons serves as output where their states are observed from the outer world to be interpreted as a network's response to the inputs. All the other neurons will be referred to as hidden neurons.

As in Hopfield networks, an energy is assigned to each Boltzmann machine state. This energy is defined by

$$E = -\sum_{i \leq j} w_{ij} o_i o_j + \sum_i \Theta_i o_i \quad (3.14)$$

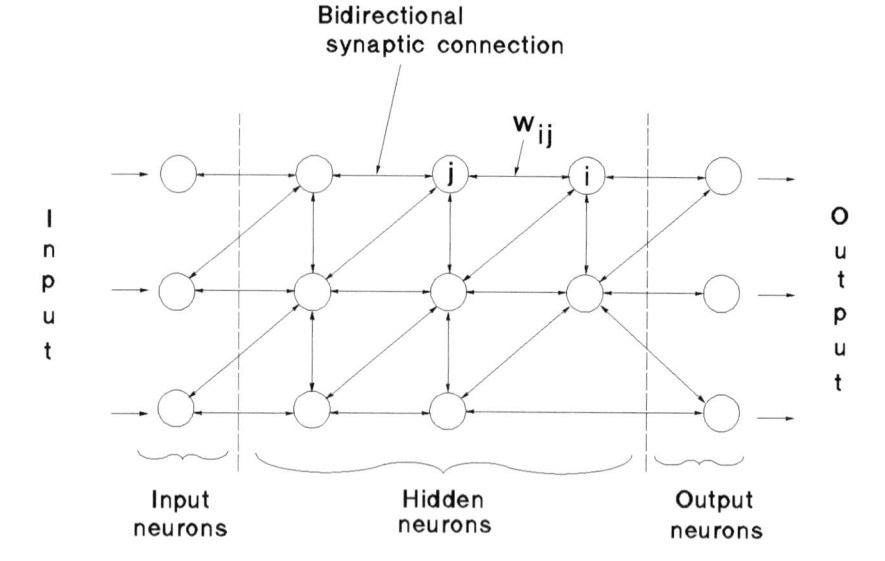

Figure 3.8 *Boltzmann machine topology*

where o_i denotes the activation, state or output ($a_i(t) = o_i(t)$) of neuron i, w_{ij} is the bidirectional synaptic weight between neurons i and j, and Θ is a certain threshold value. A neuron may adopt either state "0" (off) or state "1" (on). If no neuron is forced from outside to adopt a certain state, the whole network moves into a local energy minimum. However, in Boltzmann machines, noise is used to escape from local minima. The change of network energy by switching a single neuron k from an off-state to an on-state is calculated by

$$\Delta E_k = E(k = off) - E(k = on) = \sum_i w_{ik} o_i - \Theta_k. \quad (3.15)$$

If this change in energy is positive, *i.e.* the total input from other units and from outside the system exceeds threshold Θ_k, neuron k has to be switched on for energy reduction. Now, to avoid local minima a simulated annealing procedure is introduced. A neuron's state is activated (set to state "1"), regardless of its previous state, with probability

$$p_k = \frac{1}{1 + e^{-\frac{\Delta E_k}{T}}}. \quad (3.16)$$

Thereby, T is an annealing parameter (temperature). It can be shown mathematically that the global energy minimum is reached by reducing the annealing parameter with infinitely small increments. In reality this cannot be done, due to the infinitely long computation time it would take, but with a careful reduction of temperature T it is probable to reach a local minimum near to the global minimum.

Like Hopfield networks, Boltzmann machines can be used to solve optimization problems with weak constraints if one is able to formulate an optimization problem as a neural network topology. In this case, all local minima of the energy surface belong to feasible solutions of the optimization problem [Hin84, Aar89].

However, Hinton et al. found another interesting feature of Boltzmann machines. In [Hin84] and [Ack85] they describe a learning algorithm to obtain a weight set for a Boltzmann machine in that way that the network generates an internal model of its environment (supervised learning). Weight updates are done according to

$$\Delta w_{ij} = \alpha(p_{ij} - p'_{ij}) \quad (3.17)$$

where p_{ij} is the probability of neurons i and j both being in the on-state while the inputs and outputs are clamped to desired values from the outside world. In contrast, p'_{ij} is the probability of both corresponding neurons being "on" when the network runs with clamped inputs but without clamping output neurons from outside. It is important, however, to run the network in its "thermal" equilibrium when gathering statistics on p_{ij} and p'_{ij}. The learning procedure was derived for neurons which asynchronously update their states. In parallel hardware simulations, synchronous updates are usually necessary to simplify circuitry. Azencott [Aze89] describes a variety of the Boltzmann machine algorithm that yields better learning capabilities (faster convergence) in synchronous neuron updating. He proposes to gather weight update statistics in both clamped and nonclamped modes according to

$$p_{ij} = \left(\frac{1}{N}\right)\left[\sum_{t=1}^{N} o_i^{t-1} o_j^t + o_i^t o_j^{t-1}\right] \quad (3.18)$$

with N as the number of counts needed to gather statistics and o_i^t the activation of neuron i observed at time step t (the activation may either be "ON" or "OFF").

With respect to hardware implementation, the Boltzmann machine shows some very characteristic features. On the one hand, the learning algorithm given by Equation 3.17 only needs local information. To determine a learning update, a synapse has to observe no more than the states of the two neurons it is connecting. Thus, for learning, each synapse must have some circuitry to gather state statistics. Furthermore, Boltzmann machines can cope with low weight accuracy. Investigations have showed that even 3-7 bit weights are sufficient to solve some simple problems [Als87]. On the other hand, Boltzmann machine algorithms request random events. Equation 3.16 describes a probability to determine a neuron's state. Therefore, each neuron needs an independent random event source to calculate its new state. Other problems are the realization of bidirectional synapses, which is not as simple as unidirectional circuitry, and sophisticated network control through an annealing parameter. Only a few Boltzmann machine hardware implementations with on-chip learning have been done, so far.

3.2.4 Kohonen Self-Organizing Feature Map

Self-organizing feature maps are networks with unsupervised learning algorithms developed by T. Kohonen [Koh88]. It is a single layer network with lateral inhibition. This lateral inhibition serves to enable "competition" between neurons (see Figure 3.9). Each neuron in the network has a set of weights that is compared with the applied network input data. The more similar a neuron's weight set is compared with the input vector, the more the neuron will be activated. Through lateral inhibition only the most strongly activated neuron will respond. Thus, self-organizing feature maps belong to the competitive network category. For similarity measurement an arbitrary metric may be chosen which is application dependent. Frequently used are the normalized or unnormalized correlation

$$a_i = \sum_{j=1}^{n} w_{ij} x_j \qquad (3.19)$$

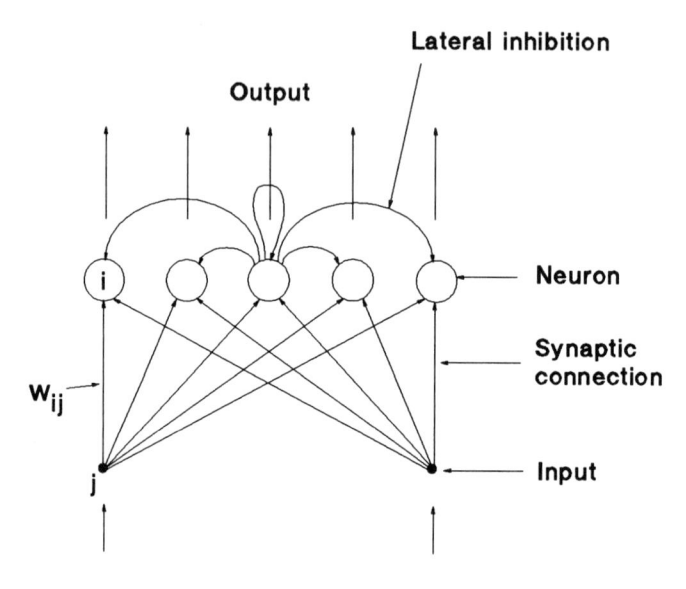

Figure 3.9 *Topology of the Self-Organizing Map from Kohonen*

or Euclidean distance

$$a_i = \sqrt{\sum_{j=1}^{n}(x_j - w_{ij})^2}, \qquad (3.20)$$

where a_i is the activation of neuron i and w_{ij} is the synaptic weight between neuron i and input j. The j-th component of input vector x is denoted by x_j. The responding neuron m is the one closest to input vector x

$$||x - w_m|| = \min_{j} ||x - w_j|| \qquad (3.21)$$

where w_m is the weight vector of neuron m and $||a-b||$ defines the distance of elements a and b in the chosen metric. Now, a neuron output o_i is different from its activation a_i since

$$o_i(t) = \begin{cases} 1 & \text{for } ||x(t) - w_i(t)|| = \min_j ||x(t) - w_j(t)|| \\ 0 & \text{else} \end{cases}. \qquad (3.22)$$

To train self-organizing feature maps, a clustering algorithm is used. The weights of the neuron closest to the actual teaching pattern x are changed to better fit the input vector (to become more similar with respect to the chosen metric). In addition, weights of neurons in the near vicinity N_m of the "winning" neuron are updated, *i.e.*

$$\frac{dw_{ij}}{dt} = \begin{cases} \alpha(t)\,[x_j(t) - w_{ij}(t)] & \text{for } i \in N_m \\ 0 & \text{otherwise} \end{cases}. \qquad (3.23)$$

The neighborhood N_m of winning neuron m must be defined, and is usually a rectangular window, a triangle or a mexican hat function. Furthermore, N_m is a function of time; during learning the neighborhood becomes smaller to make weight updates more selective. Through updates in a winning neuron's neighborhood, a feature map operates topology preserving, *i.e.* topological relations in input data will still exist at network outputs. In the time discrete case the update procedure is

$$w_i(t+1) = \begin{cases} w_i(t) + \alpha(t)\,[x(t) - w_i(t)] & \text{for } i \in N_m \\ w_i(t) & \text{otherwise} \end{cases}, \qquad (3.24)$$

with $w_i(t)$ being the weight vector of neuron i at time instant t.

Compared with error-backpropagation learning and Boltzmann machine learning, the feature map adaptation algorithm described is simpler to map onto hardware, especially if some simplifications are done. Such simplifications may be to use rectangular neighborhood windows, to use similarity criteria which are easier to implement than Euclidean distance, or to postulate weight updates of a fixed magnitude. However, such simplifications may affect convergence and overall performance. A big advantage is that no very accurate weight storage is necessary, permitting the use of analog storage techniques.

3.2.5 Radial Basis Function Networks

Radial Basis Function (RBF) networks can be interpreted as three-layer networks of different types of neurons. The first layer serves to propagate input values to the second layer of neurons. This second layer consists of radially limited neurons. Each neuron i has a vector w_i of synaptic weights, with element w_{ij} connecting input j to neuron i of the second layer. In contrast to multilayer perceptrons, neurons of the second layer may perform different tasks depending on the type of RBF network. The activation of neuron i may, for example, be obtained by the outer product between input x and weight vector w_i, or by measuring their distance with respect to an appropriate metric (Euclidean distance, Manhattan distance, etc.). Then its output is obtained by applying a radial basis function. Figure 3.10 shows two popular RBFs in one dimension, namely the signum RBF and an exponential RBF. Thus, a second layer neuron output is defined by

$$o_i = F_1(d_i) = F_1 \left(\sqrt{\sum_{j=1}^{N_1}(x_j - w_{ij})^2} - \Theta_i \right) \quad (3.25)$$

if Euclidean distance is chosen to compare neuron weights with network inputs. $F_1(d_i)$ is a radially limited function applied on the calculated distance d_i (see Figure 3.10) and N_1 is the number of input neurons (network inputs). In the case of the signum function, this means that a neuron i is activated only if the distance d_i between its weight vector w_i and network input x is smaller than a certain radius.

Network outputs from the second layer are weighted and summed up

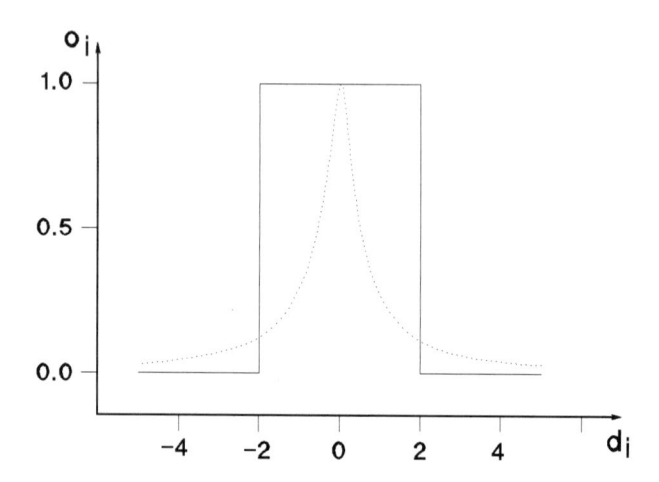

Figure 3.10 *One-dimensional signum and exponential type RBF (adapted from [Holle92])*

Artificial Neural Networks 53

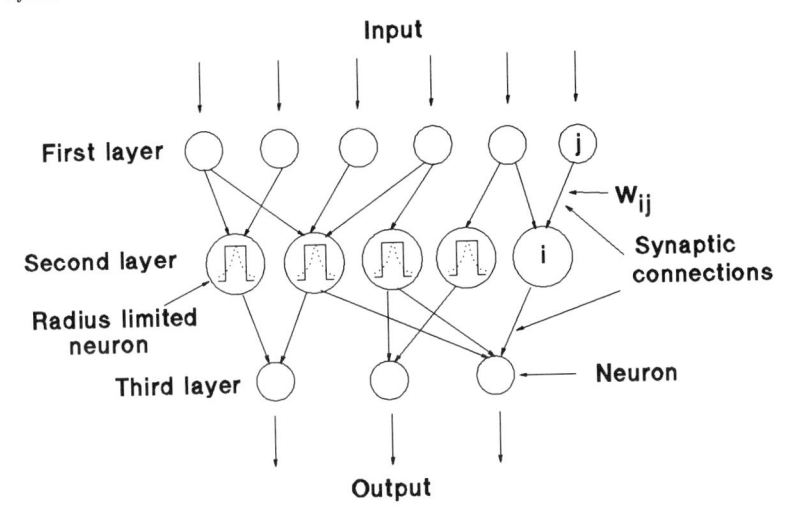

Figure 3.11 *General RBF network architecture*

through neurons in a third layer. The whole network architecture is depicted in Figure 3.11. Outputs of neurons in the third layer are calculated by

$$o_i = F_2 \left(\sum_{j=1}^{N_2} w_{ij} x_j \right) \qquad (3.26)$$

with N_2 as the number of neurons in the second layer.

By appropriately choosing distance metrics in the network layers and by selecting different functions F_1 and F_2, several varieties of networks can be realized, e.g. probabilistic neural networks (PNNs) [Spec88, Spec92], restricted coulomb energy (RCE) networks [Rei82, Sco91] and probabilistic RCE networks (P-RCE) [Sco87].

RBF networks are used as classifiers. In contrast to iterative neural network training procedures, RBF algorithms like PNN algorithms and RCE algorithms are extremely fast during the training phase. Only one or a few training sweeps through the training set is necessary to adapt the whole network. The above described network architecture is well apt for hardware implementation. In many real classification applications it is sufficient to represent a feature value which is one element of the network input with an accuracy of a few bits [Sco91]. Thus, analog weight storage is possible. For comparison metrics like the Manhattan distance, no area consuming multiplication circuitry is necessary since only subtractions and additions are needed. This enables high parallelism on low cost hardware. For some algorithms, weights from the second to the third layer are unity, which then do not need multipication circuitry, either.

3.2.6 Other Network Algorithms

Many neural network paradigms have been developed in the last decade, ranging from simple associative memory concepts to sophisticated network architectures with complicated learning schemes. But the authors did not intend to go into neural network mathematics and algorithms in depth. The interested reader is recommended to read literature on neural network mathematics (e.g. [Her91]). In many cases, other network architectures and algorithms are based on the principles of those described above.

3.3 Summary

Organic neural networks are highly complex systems with manifold electrochemical dependencies between neurons and synapses. The principal mathematical abstractions that are made for their simulation is that synapses perform simple multiplications or value comparisons, whereas neurons sum up arriving signals and perform a nonlinear operation. These mathematical operations have to be done by dedicated neural network hardware. In many cases it is questionable as to whether there remains some biological evidence in these mathematical abstractions. The error backpropagation algorithm, which is a steepest descent minimization method, or the simulated annealing algorithm do not have much in common with the effects occuring in a nervous system. But at the moment, where only a little or no knowledge is available on the complex behavior of nervous systems, such mathematical abstractions are necessary to try to understand the basic mechanisms of self-organization and learning in a massively interconnected network of simple processors.

Artificial neural network paradigms mainly differ in network topology. Adding feedback or lateral inhibitory connections to a simple feed-forward network completely changes its behavior. Furthermore, networks differ in the type of nonlinear operation done by neurons, in synapse operation (multiplication, value comparison) and in their learning algorithms. Due to these differences, demands to hardware acceleration are different. Algorithms like the error-backpropagation algorithm ask for high precision calculations and a continuously differentiable neuron activation function. In contrast, RCE-learning or LVQ-learning can succeed with 5 bit accuracy only. The demands of the algorithms to be simulated often dictate the type of hardware architecture to be used. The more flexibility needed, the more complex it has to be with less parallelism.

The artificial network algorithms presented in this chapter belong to the group most frequently used in technical applications. Nearly every dedicated hardware platform supports at least one of them.

4

Digital VLSI Building Blocks

4.1 Introduction

Today, most VLSI circuits are implemented in complementary MOS technology (CMOS technology). This shift from formerly preferred NMOS to CMOS circuits occurred because of specific CMOS features [Wes85]:

- high performance
- low power consumption
- scales well to small feature size.

Due to the significant advantages of CMOS technology over other technologies, it has spread into many areas of system design. A large variety of already designed circuits as well as excellent design tools like schematic entries, placement and routing tools, and circuit simulators (for logical and physical circuit behavior) make it easy and comfortable to design digital CMOS ASICs (Application Specific Integrated Circuits). Therefore, in the following sections, CMOS circuits for the realization of basic building blocks relevant for dedicated neural network hardware are described. A circuit's size will be measured by its number of transistors or gates. For digital circuits, in most of the cases minimum size transistors are sufficient to build up larger circuitry. Principally, such a transistor consists of a diffusion line on a lower layer which is crossed by a polysilicon line on an upper layer. Since modern fabrication lines offer fabrication processes with a feature size of less than $1\mu m$, a minimum size transistor including some distance that is required to the next element, occupies an area of not more than a few square microns. A gate is a simple circuit consisting of a few transistors. Basic gates for circuit design are the NOR and NAND gates. Figure 4.1 shows an inverter together with a NOR and a NAND gate. If circuit complexity is measured by the number of gates used, one gate corresponds to four transistors. In this section we do not intend to teach digital VLSI design, but to introduce important VLSI circuits briefly, and to discuss them from the point of view of a neural network hardware designer. For more

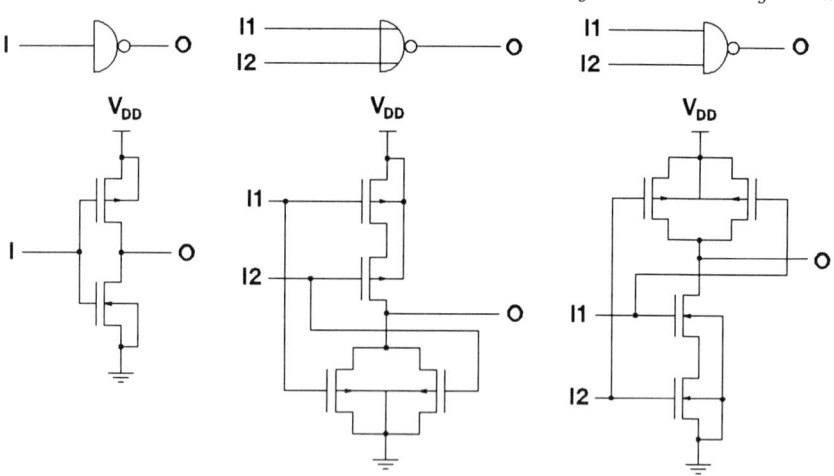

Figure 4.1 *Inverter, NOR gate and NAND gate*

detailed information, Neil Weste and Kamran Eshraghian's book "Principles of CMOS VLSI Design" [Wes85] can be recommended, as it covers the subsequently mentioned circuits.

4.2 Summation

In many digital systems, adders and counters are important components. Several principles for adder design exist to form adders with specific features. A one bit adder stage possesses three inputs and two outputs. Inputs are the carry input C from the preceding stage and two inputs A and B for the bits to be added. Outputs are the sum bit S and a carry bit feeding the carry input of a successive adder stage. Well known adder circuits are:
- simple combinational adder
- dynamic adder
- transmission gate adder
- carry lookahead adder
- manchester carry adder
- binary lookahead carry adder
- carry select adder.

Figure 4.2 shows the gate schematic and transistor schematic of a one bit combinational adder stage to implement logic functions required, which are:

$$SUM = ABC + A\overline{BC} + \overline{A}B\overline{C} + \overline{AB}C \qquad (4.1)$$
$$CARRY = AB + AC + BC. \qquad (4.2)$$

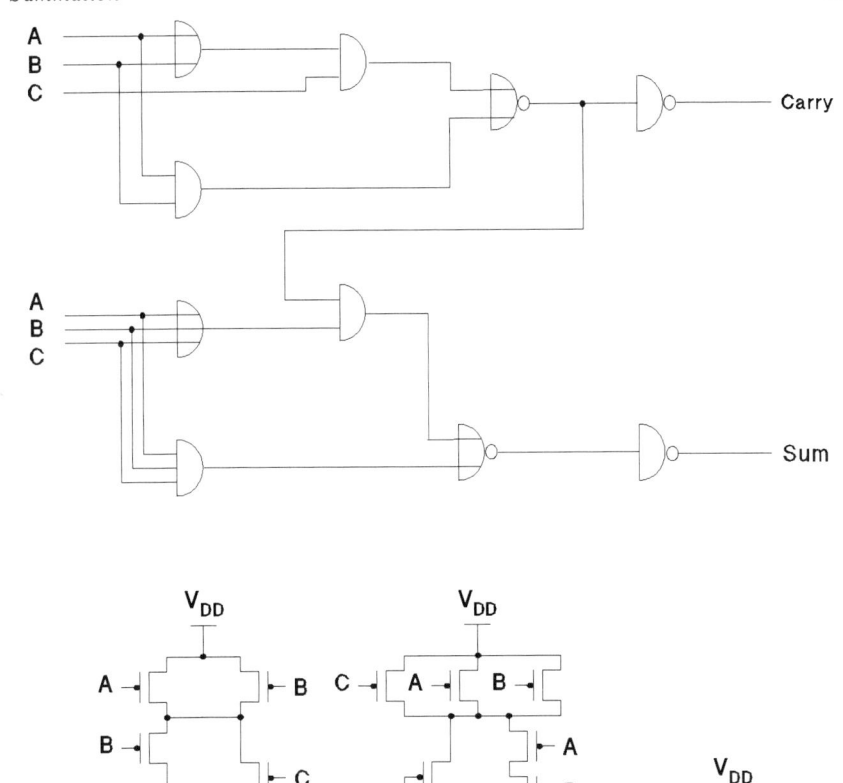

Summation

Figure 4.2 *Gate and transistor schematic of combinational adder stage (adapted from [Wes85])*

The first question for a designer is whether to implement a serial or a parallel adder. An adder stage may be used for each bit of two numbers to be added (see Figure 4.3). Since a carry bit generated by one stage is fed

58   *Digital VLSI Building Blocks*

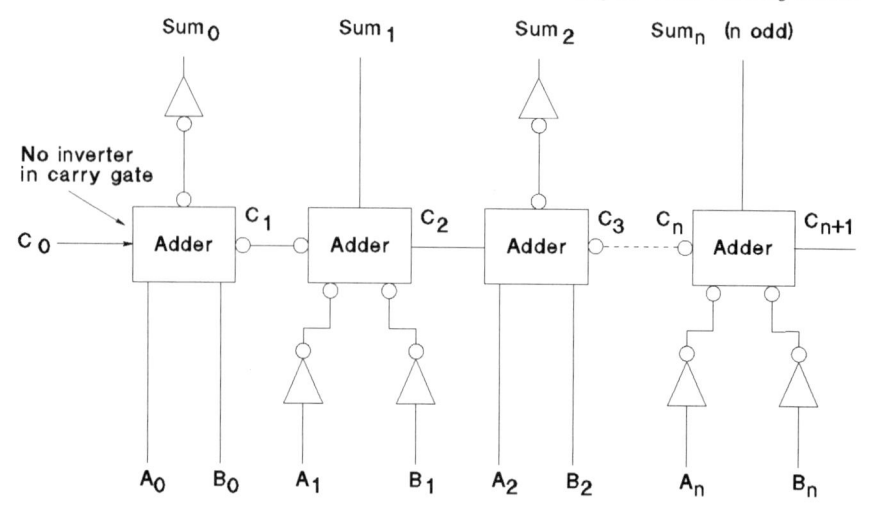

Figure 4.3 *n-bit ripple carry adder (adapted from [Wes85])*

into the carry input of the next stage, this structure is called a "ripple carry adder". A serial adder approach is given in Figure 4.4. For the serial adder approach, three shift registers are required to store addend, augend and sum, as well as a flipflop for the carry bit. A big disadvantage of the parallel ripple carry adder is the flow of the carry signal which has to ripple from input through all adder stages to the output of the last stage, thus limiting the overall speed of operation. Transmission gate adders use exclusive-or (XOR) gates constructed by means of transmission gates [Wes85]. This

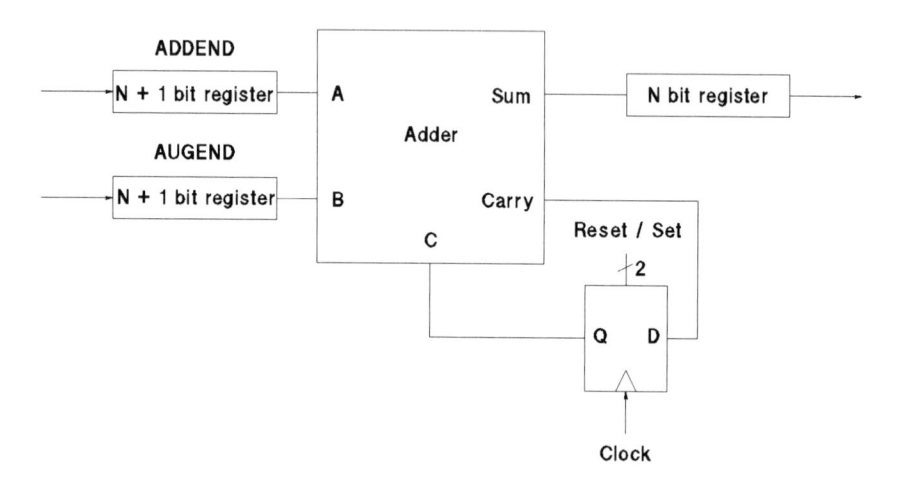

Figure 4.4 *Serial adder (adapted from [Wes85])*

adder is of the same size as a combinational adder (24 transistors), but has the advantage of equal SUM and CARRY delay times. As in the case of a standard combinational adder, however, carry delay is linearly growing with the size of input words. That problem may only be solved by calculating the carry to each stage independently of the results of previous stages, which is done in carry lookahead adders. These adders benefit from the fact that so-called generate (G) and propagate (P) signals may be formed from inputs A and B without using the results of previous stages:

$$G_i = A_i \cdot B_i \quad \textit{generate signal} \tag{4.3}$$

$$P_i = A_i + B_i \quad \textit{propagate signal.} \tag{4.4}$$

Then, the carry to stage i may be expressed as

$$C_i = G_i + P_i G_{i-1} + P_i P_{i-1} G_{i-2} + \cdots + P_i \cdots P_1 C_0. \tag{4.5}$$

It is clear that the number of gates to implement such a carry lookahead adder depends on the number of stages. As a result, in many designs the number of stages is limited to about four [Wes85]. Manchester carry adders work with a chain (domino carry chain) of precharged carry nodes. Similar to carry lookahead circuitry, there is a limitation in the length of a domino carry chain due to serial transistors with a finite conductance, which have to pull down all carries up to the last one (worst case) within one clock cycle. Another approach to fast adders is the binary lookahead carry adder. Other logic functions are used to evaluate carries, in this case implemented in a binary tree structure to minimize the number of preceding stages for the generation of carries [Wes85]. This method is suitable for adders that are larger than 16 bits. The carry select adder performs an addition twice in one stage. Thus, the first addition is done with an input carry of zero, whereas the second addition assumes a carry of one. Then, if the carry of the preceding stage is evaluated, the correct sum is selected using a multiplexor.

Counters are devices with one data input which are used to generate a sequence of binary numbers. Counters may be built up by adders and registers or by cascaded flipflops. They are not appropriate for additions, but for accumulations. In binary networks, accumulations are the operations needed to realize a neuron input (binary additions).

For neural network implementations, three features are of special importance: speed, accuracy and space requirements. Clearly, maximum speed will be achieved by parallel adders. However, in favor of speed these circuits expend area. Therefore, if a computational accuracy of many bits is required, fast parallel adders cannot be implemented on a reasonably small area. On complex, flexible processors which are used for neural network simulation, it is possible to implement such parallel adders (e.g. signal processors from Texas Instruments), since only one processor containing one adder is implemented on a chip. The same is valid for special neural network acceleration boards. However, if one is interested in many processors on one chip, as in area efficient multi-processor architectures, bit serial adders or counters have to be used, since these may be realized on a much smaller area. In most cases, even this does not cause low computational power, since data has to enter chips sequentially via a limited number of pins.

4.3 Multiplication

Multiplications have to be performed in many signal processing tasks, not only in neural network applications. In digital systems, the traditional way in which to accomplish a multiplication is by taking multiplier bits as condition for shifted additions of the multiplicand. Therefore, multiplication may be separated into the evaluation of partial products and the accumulation of the shifted partial products. Evaluating a partial product is a multiplication of the multiplicand with one bit of the multiplier, which is equivalent to a logical AND operation. So the whole multiplication operation is no more than ANDing the multiplicand with the relevant multiplier bit and accumulating the result to the shifted result of the preceding multiplication step. Different methods exist to perform this procedure. These methods differ in speed, accuracy and implementation area. The following multiplier architectures exist:

- serial
- serial/parallel
- parallel.

Figure 4.5 sketches a basic serial multiplier (C_i stands for carry in, C_o for carry out). It consists of an adder, AND gates $G1$, $G2$, a delay element, and a serial to parallel register. Numbers Y (n bit multiplicand) and X (m bit multiplier) are presented to the multiplier serially. At one cycle, one bit of the register, the ANDed bits of multiplier and multiplicand, and the carry from the previous cycle are added. To generate one partial product, it is necessary to perform that operation for n cycles. The whole $m+n$ bit result will be obtained after $m \times n$ clock cycles. Required shift operations may thus be achieved automatically by choosing an appropriate size for the serial to parallel register. An extension of a simple serial multiplier is given in Figure 4.6. Multiplier X is serially presented to the horizontal input which, owing to delay elements, performs a shift of the multiplier along the AND gates, whereas multiplicand Y is presented in parallel. After m cycles the multiplier completely enters the horizontal input line, thus guaranteeing that all shifted partial products have been generated. Then, n additional cycles are necessary to complete summation done by the n full adders which automatically shift their results to the output. The whole

Multiplication

multiplication needs only $m+n$ clock cycles, which is significantly less than the $m \times n$ cycles required by a fully serial multiplier. Faster multiplications may only be done by a parallel multiplier. A partial product consists of n elements that are ANDed bits from multiplier and multiplicand, each. Such a pair can be formed independently if $n \times m$ AND gates are available. For a $n \times n$ multiplier which requires $n(n-2)$ full adders, n half adders and n^2 AND gates, the worst case delay is $(2n+1)\tau$, with τ being the adder delay [Wes85]. Figure 4.7 delineates the structure of a parallel multiplier array.

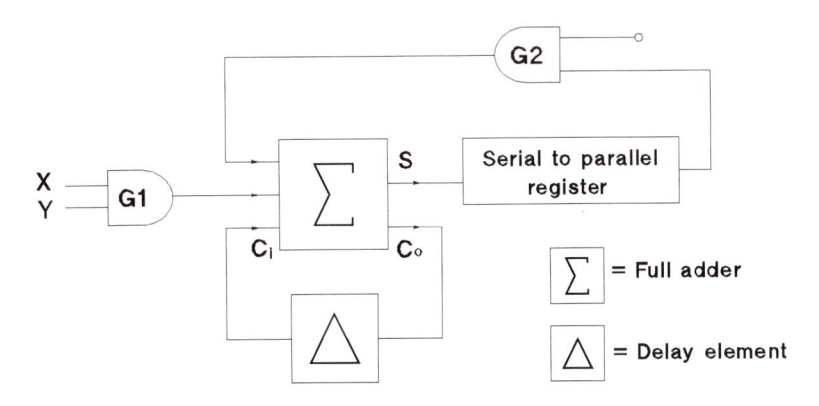

Figure 4.5 *Serial multiplier (adapted from [Wes85])*

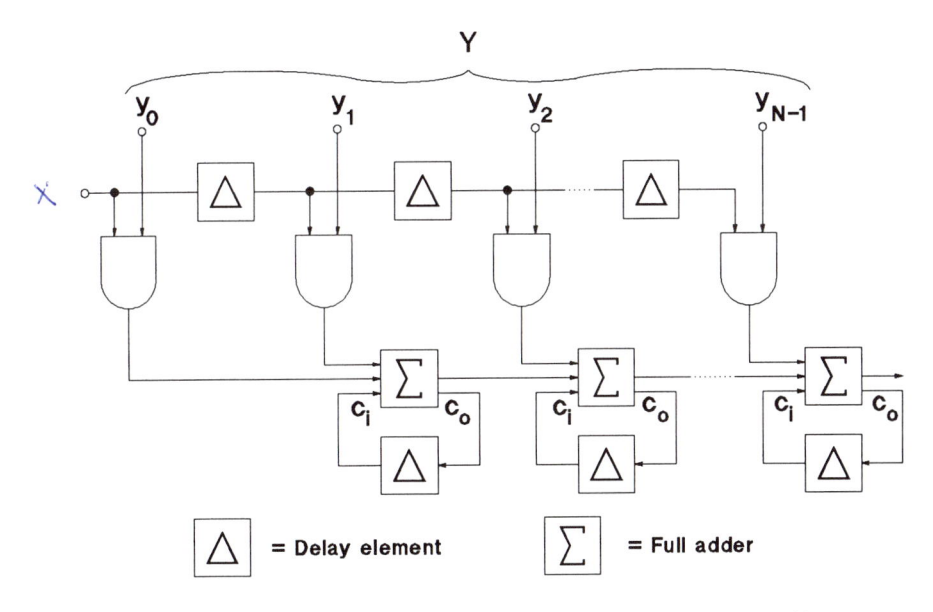

Figure 4.6 *Serial/parallel multiplier (adapted from [Wes85])*

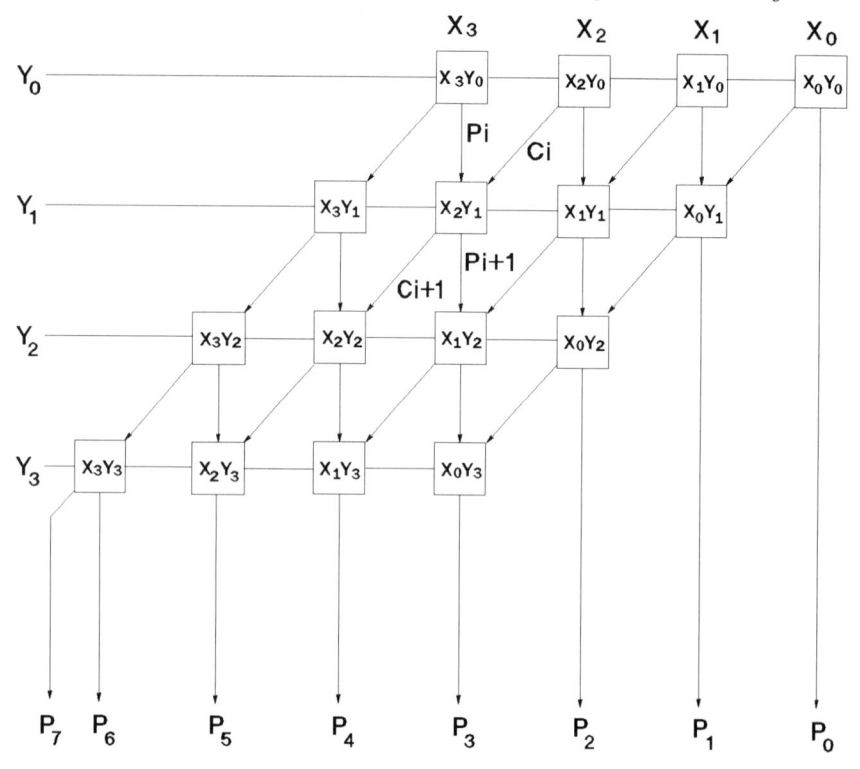

Figure 4.7 *Parallel multiplier array (adapted from [Wes85])*

Multiplication becomes a very simple task if only binary synapses and binary neuron outputs are used. In this case, a multiplication corresponds to the logic AND operation. Thus, a neuron with its receiving synapses may simply be imitated by consecutive logic AND operations (multiplication) and accumulations (summation).

For neural network multiplication circuitry the same statements are valid as given above for adder circuits. If only one complex processor is implemented on a chip which performs many tasks, fast parallel or serial/parallel multipliers should be chosen. However, in a bit slice architecture or another approach using massive parallelism, there will not be sufficient silicon area for the implementation of several, very area consuming parallel multipliers. Therefore, serial multiplier circuits will be preferred in such designs.

4.4 Nonlinearities

Depending on the network type to be realized, very different nonlinear activation functions for neurons are required. Some models need no more

Nonlinearities

than a simple hardlimiter threshold function like the neuron model used by Widrow and Hoff for their Adaline system [Wid60]. In other models (e.g. networks with backpropagation learning), more complex nonlinearities are involved like the sigmoid function [Rum86]. Rumelhart *et al.* used the logistic function

$$a_i = \frac{1}{1 + e^{-(\sum_j w_{ij} o_j + \Theta_i)}} \qquad (4.6)$$

for most of their experiments [Rum88]. Some important activation functions are given in Figure 4.8. To decide a neuron's binary state, in Boltzmann machines the Fermi distribution has to be evaluated (see Equation 3.16). A straightforward approach to obtain these functions is using circuits for full calculations, *i.e.* multipliers, dividers, adders, comparators and others. However, this may be a very time consuming and/or area consuming approach. To avoid unnecessary computations, a very common method is to use look-up tables. In most of the networks, the input space as well as output space of the activation function is confined to a small range. Furthermore, in many cases it is possible to discretize output values with rather large quantization steps. So only a few values have to be stored in a small look-up table, which therefore provides a fast and efficient solution. Additional requests, like very small quantization steps or differentiability, however, may cause some trouble. The smaller a quantization is, the more values have to be stored and the larger a look-up table will become. If differentiability is requested (e.g. backpropagation algorithm), additional circuitry may help to perform interpolation between stored points of a function. Myers *et al.* proposed the use of a seven segment piecewise linear approximation to the sigmoid which is used in backpropagation learning [Mye91] that can easily be implemented in VLSI technology [Mye89]. An appropriate method has to be found individually, since the demands of network types are diverse. Even different applications of the same network type may request different solutions.

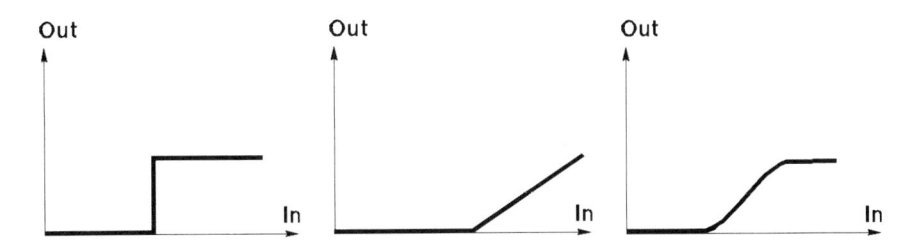

Figure 4.8 *Activation functions for artificial neurons*

4.5 Storage Elements

The question of storage is crucial for neural network realizations. For a fully connected feedback network of n neurons, n^2 synapses exist. A correlation matrix memory of n neurons with m inputs contains $n \times m$ synapses. This shows clearly that weight storage has to be extremely area efficient due to the large number of synapses. In digital technology there exist several principles to store information. Since most networks work with learning algorithms, or at least it should be possible to preload a network with specific synaptic interconnections, programmable solutions are of special interest. To store one bit of information one may implement small static or dynamic cells which are used in standard RAM chips. Figure 4.9 illustrates the basic static RAM cell (left). Two inverters are crosscoupled to hold a value imposed by external signals. The *Word* lines serve to connect and disconnect the cell from lines Bit and $\overline{Bit}$, which are used to transfer data to and from cells. Information in such a cell is retained as long as the circuit is supplied with electricity. Much smaller cells may be realized using dynamic storage techniques. The right part of Figure 4.9 shows an extremely small one-transistor dynamic storage circuit. A small capacitor that can be accessed by a transistor carries the memory value. Sense amplifiers sense a small voltage change if the capacitor is switched onto the Bit line. These circuits have to be refreshed after a short period, since charge is flowing from capacitors due to finite resistances, which makes them difficult to handle for a designer.

Storage cells may be configured to form storage for synaptic weights of arbitrary accuracy (the more accuracy requested, the more silicon area has to be spent). For neural network implementations, dynamic storage cells are very attractive due to their small size. However, for a dedicated chip, this

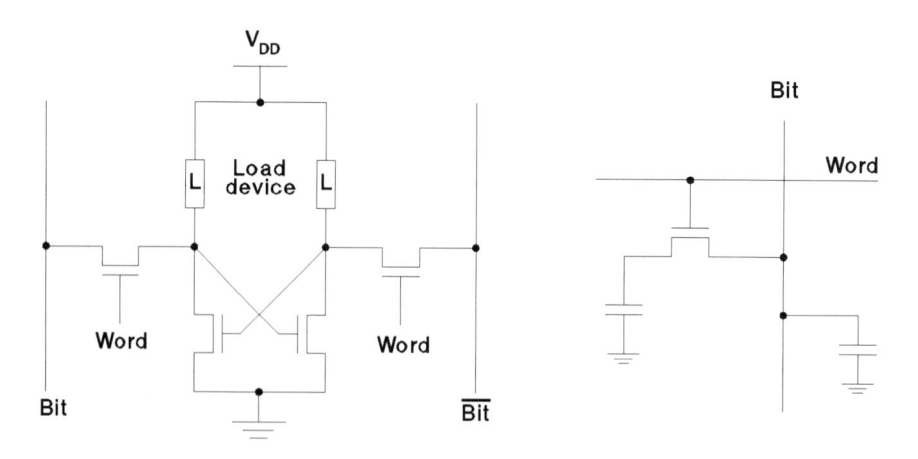

Figure 4.9 *Static and dynamic RAM cell (adapted from [Wes85])*

technology is too cumbersome. Therefore, some designs use commercially available RAM chips to benefit from a high storage density, which then have to be cascaded with dedicated neurochips. "Neuro"-designers usually use static RAM cells on their chip designs.

4.6 Other Elements

Some additional circuitry may become necessary for implementations, depending on implemented network types and architectures. One important element to be mentioned are random number generators. Stochastic algorithms as in a Boltzmann machine or some Hopfield type networks need random events. Two methods for random number generation are used in digital technology:

- shift registers with feedback via XOR-gates
- tables with a large number of random numbers.

In the shift register approach, the values of several register bits are taken and logically combined with each other through XOR-gates (see Figure 4.10). The result obtained is fed back into the input bit. Such a register which is fed back generates cyclic bit patterns. If feedback logic is chosen appropriately and the register is large enough, large cycles of pseudo random numbers will be generated. For the second approach, random numbers are generated externally and stored in memory. To generate a series of random numbers one just has to start at an arbitrary memory position and to read the contents of memory positions consecutively. This method also generates cycles of pseudo random numbers. The size of a cycle depends on the memory size. Both methods (especially the memory solution) are rather area consuming if good random numbers have to be obtained. Unfortunately, for all important algorithms, statistically independent random number generators are requested, which causes additional problems.

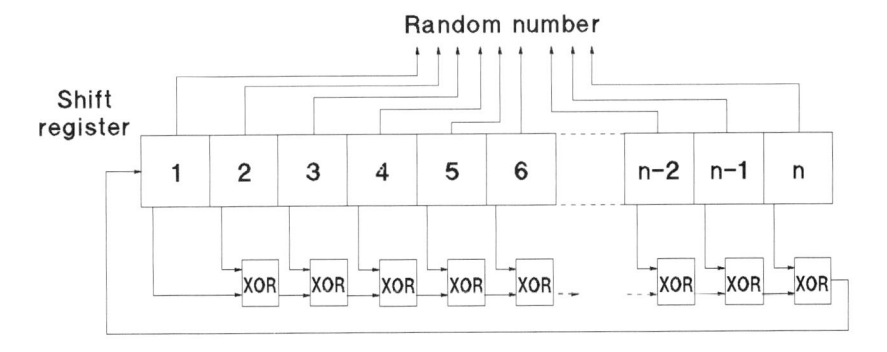

Figure 4.10 *Shift register and XOR-gates as random number generator*

Therefore, an independent random number generator would be necessary for each neuron of the Boltzmann machine.

Digital random number generators are very difficult to implement. Only pseudo random events are generated, and existing circuits are rather large. Statistical independence is nearly impossible to achieve, at least if many random events are requested, since the circuits described create cycles of random numbers. Better random events may be obtained by using analog techniques (e.g. operational amplifiers producing noise).

4.7 Summary

In this chapter the use of digital building blocks is discussed. The task of the building blocks is to perform those mathematical operations needed to simulate artificial neural networks as presented in Chapter 3, and to provide synaptic weight storage. To form a simulation platform the necessary building blocks are put together forming a data path for algorithmic operations. Information between modules or subsystems is transformed synchronously through busses. The information flow through building blocks is controlled via a global controller. Digital architectures and neurocomputer systems made from building blocks are the topic of Chapter 7.

The advantages of digital CMOS technology for neural algorithm simulation are simple and cheap fabrication, high flexibility, and high signal-to-noise ratio. RAM circuitry enables simple weight storage with easy access to the weights stored. This feature is especially crucial for the implementation of learning algorithms, since learning needs the controlled change of weight values. At the expense of area in parallel operation mode or speed in sequential operations, an arbitrary accuracy of mathematical operations may be achieved. The use of a floating point format allows one to realize extremely flexible systems that may simulate a large variety of algorithms.

On the other hand, a simple adder or multiplier circuit consists of hundreds or even thousands of transistors which occupy a significant amount of silicon area, thus reducing the achievable amount of parallelism. The controller, as well as busses for information exchange, needs additional area. Furthermore, digital systems are usually clocked. However, a time discrete evaluation of networks with feedback is very inefficient in terms of simulation time. Hence, an asynchronous evaluation of neural network paradigms including feedback (e.g. Hopfield type networks) may be much more efficient than a time discrete simulation on digital circuitry.

5
Analog Building Blocks

5.1 Introduction

An important alternative to digital techniques in artificial neural network design are analog implementations. This is due to the features of analog technology, which are: efficient data transmission through multilevel signals (not only binary), high speed through asynchronous circuitry, and extremely small computational circuit implementation by exploiting physical effects. These features make analog VLSI technology well suited for the implementation of fast and area efficient artificial neural network systems with low power dissipation. Exploiting basic physical effects to model the weighting of inputs from interconnected neurons is a special feature that can be identified even in early designs of analog neural nets.

As in the case of digital VLSI implementations, the basic building blocks of dedicated analog hardware realizations may be divided into:

- circuits for summation
- circuits for multiplication
- circuits for weight storage
- circuits for nonlinearities
- other circuits.

However, in contrast to digital implementations, it may become far more difficult to distinguish between different elements and their function. For example, a simple MOS transistor may serve to store information and to operate as a multiplier. Thereby, synaptic weight information can be stored as a charge on its gate, whereas the transistor realizes an adaptive resistor whose resistance is controlled by gate voltage (*i.e.* the amount of charge on the gate). The storage effect is caused by the fact that each MOS transistor gate consists of two layers of conducting material separated by a thin layer of isolating oxide, thus forming a small parasitic capacitor. Hence, a MOS transistor may be modeled by a small capacitance and a channel whose resistance is controlled by the capacitor voltage (this is a very simple model, neglecting many physical effects). In fact, two elements are present, a parasitic capacitor used for synaptic weight storage and a voltage controlled channel which may be used for multiplication ($I = G \cdot U$, with I the channel current, G the voltage dependent channel conductivity, and U the drain-to-source voltage which is proportional to the stored weight value). Thus, if an analog circuit is analysed, the user has to seriously consider how the circuit operates and what it consists of, to distinguish the different operations performed by it.

Compared with fully digital implementations, analog circuitry is much more sophisticated and difficult to design. On the one hand, this is caused by the large variety of materials and design technologies available for the analog designer. On the other hand, if a specific implementation and design technology has been chosen, not only a configuration of specific elements affects circuit behavior but also many parameters of each individual element. Such parameters may be fabrication dependent parameters (e.g. doping) which cannot be influenced by a designer and just have to be taken into account. Another example is user defined parameters like channel length and width of a MOS transistor. To exploit special digital and analog features, mixed analog/digital chips have been implemented. Due to the large variety of analog implementations, in subsequent basic building block sections one has to distinguish properly between design principles and implementations. A design principle will thus be a specific circuitry to perform a specific operation. An operational amplifier may be such a circuit (design principle) that is realized by an arrangement of transistors. Within its linear range an operational amplifier with gain control may be used as a multiplier. Within its full range (beyond linear region) it may serve as a nonlinearity. A practical implementation of an operational amplifier, however, may be done by bipolar transistors or by MOS transistors operating in subthreshold mode, which are two completely different implementation technologies.

The following description of analog circuitry and design techniques is not complete. Furthermore, descriptions of each circuit mentioned may not be profound enough for every reader. More detailed information can be taken from referenced articles or books on analog VLSI technology.

5.2 Summation

Summation of analog signals is quite simple compared to summation in digital circuitry. Most of the analog neural network implementations are working with synapses which produce currents or charges while synaptic inputs are voltages.

5.2.1 Kirchhoff's Current Node

A straightforward summation of currents can be realized by exploiting Kirchhoff's current law. This law says that "The sum of all currents towards a node must be zero at any time" [Millm87].

$$\sum_k I_k = 0 \qquad (5.1)$$

Equation 5.1 describes Kirchhoff's current law. Thus, a simple current node in a circuit performs a summation. This is a very convincing example of the advantages of analog circuitry on digital implementations. A smaller adder than a simple analog current node cannot be implemented in VLSI technology. Such an exploitation of simple physical laws for realizing computational entities enables fast computations on a very small area. In an analogous way, one can derive a similar equation using the law of conservation of charges for the summation of charge inputs. Conservation of charges means that an amount of charge cannot emerge or disappear suddenly. If several charges flow to a node, the node's charge increases by the sum of receiving charges. The principles of Kirchhoff's current law and the law of charge conservation may be exploited to realize a neuron's input (see Figure 5.1).

5.2.2 Current Subtraction with Cascode Current Mirror Circuit

To subtract excitatory and inhibitory signals represented on two current lines, Mann et al. propose a cascode current mirror circuit [Man87, Man88a], as depicted in Figure 5.2. An additional difference amplifier at the circuit output ($I_+ - I_-$ output) guarantees that a constant potential is present at all synaptic devices connected to a current summing line. This current subtraction circuit was designed to operate together with a synapse circuit in

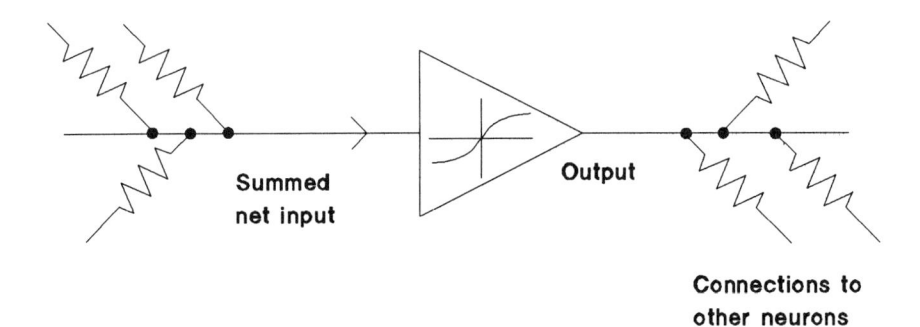

Figure 5.1 *Analog neuron model (adapted from [Jac87b])*

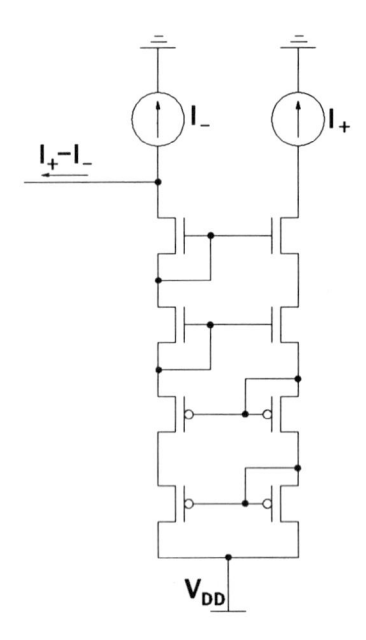

Figure 5.2 *Current mirror cascode for current subtraction (adapted from [Man88a])*

the form of a multiplying digital/analog converter (MDAC), also proposed by Mann *et al.* (see Figure 5.10).

5.2.3 Charge Summation on a Capacitor

Simple circuits for performing mathematical operations on analog signals may also be implemented using pulse stream techniques. In such a system, signals are transferred via pulses. Information is coded by means of varying pulse frequency (pulse frequency modulation) or varying pulse width (pulse width modulation). Then, a low pass filter circuit with a capacitor may be used as a summing element that accumulates charges (positive charges are flowing to the capacitor, negative charges are removed from the capacitor). Such a technique was used, for example, by Murray to design an analog synapse circuit [Mur89b]. The principle is sketched in Figure 5.3, where two input lines with pulse stream signals control transistors T1 and T2. The pulse stream on the gate of T2 serves as a specific discharge level. Depending on the pulse width of the pulse stream signal arriving at T1, the capacitor receives a certain amount of charge or loses charge, thus allowing positive and negative signals to be summed (positive or negative signs are encoded by pulse width).

Cotter *et al.* [Cott88] proposed a circuit design that accepts either pulse

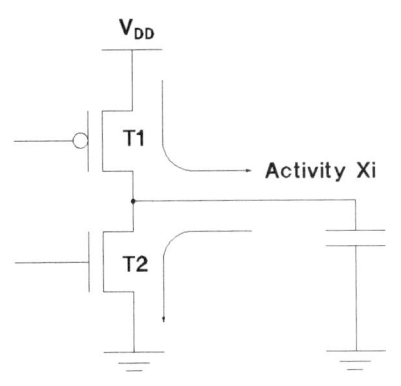

Figure 5.3 *Summing element used by Murray et al. (adapted from [Mur89a])*

width modulated signals or analog levels as input. The output of the low pass filter is a slowly varying signal, proportional to the duty cycle of the sum of the input signals. Inverting and noninverting outputs are provided for use in multiplication circuits.

5.2.4 Summation of Charges in CCD Chains

In effect, CCDs are long channel MOSFETs with closely spaced gate electrodes between source and drain. Each gate area of a MOS transistor forms a MOS capacitor that can store electrical charge. A CCD chain is a chain of special MOS transistors controlled by specific clock schemes to move charges stored under the gates along the chain. However, no single-polysilicon digital CMOS process may be used (as, for instance, in the twin capacitor cell solution of Schwartz *et al.*, which is very similar to CCD implementations), since this causes high parasitic capacitances to the substrate from the diffusion connecting transistors in a charge transfer string of a CCD chain. In CCD technology, high transfer efficiency is required to guarantee the survival of charge packets over many shift operations without distortion. A CCD circuit is operating with time-varying voltages at the gate electrodes in such a way that packets of minority carriers in the silicon (stored charge packets of the underlying capacitor) are transferred from capacitor to capacitor. The upper limit of the clock frequency (1 to 30 MHz) is determined by the maximal allowable power dissipation caused by charging capacitances and the permitted distortion of transferred charge from one capacitor to the next. In addition to very low CCD memory access times compared with standard RAM circuits, stored information is analog, thus permitting a high data transmission speed. There are several implementations of analog neural networks which use CCDs as basic building blocks.

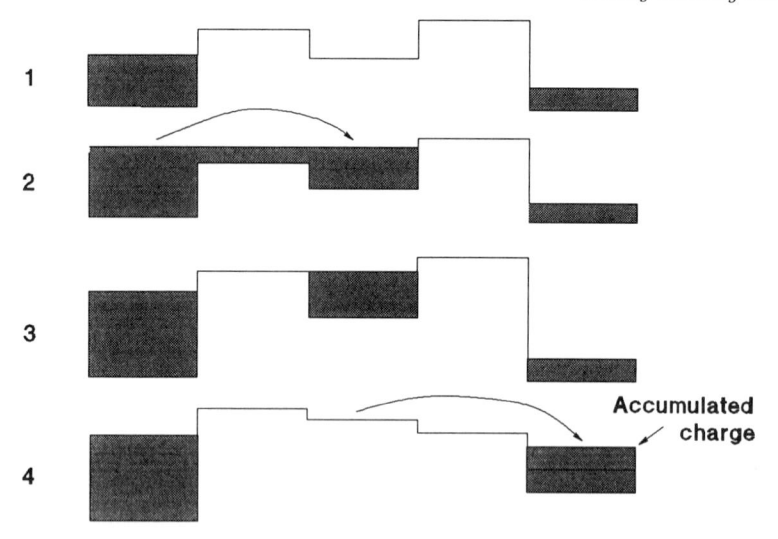

Figure 5.4 *Summation through charge accumulation at the end of a CCD chain (adapted from [Sag86])*

Applications of CCDs are also encountered in the areas of solid-state visible images and digital signal processing systems.

Since every CCD element has the capability to form a potential well under its gate, summation may be performed by simply accumulating charges in such a potential well. Figure 5.4 sketches a CCD chain. The potential of the last element is kept at a constant value (through a constant gate voltage) which is deep enough to keep a certain amount of charge. Through changing the gate voltages of preceding CCD elements via appropriate clock signals, their charges are moved towards the final CCD element. If reaching there, they "fall" into its deep potential "trap" accumulating its charge. Finally, by changing the gate voltage the potential may be increased and the accumulated charge shifted out for further processing.

More basic information on CCD technology can be taken from [Bey80] or [How79]. A short overview on the use of Junction Charge Coupled Devices for neural network emulation can be found in [Hoe91].

5.2.5 Charge Accumulator

The accumulation of weighted pulses to a neuron is represented by the calculation of the area underneath the pulse stream in an analog/digital implementation, which is geared to the processing of frame-based data [Wal90]. The calculated area can be easily translated into a current. Concerning the charge holding capacity, a single capacitor cannot be used for

Multiplication

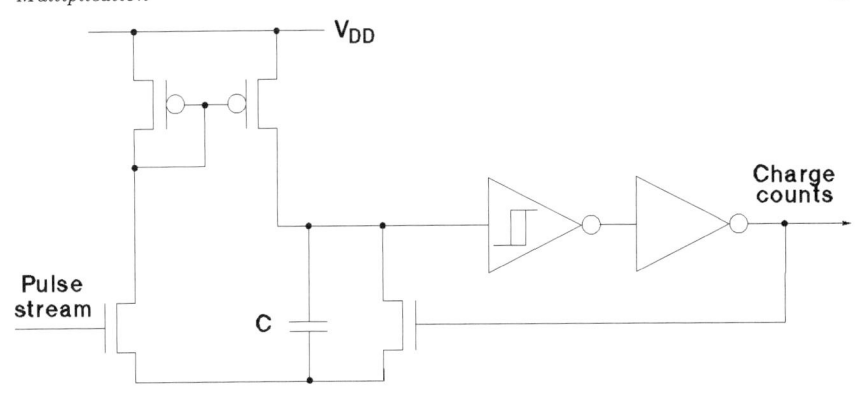

Figure 5.5 *Charge accumulator (adapted from [Wal90])*

the accumulation, because of the variable frame time. The circuit proposed by Waller *et al.* [Wal90] (see Figure 5.5) converts the pulse area into unit charge counts which can be accumulated by a digital counter. A current mirror charges capacitor C situated in a branch of it, proportional to the area underneath the pulses coming from the synapse. These pulses control a MOS transistor switch placed in the other current mirror branch. The capacitor is connected to a Schmitt trigger. As the voltage of the capacitor reaches the upper threshold of the Schmitt trigger [Millm87], the output state will be changed. The output of the Schmitt trigger is inverted again to activate the MOS transistor, which discharges the capacitor that is connected in parallel. After discharging the capacitor, the lower threshold of the Schmitt trigger is reached. Then the output state will be changed again, leaving the capacitor initialized.

5.3 Multiplication

Analog multipliers are classified as one-, two- or four-quadrant systems. A one-quadrant analog multiplier forms the product of two positive signals. A two-quadrant multiplier delivers the product of a positive signal and a signal of either polarity. Both signals may be of either polarity in a four-quadrant multiplier. A multiplication of an analog signal with a constant is no more than a simple linear relationship between an analog input and an analog output. The value of the constant to be multiplied with the input signal corresponds to the slope of the linearity between input and output. To multiply two varying analog signals it is necessary that one of the analog input signals controls the slope of the linearity. Several elements and microelectronic circuits show a linear or approximately linear behavior between input and output signals. Simple elements, for example, are passive resistors. Another element with approximately linear behavior (at least in a definite range) is the MOS transistor. Its channel realizes a resistor whose resistance may even be controlled by the gate voltage. More complex circuits with a linear input/output relation can be found in some amplifiers. In a small range their output nearly linearly depends on their input. The slope of this linearity is the amplifier gain, which may be controlled by other inputs. Some simple two-quadrant multipliers are the emitter-coupled pair [Gray84] and the transconductance amplifier. The restriction of two-quadrant operation, however, is a severe one for many applications, and most practical multipliers (e.g. the Gilbert amplifier) operate in all four quadrants.

Due to many different implementation technologies and the large number of elements offered to designers, many analog circuits may be used to realize analog multipliers. These different implementations offer very different features. The best to be chosen for a specific system has to be found by considering several factors, such as the required accuracy for calculations, maximum implementation size, implementation costs, *etc.* In the following, realization principles will be considered, beginning with very simple mixed analog/digital ternary synapse circuits and simple passive resistive elements. Due to different implementation technologies and methods provided by different analog fabrication lines, the scope of multiplier realizations is much wider than in digital approaches.

5.3.1 Simple Analog/Digital Ternary Synaptic Multiplication

Combined with digital technology for simple adaptive weight storage, ternary synapses have been used in some early implementations. A ternary synapse may adopt the three states $(-1, 0, +1)$. Figure 5.6 shows two circuits for ternary synapses. Signals are transmitted from neuron j to neuron i. The value of the synaptic weight is stored in elements *Mem1* and *Mem2* (*Mem1* and *Mem2* together implement one weight; each cell contains one bit of information about the weight value). To realize *Mem1* and *Mem2*, standard digital RAM cells are used (see the section on digital storage elements). The left synapse of Figure 5.6 generates a current which is excitatory, inhibitory or zero, depending on the state of the connecting synapse (*Mem1* and *Mem2*) and the output of neuron j [Graf87b, Graf87c, Ver89a, Ver89b]. Problems are caused by different n- and p-type transistors, which are used to generate the output current. It is impossible to guarantee excitatory and inhibitory currents of absolutely equal magnitude, and therefore an excitatory current will never completely compensate an inhibitory current. The more synapses that are used, the larger the amount of uncompensated currents may become, which prevents the realization of large networks. Performance of the second ternary synapse is straightforward; however, receiving neuron i has to possess two inputs, one input for excitatory signals and another input for inhibitory signals

Multiplication

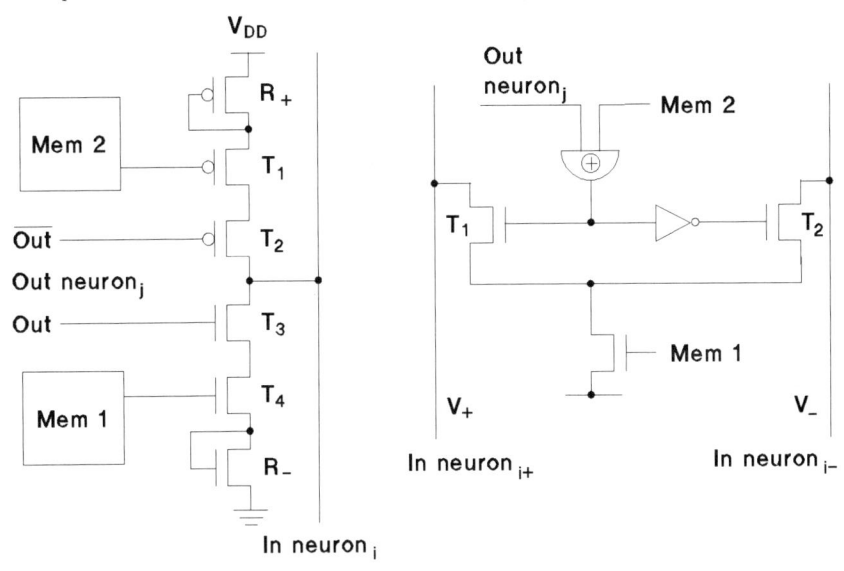

Figure 5.6 *Ternary synapse circuits (adapted from [Graf87c] and [Ver89b])*

[Ver89a, Ver89b]. Since transistors are of the same type, excitatory and inhibitory currents are equal in magnitude.

5.3.2 Multiplication with Passive, Resistive Elements

The simplest method of analog multiplication is based on the basic theories of physics. According to Ohm's law, voltage V across a passive, resistive element is proportional to current I passing through it ($V = I \cdot R$). The constant of proportionality, resistance R, may be interpreted as the strength of a connecting element (synapse) between two neurons. Whereas some early neural network implementations or neural network like systems even made use of large discrete resistors and potentiometers (e.g. the network from Edmonds and Minsky, or the "Adaline" system from Widrow and Hoff), in the following, VLSI elements will be discussed exclusively, since only these are of interest with respect to powerful implementations for real applications.

Undoubtedly, one of the simplest devices that couple two neurons through a weighted connection is a simple linear resistor. However, an area efficient linear resistor is difficult to fabricate with a standard silicon process. If an implementation with a highly integrated state-of-the-art fabrication process (feature size < 1 μm) is considered, power dissipation of individual elements has to be very low. This is due to a fixed maximum power dissipation of a chip with standard packaging and no special cooling. The more neurons to be implemented on a single chip, the higher synaptic resistances have to be to keep overall power dissipation low. At fixed voltages, reducing the power dissipation of a passive resistor can only be achieved by increasing its resistance. In standard MOS/CMOS processes, polysilicon, p-/n-diffusion areas and metal are used to form conducting lines (for more information read [Wes85]). The material with the lowest conductance are diffusion areas. However, even this conductance is high enough for very long and narrow diffusion channels to be necessary to realize a resistance of a few thousand Ohms. Furthermore, large fabrication tolerances in doping concentration occur that prevent the implementation of resistors with accurately determined resistance. Therefore, no reasonable resistors can be designed directly from diffusion lines.

In some implementations amorphous-silicon has been used to form resistors. This technique permits the realization of resistors of large resistance which are more accurate and small enough for VLSI implementation. Graf et al. implemented an analog neural network of 256 neurons using fixed amorphous-silicon resistors [Graf86, Graf87b]. The typical resistance of small amorphous-silicon resistors is in the range of several hundred kΩ up to a few MΩ. Graf et al. shaped resistors with electron-beam lithography and reactive-ion-etching. Thus, amorphous-silicon resistors showed good linearity and a resistance variation of not more than 5% across the whole chip [Graf86].

In other recent implementations, current sources are used for connecting elements instead of resistors (see Figure 5.8), controlled by the output of the connected neuron. Even in these designs, the basic model of the analog neuron described in Figure 5.1 remains the same.

5.3.3 Multiplication with a MOS Transistor

The MOS transistor may operate in three different modes, which are controlled by gate-to-source voltage V_{GS} and drain to source voltage V_{DS}. If V_{GS} of a NMOS transistor is very low, a digital circuit designer assumes the transistor to be "cut off". However, this is not correct. In fact a drain current I_D still exists depending on V_{GS} and V_{DS}. This current may be calculated by Equation 5.2 (I_0 is a complex transistor constant):

$$I_D = I_0 e^{-\frac{qV_{GS}}{kT}} \left(1 - e^{\frac{qV_{DS}}{kT}}\right) \qquad (5.2)$$

However, this current is in the range of 10^{-12} A to 10^{-8} A with gate to source voltages of 0.3 V to 0.8 V (subthreshold region). Hence, if MOS transistors operate at gate voltages below threshold voltage V_T ($V_T \approx 0.9$ V), this current may be neglected and the transistor assumed to be "cut off". If voltage V_{DS} slightly rises above threshold voltage V_T at low drain to source voltages, the transistor enters an ohmic region with nearly linear

Multiplication 77

resistive behavior between drain current I_D and drain to source voltage V_{DS}. If V_{DS} is now increased, I_D increases linearly up to a certain amount where I_D becomes nearly constant. At this point, the transistor becomes saturated and enters the saturation region. The slope within the ohmic region may be controlled via gate to source voltage V_{GS}. Figure 5.7 shows the drain current as a function of drain-source voltage for several values of gate-source voltage.

The transistor is in the ohmic region if $V_{GS} - V_T > V_{DS}$ and if gate-to-source voltage $V_{GS} > V_T$. Then, Equation 5.3 determines drain current I_D:

$$I_D = \frac{k'}{2}\left(\frac{W}{L}\right)[2(V_{GS} - V_T)V_{DS} - V_{DS}^2.] \tag{5.3}$$

The aspect ratio of the transistor is given by the fraction of its channel width W and length L, whereas $k' = \mu_n C_{ox}$ is a constant depending on process parameters (μ_n describes electron mobility, C_{ox} is the gate capacitance). At low drain-source voltages, the term V_{DS}^2 may be neglected which obtains a linear relationship between drain-source voltage and drain current. Furthermore, channel conductivity is controlled by gate-source voltage V_{GS}.

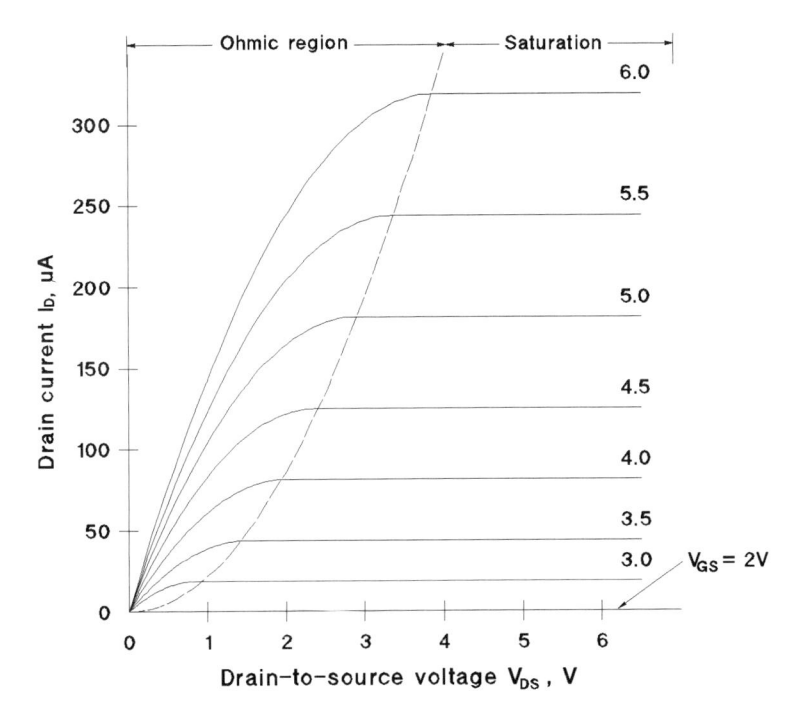

Figure 5.7 *Behavior of MOS transistor (adapted from [Millm87])*

The saturation region is entered for $0 < V_{GS} - V_T < V_{DS}$. Then, drain current I_D becomes a nearly constant saturation current I_{Dsat}. This situation may be described by Equation 5.4:

$$I_D = \frac{k'}{2}\left(\frac{W}{L}\right)(V_{GS} - V_T)^2 \equiv I_{Dsat}. \tag{5.4}$$

Now, I_D fully depends on the effective control voltage $V_{GS} - V_T$.

A more detailed discussion of the MOS transistor is given in [Millm87]. The MOS transistor is the most important element in current VLSI designs.

MOS transistors in the subthreshold area are not used for simple passive resistors due to their nonlinear behavior.

In the ohmic region a MOS transistor operates approximately as a linear passive resistor which can be controlled by gate-source voltage V_{GS}. Thus, a multiplication between V_{GS} and V_{DS} occurs, which may be seen from Equation 5.3. However, this multiplication is not very linear depending on the value of V_{DS}. The smaller V_{DS}, the more accurate multiplication results will be. However, fabrication parameters have a significant influence on drain current I_D, which makes it difficult to use a simple MOS transistor for direct use as a multiplier. With constant gate-source voltage the resistance of the channel may be modified by changing the width to length ratio $\frac{W}{L}$. However, resistances obtained are too low for large networks with many synapses (power dissipation problems). Furthermore, the influence of fabrication parameters permits only modest resistance accuracy, corresponding to a few bits (typically 4 bits or less).

A saturated MOS transistor is a quiet good current source due to nearly constant saturation current I_{Dsat} (see Equation 5.4). In combination with digital weight storage in ternary synapse circuits, saturated MOS transistors are used to generate positive and negative currents. This is not real analog multiplication, since only a positive, negative or no current is generated and injected into a summation line (see ternary synapse circuits in Section 5.3.1). Problems may be caused by the influence of fabrication parameters. If p- and n-type transistors are used to generate positive and negative currents, it is impossible to guarantee that both currents are nearly equivalent in magnitude. P-type material conducts less than n-type material, which has to be compensated by different doping or different transistor sizes. The control of doping during fabrication, however, is very difficult. Hence, conductivity of n-type and p-type material may never be predicted accurately. For a designer it is not possible to completely compensate low p-type conductivity exactly by increasing aspect ratio $\frac{W}{L}$ of p-type transistors.

5.3.4 Transconductance Amplifier

The current mirror (dashed part of Figure 5.8) [Millm87] is a device widely spread in analog circuitry. A drain and gate shorted (diode connected) MOS transistor acts as a simple current to voltage converter. Transistors with equal aspect ratios to which the output voltage ($V_{DS} = V_{GS}$) is applied are operating in the saturation region to copy the reference current into another circuit branch. However, variations in substrate voltage, geometry or doping can produce variations in the output current. Other applications of current mirrors are inversion and the scaling of currents.

A general MOS differential amplifier consists of a differential pair (see e.g. [Millm87]), also known as a source coupled pair (circuit outside dashed area of Figure 5.8), and active loads on top of it. The output of the differential amplifier is affected by the specific implementation of active loads. Transconductance amplifiers use current mirrors to form active loads. The

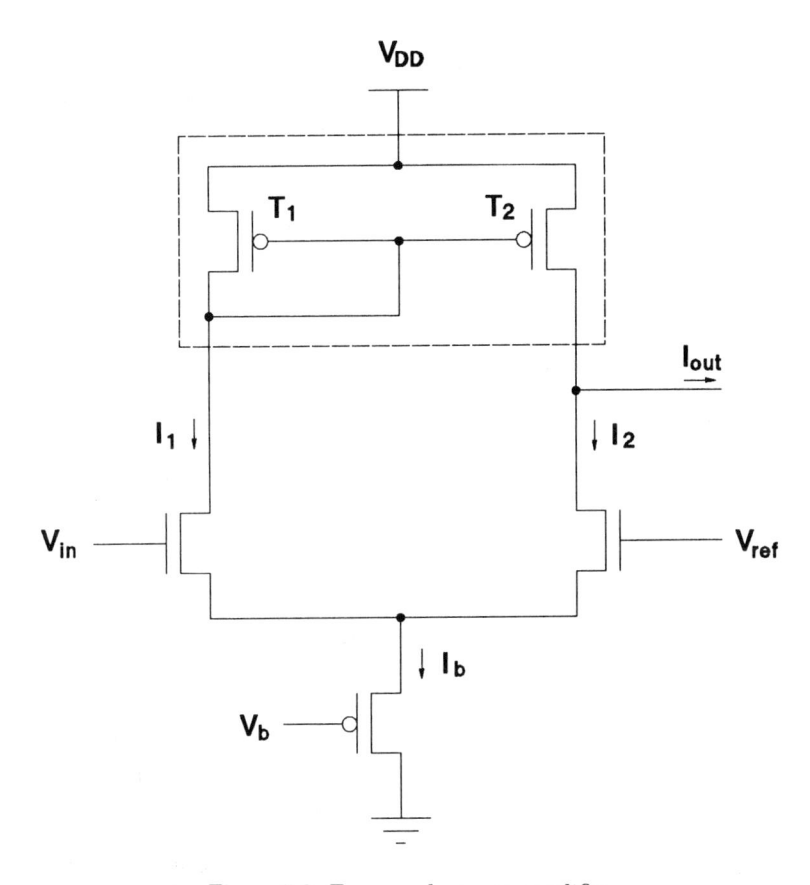

Figure 5.8 *Transconductance amplifier*

advantage of this configuration is that the differential output of the pair is converted into a single signal with no extra components required.

The transconductance amplifier delivers a current output that depends on the differential voltage input $V_{in} - V_{ref}$ and gate voltage V_b of the bias transistor (see Figure 5.8). If a differential voltage $V_{in} - V_{ref}$ is applied between the gates of the source coupled pair, it can be shown that half of it is applied between the gate and source of each transistor. Changes in the input voltage difference result in current changes ΔI of equal magnitude but different sign of currents I_1 and I_2. The current mirror copies reference current I_1 of T_1 into the channel of transistor T_2 (if aspect ratios W/L of transistors T_1 and T_2 are identical). Thus, by applying Kirchhoff's current law, output current I_{out} is obtained by subtracting I_2 from I_1:

$$I_{out} = I_1 - I_2 = 2 \cdot \Delta I. \tag{5.5}$$

Therefore, transconductance $G_{trans} = \frac{I_{out}}{(V_{in} - V_{ref})}$ of the circuit is the same as that of a single transistor.

By using the fact that the saturated drain current is quadratic with the gate-to-source voltage, one can show that I_{out} is proportional to the product of gate voltage V_b of the bias transistor and the differential voltage input $(V_{in} - V_{ref})$.

The gate capacitance (parasitic capacitance) of the bias transistor can be used to store a synaptic weight, if the stored charge can be refreshed compensating the decay due to current leakage. Since no purely analog memory refresh method exists, some sort of discretization must be applied before refreshing is performed [Cav90].

Output current I_{out} of the transconductance amplifier can be of either positive or negative polarity, but not bias voltage V_b. Hence, the stored weight (stored as a charge on the parasitic gate capacitor of the bias transistor) can only be positive. Four-quadrant multiplication can be realized by using each of the currents I_1 or I_2 from the source coupled pair as bias currents I_b to two other pairs. This circuit with three differential pairs is the CMOS version of the Gilbert multiplier (see also Figure 5.9).

5.3.5 Gilbert Cell

The Gilbert cell may be considered as a modified version of a differential amplifier or an emitter coupled pair. The DC transfer characteristic of the amplifier is the product of the hyperbolic tangent of the two input voltages.

Three application areas of the Gilbert cell can be identified [Gray84]. If both input voltages are large compared to thermal voltage $V_{th} = \frac{k \cdot T}{q}$, the amplifier is used for the detection of phase differences between two amplitude-limited signals in phase-locked loops. The second class of applications can be distinguished by applying only one input that is larger than V_{th}. Then, the circuit, acting as a modulator, multiplies the smaller signal

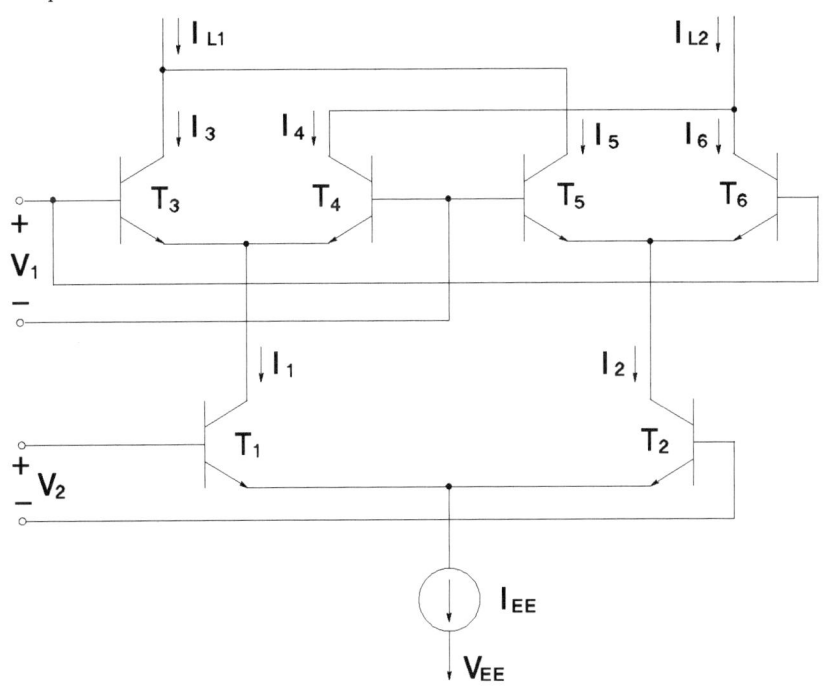

Figure 5.9 *Gilbert cell (adapted from [Gei90])*

by a square wave [Gray84]. In the third class of applications, if both signals are kept small with respect to V_{th}, the hyperbolic tangent function can be approximated as linear and the amplifier behaves as a multiplier. The range of input voltages over which linearity is maintained can be widely extended by including a nonlinearity to compensate the hyperbolic tangent function. The required nonlinearity that predistorts input signals has an inverse hyperbolic tangent characteristic.

Figure 5.9 shows a bipolar version of the Gilbert cell. This cell allows for four-quadrant multiplication. It is the basis for most multipliers used in analog integrated circuits. If the difference of currents I_1 and I_2 is converted into a voltage V_{out} through an appropriate current-voltage converter, this voltage can be described as

$$V_{out} = K V_1 V_2 \qquad (5.6)$$

with a constand K, if the cell is driven in its linear operation mode.

5.3.6 Multiplying D/A Converter (MDAC)

In some implementations analog computation is used only internally. Inputs, outputs and weights are digital, which makes integration in a digital system straightforward. This combination of analog with digital technology is done to benefit from simple adaptive digital weight storage with high accuracy. Then, a digital-to-analog (D/A) conversion is needed at each interconnection. A D/A converter which may use a controllable analog input voltage V_{in} instead of a fixed reference voltage can be considered as a multiplying D/A converter (MDAC). Connections to a neuron can be implemented with an array of MDACs [Man88a, Man87] so that digital weights may be directly used for computations. Figure 5.10 shows a schematic of a multiplying D/A converter. All input MOS transistor pairs controlled by voltage input V_{in} operate as current sources. Their width to length ratios are chosen to deliver a current of 1, 2, 4 and 8 times the basic current delivered by the transistor responsible for the least significant bit (1:1 ratio). N-channel devices are used as current sources because of their relative insensitivity with respect to channel length modulation as

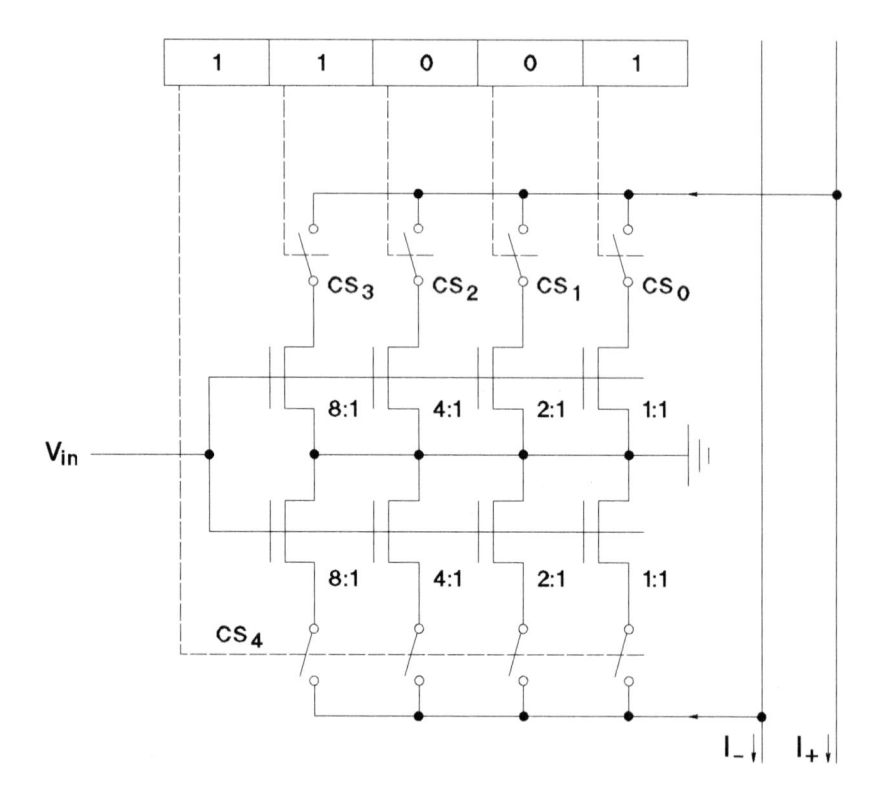

Figure 5.10 *Multiplying D/A converter (MDAC) (adapted from [Man87])*

compared to p-channel devices. For a digital weight value stored as a one's complement number, control switches CS_0 through CS_3 are switched corresponding to the stored bit pattern. Thus, a switch, which corresponds to an active bit, is closed to connect the respective current source to the positive summing wire I_+. If the weight has a negative value, sign bit CS_4 will close all the bottom switches, drawing a current from the negative summing wire I_- producing a one's complement representation on the positive and negative current summing lines. The contributions from all of the interconnections to the neuron are summed on the two wires. In a network, both currents are subtracted from each other in a current mirror to obtain the weighted net input which is presented to the nonlinearity.

5.3.7 The Emitter-Coupled Pair

The emitter-coupled pair can be considered as a simple two-quadrant multiplier in bipolar technology. The circuit is similar to its CMOS counterpart, the differential amplifier (see Figure 5.8) with input voltage V_{i1} corresponding to differential voltage $V_{in} - V_{ref}$ in the transconductance amplifier. The bias current for the emitter-coupled pair is provided by a bipolar current

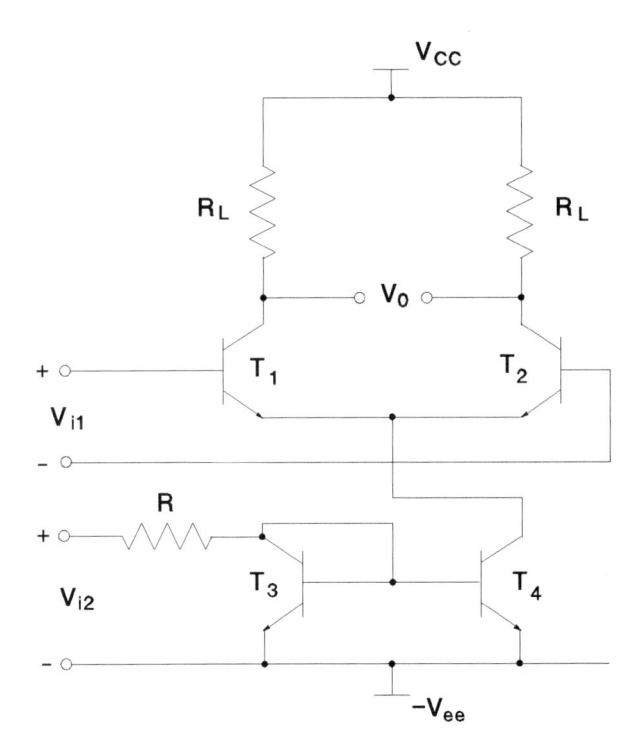

Figure 5.11 The emitter-coupled pair as a multiplier (adapted from [Millm87])

mirror to which the second multiplier input, voltage input V_{i2}, is applied. Both loads R_L realize resistances of an equal magnitude. A circuit to make a simple multiplier by means of an emitter-coupled pair is depicted in Figure 5.11. A signal nearly proportional to the product of V_{i1} and V_{i2} can be obtained between the collectors of T_1 and T_2 (output voltage V_o).

The bipolar version of the Gilbert multiplier can be obtained by connecting an emitter coupled circuit in series with two cross coupled circuits of emitter coupled pairs [Millm87].

5.3.8 Switched Capacitor Circuits

A capacitive element, switched between two circuit nodes at a high switching frequency, is the basic cell used in the switched capacitor technique. Due to the exchange of a specific amount of charge in each (well defined) switching cycle, the behavior of the switched capacitor is equivalent to that of a passive resistor. Thus, the effective resistance may be determined by capacitance and switching frequency.

Elements INT_2, C_3, C_2, rst_2 and switches clocked by signals ϕ_1, ϕ_2, ϕ_x and ϕ_y in Figure 5.12 form a switched capacitor integrator. If $\phi_x = \phi_2$ and $\phi_y = \phi_1$, with ϕ_1 and ϕ_2 being two nonoverlapping two-phase clocks, it is simple to calculate the moved charge assuming that switched capacity C_2 is small enough to be able to completely charge or discharge within

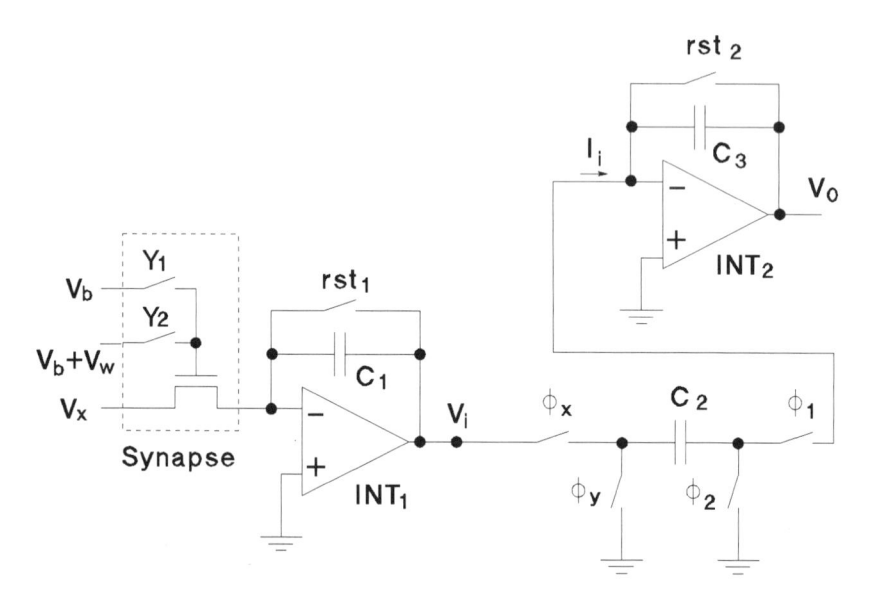

Figure 5.12 *Multiplier based on the switched capacitor technique (adapted from [Mek90])*

Multiplication 85

one clock cycle. Then, within one clock cycle, a total amount of charge Q of $Q = C_2 \cdot V_i$ is moved, corresponding to a current $I = C_2 \cdot V_i \cdot f$ (f is clock frequency). Hence, the switched capacitor is forming a resistor with resistance R determined by

$$R = \frac{V_i}{I_i} = \frac{1}{C_2 \cdot f}. \tag{5.7}$$

Therefore, time constant τ of switched capacitor integrator INT_2 can be determined by

$$\tau = \frac{C_3}{C_2 \cdot f}. \tag{5.8}$$

Clock frequency f can be generated with an accurate oscillator. Capacitors fabricated with a typical tolerance are suitable, since only the ratio of capacitances affects time constant τ. Hence, if two capacitors are implemented near to each other on the die, it can be assumed that they are affected in the same way by changes in the fabrication parameters. Thus, parameter influences may be neglected in capacitor ratios. This also facilitates the use of small capacitors, reducing implementation size.

The multiplier circuit depicted in Figure 5.12 was proposed by Mekkaoui et al. [Mek90]. It consists of two integrators connected in series and one transistor together with two switches. Input V_x, which is connected to the transistor drain, is multiplied by voltage V_w, which affects the transistor gate voltage. Voltages V_w and V_x may adopt both positive and negative values, permitting four-quadrant operation. The first switch is connected to bias voltage V_b, whereas V_b+V_w is applied to the second switch. Together with signal ϕ_1, the second switch becomes active (input $V_b + V_w$), and with ϕ_2 the first becomes active (input V_b). Integrators can be reset using rst_1 and rst_2, respectively.

During ϕ_1, current I_1 flows through the input transistor. If this MOS transistor is operated beyond the threshold but before saturation, its drain current I_1 is given by

$$I_1 = k\frac{W}{L}\left[2(V_b + V_w - V_t)V_x - V_x^2\right]. \tag{5.9}$$

Assuming that the input voltage V_x is small, the quadratic term may be neglected, yielding

$$I_1 = C(V_b + V_w - V_t)V_x \tag{5.10}$$

where C denotes a constant including fabrication dependent constant k, transistor width to length ration $\frac{W}{L}$, and the factor 2 in Equation 5.9. On the other hand, during ϕ_2, current I_2 flows through the transistor channel that can be derived in the same way as

$$I_2 = C(V_b - V_t)V_x. \tag{5.11}$$

With $\phi_x = \phi_1$ and $\phi_y = \phi_2$ one can guarantee that the second integrator is operating in a noninverting mode at the end of the ϕ_1 cycle. Then, voltage V_o appearing at the output of INT_2 is proportional to $I_1 \cdot T$, where T is the integrating time. After resetting INT_1, ϕ_2 becomes active. By changing the switching signals of INT_1 to $\phi_x = \phi_2$ and $\phi_y = \phi_1$, the inverting mode operation of INT_2 at the end of the ϕ_2 cycle is achieved. Then, at the end of cycle ϕ_2, output voltage V_o is proportional to $T \cdot (I_1 - I_2)$. Therefore

$$V_o = T\left(C(V_b + V_w - V_t)V_x - C(V_b - V_t)V_x\right) = TCV_wV_x \qquad (5.12)$$

follows, which is the desired proportionality of output voltage V_o to the product of input voltages V_w and V_x.

Nonlinearity due to mismatches caused by using the same transistor and integrators to control both I_1 and I_2 is a drawback in this design. Performance can also be affected by clock feed-through and switch charge injection [Mek90], which that are common to all switched capacitor circuits. The selection of proper switch sizes and optimum layout can minimize these effects. This multiplication circuit was integrated in a winner-take-all system for classification tasks [Mek90]. More synapses can be connected to the summing junction between the input transistor and operational amplifier INT_1. Thus, the input node of the first integrator serves as a summing node to sum up arriving currents (Kirchhoff's current law).

5.3.9 Multiplication of Pulse Modulated Signals

A comparator with complementary outputs plays a key role in a multiplier of a pulse stream network described by Cotter et al. [Cott88]. It converts analog voltage inputs to pulse width modulated (PWM) signals. The output of the comparator becomes active when the input voltage is higher than the reference voltage. The reference signal is thus a time varying triangle wave with both positive and negative values (see Figure 5.13). With each cycle of the reference signal, a rectangular current pulse is produced. The width and DC components of the pulse are proportional to the analog input voltage. A stored analog weight value w_{ij} (represented by an analog voltage) is preprocessed using the comparator circuit to convert it into a PWM signal representing its synaptic strength. The complementary outputs of the comparator carrying pulse width modulated weight signals are used to control CMOS switches through which output voltages $+V_j$ and $-V_j$ of the preceding neuron j are passed to the summing element. Hence, complementary comparator outputs and dual signal representation of the output voltage of a neuron is essential for four-quadrant multiplication.

Another technique for multiplying analog pulse modulated signals becomes interesting in combination with digital weight storage. This technique is sketched in Figure 5.14, and was used by Murray et al. in some early designs [Mur87, Mur89b]. Chopping clocks are used to gate a neuron's output signal o_j (from neuron j). For each bit, except the sign bit, of

Multiplication 87

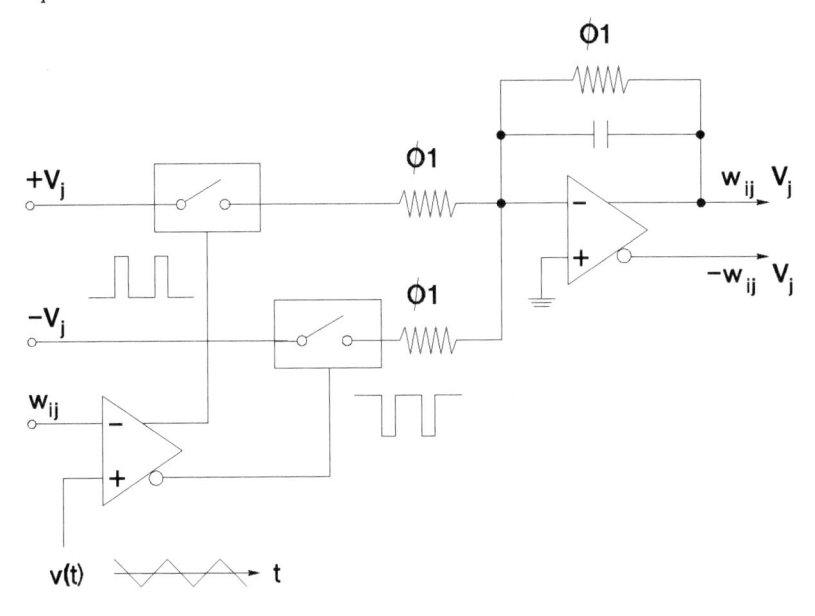

Figure 5.13 *Pulse width modulation multiplier (adapted from [Cott88])*

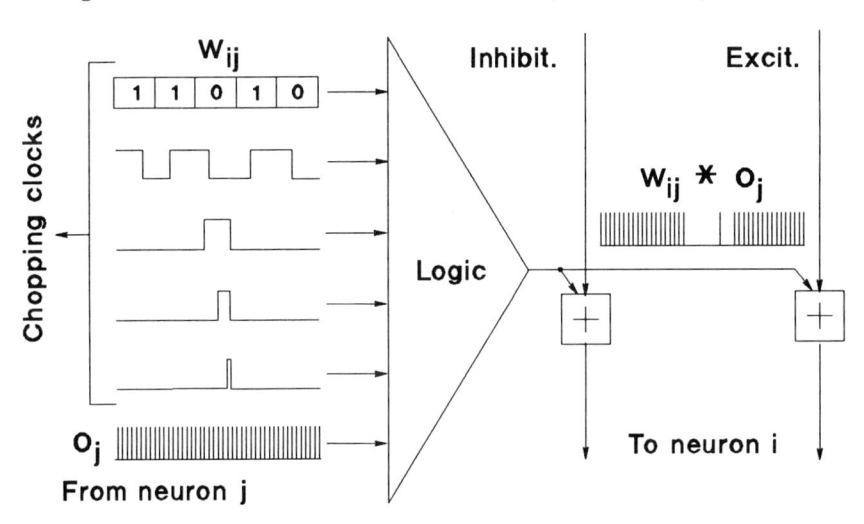

Figure 5.14 *Multiplication by gating signals with chopping clocks (adapted from [Mur89b])*

a digitally stored weight w_{ij}, one clock signal exists. Clocks for the bits are ratioed 1:1 (most significant bit), 1:2, 1:4, 1:8 (least significant bit in Figure 5.14), *etc.* Each cycle of a chopping clock defines a time interval for gating a pulse modulated (pulse width modulated or frequency modulated) signal from a preceding neuron. If a weight bit is zero, the respective chopping clock becomes zero, too. The sign bit of the stored synaptic weight serves to control whether the gated signal is transferred to the inhibitory or excitatory line, thus forming a two-quadrant multiplier. Additional circuitry is necessary to realize four-quadrant multiplication.

To benefit from area efficient analog storage, Murray et al. also developed a fully analog synapse circuit for analog multiplication. Thus, the output o_j of neuron j is determined by frequency f of signal pulses with a constant width D_{const}. Special analog circuitry which is described in more detail in the implementation part of this book (Chapter 8) can form pulses of width $D = D_{const} \cdot w_{ij}$ (w_{ij} is a synaptic weight stored as analog voltage) with frequency f, thus if transformed into a current by means of a current source, carrying a charge proportional to the product of synaptic weight w_{ij} and neuron activity o_j of neuron j.

5.3.10 Multiplication with CCD Elements

A very simple multiplication of a binary input signal with an analog weight may be realized using CCD technology. Here, weight information is stored as a potential well under a CCD element gate. Figure 5.15 sketches a three-gate CCD circuit. CCD elements with gates G_i (input) and G_o (output) serve to either connect CCD element W to the input or output. The depth of the potential well under gate W encodes an analog weight value. The deeper the potential, the larger the corresponding weight value. This well may be obtained via an MNOS element or by simply applying a constant voltage on gate W.

To perform a multiplication, the input (diffusion area D_i on the left side) has to maintain a constant charge potential. At the beginning of the multiplication procedure, high potential barriers are kept under access gates G_i and G_o (step 1). Thus, the potential well under gate W contains no charge. In a second step, the voltage of gate G_i is changed to reduce its potential barrier a little. By controlling gate G_i through the output o_j from preceding neuron j a simple multiplication of a binary value with an analog weight represented by the potential on gate W may be accomplished. If a high charge potential is present at D_i, a certain amount of charge flows under gate W. This amount corresponds to the depth of its potential well, and thus to the stored weight value. If the preceding neuron output o_j is low, no charge can surmount the potential barrier G_i, and no charge will flow under W. Now potential barrier G_i will be increased (step 3) and barrier G_o decreased (step 4). By lifting the potential under gate W during step 4, the charge trapped there will flow to diffusion area D_o, where it can be accumulated with charges from the output of other three-gate CCD elements. Simple multiplications of binary values with analog weights are

Multiplication

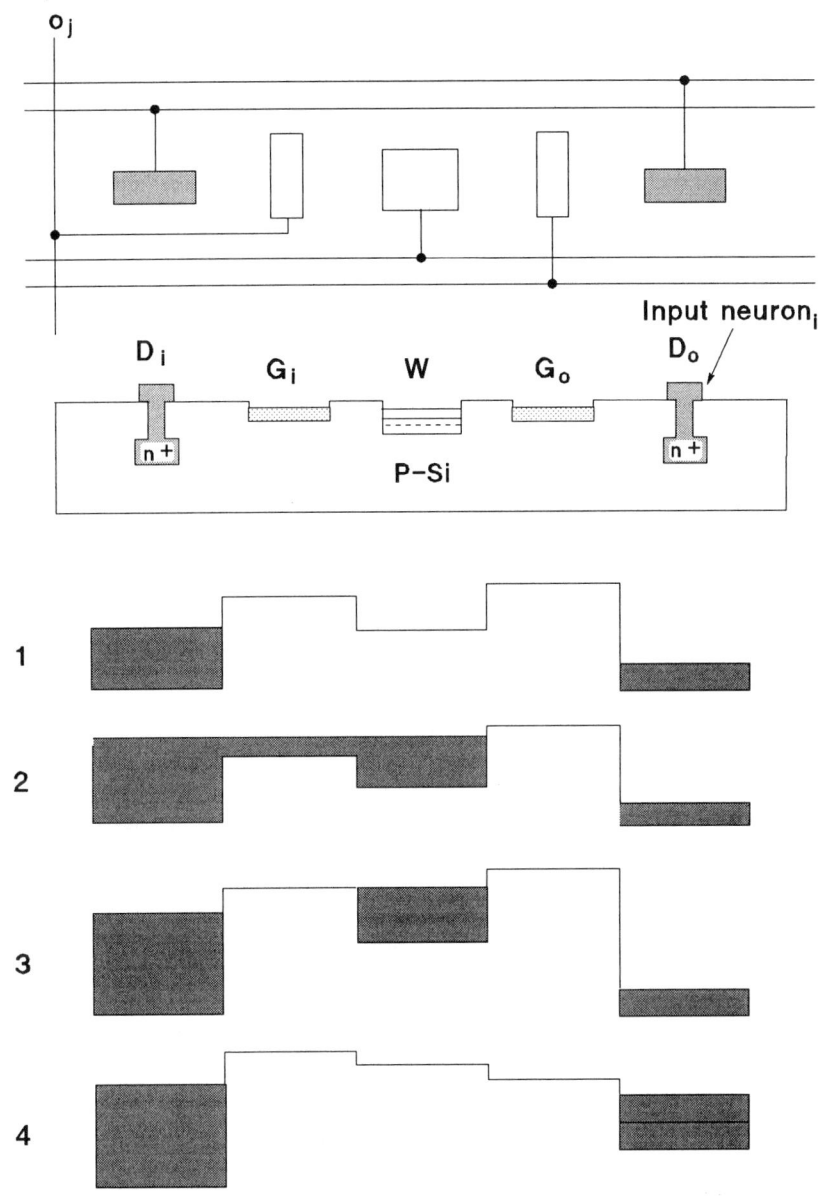

Figure 5.15 *Channel potentials of a three-gate CCD element (adapted from [Sag86])*

performed and the outputs accumulated to calculate a neuron activation potential.

5.4 Analog Storage Elements

Compared with digital technology, analog storage elements may encode far more information on the same area. This is as a result of several signal states which can be produced in contrast to only two states, "on" and "off", in digital signal circuitry (theoretically, analog technology allows an infinite number of different states, which in fact is reduced to a finite number of distinguishable states depending on the accuracy of signals). However, the implementation of analog storage cells has some significant drawbacks compared to digital storage elements. Therefore, one of the major challenges in analog realizations of neural networks is the analog representation and storage of synaptic weights. Whereas this is quite simple for weights which are defined and fixed during fabrication, many problems are caused by designing adaptive weight storage elements. Adaptive weights are a prerequisite for user defined network configurations. Furthermore, on-chip learning requires a continuous updating of synaptic weights, requesting adaptive storage cells. In adaptive, fully analog circuits, weight information is coded by analog voltages or charges on capacitors or potential wells under gates (see the section on CCD technology). Such a type of neural network hardware may interact with its environment and adapt its weights continuously. In many cases, even sophisticated hardware with adaptive weight storage does not contain on-chip learning support, since additional circuitry to update analog weights is extremely difficult to realize. In most cases, adaptivity means that the user may define the network topology and weight values to configure his hardware. Weight values therefore have to be found by off-chip simulation on other hardware media (like conventional sequential computers). Even without on-chip learning, adaptive circuits cause many problems. A standard capacitor is only suitable for short term memory because of its charge leakage. A major difficulty in implementing long-term dynamic analog memories is how to refresh the stored charge. In the following, the main building blocks for analog information storage will be described and discussed.

5.4.1 Fixed Resistors

As previously described, a simple multiplication may be performed exploiting Ohm's law for simple passive resistive elements, like amorphous silicon resistors or MOS transistors in a specific operation mode. Resistor implementations in the form of simple diffusion lines cannot be used, since a low specific resistance will either require the design of long narrow lines (area consuming) or the implementation of low resistance resistors (causing heat problems on a chip). Hence, resistances are usually realized by single MOS transistors or MOS circuits, or by amorphous silicon technology.

Using resistors, a variable input signal is multiplied by a constant that is represented by the element's resistance. Therefore, these elements also serve for weight storage. The weight value is represented by a resistive element's resistance. In the case of amorphous silicon resistors, the resistance is defined by the cross-section and length of a resistor element. The larger the cross-section and the shorter the length, the smaller its resistance will be. With a fixed thickness, the resistance is defined by the length to width ratio. The same is valid for a MOS transistor with a fixed gate-source voltage. Its resistance depends on the aspect ratio, *i.e.* the length to width ratio of its channel area (and channel doping, which is fabrication dependent), assuming that its operation region (saturation or ohmic region) is not left. Thus, accuracy of resistances within a chip is affected by the accuracy of geometric forms that can be realized by lithographic methods and the conductivity accuracy of materials used. Resistors with an overall accuracy of not more than 5% are realized with state-of-the-art fabrication processes, permitting a weight representation accuracy of a few bits. The main disadvantage of such a weight representation, however, is that resistances are fixed during fabrication. Hence, no later user defined changes can be made. Neither on-chip nor off-chip learning is possible. Some attempts have been made to develop adaptive passive resistive material such as bismuth compounds for the realization of user programmable resistors [Spen86], but this needs technologies which are not offered by commercial fabrication, and is still unreliable.

5.4.2 Resistors of Bistable Bismuth-Oxygen Compounds

A system of crystalline bismuth-oxygen compounds Bi_2O_3, $Bi_{12}GeO_{20}$, $Bi_{12}SiO_{20}$ and $Bi_4Ge_3O_{12}$ was investigated for use as electrically programmable resistors and bistable switches in neural hardware [Spen86]. These materials, based on bismuth sesquioxide, show remarkable crystallographic, optical and ultrasonic properties. They melt congruently and grow readily from the melt. This technology has developed during the last decades, expanding its applications (e.g. large $Bi_4Ge_3O_{12}$ crystals are produced for nuclear scintillation counters).

Under stoichiometric conditions, $Bi_{12}GeO_{20}$ has a specific resistance in the order of 10^{10} to 10^{13} Ohm/cm. Hence, it can be treated as an insulating material. The application of a single or a series of pulses to the system causes an increase in oxygen vacancies in the crystal, known as the off stoichiometry oxygen defect. Then, electrons start moving in a direction defined by an applied electric field causing a finite conductivity. By controlling the number of oxygen vacancies by regulating the number and the strength of pulses, it is possible to program the resistivity over many orders of magnitude.

In the absence of a bias voltage or the applied electric field, the resistivity of the element remains the same despite the application of input pulses.

The strength of pulses which increase element conductivity (if desired, bias voltage is applied) is of a magnitude of 3.5 V. The programmable resistors behave ohmic for pulses or computing voltages (normal input to the synaptic element in operation mode) below a critical value of 1V. By applying reverse pulses, the material can be returned to its insulating initial stage.

Test structures consisting of a longitudinal conducting stripe over the bismuth oxide deposits were investigated by Spencer [Spen86]. Initial tests were carried out for 20 resistors or switching elements using 100μm wide gold conductors and approximately 3000Å thick films of $Bi_{12}GeO_{20}$. By applying DC voltages of 1V to 5V with currents in the mA range, the device behaves as a switching element. Because of some irregularities observed at voltages much smaller than that required for switching, testing measurements were carried out using thinner conductors (1μm) in order to reduce the currents. Equation 5.13 gives the resistance of a uniform material with a specific resistance ρ (Ωcm), thickness L, and cross-sectional area A:

$$R = \rho \cdot \frac{L}{A} \tag{5.13}$$

Use of this technology in switching and in electrical programming of resistors is evaluated with low voltages at about 50 mV and with currents in the nA range. Usually, resistances are in the order of $10^6 \Omega$ to $10^9 \Omega$ in the OFF state and of $10^4 \Omega$ to $10^5 \Omega$ in the ON state. However, there are several difficulties in applying this technology to produce large scale arrays of synaptic elements (e.g. small differences in the operating parameters among synaptic elements in the array). These problems will only be removed by improved fabrication methods.

5.4.3 Weight Storage on Capacitors

The capacitor is an excellent element on which to store analog information. Here, information may be coded as a certain amount of charge Q which is proportional to a capacitor's capacitance C and the applied voltage V ($Q = C \cdot V$). Using VLSI technology, a capacitor may be simply implemented by two layers of conducting material which are isolated by a thin layer of silicon oxide. Even a standard MOS transistor may be modeled by a small capacitor which is formed by its isolated gate and an "ideal", voltage controlled transistor, thus realizing a small simple storage cell which can also be used for crude mathematical operations (see the multiplication section above).

Unfortunately, only small capacitors of an acceptable size are implementable with only a low accuracy. Due to this small size and finite isolation, leakage currents may discharge such a capacitor within a few milliseconds. For analog storage with high precision, loss of charge should not be larger than 1% during all necessary calculations. The leakage current

Analog Storage Elements 93

may be reduced by operating a circuit at a very low temperature. By cooling a chip with liquid nitrogen a data retention time of a few minutes may be achieved with a charge loss of less than 1%.

Schwartz *et al.* used a differential voltage stored on a capacitor pair as a weight storage element for a programmable analog neural network chip [Sch89]. Figure 5.16 shows their simplest storage cell, consisting of two MOS capacitors and five MOS transistors of different size. A stored weight w_{ij} is represented by the voltage difference between the two capacitors:

$$w_{ij} \propto V_+ - V_- \tag{5.14}$$

On the one hand, this offers the advantage of simple representation of positive and negative values, which is a problem in other implementations. For their fully analog synapse circuits, Murray *et al.* needed special circuitry to set an analog threshold which separates positive from negative values on the capacitor that stores the weight [Mur89b]. On the other hand, the negative influence of charge leakage is reduced. Of course, each capacitor loses charge through leakage currents, but if both capacitors are of equal size and are carrying a similar amount of charge, leakage currents are of nearly the same magnitude. Hence, a voltage difference between them remains quite unaffected, thus extending data retention time. Transistors TA (access transistors) of Figure 5.16 serve to access the capacitors, whereas TC is a transistor used for small weight changes by means of charge injection. This is done together with isolation transistors TP (positive node) and TM (negative node). By activating TP and TC, a small amount of charge flows into the long and narrow channel area of TC. After reaching equilibrium, TP is switched off, TM (minus node) is activated, and the charge stored in the channel of TC may be transferred to the second capacitor by slowly turning off transistor TC. With a more elaborate circuit, even gradual weight decay may be realized [Sch89]. With experimental measurements on a MOS accumulation mode capacitor with an access transistor TA, which was optimized with respect to small leakage currents, Schwartz *et al.* found that a temperature of -8 °C increases data retention time by a factor of over 100 as compared to room temperature. Then, data may be kept on a capacitor for about 100 seconds with a loss of less than 1%.

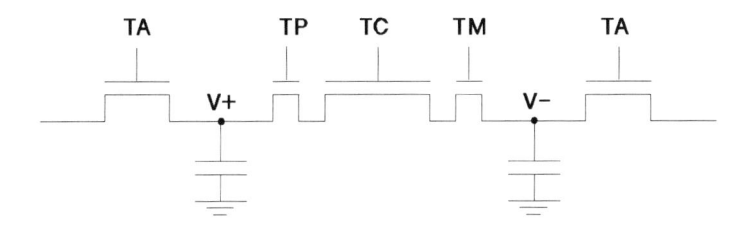

Figure 5.16 *A simple twin capacitor storage cell (adapted from [Sch89])*

However, a special clock scheme has to be generated for different operations [Sch89], and the programming characteristic of weights is nonlinear, due to semiconductor physics.

Another technique to cope with leakage currents is to refresh a capacitor periodically. This means that the initial charge is put onto the capacitor periodically, requiring active circuitry. Several circuits with active charge refresh mechanisms for neural networks were proposed by Horio et al. [Hori90]. They propose active analog memories based on charge pumping, on a master-slave concept, on a frequency locked loop, and on voltage difference sensing between two capacitors. The charge pumping method uses two capacitors which are charged and discharged, respectively. Additional circuitry allows to pump charge from one capacitor to the other. The authors claim that the charge loss on the storage capacitor may be compensated by this circuit.

In the master-slave concept, synaptic weights are stored on identical capacitors which are connected to current sources and sinks via switches. Switches are controlled by two clocks. A reference capacitor which is identical to weight storage capacitors serves to "simulate" the charge loss of storage capacitors. Only this reference capacitor is equipped with charge leakage sense circuitry which generates two clocks that can be used to

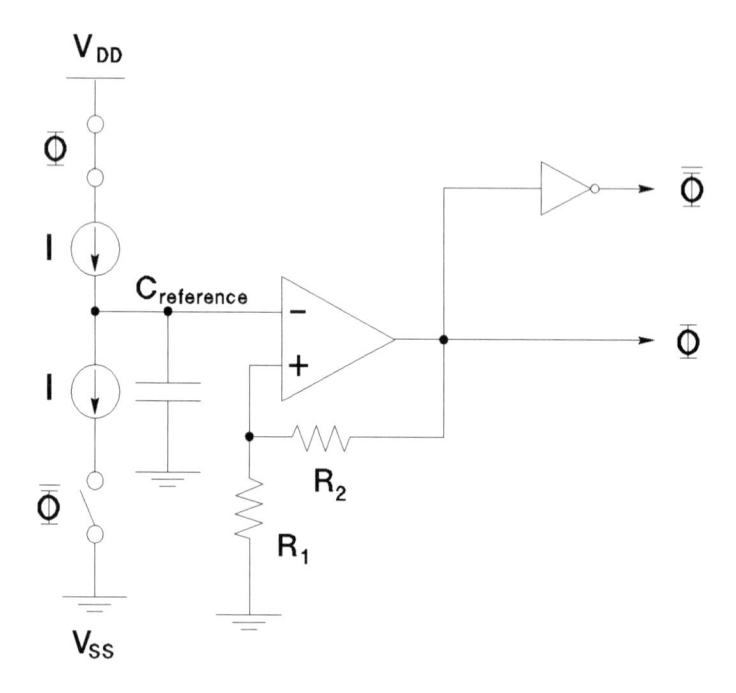

Figure 5.17 *Master circuit (adapted from [Hori90])*

Analog Storage Elements

compensate charge loss on storage capacitors. The whole circuit is depicted in Figures 5.17 and 5.18, with reference capacitor and charge leakage sensing circuitry (master) depicted in Figure 5.17 and memory circuits (slaves) depicted in Figure 5.18. Clocks Φ and $\overline{\Phi}$ are modified by charge losses on reference capacitor $C_{reference}$. By an individually controlled signal L_{ij} (and $\overline{L_{ij}}$) each slave capacitor may be preloaded with the respective weight information w_{ij}.

The frequency locked loop circuit consists of a voltage controlled oscillator, a frequency to voltage converter, and a delay element which are assembled in a loop that is connected to the weight capacitor. Because of the loop, the frequency and thus the capacitor voltage are locked.

Two disadvantages of the previously described twin capacitor storage element from Schwartz et al. [Sch89] are the finite storage time due to leakage currents, and nonlinear programming. Horio et al. [Hori90] propose an analog storage circuit where weight information is stored as a voltage difference V_{diff} between two identical capacitors, as in the implementation of Schwartz et al. The upper part of Figure 5.19 gives a conceptual sketch, while a concrete circuit example is shown in the lower part. Identical capacitors C_1 and C_2 carry weight information as a voltage difference between them. A comparator in the circuit senses whether capacitor C_2

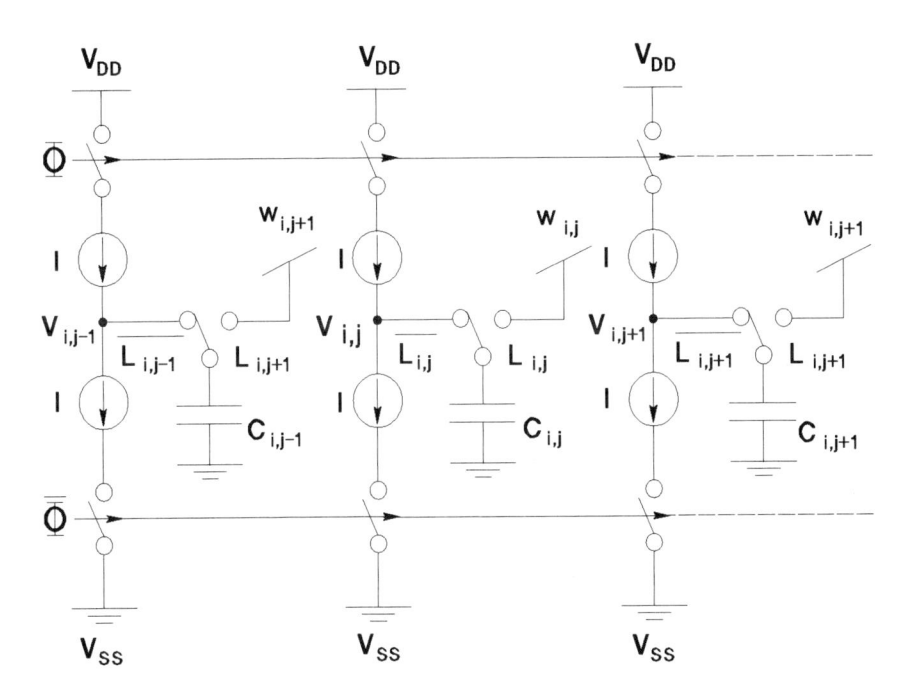

Figure 5.18 *Slave circuit (adapted from [Hori90])*

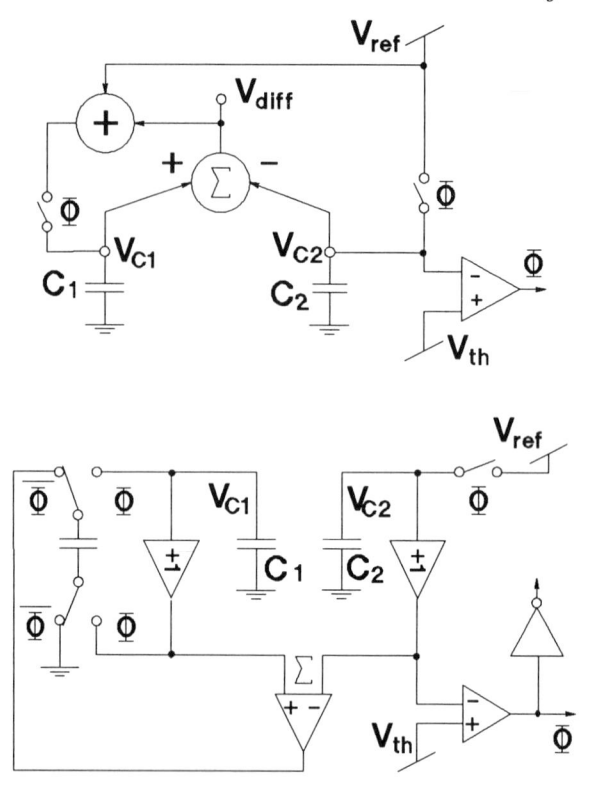

Figure 5.19 *Analog voltage difference sensing between two capacitors (adapted from [Hori90])*

has reached threshold voltage V_{th}. After this has occurred as a result of leakage currents, a signal Φ is generated which charges up C_2 to reference voltage V_{ref}, whereas C_1 is charged up to voltage $V_{ref} + V_{diff}$.

All circuits proposed by Horio *et al.* are much more complex to integrate than a single capacitor. They have been mounted and tested only with discrete elements. According to Horio *et al.* [Hori90], mathematical stability still has to be proved since all circuits are operating with feedback. Furthermore, very optimistic assumptions have been made, like identical capacitances, identical leakage currents, *etc.* which is not achievable in real implementations. Hence, mismatch effects, and how they affect performance, have to be considered.

The circuits described are only a few approaches to coping with leakage currents and providing periodic charge refresh. For example, several circuits to enable short and medium storage times on capacitors for neural network weight storage have been proposed by Vittoz *et al.* [Vit90] and other researchers working on analog implementation technologies.

Analog Storage Elements 97

5.4.4 Floating Gate Elements

In contrast to a standard MOS transistor, floating gate devices employ an additional gate between the silicon and normal MOS gate. This additional gate is completely isolated, and thus may store a charge (encoding weight information), affecting channel conductance. Several types of floating-gate elements exist.

Double-Gate MOS Transistor (EPROM)

Erasable Programmable Read Only Memories (EPROMs) are state-of-the-art technology. Figure 5.20 shows a MOS transistor with two gates which is used to realize a single EPROM cell [Millm87]. Such a transistor is also termed a Floating-gate Avalanche-injection Metal Oxide Semiconductor (FAMOS). Gate 1 (lower gate in Figure 5.20) is completely surrounded by SiO_2 and thus electrically isolated from its environment. By applying a large positive voltage between gate 2 (upper gate in Figure 5.20) and drain of the MOS transistor, high-energy electrons which can penetrate the insulation layer between channel and gate 1 are generated in the channel area. Hence, a negative potential emerges on gate 1 affecting channel conductance in normal operating mode (low voltages on gate 2 and drain). This potential varies only slightly over time, allowing information storage for a long time. A measurable indicator of charge stored is threshold voltage V_T of the device. V_T is the gate voltage at which the device begins to conduct. If electrons are added to the floating gate, the effective voltage of the floating gate decreases. Hence, a more positive control gate voltage V_T is required to make the device conductive. Therefore, an increase in V_T corresponds to the number of electrons added. Charge, and thus information, may be removed by exposing the gate area to UV light, which reduces the extremely high resistance of SiO_2.

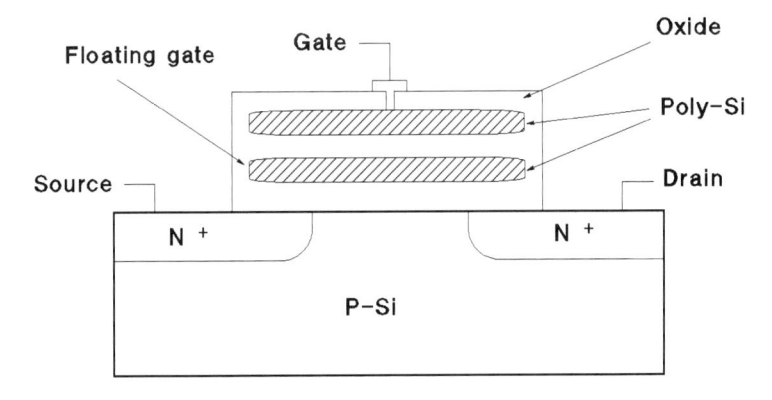

Figure 5.20 Double-gate MOS transistor (adapted from [Millm87])

Double-Gate MOS Transistor with Thin Isolation Layer (EEPROM)

A disadvantage of double-gate MOS technology is the long deletion time required by UV illumination. By reducing the thickness of the SiO$_2$ insulation layer between the floating gate and transistor channel in Figure 5.20 to about 100 Å, a relatively low voltage of about 10 V applied between the two sides of the extremely thin SiO$_2$ layer causes a current flow to gate 1 by a type of quantum-mechanical tunneling (Fowler-Nordheim tunneling). This effect is used for relatively fast erasure of stored charge by applying a voltage of the opposite polarity (compared with voltage applied for programming) between the drain and gate 2. EEPROMs are generally based on this double-gate MOS structure with a thin SiO$_2$ layer.

There are slightly different implementations of EEPROMs, which basically depend on the same structure as described above. A variation is the floating-gate tunnel oxide cell (Flotox cell) [Gos90]. After many program and erase operations, the thin layer oxide degrades, affecting channel conductance. The Flotox cell depicted in Figure 5.21 has a thick oxide layer with a small thin layer tunnel oxide area placed directly over the drain to prevent degradation of the tunnel oxide from affecting the transistor's operation.

To emulate neural operations, a VLSI synapse based on the Flotox cell developed at Intel was proposed by Card *et al.* [Car89]. It uses logarithmic neural signals to enable on-chip learning. This requires a logarithmic amplifier for each neuron. Furthermore, the voltage must be multiplied by an additional constant to ensure that the logarithm of the voltage remains positive.

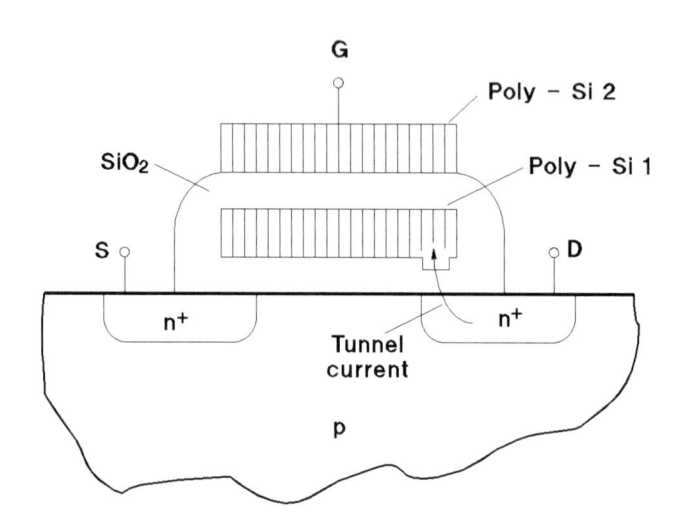

Figure 5.21 *Cross-section of Flotox cell (adapted from [Gos90])*

Analog Storage Elements 99

MNOS Elements

A technology related to floating gate implementations is MNOS technology. Like floating gate devices, Metal Nitride Oxide Semiconductor (MNOS) structures are well suited to the storage of electrically programmable non-volatile analog synaptic weights in the form of an electrical charge.

A cross-section of an MNOS element is shown in Figure 5.22 [Sag86]. In comparison with a floating-gate device, it consists of a silicon nitride layer as the main gate insulator and a thin (25 Å) silicon oxide layer. No second gate is present. However, electrical charge that can be trapped at the border between the SiO_2 and nitride insulator under certain conditions plays a significant role in modulating the effective gate voltage, which controls the size of the synaptically transferred charge packets. Hence, this insulation border operates in a way similar to a floating-gate. If a high positive voltage is applied to the gate with the presence of a charge packet in the underlying silicon, a high field develops across the dielectric, causing electrons to tunnel from the silicon to traps in nitride, and holes to tunnel from the traps to the silicon via the thin oxide layer, causing a positive potential shift in the trap area (border between SiO_2 and nitride layer). In the case of a large negative gate voltage, carriers tunnel in the opposite direction, causing a negative shift in the traps. Therefore, synaptic weights represented by charges can be programmed electrically at any time by changing the amount of trapped charge in the nitride layer.

Trapped charges are stable over a long time, unless the gate voltage does not exceed 10 V. A major disadvantage of MNOS synaptic elements is that they cannot handle bipolar values of weight coefficients. Some problems are caused by charge migration effects changing trapped charges within longer time periods. These effects may be accelerated through exposure to high temperatures.

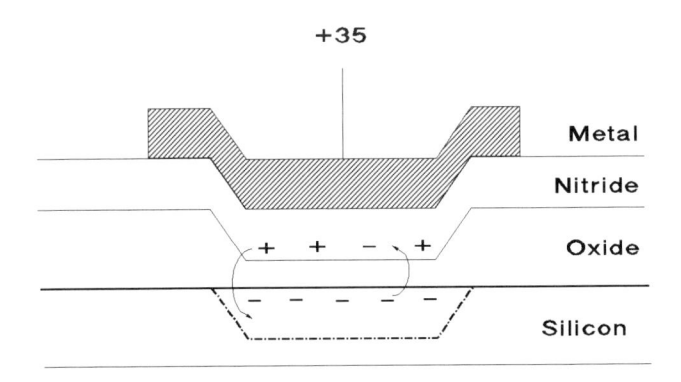

Figure 5.22 *Cross-section of a MNOS element (adapted from [Sag86])*

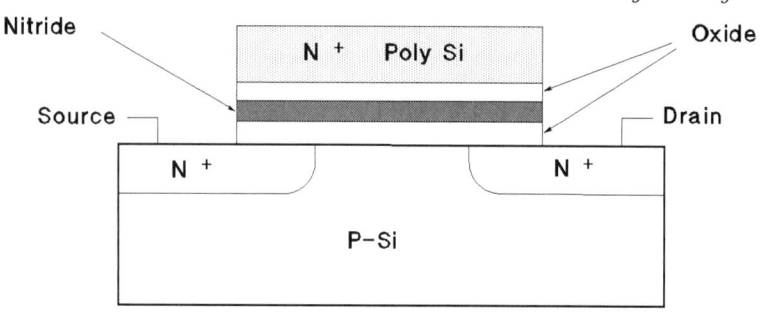

Figure 5.23 *ONO-EEPROM structure (adapted from [Cha87])*

Oxide-Nitride-Oxide Element

The Oxide-Nitride-Oxide (ONO) based implementation proposed by Chan et al. [Cha87] has improved data retention capabilities compared with MNOS implementations. Furthermore, the silicon area occupied by an ONO-EEPROM is half the area of a conventional EEPROM (Figure 5.23). The silicon nitride dielectric sandwiched between two oxide layers is used as the storage medium for trapped hot electrons generated in the high field region near drain diffusion. Hot holes are injected through the bottom oxide (60 Å) near the drain, using the deep-depletion-mode drain breakdown to erase the ONO-EEPROM device. The top oxide layer with a thickness similar to the bottom layer insulates the nitride layer from the polysilicon gate. This improves data retention time in comparison with an MNOS element.

5.4.5 Charge Storage on CCD Elements

Principally, CCD elements may be used to store weight information. To do this, potential wells of a constant depth are generated under the gates of several elements. This is done by applying the same voltage to all their gates. Then, each potential well can store a certain amount of charge corresponding to a weight value. Problems, however, are caused due to the net generation of currents distorting stored charges. For Junction Charge-Coupled Devices, Hoekstra [Hoe91] mentions a current of $1nA/cm^2$ caused by the net generation of electron-hole pairs due to nonthermal equilibrium conditions. Without restoring weight information within about 1 second, 10% of the charge potential can be filled by this current.

5.5 Nonlinear Elements

In contrast to digital realizations, analog technologies are suited to the implementation of smoothly shaped input/output characteristics. Whereas

Nonlinear Elements 101

all digitally simulated discriminator functions consist of a more or less large number of steps, perfectly smooth slopes may be realized with analog circuitry. Hence, most of the analog implementations use sigmoid shaped nonlinearities at neuron outputs. Moreover, with fully analog circuitry a perfect hard limiting threshold function (activation function) cannot be realized.

5.5.1 MOS Inverter as a Nonlinear Element

The ideal MOS inverter used for digital circuits has a voltage transfer characteristic as sketched in Figure 5.24 (left). If the input voltage rises smoothly from 0 V, suddenly, at a voltage of $V_{DD}/2$, its output voltage changes from V_{DD} to 0 V. However, a real inverter has a voltage transfer characteristic which shows significant deviations from this ideal case [Millm87]. Such a realistic characteristic is depicted in the right part of Figure 5.24. Thus, MOS inverters may be used to imitate a neuron's activation function. MOS inverters are used as nonlinear elements in the neural architecture proposed by Boahen et al. [Boa89]. Bipolar currents received from the synapses are integrated over time by the interconnect capacitance. Neuron states switch to +1 or −1 if the voltage of the capacitor exceeds or falls below the inverter's threshold voltage, respectively. The state of the neuron remains unchanged if the input current is zero.

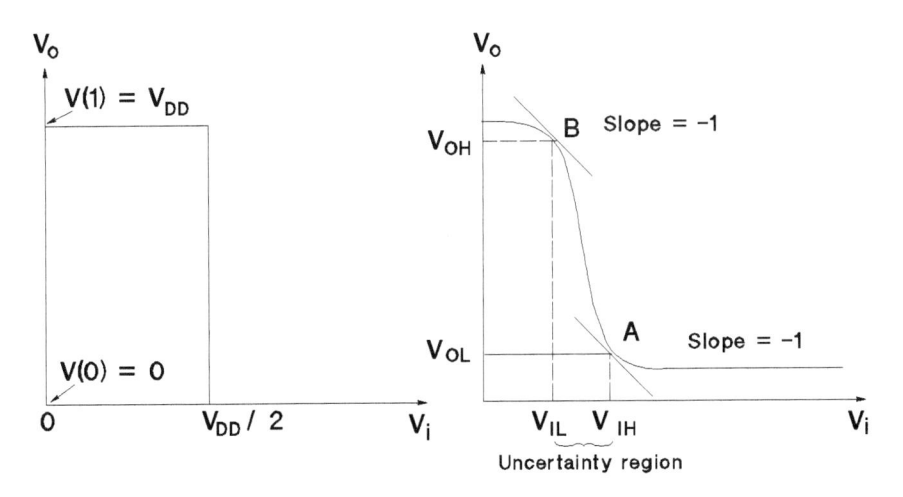

Figure 5.24 *Ideal (left) and real (right) MOS inverter characteristic (adapted from [Millm87])*

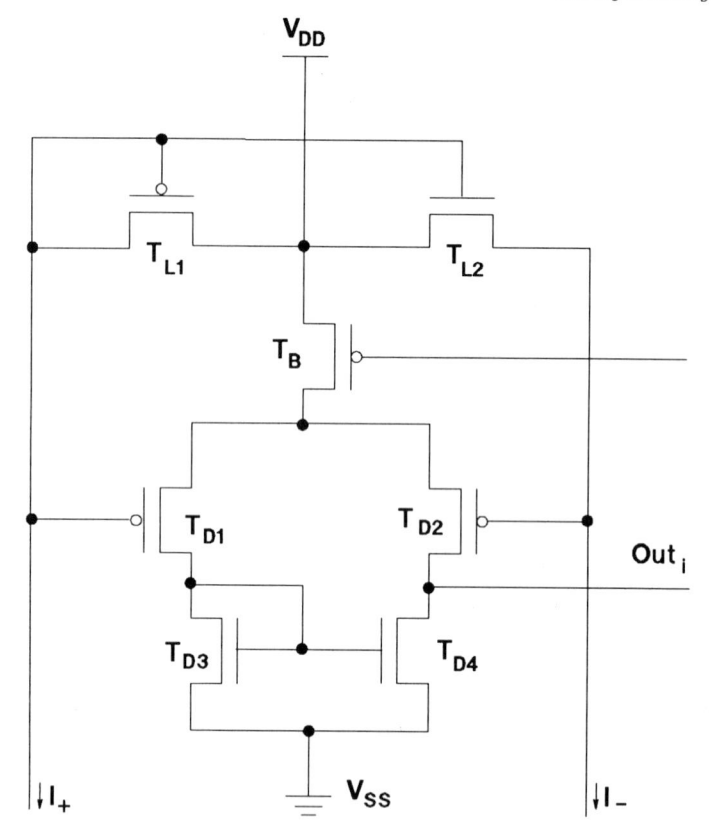

Figure 5.25 *Current subtractor based on a differential amplifier (adapted from [Ver89a, Ver89b])*

5.5.2 Discriminator Based on Voltage Comparison

In other analog neural network implementations, subtraction of currents is done by converting them to voltages which are compared. The currents to be compared are converted into voltages across transistors T_{L1} and T_{L2} (Figure 5.25 shows a circuit proposed by Verleysen et al. [Ver89a, Ver89b]). These voltages are compared in the differential amplifier formed by transistors T_{D1} to T_{D4}. Output Out_i provides voltage V_{SS} in the case of $I_+ > I_-$ and voltage V_{DD} otherwise.

5.5.3 Double Differential Amplifier

If two voltage signals have to be added before the nonlinear operation, a double differential amplifier may be used. Such a solution was proposed by Alspector [Als88a]. He used this approach to add noise represented by a

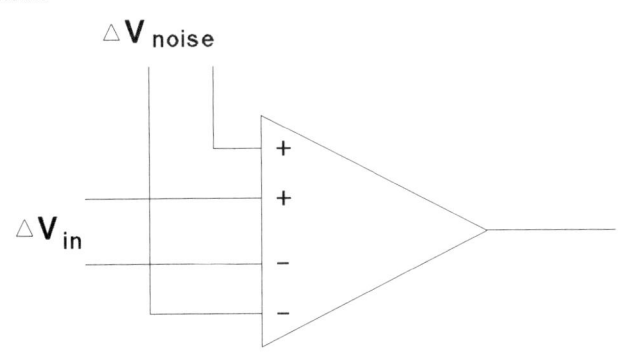

Figure 5.26 *Double differential amplifier used as nonlinear discriminator (adapted from [Als88a])*

voltage to a neuron's potential (also represented by a voltage). The nonlinear function used at neuron outputs is of the type *tanh*. This is implemented as a double differential amplifier, as shown in Figure 5.26. Separate differential inputs ΔV_{noise} and ΔV_{in} are summed at low gain. The differential outputs of the low gain summing stage are converted to a single output by a high gain stage. This is fed to a switching system that selects either the amplifier output or an external clamping signal (to realize input and output neurons). The output of the switch, which is the present state of the neuron, is further amplified before driving the following neurons of the network. The final output represents a two-state binary neuron.

5.6 Other Elements

As in the case of digital implementations, additional circuits are necessary to generate, for example, noisy signals. On the one hand, the need for such additional circuitry depends on the specific neural algorithms to be simulated; on the other hand, it depends on the integration of analog circuitry into a digital environment (which is always the case if a digital host computer is used to embed analog VLSI subsystems). Some important circuits are mentioned in the following.

5.6.1 Noise Amplifier

The noise amplifier used before entering the double differential amplifier of Figure 5.26 amplifies the random thermal noise in a transistor channel with a gain of nearly one million. Low pass negative feedback in three stages serves to stabilize the DC output (see Figure 5.27). An annealing procedure as requested by the Boltzmann machine algorithm is realized by reducing the strength of the anneal input. Thus, it is possible to control

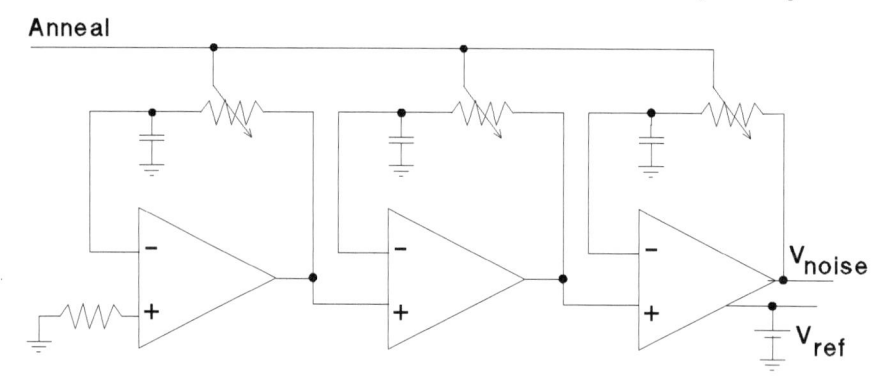

Figure 5.27 *Noise amplifier (adapted from [Als88b])*

both strength and bandwidth of the noise by varying feedback in the stages. The main disadvantage of this amplifier is its instability at high gain.

5.6.2 Current Inverter

In some building blocks of neural implementations, current sources and sinks are needed. A current mirror which is ideally suited for duplicating currents can be extended to obtain a current sink that is equal in amount to

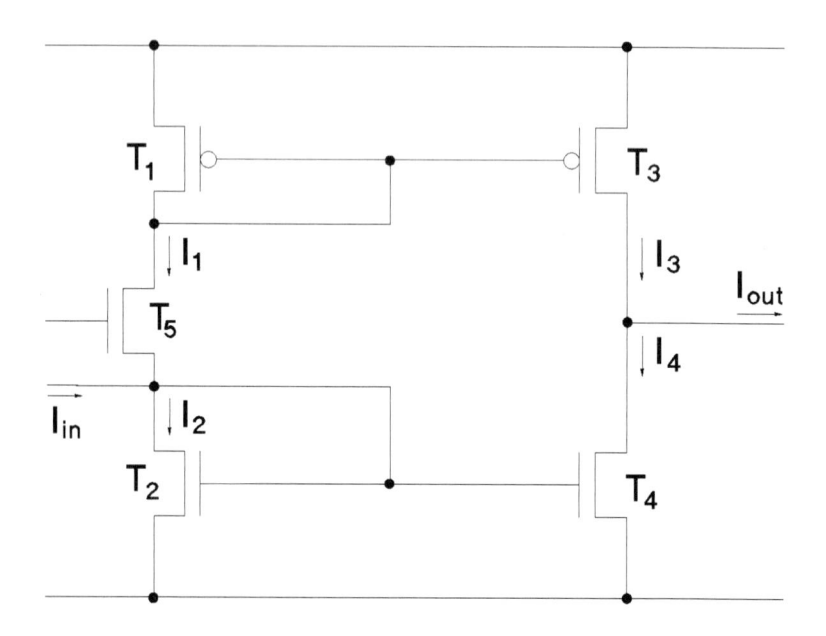

Figure 5.28 *Current inverter*

Other Elements 105

a given current source. An extended CMOS current mirror that operates as a current inverter is given in Figure 5.28. Transistor pairs T_1, T_3 and T_2, T_4 constitute current mirrors consisting of transistors with the same aspect ratio, *i.e.* $I_1 = I_3$ and $I_2 = I_4$. Considering Kirchhoff's current law, one can easily come to the conclusion that $I_{out} = -I_{in}$. Transistor T_5 may be used to switch the current inverter on and off.

5.6.3 Analog Multiplexor

An analog multiplexor in a module chip with 16 neurons was used by Mueller *et al.* to provide the A/D converter connected to the host computer with time segments of all the neuron outputs [Mue89]. The host computer uses this data to monitor network performance and to enable off-chip learning without interfering in the functioning of the analog neurons.

The outputs of 16 neurons are sequentially connected to a common output line by analog switches in the multiplexor. The switches are addressed by a 16-bit shift register that shifts a "1" according to the two-phase clock derived from the master clock of the host computer. After the last neuron has been read, a control pulse is generated and the next module will be ready to start sending its outputs to the host computer. Digital outputs are stored in the host computer for further processing.

5.6.4 Winner-take-all Circuits

For competitive neural network algorithms such as Kohonen's self-organizing feature map or learning vector quantization (LVQ) networks, it is required to find the most active unit out of a neuron layer. Digital realizations always need several computation steps to find a winning neuron. Even on massive parallel digital computer arrays, this cannot be done in one step, since global information exchange is necessary to compare neuron activations distributed over many processor nodes with each other. A much faster solution may be provided by analog hardware. Different analog approaches were proposed to find a winner. In most cases, currents are compared to each other using MOS transistors controlled by a common reference signal (e.g. see Vittoz [Vit89a] and Mann *et al.* [Man88a]). If one input to the winner-take-all circuit wins, other inputs are inhibited through lateral feedback.

In an early analog Kohonen feature map implementation, Vittoz *et al.* realized a mexican hat function through a network of lateral resistor/conductor elements [Vit89b]. The idea is to use two linear resistor/conductor networks as depicted in Figure 5.29. Each of the networks is producing a voltage distribution similar to a Gaussian if a node is connected to a high potential. The potential decreases with an increasing distance from

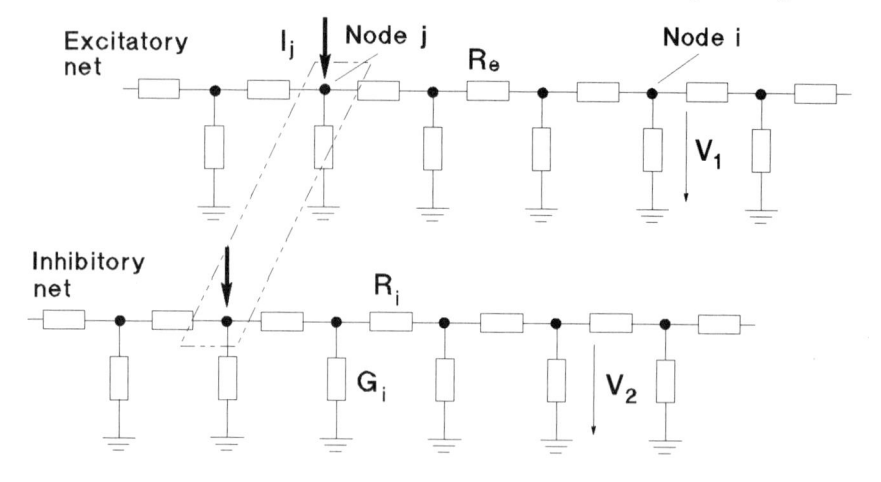

Figure 5.29 *Two networks of resistors and conductors (adapted from [Vit89b])*

the activated node. Now, Vittoz et al. generate two different voltage distributions on the two sketched lines which are then subtracted from each other (e.g. through a transconductance amplifier). Therefore, the first net is called an excitatory net, whereas the second is the inhibitory net. Figure 5.30 shows the two individual potential distributions and the resulting mexican hat function after subtraction. Resistors and conductors are realized by MOS transistors. By driving MOS transistors into different operation modes via changing gate potentials, voltage distributions may be affected.

A simplification is to replace the inhibitory net by a constant potential.

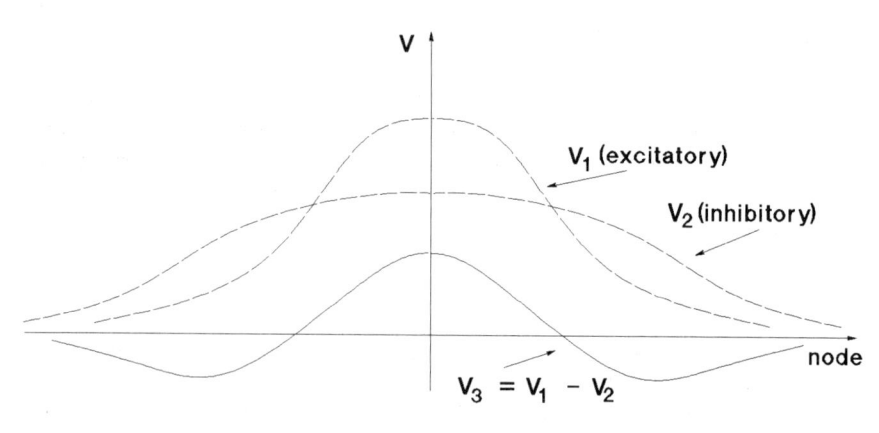

Figure 5.30 *Generation of "Mexican Hat" function through subtraction of two potential distributions (adapted from [Vit89b])*

Summary

Since the Kohonen feature map is rather invariant against small changes, this may be tolerable in some applications.

5.7 Summary

Compared with digital circuitry, analog technology may provide much faster and much more compact solutions in realizing the basic computational units needed for neural network simulation or emulation. This is due to the exploitation of physical laws to perform mathematical operations on extremely small elements, and the asynchronous evaluation of circuit outputs without a global clock scheme.

The two main problems in using analog techniques with respect to the simulation of neural algorithms are realizing a good four quadrant multiplication and storing synaptic weights. For multiplication one needs a circuit with variable linear input/output characteristics. By changing the slope of the input/output behavior, a multiplication can be performed. However, linearity of the characteristic as well as noise affect the accuracy of the calculation. Due to noise and changing fabrication parameters, which have a significant influence on analog circuit behavior, the achievable accuracy is limited to a maximum of about 7 bits. The problems associated with analog weight storage are twofold. Most implementations operate with charge storage on a capacitor or a potential well. Then, leakage currents destroy the information stored within a few seconds, or even in a split second. These can only be minimized at low operating temperatures or compensated by means of additional circuitry. The second problem involved in charge storage is the controlled change of small portions of charge, which is necessary to implement neural network learning. Using EEPROM technology for weight storage solves the charge destruction problem through leakage currents (but smaller charge migration problems are present). But the controlled change of small charge units is even more difficult, since high energy hot electrons must be generated.

Due to the accuracy problems, most purely analog architectures only realize the feed-forward phase of neural computations. On-chip learning can be provided for LVQ algorithms, the self-organizing feature map, and some radial basis function networks which are not very critical in terms of computation accuracy. On-chip backpropagation learning, however, will not be found working properly on fully analog circuitry.

Some researchers try to combine the virtues of digital and analog circuitry in mixed analog/digital architectures. In most of these cases, weight storage is done digitally whereas signal evaluation occurs on analog parts. Chapter 8 discusses some architectures that combine analog building blocks for asynchronous neural network emulation. That chapter also contains examples of how analog building blocks may be combined with digital parts.

6
Optoelectronic and Optical Building Blocks

6.1 Introduction

Optical computing is another, very exciting way in which to carry out signal processing. Due to the high speed of light beams, extremely fast computers may be built. Another feature of light as an information carrier is that light beams may cross without interfering with one another. Therefore, information channels can cross each other arbitrarily without losing information. This feature is of particular value to neural computing, since processors are heavily interconnected.

In the following, only a brief introduction to optical processing is given, since the focus of this work is on microelectronic implementations. Compared with microelectronics, optical computing shows many similarities to analog VLSI circuits. As in analog VLSI circuitry, physical effects are exploited to perform mathematical computations. A large variety of different approaches are already known to perform calculations, and certainly many others will be found within the next few years. As with analog VLSI, extremely high computational power can be realized in rather small pieces of hardware, but at the expense of computational accuracy as compared to digital approaches. Furthermore, only experts may handle the necessary circuit and device technology, which is tricky to design and, at least at the moment, extremely expensive to manufacture.

Optical realizations may be separated into two classes: pure optic solutions (holographic), and optoelectronic approaches. In fully optical solutions, coherent laser light is usually used to carry information. Light beams are directed through complex lens systems, mirrors and masks. This technology needs high precision mechanical devices and leads to large laboratory systems. Much smaller designs may be achieved using optoelectronic technologies. These systems use optical technologies to realize operations of the synaptic field and electronic technologies to realize neurons and input/output operations to the world outside the neural network. Therefore, a conversion from electrical signals to optical signals, and *vice versa*, has to be done. LEDs serve as light emitting parts (incoherent light) to optical circuitry, whereas phototransistors are responsible for generating electrical signals from optical inputs.

In all optical parts spatial light modulators (SLMs) are used to generate and modify light. There exist a large variety of SLMs which can be used for different tasks [Horn87]. The general characteristic of a SLM is that it modifies light passing through it. This modification can either be done in a linear way (to implement a synaptic multiplication) or in a nonlinear way (to implement the nonlinear neuron threshold function).

6.2 Summation

As in analog VLSI technology, the summation of signals is a simple task. In fully optical systems several light beams may be projected onto a single spot. There, the total illumination or brightness corresponds to the sum of the single beams. Thus, a summation can be performed on an extremely small spot (comparable to a current node in analog VLSI, where Kirchhoff's law desribes the summing behavior). The same principle is applicable to optoelectronic realizations. Several light beams may be projected onto a single phototransistor or photodiode. If the phototransistor is operated in its linear operation region, the sum of the entering light beams may be transformed into an electrical signal.

6.3 Multiplication

Signal multiplication can be achieved by signal-multiplying SLMs. In general, these are three-port devices with an input for the signal to be modulated, an output for the modulated signal, and another input to control the modulation. Images (a) through (c) of Figure 6.1 depict the principles of signal-multiplying spatial light modulators. Image (a) shows the amplitude modification of an image reflected at a mirror (right side of the mirror). The reflectance of the mirror is influenced by charges generated from an image projected onto the left side of the mirror layer. Depending on the kind of SLM used, binary or multivalued multiplications are possible. Examples for signal-multiplying SLMs are the microchannel plate device (see Figure 6.2), liquid-crystal devices, the photo deuterated potassium dihydrogen phosphate light valve *etc*. A significant difference to electric implementations is that no light with a negative sign can be generated. Therefore, architectural measures have to be taken to represent negative weights. As in some analog implementations, this is done by providing two synaptic fields, one representing positive, the other representing negative values. In optoelectronic realizations, results from the first field are added to a neuron's potential, whereas results from the latter are subtracted.

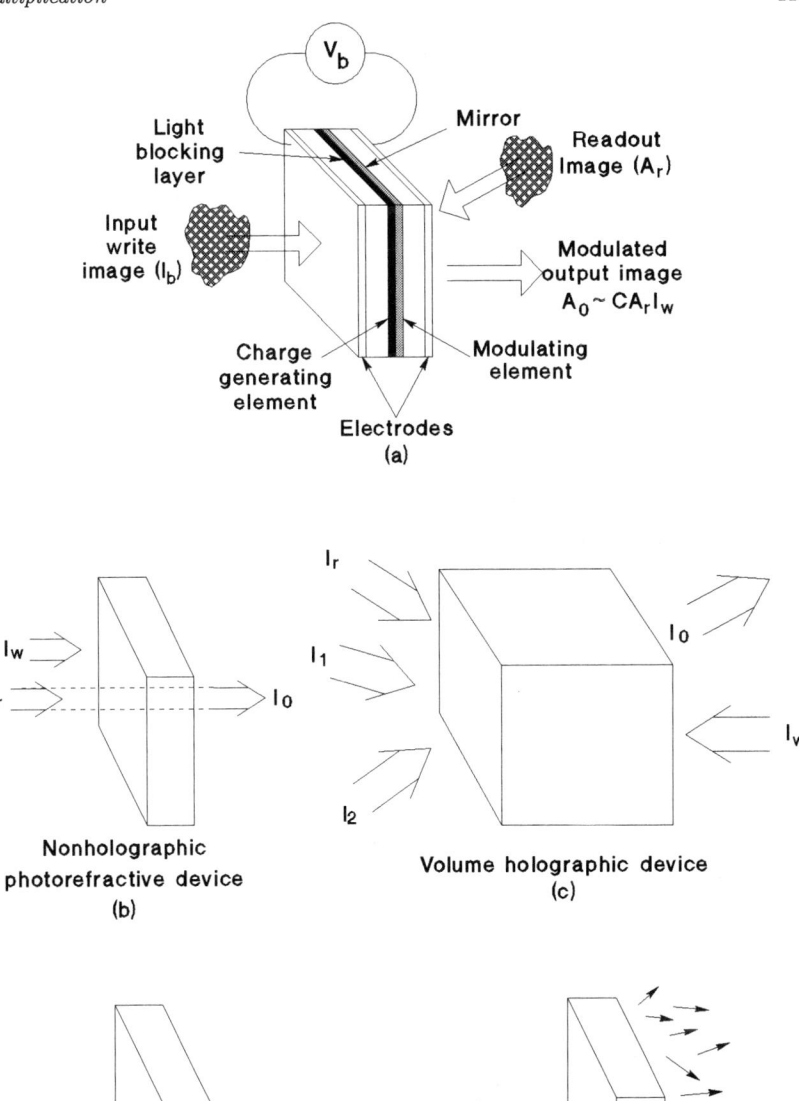

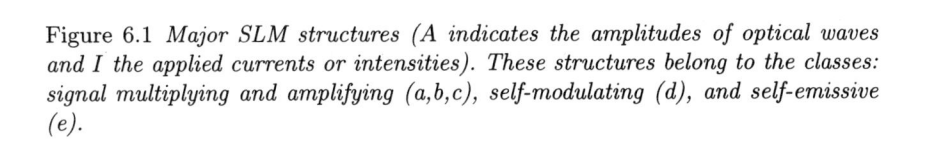

Figure 6.1 *Major SLM structures (A indicates the amplitudes of optical waves and I the applied currents or intensities). These structures belong to the classes: signal multiplying and amplifying (a,b,c), self-modulating (d), and self-emissive (e).*

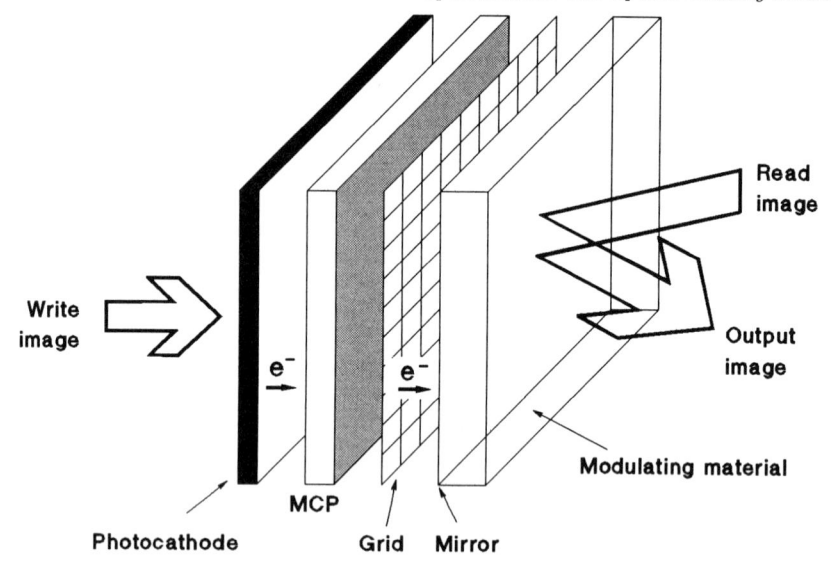

Figure 6.2 *Generic structure of MSLM and PEMLM incorporating photoemission and microchannel plate electron amplification*

6.4 Nonlinearities

Nonlinearities may be realized by means of self-modulating spatial light modulators. These are two-port devices, as indicated in image (d) of Figure 6.1. Usually, they are made of materials that perform a simple nonlinear function. Hard-limiter thresholding is possible, as well as linear or sigmoid shaped functions with or without hysteresis.

6.5 Weight Storage and other Tasks

Weights may also be stored in some SLMs. For example, a neural network's interconnection scheme may be represented by a hologram (a discussion on the storing capacity of holographic associative memories is given in [Hon86]). Another possibility is to store the weight matrix as a charge distribution in a layer adjacent to a voltage sensitive light modulation layer. These are only two examples for possible weight storage.

To generate and control light beams other elements are necessary in optical computing. Incoherent light is generated by simple self-emissive devices (see image (e) in Figure 6.1) like an array of light emitting diodes. The use of laser diodes is a way in which to produce coherent light.

Differing from approach to approach, other devices like lenses, mirrors, *etc.* may be used.

6.6 Summary

Most of the characteristics of analog circuitry also apply to optical solutions. The exploitation of optoelectronic and optical technologies may lead to systems of extremely high performance, but compared with digital and analog VLSI technology, optoelectronic and optical computing is much less mature and still a topic of basic research. Chapter 9 discusses a few optoelectronic architectures and one purely optical solution.

7
Digital Neurocomputers

7.1 Introduction

After presenting the principles and basic building blocks of artificial neural network hardware systems in the previous chapters, this and the following chapters are devoted to customized neural network hardware and important proposed hardware architectures. No implementation principles which have already been described in Chapters 4, 5 and 6 will, therefore, be discussed. Rather, the aim is to give an overview of important architectures, fabricated designs and commercially available chips, which will be assessed for their implementation size, speed, flexibility and cascadability. As mentioned in the preface and first chapter, not every architecture proposed and chip fabricated can be mentioned in this book, but the authors tried to cover all the important types of architecture and implementation technologies.

7.1.1 Implementation Size

This is a feature which is simple to assess. Most current neural network implementations are done on silicon. The silicon area used is a direct measure for network size. It is also possible to give the number of implemented transistors or gates, at least for digital approaches, since transistor size is nearly constant in the whole circuit. If the number of neurons and synapses per chip is given, however, one has to bear in mind features like network type and the accuracy of computations. Clearly, it is easier to implement a parallel associative correlation matrix memory with binary synaptic weights on a small chip area than a parallel backpropagation network with 32 bit floating point precision.

7.1.2 Speed

Since speed is one of the most important features of each neural network hardware implementation, if possible, a performance figure will be given for every chip and architecture described. Most performance figures are taken from publications, and therefore have to be viewed with caution. Hardware approaches are very different, which makes it impossible to run the same benchmark on all systems. For flexible digital architectures which support neural network learning, the backpropagation algorithm is usually used as a benchmark. During learning this algorithm iteratively performs two phases: a forward phase to calculate the activation of neurons, and an error-backpropagation phase to calculate weight updates. To obtain a performance figure, a network is trained with arbitrary data, and the average number of weight updates per second (called connection updates per second = CUPS) is evaluated. In spite of this, machines reported to work with the same number of CUPS may have different computational power. On the one hand, this is due to implementation differences of benchmark algorithms. It is possible that a programmer implements an algorithm efficiently, whereas another does not fully use the computational power of his system. On the other hand, the accuracy of calculations has to be taken into account. Two architectures working with the same number of connection updates per second do not show the same performance if one, for example, is using 8 bit arithmetic and the other works with 16 bit precision. Another consideration has to be whether area saving fixed point arithmetic circuitry is employed or more sophisticated floating point arithmetic. Furthermore, large networks may be implemented more efficiently than small networks, resulting in higher performance for large networks. An example of two different implementations of a backpropagation algorithm on dedicated hardware can be found in Pomerleau *et al.*'s approaches on a Warp systolic array [Pom88]. One implementation used memory on single Warp processors for weight storage (network partitioning), whereas the second implementation used Warp memory for storing training vectors and a separate cluster memory for synaptic weight storage (data partitioning). The second implementation was much more efficient for the simulation of large networks. An optimally implemented backpropagation algorithm may run many times faster than a less efficient implementation, resulting in a much higher CUPS value.

Many architectures do not support learning algorithms. Hence, it is necessary to find benchmarks or performance criteria other than the backpropagation algorithm. Usually the speed of the forward phase, *i.e.* the number of synaptic multiplications per second, is given (called interconnections per second or connections per second = CPS). As in the case of the backpropagation benchmark, one has to take into consideration the precision of calculations. Clearly, a network using binary synaptic values may reach a higher number of interconnections per second than a network with 16 bit accuracy in computations.

Hence, to assess a given performance figure the following questions first have to be considered:

1. What kind of benchmark was used?
2. How is the benchmark algorithm implemented?
3. Which accuracy is achieved in calculations?

Even with this knowledge, it is often difficult to assess numbers given, due to implementation differences among benchmarks. In the literature there is usually little or no information given on benchmarks.

7.2 Sequential Computers

Even so, most neural network simulations are done on conventional sequential computers. Figure 7.1 shows the concept of a von Neumann machine. One processor, called the central processing unit (CPU), is responsible for any kind of data processing. Thus, data is stored outside the CPU in special memory chips. In addition to storing data, memory serves for the storage of programs (instructions to control the CPU). Furthermore, input/output interfaces are used to communicate with the external world. This architecture has very characteristic features. Due to the single processor involved, control is very simple. It is not necessary to distribute data to several more or less independent processors and, more important, to control dataflow between processors. Even with few available program development tools, a user may work successfully with a sequential machine. However, the conventional dataflow in a sequential computer is not well suited to neural network simulations. Operations to be performed in a network are only few and rather simple. Most of the neural network algorithms perform matrix multiplications to input vectors (floating point multiplications) with a following

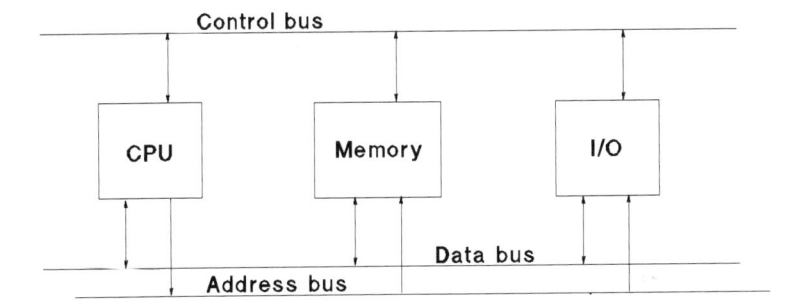

Figure 7.1 *Conventional computer (von Neumann machine)*

summation and nonlinear threshold operation. So the processor power is used only partially. Furthermore, weight matrices (synaptic weights) may become very large, even in moderate size networks, requiring weight storage in large memory chips. For each multiplication a weight value has to be transferred from memory chips to the CPU. Most of the simulation time is therefore spent in floating point multiplications and weight transfer from relatively slow memory to the CPU. The performance of neural network implementations on conventional, sequential computers is roughly between 25,000 and 250,000 interconnections per second [DAR89]. Principally, two methods exist to speed up simulations. First, one may involve several processors in the sharing of computations (parallel computing), and second, one may attempt to construct hardware working on a larger bus width or at a higher clock frequency. To avoid the problems of parallel computing, special acceleration boards which also work sequentially have been developed and commercially produced to speed up neural network simulation. Extremely fast floating point ALUs and high speed memory for weight storage are mounted on boards with a VME bus interface or an interface to IBM PCs. Examples are the Delta Floating Point Processor from the Science Applications International Corporation (SAIC), or the neurocomputing coprocessors from Hecht-Nielsen Computers (HNC) [Hec88]. They are both sequential systems with no more than a minimum parallelism by means of a pipelined architecture (e.g. floating point calculations by separate addition and multiplication parts on the SAIC Delta II FPP vector processor, or a 4-stage pipelined Harvard architecture on the HNC ANZA Plus board). The original Delta processor runs with a calculation speed of 2 million CUPS (backpropagation during learning) [Wor88] or 10 million connections per second without weight update, thus providing speed up by a factor of between 10 to 100 compared with a standard computer. Performance of the HNC ANZA Plus board is reported with 1,800,000 CUPS in learning [Atl89]. More products are now on the market, especially products using fast DSPs and processors with floating point arithmetic like the Motorola 68020 and Motorola 68881 (Mark III and Mark IV neurocomputer from TRW with 450,000 and 5 million interconnections per second [Kuc88]), or the Intel i860 RISC processor (Myriad MC860 board). One of the recently emerged acceleration boards is the Balboa 860 board from Hecht-Nielsen Computers, Inc. It uses the Intel i860 processor, and shows a performance of about 7 million CUPS (backpropagation learning) [Hec91]. More information on acceleration boards and other tools for neural network simulation can be taken from [Wil89]. The advantages of sequential computers are their general availability, the large number of existing software and hardware tools and, therefore, their high flexibility. Most acceleration boards are not restricted to use for neural network simulations only. There exist compilers (e.g. SAIC's "Delta C" compiler), usually C compilers, and algorithm libraries (e.g. HNC's scientific algorithm library SAL) to

Digital Signal Processor Arrays 119

accelerate computations, opening the application of acceleration boards to speed up data preprocessing which will be required in most neural network applications. Otherwise, data preprocessing will become the computational bottleneck. But, due to their high flexibility and general availability, even future sequential computers will probably serve for most neural network prototyping.

7.3 Digital Signal Processor Arrays

The performance of sequential systems may be increased up to a certain degree by increasing the bus width and clock frequency. At present, the fastest systems commonly work with 32 bit busses and a clock frequency of up to 60 MHz. Physical parameters and effects such as chip size or wave reflections limit the maximum computational power that may be achieved. Further improvement of system power can only be done by parallel components. One way is to use several processor chips of conventional, sequential computers and fit them together on several boards connected with each other, thus having the power of several sequential machines. Since most neural network algorithms make use of many floating point multiplications, processors should be able to perform fast multiplications, thus making digital signal processors (DSPs) with floating point units good candidates for implementation. A big disadvantage of such processors, originally designed for use in sequential systems, is their lack of communication facilities with neighboring processors. A large amount of information is exchanged between neurons (even neurons in the far neighborhood) of a network, requiring an extensive exchange of information between processors. This problem may be solved by providing each processor with a large amount of private memory (off-chip) for weight storage and off-chip communication facilities.

7.3.1 DSP Array Architecture from Cruz et al. (IBM)

One of the first massively parallel DSP architectures developed and proposed for the simulation of neural network related algorithms emerged from the IBM Palo Alto Scientific Center [Cru87]. Since 1981 a group at the IBM center studied so-called "flow-of-activation networks" (FANs). FANs are very similar to neural networks in that a large number of simple processor nodes communicating with each other through directed point-to-point channels process information in massively parallel way. C.A. Cruz et al. [Cru87] describe flow-of-activation networks as an abstraction of neural networks. Like neural networks, FANs consist of nodes and links which may be configured in an arbitrary topology. Each node possesses a state-variable called the "activation level". Links and nodes may be adaptive, their transfer function can change over time. Node communication is done by transmitting node activation levels to each other through unidirectional paths. The research group at IBM developed software programs (GNL network compiler) to construct networks from a structured high level description and to run them (IXP network emulation program). Furthermore, a parallel, digital signal processor-based emulation engine was designed (called "NEP"). Software and hardware constitute the "Computational Network Environment" (CONE) for an IBM PC/XT or PC/AT. The CONE environment is a flexible environment for network design, network debugging, network analysis and network execution.

The Network Emulation Processor (NEP) is a cascadable parallel coprocessor for IBM PC compatibles. Figure 7.2 sketches the basic architecture of a NEP card. Each NEP was planned to be able to simulate

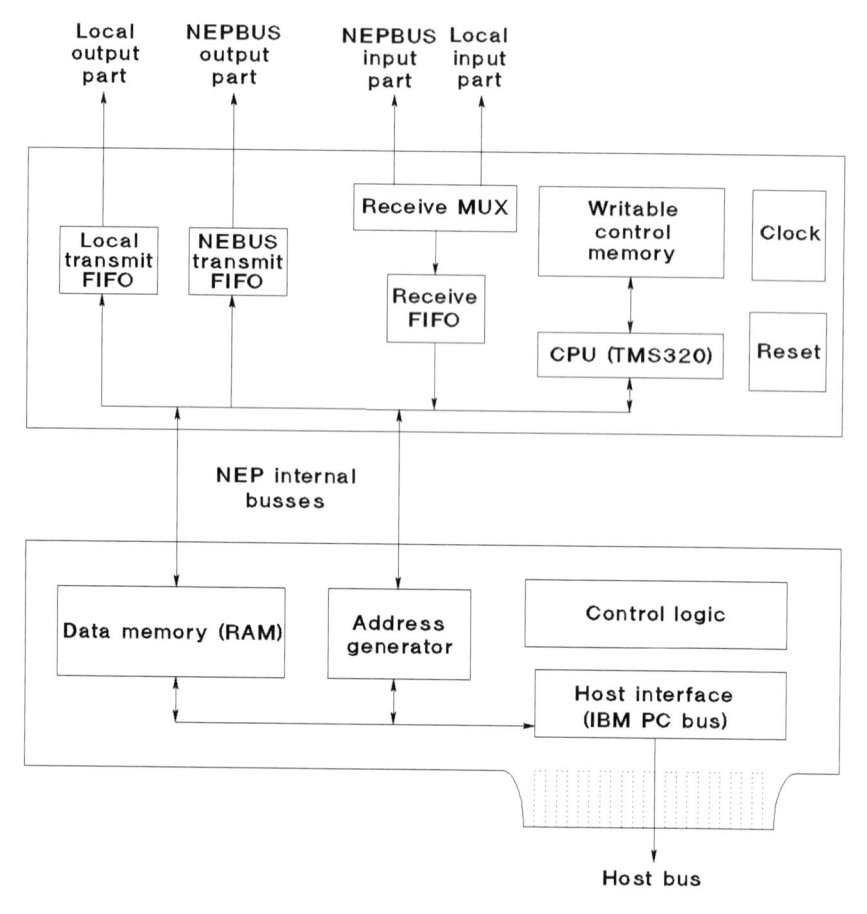

Figure 7.2 *Architecture of the Network Emulation Processor (NEP) (adapted from [Cru87])*

4000 nodes and 16,000 adaptive links, with at least 30-50 total network updates per second, thus corresponding to a speed of about 48,000 CUPS to 80,000 CUPS (per NEP board). However, the actual speed depends on the type of DSP (integer arithmetic or full floating point processor) used in the NEP board. More nodes and links on a board can only be simulated by using fixed-weight links. Larger networks, however, may be distributed on several NEP boards. A high-speed interprocessor communication network called "NEPBUS" allows up to 256 NEPs to be cascaded, thus allowing the implementation of networks containing up to 1 million nodes and 4 million links. For fast data exchange, each NEP contains high-speed local input/output devices. The NEPBUS and local I/O interface are FIFO buffered to allow a group of NEPs to asynchronously update the state of their respective portions of a large network. Cascading different NEPs via the NEPBUS interface is illustrated in Figure 7.3.

The NEP architecture is a very flexible architecture. Hardware may be configured to form processor arrays of requested size (up to 256 PEs). This system is able to run any algorithm which can be implemented on parallel hardware. Software tools enable fast and user-friendly prototyping.

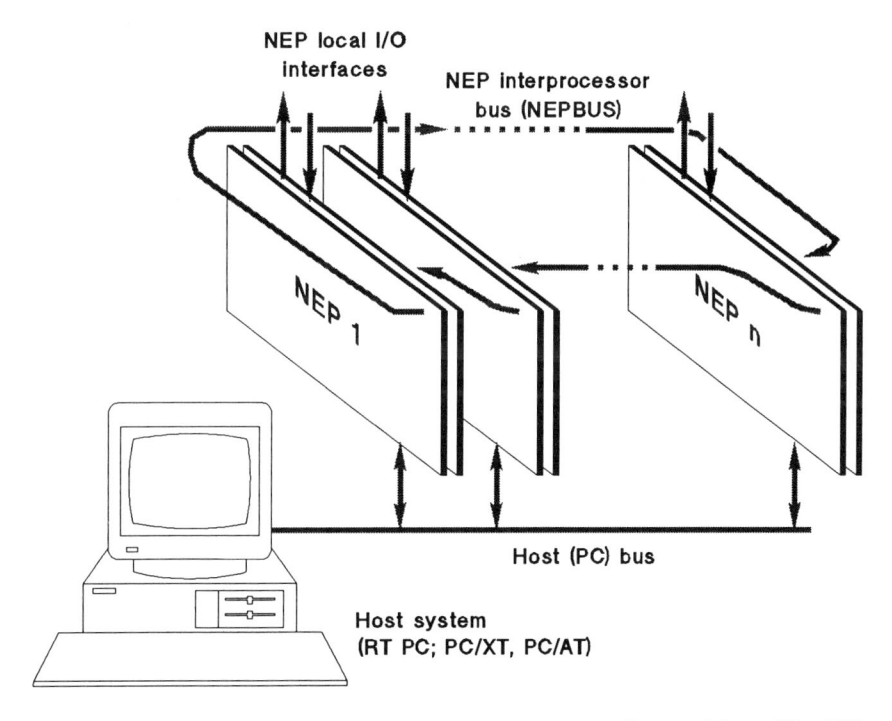

Figure 7.3 *NEP system consisting of several NEP boards (adapted from [Cru87])*

7.3.2 Digital Signal Processor Array (Fujitsu)

Another parallel processor system based on DSPs was implemented by Kato et al. at Fujitsu Laboratories [Kat90]. As the processor they chose the floating point digital signal processor TMS320C30 from Texas Instruments. To make processors more suitable for neural network simulation, each of them is provided with external high speed memory (off-chip) and a "tray" for fast information exchange. Figure 7.4 shows the basic architecture. All neurons (with their receiving synapses) in one network column are mapped onto a single processing element (PE) realized by a signal processor. No physical layer structure exists in the hardware architecture. For a three layer backpropagation network the number of PEs corresponds to the number of neurons in the hidden layer. This is due to the chosen weight storage on the processor memory and information exchange by means of processor trays. Thus, all a neuron's receiving synaptic weights are stored on the corresponding processing element's off-chip local memory (see Figure 7.5). This is to obtain maximum performance. However, since one PE may simulate several neurons, depending on the implementation chosen, it is also possible to simulate very large networks which have more neurons in one layer than PEs that are available.

Figure 7.5 sketches the dataflow within the processor system during the forward (or recall) phase of the error backpropagation algorithm [Rum86]. Suppose the network of Figure 7.4 is implemented on the machine, W is

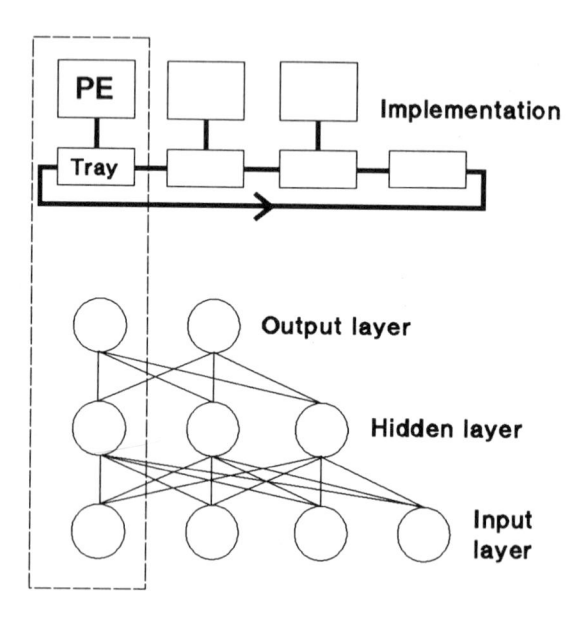

Figure 7.4 *Basic architecture of Fujitsu's DSP solution (adapted from [Kat90])*

Digital Signal Processor Arrays

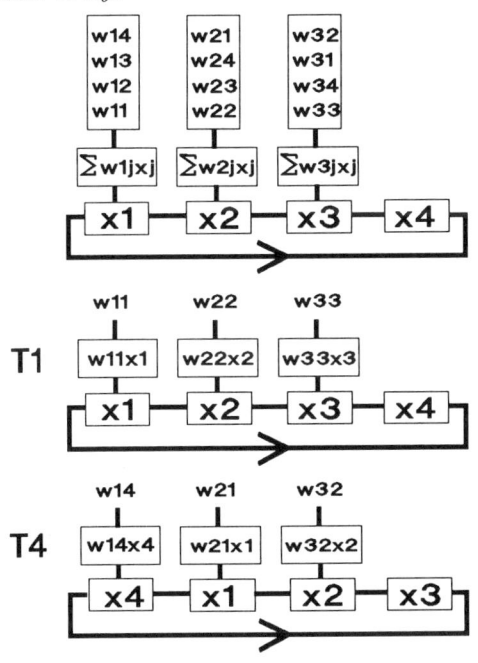

Figure 7.5 *Data flow during recall phase (adapted from [Kat90])*

a four by three matrix of weight elements between the input and hidden layer, with w_{ij} the weight from neuron j of the input layer to neuron i of the hidden layer. Signals x_j (neuron output values) propagated from the input layer to the hidden layer are kept in the trays and rotated counter-clockwise to provide each PE with all neuron outputs from the preceding layer. Summation of partial sum $\sum_j w_{ij} x_j$ of neuron i is done in an accumulator on its corresponding PE. In the example, after four cycles all computations are done and the machine may proceed to the next layer (after thresholding partial sums).

For error backpropagation, $W^T y$ has to be computed with y being the generalized error (three element vector in the example), which is back-propagated from the output layer. Figure 7.6 shows the data flow for error backpropagation. Now the roles of trays and accumulators are swapped. Partial sums are circulated through the tray ring and error y_i is held in the ith PE. The whole architecture is comparable to a SIMD array with very complex processing elements, since each PE is performing exactly the same task but on different data. It is disadvantageous that the fixed length of trays makes the required computation time for each network layer exactly the same, regardless of the number of neurons to be simulated. Thus, without a dynamic change of ring size, the performance of the machine becomes

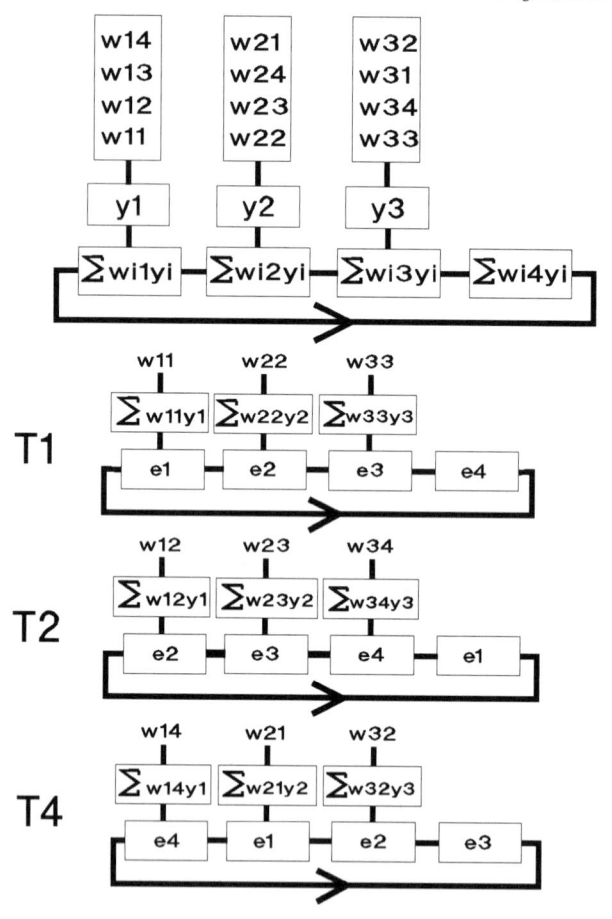

Figure 7.6 *Data flow during error backpropagation (adapted from [Kat90])*

worse from layer to layer, if the layer size, *i.e.* the number of neurons in the layer, is decreasing.

At Fujitsu Laboratories a prototype system with 256 processors called Sandy/8 was developed. Each DSP (2K words internal memory) is provided with 32K words of external high speed memory. The word width of the internal and external memory is 32 bits. Within 60ns one 32-bit floating point multiplication and addition can be performed. Trays are implemented on custom gate-array chips (2000 gates). The whole system is connected to a Sun station via a VME bus, as depicted in Figure 7.7. With a ring network width of 32 bits and 60ns cycle time, a bandwidth of 67 MB/s is obtained. A system with 64 PEs (Sandy/6) worked with 118 million CUPS in the NETtalk application [Sej86] and a maximum speed of 141 million

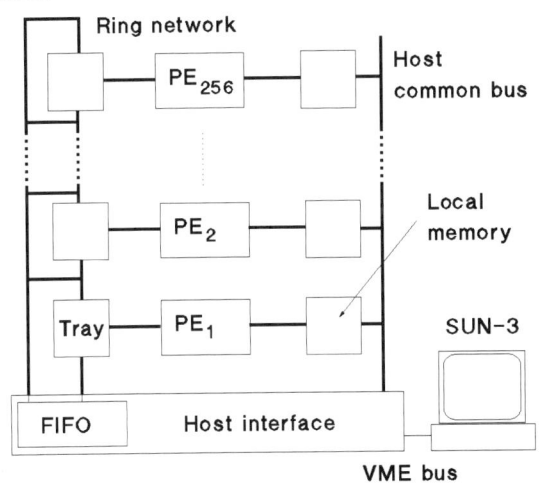

Figure 7.7 *Prototype system Sandy/8 (adapted from [Kat90])*

CUPS [Kat90]. The 256 PE system Sandy/8 was expected to work with up to 567 million CUPS in large networks [Kat90]. At that time, this machine was reported to be the world's fastest neurocomputer.

Such a system needs an enormous amount of hardware; however, its big advantage is high flexibility. It may be used for neural network simulations as well as for other computationally intensive tasks like image processing that may benefit from tightly interconnected processor arrays.

7.4 Transputer Networks

The implementation of neural network algorithms on transputer networks is comparable to their implementation on networks of digital signal processors. A transputer is a rather complex processing element which has not been designed for exclusively simulating neural networks. One advantage of transputers over standard digital signal processors with respect to neural network simulation is the fact that transputers possess more on-chip memory, an external memory interface, and communication channels. Figure 7.8 shows a block diagram of the Inmos T800 transputer from the famous Inmos transputer family (T414, T424 and T800). The T800 transputer is a 32 bit CMOS microcomputer with a 64 bit floating point unit and graphics support [INM89]. High speed on-chip memory of 4 Kbytes supports high speed processing. If this memory is not sufficient, which will be the case in simulations of medium and large size neural networks, additional external memory may be easily accessed via an external memory interface. Four standard Inmos communication links can form independent data channels for fast, direct data exchange between neighboring transput-

126   *Digital Neurocomputers*

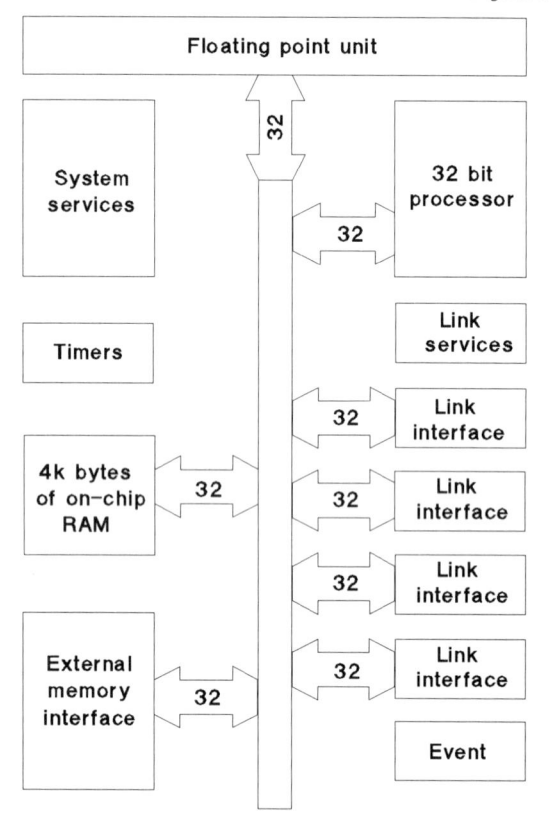

Figure 7.8 *Transputer block diagram (Inmos T800) (adapted from [INM89])*

ers. Direct data exchange means that transputers can directly be connected to each other without the need for additional external logic. Thus, networks of transputer family products can be easily formed. The IMS T800 links support a standard operating speed of 10 Mbits/sec, but also operate at 5 or 20 Mbits/sec. Unidirectional as well as bidirectional data transfer is possible. Each link can transfer data bidirectionally up to a speed of 2.35 Mbytes/sec.

Network mapping on transputer networks is neuron oriented, since transputers are complex and large processing elements. Figure 7.9 sketches a typical mapping of network nodes onto a transputer network (e.g. see [Erno88]). The transputer concept is very flexible and with the Occam language there exists a software environment for parallel computing. However, there is a trade-off in the use of Occam for programming transputer systems. Occam facilitates the implementation of parallel algorithms significantly. But this has to be paid for by lower performance compared

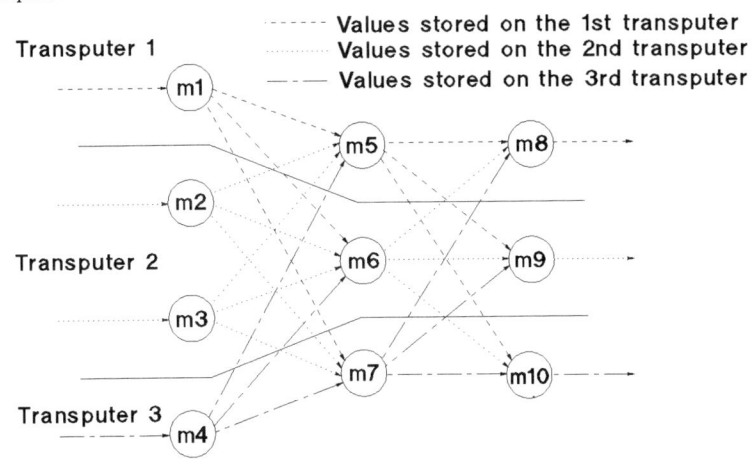

Figure 7.9 *Mapping of networks on transputers*

with a dedicated "hand made" algorithm implementation. Furthermore, Occam does not support C-like functionality like dynamic memory allocation (dynamic data structures), records and lists. Therefore, some people working with transputers have developed their own C library routines [Erns90].

As in all algorithm implementations on parallel hardware, a certain computational overhead has to be considered for information exchange, management tasks between processing elements of the parallel network, and management tasks between parallel network and host computer. Therefore, it is difficult to predict the performance of neural network algorithms on parallel hardware. The better the implementation and the larger the network to be simulated, the faster the whole system will run. This statement is also valid for transputer networks. C. Ernoult [Erno88] reports that a network of 2480 neurons with 921,600 links simulated on a 16 transputer system (Inmos T800) runs 14 times faster than the sequentially executed network (on a single transputer). During simulation, she obtained weight updates with a speed of about 575,000 CUPS. On the whole, similar results can be found in other publications (e.g. H.P. Ernst *et al.* [Erns90]). Most neural network simulations have been done on rather small transputer networks of 4 to 16 transputers. With a backpropagation implementation (network with 74,996 connections) on a four transputer network (Inmos T800 transputers), Ernst *et al.* [Erns90] obtained a performance of about 250,000 CUPS.

Summarized, transputers are very flexible processors. They may be configured to linear or 2-dimensional networks of processing elements for neural network simulation as well as any other algorithm that may be mapped onto several processors. Thus, transputer networks are also well suited for image processing applications or data preprocessing for a neural network input. Transputer arrays are a flexible, low cost, modest performance solution for neural network simulation.

7.5 RISC Arrays

The justification for all dedicated hardware developments is to achieve higher performance by keeping as much flexibility as possible. One way to speed up sequential processors is to use data busses of a larger width to increase clock frequency, and to implement special circuits on silicon that are extremely fast or able to perform complex tasks in one machine cycle (by using high speed on-chip memory, fast floating point circuits, *etc.*). This method has been pursued by developers of digital signal processors. However, there exists another possibility to make processors faster [Goo89]. This is by reducing the time data need to pass through the critical data path in the processor hardware. A reduction in the number of instructions, addressing modes and data types eliminates the need for a large control area. In standard processors, the control area is usually occupied by a microprogrammed controller containing the microprogram to control processor activities. If only a few simple operations (most of which need one machine cycle) have to be executed, the controller will be small and may be hard-wired. Furthermore, the migration of complex functions from the executing processor to the compiler contributes to simple instructions and shorter cycle times. Therefore, complex operations, such as "multiply", are interpreted, *i.e.* the operation is performed by a sequence of simpler instructions. Architectures with this basic concept are called "reduced instruction set computers" (RISC). The RISC philosophy, however, includes more than a reduced instruction set processor with a very fast, hard-wired controller. The processor architecture also has a better compiler interface.

Boundaries between different hardware approaches are not always easy to define. This is especially the case with RISC processors. Not all of the above-mentioned features are very good for classification. For example, the question arises as to "What is a better compiler interface?". Furthermore, what happens if only one of the above aspects is not fulfilled? Is a processor with only a few operations that can be executed in a few cycles not a RISC processor if it does not contain a hard-wired controller? So on one side there is a smooth transition between RISC and CISC (complex instruction set computer) processors. Early digital signal processors had been designed to solve specific tasks with a rather small set of instructions. However, modern DSPs distinguish themselves by a larger set of instructions for flexible applicability, by area consuming hardware circuits for fast data processing (circuits for addition and multiplication), and by large register banks (for fast data processing like vector processing). On the other side, towards decreasing processor complexity, it becomes difficult to distinguish RISC processors from dedicated processors used to implement systolic arrays or SIMD arrays (single instruction multiple data). A SIMD array processor is a kind of RISC processor. Only a few instructions, depending on the complexity of a processing element, can be performed. However, a SIMD processor does not possess an independent controller, since each processing element of a SIMD array performs the same task (*i.e.* the same instruction) at the same time (on different data). Thus, one single controller may serve to control a whole array of hundreds or thousands of processors. The situation becomes more obscure if processors of general systolic arrays are considered. Principally, a systolic array processor is a more or less complex RISC processor. It performs a limited number of instructions. In all known applications this number is much smaller than that of commercially available state-of-the-art RISC processors such as the Intel 80860.

7.5.1 Neural RISC

A neural RISC processor-based architecture has been developed by M. Pacheco and P. Treleaven *et al.* [Pac89, Tre89] at University College London. Such a RISC machine may serve to build a parallel MIMD general-purpose computer. In contrast to SIMD arrays, each processor of a MIMD machine is an independent processing unit with its own controller which is principally able to solve problems independently. Therefore, a MIMD computer is a very general and flexible system.

Pacheco's Neural RISC architecture has a 16-bit RISC processor unit with local memory and a communication unit on one chip [Tre89]. The network architecture of the Neural RISC network is shown in Figure 7.10. Each chip contains several processing units (PUs). Thus, processor density benefits from the simplicity of RISC processor units. The processor performs no more than 16 different instructions. To prevent interconnection problems and expensive packages with a large number of pins, processors are connected in the form of a linear array. Such an interconnection scheme was used in several successful architectures like the Warp array used by Pomerleau *et al.* [Pom88]. It has the advantage of simplified wiring and placement of PUs on the chip area (efficient use of costly silicon area, reduced pin numbers). Moreover, cascadability and therefore extension of the processor array beyond the chip boundaries is very simple. Furthermore, the control of information exchange between processors is not difficult. A whole network, as illustrated in Figure 7.10, consists of linear processor arrays connected in the form of rings to a multi-ring interconnect module, forming a cluster.

Each RISC-array ring ends up in an interconnect module. Pacheco *et al.* [Pac92] report that each ring may be of an individual size. The interconnect module is an autonomous unit with its own microprocessor. Its

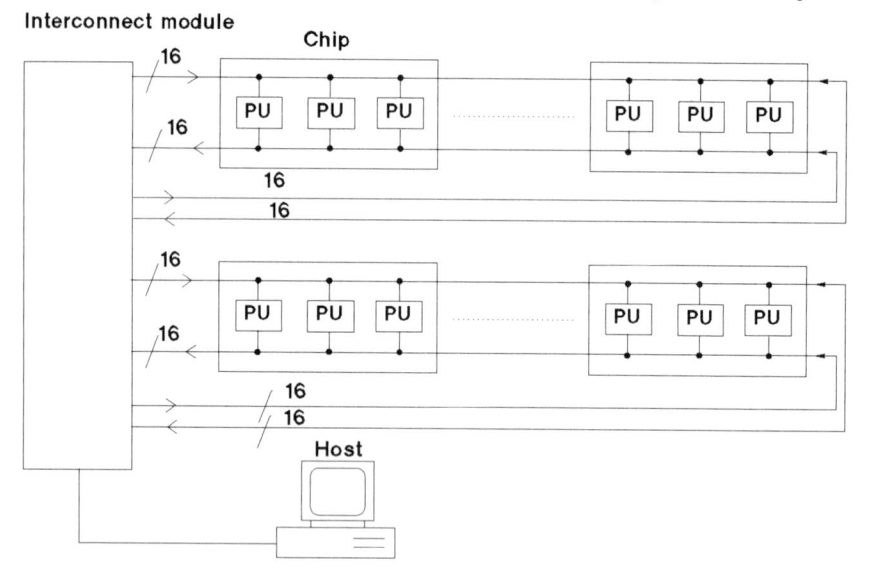

Figure 7.10 *Neural RISC network architecture (adapted from [Pac92])*

tasks are to send messages into the RISC arrays and to form an interface to the host computer. Several interconnect modules with rings, each forming a RISC cluster, may be connected to a host computer. The architecture is freely scalable allowing short rings in many clusters or long rings in a few clusters, affecting system costs and computing power [Pac92]. Through the interconnect modules, RISC-arrays may be interconnected via different topologies like rings, meshes, cubes, *etc*. A maximum number of 65,536 processor nodes is permitted by the system architecture.

Two RISC units are depicted in Figure 7.11. The RISC unit consists of a 16-bit ALU, the accumulator Ax, the instruction pointer IP, the processor status word PSW, and the multiplication auxiliary register Mpx. One Kword of SRAM is implemented on-chip for each PE (the word width is 16 bits). Furthermore, there is a communication unit and a processor PLA (controller). All instructions are of a length of one word using a fixed format with two fields: a 4-bit opcode and a 12-bit immediate value/address.

The task of the communication unit is to provide a facility for data exchange between processors. Hence, it supplies two bidirectional, point-to-point links (implemented by four unidirectional links) and a protocol to support a logical bus for broadcasting and routing data packets. Each 16-bit link is controlled by three handshaking signals. A message exchanged between processors consists of three 16-bit words, which are:

1. Neuron name or layer (to define the destination processor or group of processors).

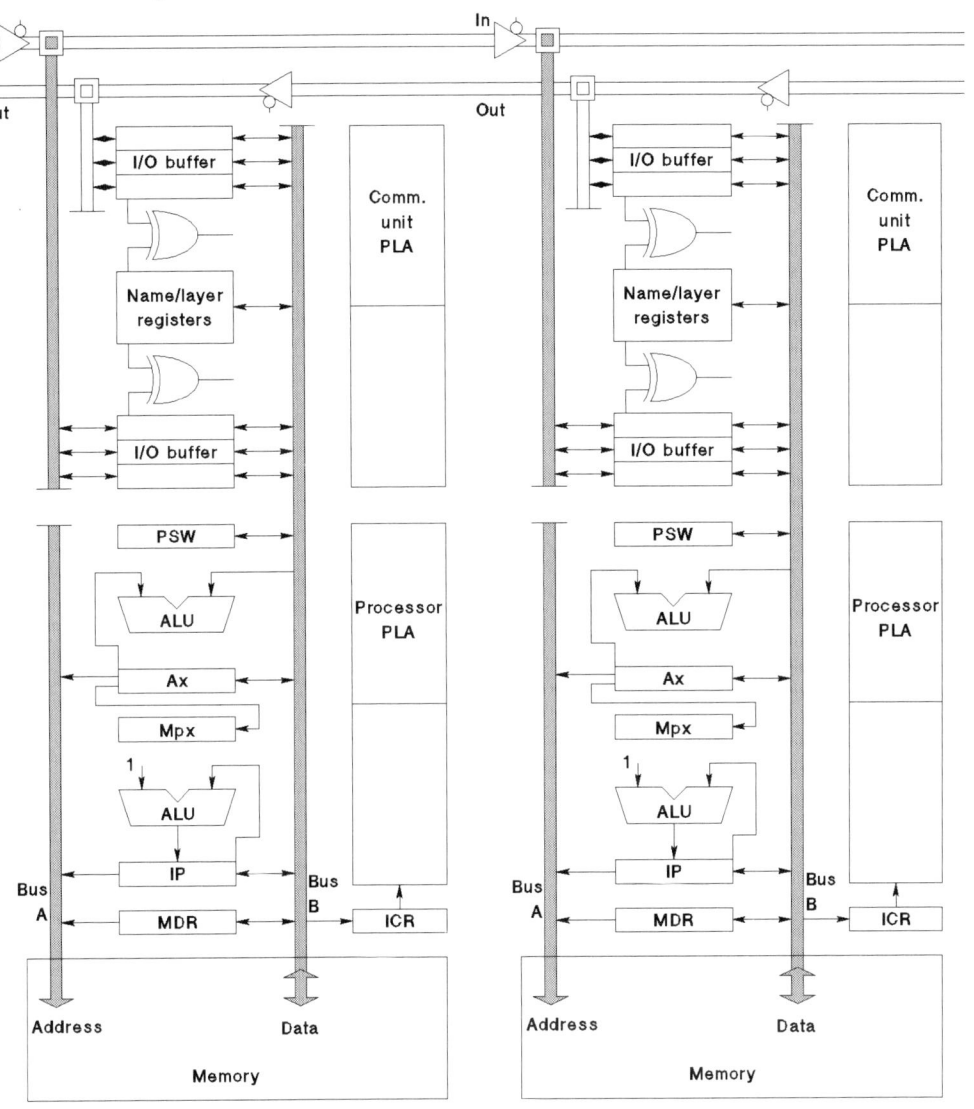

Figure 7.11 *The Neural RISC architecture (adapted from [Tre89])*

2. The dendrite (which defines the input link).
3. A signal (which defines a value associated to the input).

To perform this task, each communication unit provides two I/O buffers which are called "name register" (to identify the PE in the network) and "layer register" (to access a group of PEs), respectively. Communication is controlled by a routing algorithm on the host computer.

Since the network is a MIMD machine, the system has to be configured by downloading programs into each PU (since each RISC is an independent von Neumann machine).

A prototype implementation in 1.5 μm CMOS technology was carried out in 1990. This chip contains two PUs with 2 Kbytes of memory, running at 5 MHz. The chip fits into an 84-pin package.

7.5.2 Two-Level Pipeline RISC Array

A proposal for a complex two-dimensional mesh-connected RISC processor array for the simulation of artificial neural networks was made by Hiraiwa et al. [Hir90]. As the physical network processor they propose the Intel 80860 with 4 MBytes of off-chip memory each. Two FIFOs (first in first out memory) of 256 words (64-bit word width) serve to implement a mesh connection. The Intel 80860 is a modern state-of-the-art RISC processor with a 32/64 bit floating point multiplier and adder, 12 KBytes of on-chip memory, and a pipelined processing architecture.

Two methods to partition a network for simulation on parallel hardware exist. On the one hand, it is possible to use the parallelism existing between neurons. This means that in the case of the multilayer perceptron with backpropagation algorithm, the neurons of one layer may be mapped onto different PEs, whereas neurons of successive layers may be mapped onto the same PE. Figure 2.10 (upper right) shows this kind of mapping. It is called "network partitioning" due to the fact that concurrently operating parts of the network are partitioned into different sets. Each set is assigned to a physical processor. In Figure 2.10 it becomes clear that the network topology is partitioned, in this case into slices of neurons with their receiving synapses. On the other hand, the input/output data to the network can be partitioned. For the backpropagation algorithm an input vector from the input data set is applied to the network, fed forward through the network and its output calculated. Then, this actual output is compared to the desired output of the output data set and an error signal computed, which is backpropagated through the network to calculate weight updates. During one training sweep this procedure is done for each input/output vector pair of the training data set. Weights can either be changed after each application of an input/output vector pair, or calculated weight changes may be accumulated and network weights changed after an epoch, i.e. after the application of several training vectors without weight update (epoch update or epoch mode of learning) [Rum86]. The epoch mode of learning permits a very efficient, parallel implementation of networks. Thus, the whole network is simulated sequentially on one processor with one input/output vector pair. Simultaneously, the same network is simulated (sequentially) on another processor with another input/output vector pair of the training set. Thus, the maximum degree of parallelism achievable depends on the number of vectors in the training set. Realistic applications have vector sets in the range of hundreds or thousands of training vectors, thus allowing massive parallelism. This method will be referred to as data partitioning. It was used for a powerful implementation of large networks on the Warp systolic array by Pomerleau *et al.* [Pom88].

Hiraiwa *et al.* are combining network and data partitioning in their architecture proposal, as may be seen in Figure 7.12. Horizontal mesh connections serve for information exchange for data partitioning, whereas vertical meshes support dataflow in network partitioning. Thus, vertical PEs are sharing weights and horizontal PEs are sharing data. However, to benefit from both implementation methods for extremely fast simulations, some weights have to be stored twice, which is less memory efficient [Hir90]. Simulations of this architecture were done by Hiraiwa *et al.* to evaluate its expected performance. For a 368 neuron network (256 input units, 80 hidden units, and 32 output units) with a training set of 5120 vectors running on a 128 PE RISC array at 50 MHz clock frequency, they expect a performance of more than 1000 MCUPS [Hir90].

Like arrays of signal processors or transputers, RISC processor arrays are a very flexible general tool for parallel processing. They are not dedicated to the simulation of a specific neural network algorithm, or even to neurocomputing. Any algorithm which may be parallelized can run on them,

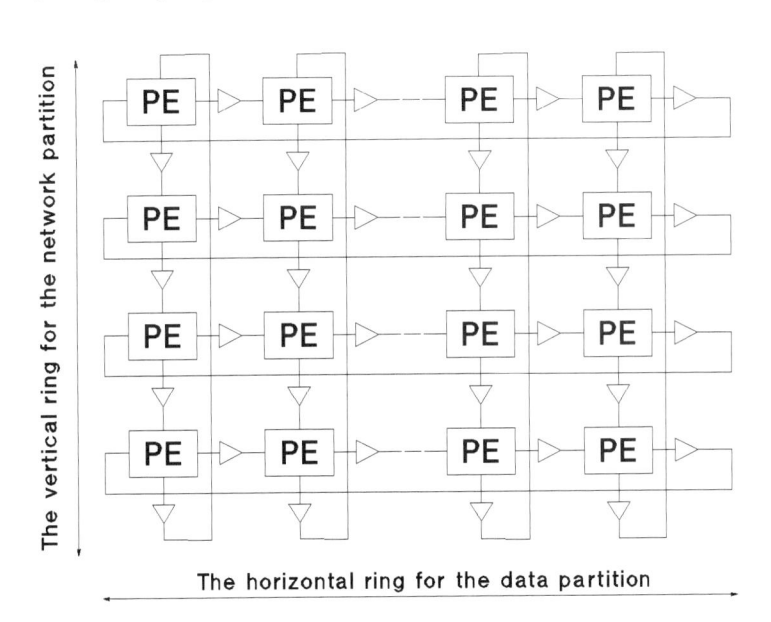

Figure 7.12 *Network and data partitioning implementation (adapted from [Hir90])*

thus allowing data preprocessing algorithms to run on the hardware as well as the neural network. Compared with digital signal processors, the expense of hardware is similar using commercial products. More efficient implementations other than DSP approaches can only be done if several customized RISC processors are implemented on one chip, to increase PE density or reduce system size and system costs. The computational power of RISC arrays is similar to that of DSP arrays.

7.6 SIMD Arrays and Systolic Arrays

Conceptually, digital signal processor arrays or transputer arrays may be extended to a very large number of processing elements for high performance. The expense of hardware, however, is significant. Each PE consists of a complex DSP chip, standard RAM chips to provide sufficient memory for weight storage, circuitry for fast information exchange with neighboring processors (e.g. FIFOs to implement mesh connections), and some additional interface and control circuitry, thus permitting the realization of no more than one or only a few PEs on one printed circuit board. A network consisting of several hundred PEs will occupy quite a lot of space. Power dissipation and therefore cooling may become problematic as well as increasing unreliability of a complex system consisting of many components. More computational power can only be provided by smaller, more specific and less flexible processing elements which are interconnected efficiently. Therefore, the processing elements and interconnection scheme are optimized to solve specific classes of algorithms. Through restriction on specific algorithms to be solved, PE complexity is reduced (every PE is a RISC processor), resulting in a higher PE density on silicon. Systolic arrays and SIMD arrays are such dedicated parallel PE arrays.

Systolic array processors are a class of very specific architectures. In contrast to von Neumann machines, systolic arrays consist of a large number of processing elements that are highly pipelined. Each processing element is a quite independent processor with its own controller, and performs a specific task. Kung [Kun88] defines a systolic array as a system of processors which is:

- **Synchronous:** Data is rhythmically computed and passed through the network.

- **Modular and regular:** The array is built up from an arbitrary number of homogeneously interconnected units (processing elements).

- **Spatially and temporally local:** Spatial locality expresses the local interconnection scheme between PEs for communication. Temporal locality means that each node (PE) has a time delay of at least one unit to allow the completion of tasks from one node to the next.

SIMD Arrays and Systolic Arrays 135

- **Pipelinability:** An $O(M)$ speedup is achieved in a system consisting of M processing elements, due to pipelining.

Thus, a systolic array is a regular and modular array of processing elements. There exist no broadcast busses which can be accessed by each PE. Rather, only local interconnections between PEs serve for information exchange. Hence, data cannot be preloaded onto individual processors but has to be "pumped" through the array (pipelining). This principle is shown in Figure 7.13, depicting a simple configuration of a systolic array [Kun88]. Pipelining has the advantage that high computation throughput can be achieved without increasing memory bandwidth. Each PE has its own controller, permitting different PEs to perform different tasks. Systolic arrays are, however, not data driven, and there exists a global clock scheme to synchronize PEs which distinguishes them from wavefront arrays. Many interconnection schemes, from simple one-dimensional linear or ring connections to more complex two-dimensional connection grids with loops, may be used to implement algorithms. Figure 7.14 illustrates the principle of the systolic array architecture. Due to the simplicity of the individual PE and the regularity of the array structure, systolic arrays are well suited for implementation in VLSI technology. Furthermore, regularity and modularity allow an easy extension of the system beyond chip boundaries, *i.e.* simple cascadability without additional off-chip circuitry.

Compared with systolic arrays, SIMD arrays are very similar systems. Like systolic arrays they consist of a large number of relatively simple processing elements. Depending on the intended application, one PE may be a simple bit-slice architecture (1-bit ALU) with a few registers (hundreds of such simple PEs may fit onto one single chip), or a more complex circuit with 32-bit IEEE floating point circuitry for fast multiplications and summations with several KBytes of its own RAM memory (with only four or eight processing elements on a single chip). However, in contrast to a systolic approach, PEs possess no individual controllers, but there is a central controller which broadcasts its control signals to all PEs simultaneously. Thus, at the same time, each PE receives the same control signal and performs exactly the same operation as its neighbors (single instruction principle), making a SIMD array a synchronous array of processors under the control of a single control unit. Another difference to systolic architectures

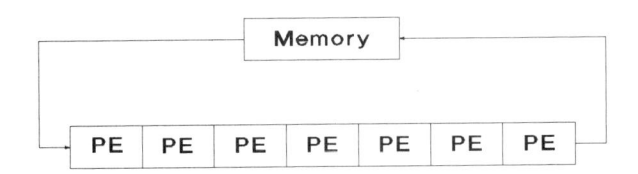

Figure 7.13 *Simple systolic array (adapted from [Kun88])*

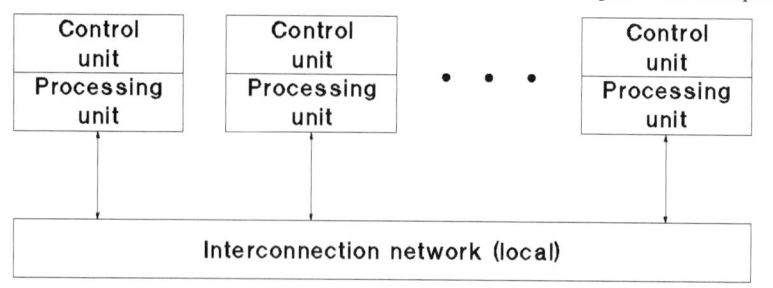

Figure 7.14 *Systolic array (adapted from [Kun88])*

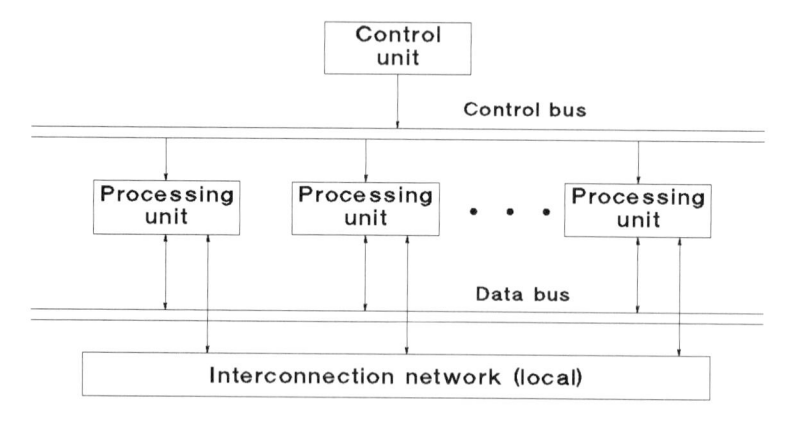

Figure 7.15 *Simple SIMD array (adapted from [Kun88])*

is the existence of broadcast busses which may be accessed by each PE. The SIMD architecture principles are sketched in Figure 7.15. PEs may be interconnected in the form of a simple linear array or in two-dimensional arrays with local interconnections in addition to broadcast busses. In contrast to systolic architectures, data is usually preloaded into local memory of PEs via a broadcast data bus or a large shift register (formed by PEs). In systolic arrays data is piped from an external host through the array, and results obtained are piped back [Kun88]. This may become an advantage for algorithms where a continuous flow of information can be achieved. Through continuous data piping the peak data transformation rate can be lower than in SIMD arrays, which have to be preloaded.

Both SIMD arrays and systolic arrays may be well suited for neural network simulations. However, some requests have to be fulfilled which also depend on the network type and size to be implemented. For many networks a computational accuracy of at least 16 bits is necessary. Better would be a 32-bit floating point format to increase flexibility (at the expense of integration density). It is important to have a sufficient amount of memory for each PE to store synaptic weight data (at least a few KBytes of RAM per PE). Therefore, SIMD arrays dedicated to image processing are usually not suitable for neural network simulation. Processing elements are bit-slice architectures, and often provide an accuracy of not more than 8 bits. They do not possess sufficient memory (only a few registers) and the necessary computation accuracy for efficient neural network simulation. Neural networks need a special type of SIMD array. A data piping facility may be an advantage for systolic arrays. If a smaller amount of training data can be stored on each PE, weights may be pumped through the systolic array, allowing external off-chip storage of the large amount of synaptic weights. Only a smaller amount of training data has to be stored in each PE (data partitioning method). This enables an efficient implementation of large networks. Pomerleau et al. [Pom88] used this method for a fast implementation of the backpropagation algorithm.

In the following, some important architectures and commercial products will be described. Some vendors do not distinguish properly between systolic arrays and SIMD arrays according to the above given definitions. This is also due to slightly different definitions of systolic arrays made by other authors. Therefore, some products offered are referred to as "systolic arrays in SIMD architecture". With the above given definitions, these are actually SIMD arrays.

7.6.1 Warp Systolic Array

An important systolic array used for an early neural network simulation is the Warp array [Arn85, Ann87]. It was designed and built at Carnegie-Mellon University (CMU), with an industrial partner, as a powerful processor array for image processing tasks [Kun85]. The Warp machine consist of three parts: the Warp processor array, the host computer, and an interface unit between host and Warp array (shown in Figure 7.16). Each Warp

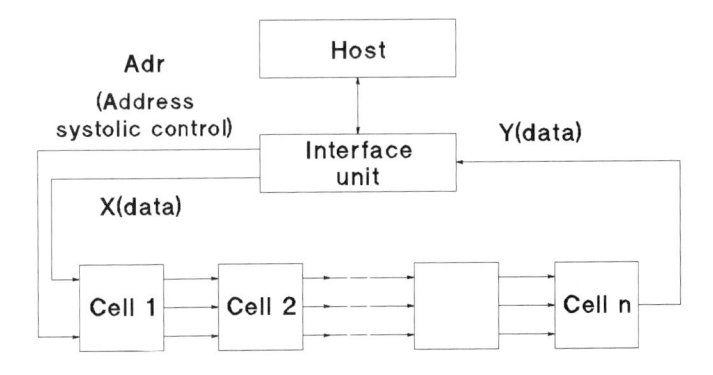

Figure 7.16 *The Warp system (adapted from [Arn85])*

cell can be used independently due to a microengine which can be programmed by the user, providing complete user control over the processor. A compiler was developed at CMU to facilitate programming. The Warp array can operate in a systolic mode to perform systolic algorithms, and in a local mode, where each PE works independently on its own data [Kun88]. Figure 7.17 shows the configuration of a Warp cell. The Warp system works with a global clock of 5 MHz resulting in a performance of 10 MFLOPS per processor. Two data paths exist to form a ring to pump data through the system. An address path provides processor cells with addresses and systolic control signals. The Warp cell used by Pomerleau *et al.* has a floating point multiplier (5 MFLOPS), a floating point adder (5 MFLOPS), an integer ALU (10 MIPS), and 32 KWords of high speed memory. A special boundary processor with bidirectional links to the interface unit, to the first cell and to the last cell may be attached to the end of a Warp array, thus enabling fast data circulation in the array without using the external host. Warp systems consist of linear arrays of 10 Warp cells and more.

The host system is responsible for communication with peripheral devices, and for providing the Warp array with data through an interface unit. To do this efficiently, the host system consists of a workstation (Sun 3/160 in the 1988 configuration used by Pomerleau *et al.*) controlling the Warp machine and an additional external host (external to the workstation) consisting of three 68020-based processors, one responsible for the

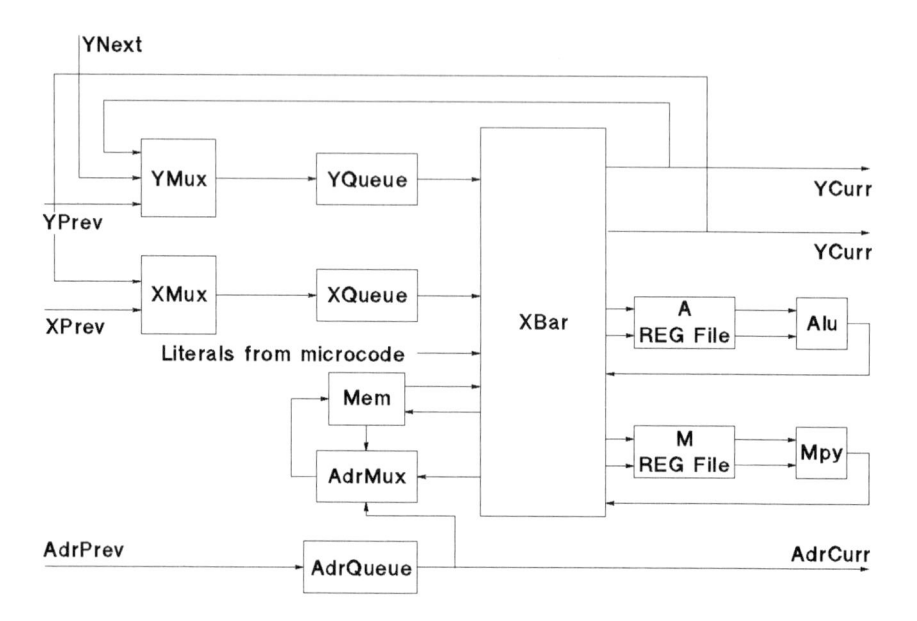

Figure 7.17 *Configuration of the Warp cell (adapted from [Arn85])*

SIMD Arrays and Systolic Arrays

control of peripheral devices (support processor), and two responsible for data transfer from and to the Warp array via the interface unit (cluster processors).

The task of the interface unit is to provide control signals for Warp processors and to organize the communication between host and processor array. The interface unit is sketched in Figure 7.18. It consists of input/output FIFOs (32 bit width, 512 word depth, each) for data buffering between host and Warp array, integer-to-floating-point (and *vice versa*) converters, input/output crossbars to allow the Warp array to receive from or send to either of the two interface unit's input/output ports, an address generator to send 16-bit addresses to the Warp (one per 100 ns), and a host interface with three 32-bit registers [Kun88].

A 10 cell Warp array is reported to perform a 1024 point complex fast fourier transform in 0.6 ms [Kun88]. Pomerleau *et al.* [Pom88] implemented the backpropagation algorithm on a 10 cell Warp array. Using network partitioning, the size of networks is limited by the Warp cell memory which has to store synaptic weights. With the available memory only small networks can be implemented. However, Pomerleau *et al.* implemented larger networks using the data partitioning method. Weights were stored on a 39 MByte cluster memory and pumped through the array efficiently. Warp

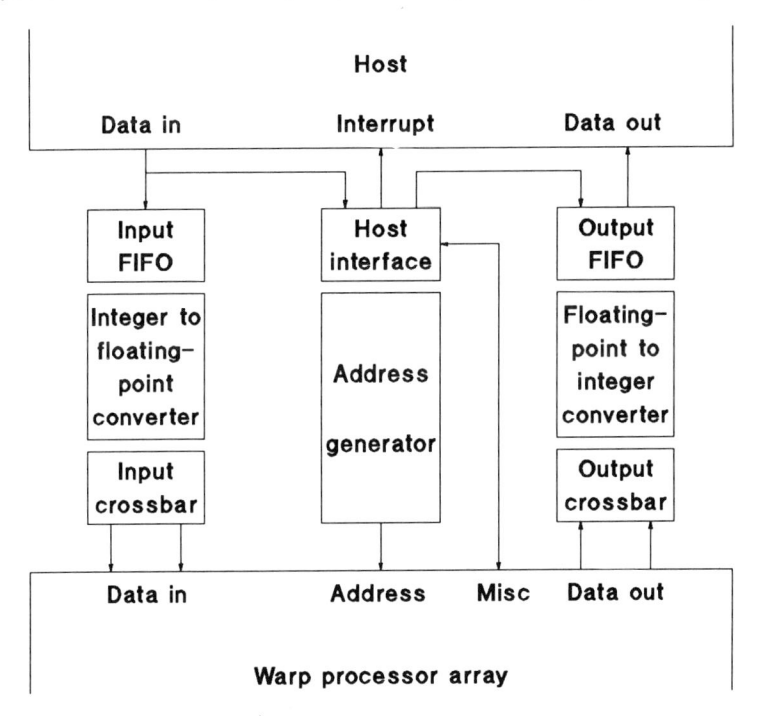

Figure 7.18 *The interface unit of the Warp system (adapted from [Arn85])*

cells had to hold only partitioned training data in on-chip memory. A performance of 17 MCUPS was obtained.

7.6.2 The MasPar MP-1 Computer

The MasPar massively data-parallel computers belong to a computer family based on the MP-1 SIMD array chips. It is a general purpose parallel computer which was not designed specifically to simulate neural networks. The main application area is in running fast numerical algorithms for real-time image processing used, for example, in electrical computer aided design. Algorithm libraries are implemented for the Numerical Algorithms Group (NAG) Fortran library used in many industrial and scientific applications [Mas90a]. However, due to a large amount of memory per processing element and 32-bit floating point operations, it may also be used for neural network simulations.

MasPar introduced the MP-1 computer in January 1990. Two series of the MP-1 computer are available, the MasPar 1100 series computer systems [Mas90b] and the MasPar 1200 series computer systems [Mas90c]. MasPar 1100 computer systems are available from 1024 processing elements up to 4096 PEs. Systems up to 16,384 PEs can be realized with the MasPar 1200 products.

The core circuit of the MasPar 1100 and 1200 series computers is the MP-1 processor chip. It consists of 32 processing elements configured in an SIMD architecture. Figure 7.19 shows the architecture of an individual processing element. It is a small RISC processor with 48 32-bit registers, 40 of which are available to the user (eight registers are used internally to implement the MP-1 instruction set). Additionally, the PMEM address unit and PMEM data unit provide an interface to access up to 16 Kbytes of external memory. Internally, the PE processes 4-bit data by means of a 4-bit ALU, a 16-bit exponent unit (EXPONENT), and a 64-bit mantissa unit (MANTISSA). Within one PE data is moved on the 4-bit nibble bus and the 1-bit bit bus. Since PEs are organized as a SIMD array, each PE receives the same control signal generated by the MP-1 array control unit (ACU). The MP-1 instruction set has been adapted for operand sizes of 8, 16, 32 and 64 bits. To perform a 32-bit or 64-bit floating point instruction, the array control unit microcode engine steps PEs through a series of operations on successive 4-bit nibbles to generate the full precision result. A 32-bit integer add requires eight clock cycles. Thus, the internal 4-bit nature of the PE is not visible to the programmer. Each PE provides floating point operations on 32 and 64 bit IEEE or VAX format operands and integer operations on 1, 8, 16, 32 and 64 bit operands. More information can be taken from [Nic90]. Thirty-two processing elements are implemented on one MP-1 chip, fabricated in two-level metal 1.6 μm CMOS technology. One chip contains 450,000 transistors on a die area of 11.6 mm by 9.5 mm. The chips are

SIMD Arrays and Systolic Arrays 141

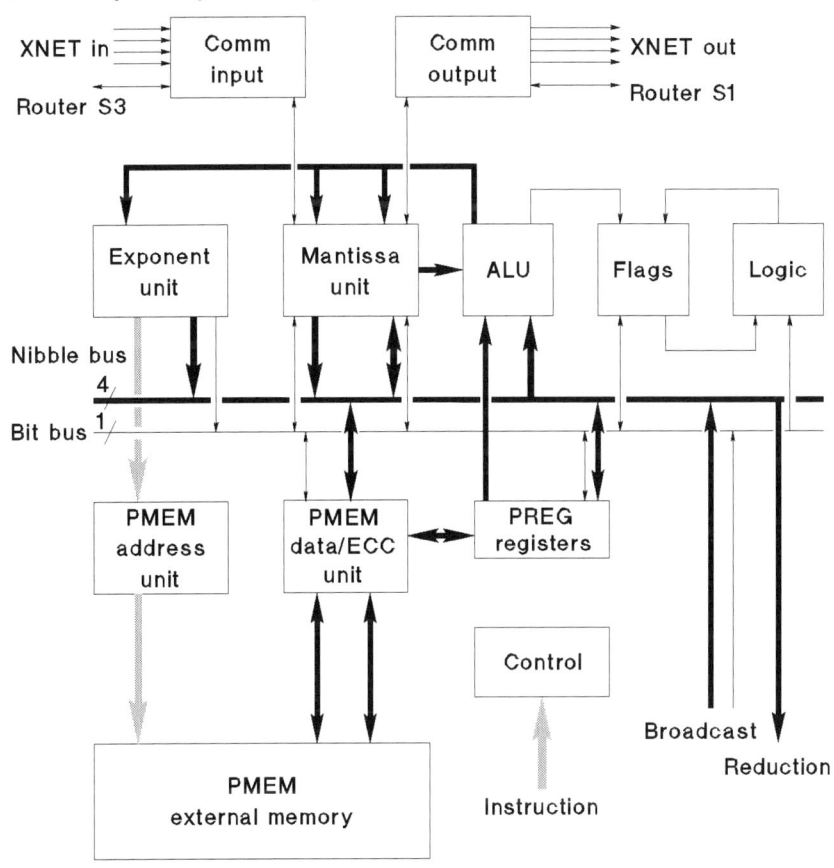

Figure 7.19 *MP-1 processing element (with external RAM) (adapted from [Nic90])*

working with a conservative clock frequency of 14 MHz to avoid problems with power dissipation.

To form a parallel computer system, PEs are ordered in a two-dimensional array. One processor board hosts 1024 processor elements with memory. A complete MasPar computer array can consist of 1 up to 16 identical processor boards. Figure 7.20 sketches a MasPar computer built from several boards. On one board PEs are arranged as 64 processor element clusters (PECs). Each cluster (PEC) consists of 16 PEs configured in a 4 by 4 array with an X-Net mesh interconnect [Nic90]. PE clusters (PECs) are also interconnected via the X-Net neighborhood mesh. Thus, for information exchange, each PE can easily access one of its eight nearest neighbors in a two-dimensional array. For the user, cluster, chip and board boundaries are not visible. Furthermore, connections at the PE array edges are

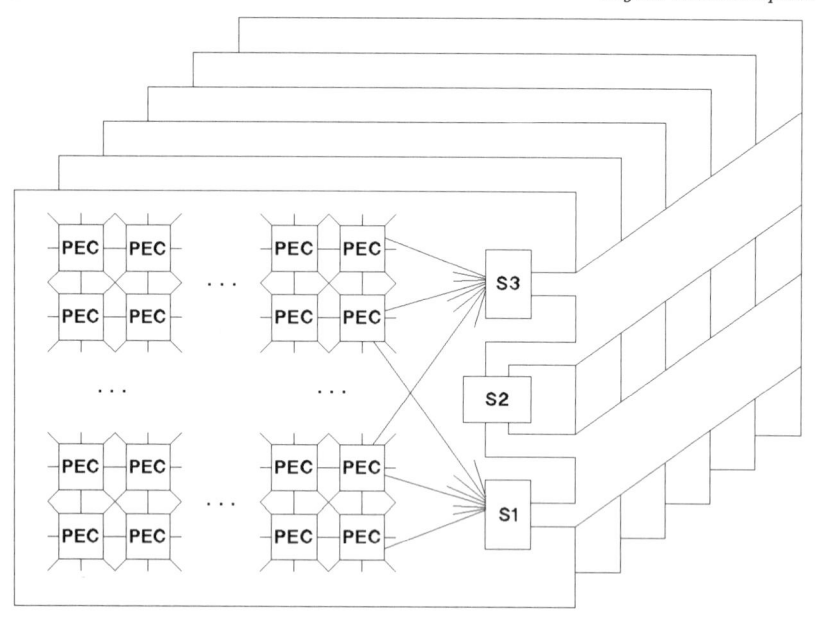

Figure 7.20 *Several boards forming a MasPar processor array (adapted from [Nic90])*

wrapped around to form a torus. The X-Net mesh interconnection uses a bit-serial implementation to minimize pin and wire costs, and is clocked synchronously with the PEs. A PE cluster is sketched in Figure 7.21 (two PE clusters are implemented on one MP-1 chip, PMEM is off-chip). Global communication between PEs is realized by a multistage crossbar interconnection network. To implement a 1024 by 1024 crossbar switch, the MP-1 system uses three router stages (S1, S2 and S3 in Figure 7.20). This also forms the basis for the MP-1 I/O system. Connections between PEs are done from the source PE via stages S1, S2 and S3 to the destination PE. Thus, each PE cluster shares a source port connected to router stage S1 and a destination port to router stage S3. Since a 16,384 PE computer system consists of 1024 PE clusters, the maximum interconnection grid of 1024 by 1024 connections may only be realized in such a large system. Furthermore, 1024 simultaneous connections are only possible if all 1024 originating and all 1024 target PEs are located in distinct clusters. Figure 7.22 gives a block diagram of a complete MasPar computer system [Blan90]. The performance of MasPar 1200 series machines is given by Table 7.1 [Mas90c]. Costs for the MP-1 family are reported to be $30 per MIPS and $625 per MFLOP in the largest MP-1 configuration [Mas90d]. Hence, the cost of a 16K PE machine with 580 MFLOPS is about $362,500. A neural network algorithm was implemented on a 4K PE machine by Grajski *et al.* [Graj90a, Graj90b]. They

SIMD Arrays and Systolic Arrays

used a 900 input units, 20 hidden units and 17 output units network with the backpropagation algorithm, applied to a speech recognition problem. The performance obtained was 306,000 CUPS. With more efficient implementations, Grajski *et al.* expect a computational power of up to several tens of MCUPS on MasPar computers.

The MasPar massively parallel computers are very flexible tools to run parallel numeric algorithms. A crucial issue for neural network simulations is the amount of memory per processor element. 16 KBytes of memory is not much, especially if network partitioning is chosen to implement a neural network algorithm on a limited number of PEs. Only small networks can be simulated. However, a computer consisting of several thousand PEs provides sufficient parallelism so that a physical PE can be assigned to each

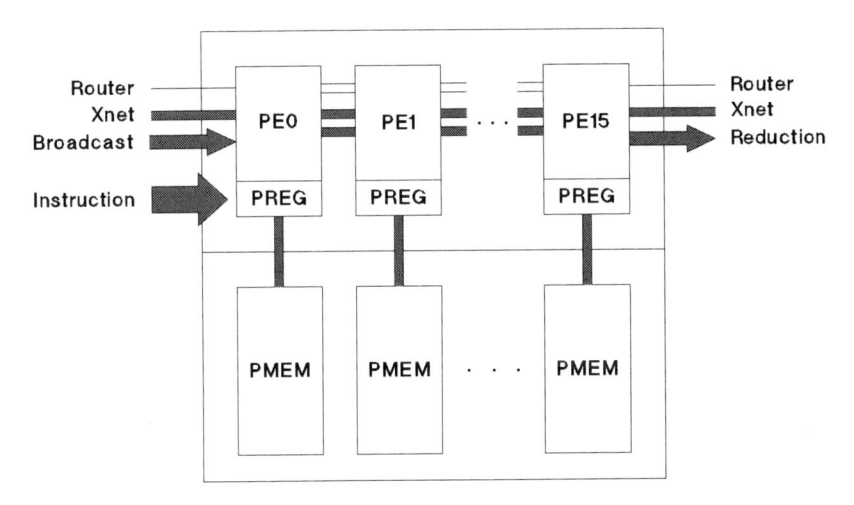

Figure 7.21 *Processor element cluster (PEC) (adapted from [Nic90])*

PE Array Size	MIPS	32-Bit MFLOPS	64-Bit MFLOPS
1K PEs	1,600	82	36
2K PEs	3,200	164	73
4K PEs	6,400	325	145
8K PEs	13,000	650	290
16K PEs	26,000	1,300	580

Table 7.1 *Performance of MasPar 1200 series computers*

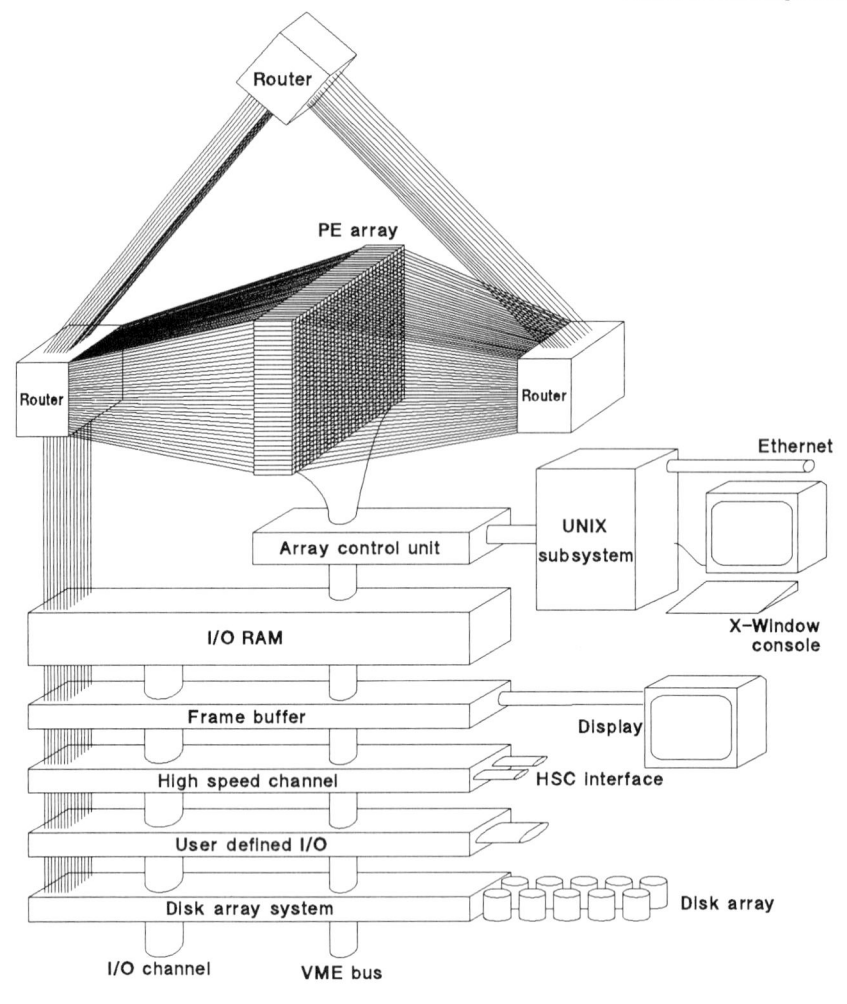

Figure 7.22 *Block diagram of MasPar system (adapted from [Blan90])*

neuron (if the network is not too large). Then, several thousand synaptic weights of receiving synapses may be stored on the memory assigned to each PE (to implement backpropagation learning, however, one has to consider that not only weights of preceding neurons but also weights of successive neurons have to be stored). A common disadvantage of general purpose parallel computers is that their interconnection scheme and processor architectures are not optimized for neural network simulation. Processor interconnections are well suited for local information exchange as in image processing. Global information exchange is often time consuming. Large local memory is another feature of dedicated neural network hardware which is not found in many general purpose parallel computer concepts.

To summarize, MasPar computers, as well as many other parallel computers, are suitable for the simulation of small and medium size networks. They are very flexible and can also perform data preprocessing tasks. Since they are commercial and mature products, software packages are available [Chr90, Mas90d]. However, dedicated neural network computers often show much better performance at less hardware expense.

7.6.3 CMOS Hopfield Network with Learning

Hopfield type networks are preferred candidates for analog implementations. This is due to their regular feedback structure and the straightforward implementation of synapses through resistive elements and neurons through nonlinear amplifiers. Furthermore, Hopfield networks may run with rather inaccurate computing devices, though at the expense of a reduced storage capacity. Early neural network VLSI implementations of the mid-1980s were mostly implementations of Hopfield type networks (see ASSOCMEM from Sivilotti et al. [Siv86] or the circuits from Graf et al. [Graf87a, Graf87b, Graf87c], for example).

An interesting fully digital CMOS realization of a Hopfield type network was done by Weinfeld [Wei89]. To simplify the circuit architecture, Weinfeld confined the characteristics of networks to be simulated. Confinements are:

- neuron outputs are binary (only output values $+1$ and -1 are allowed)
- the network size (number of neurons) must be a power of 2
- only strictly local learning algorithms are used.

The first assumption of binary neuron outputs has two advantages. First, the synaptic multiplication is reduced to a simple addition or subtraction. Second, the interconnection problem is reduced, since one-bit lines are sufficient for information exchange. The second and third assumptions facilitate the realization of learning algorithms. Usually, a normalization in the form of a division by the number of neurons is necessary to calculate the weight update in a single learning step. If the number of neurons is a power of 2, the division may be implemented by shifting the value to be divided by an appropriate number of steps.

Figure 7.23 shows the architecture of a later 64 neuron design based on the principles of the older eight neuron version. Eight processing elements, each representing the functionality of a neuron, are placed around a shifter circle. Each neuron i contains its fully corresponding weight column, i.e. the connecting synaptic weight values w_{ij} to all N network neurons ($j \in 1, ..., N$). To perform the synaptic multiplications from all receiving inputs, the ouput values (which are either $+1$ or -1) of all neighboring neurons are presented sequentially to a neuron. This is done by shifting the

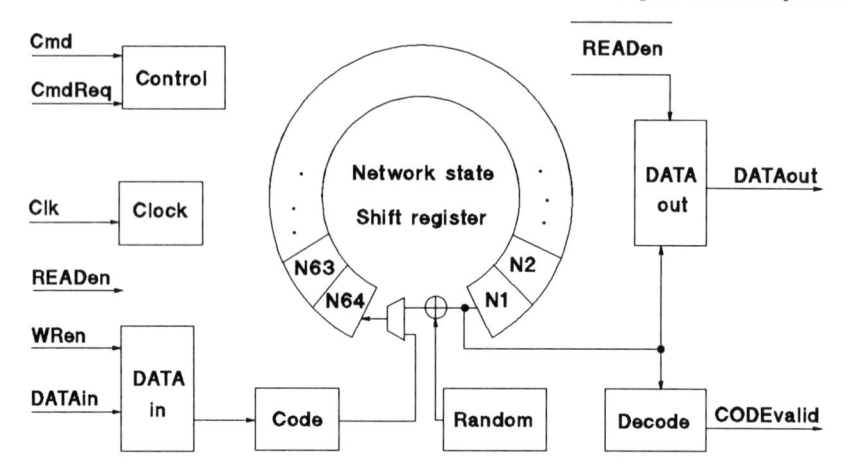

Figure 7.23 *Network architecture with neurons arranged in a circle (adapted from [Gas92])*

one-bit neuron outputs through the circle shift register carrying eight different outputs from the eight neurons. After presentation of all outputs to all neurons, which needs eight cycles, the new neuron outputs are computed and written to the circle shift register in parallel (one cycle). Then, a new computation step begins.

The architecture of a single processing element (neuron) is depicted in Figure 7.24. Due to the above stated assumptions, no multiplier/divider circuit is necessary. All operations are done by a simple adder/subtractor ALU (12 bit). The synaptic column weights w_{ij} are stored in a shift register bank (64 × 9 bit), since they are always addressed in the same sequence. Accumulator A_i accumulates the activation of neuron i. Finally, its most significant bit determines a neuron's output. Thus, a simple threshold operation is performed. In addition to the neuron's actual output $o_i(t)$, its output from the previous computation step $o_i(t-1)$ is stored. This information is needed to detect convergence during recall or learning. The two values are EXORed and this information leaves the processing element. Then, these values from different PEs can be ORed together to detect whether a bunch of neurons has converged or not. With this architecture and the above assumptions, simple learning algorithms like the Hebb rule [Heb49, Rum86] or a simplified projection rule [Per86, Wei89] may be realized, in addition to the recall phase. However, a drawback of the architecture is that it allows only limited cascadability.

A chip carrying 64 neurons of the described architecture was designed and fabricated using a 1.2 µm double metal CMOS technology [Gas92] (ARIANE-chips). The silicon containing 420,000 transistors on an area of 1 cm^2 is packaged into a PGA 176 carrier. Chips run at a clock frequency of

SIMD Arrays and Systolic Arrays   147

20 MHz. An updating cycle during learning is reported to have a duration of 6.4 μs. Since one chip contains $64 \times 64 = 4096$ synaptic weights, this corresponds to 640 million weight updates per second per chip. However, this figure cannot be compared directly to the standard CUPS rate of other machines, since usually the backpropagation algorithm is used as the benchmark, which includes a forward and backward phase and more complex operations.

Gascuel et al. [Gas92] fitted four chips and some control logic together to form a four network board based on the Macintosh Coprocessor Platform (with an M68000 processor, memory and interface ASICs). Five boards with a total of 20 networks can run on a single Macintosh II computer. For larger networks several computers may be linked together.

7.6.4 The Adaptive Solutions Neurocomputer

The X1 chip from Adaptive Solutions, Inc. (see Dan Hammerstrom et al. [Ham90]) is a SIMD array chip specifically designed for neural network simulations. Adaptive Solutions, Inc. offers a system called CNAPS (Connected Network of Adaptive ProcessorS) based on X1 chips.

The X1 architecture is a result of several compromises with respect to a number of goals. One of the goals pursued by the designers was to design a neural network hardware system supporting efficient on-chip learning. The system will support neural network research, not only a specific applica-

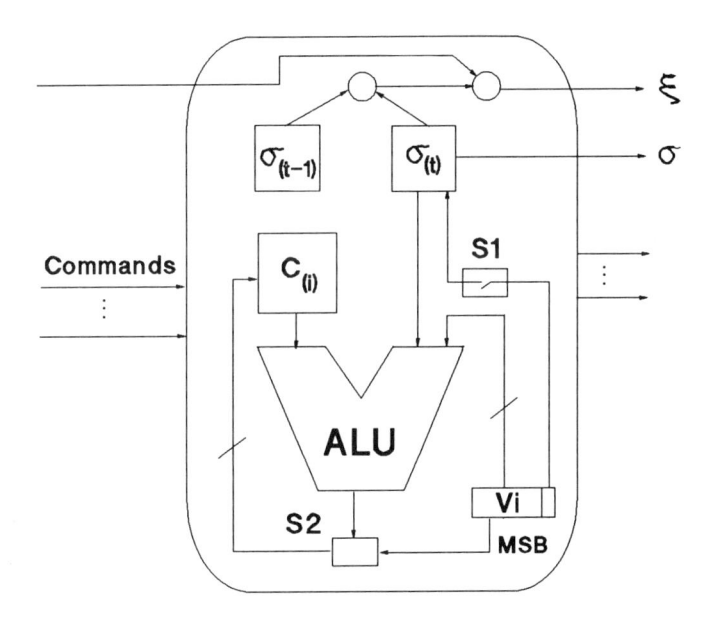

Figure 7.24 Architecture of a single neuron (adapted from [Wei89])

tion in the recall phase, hence efficient learning is an important feature. Furthermore, it should be flexible enough to support a large variety of neural network algorithms, not only one specific network type. Low cost is another feature to be considered in any commercial product. Last but not least, speed is a crucial aspect for any system that is used for neural network simulations, due to the large number of arithmetic operations to be performed.

An X1 chip consists of a number of simple processor elements configured in a linear array in SIMD architecture [Ham90]. Figure 7.25 shows the ordering and interconnection scheme of X1 processing elements. Two broadcast busses provide all PEs with the same information simultaneously. INBUS (8 bits) provides input data, whereas PNCMD (31 bits) is the processor node command bus, responsible for telling PEs what to do (each PE performs the same command simultaneously). Furthermore, neighboring PEs are connected with each other via a local 4-bit inter-PE bus. The inter-PE bus is used for efficient winner-take-all operations. By means of a decentralized algorithm, PNs cooperatively may determine which PE contains the maximum value [Ham90]. A global 8-bit output bus (OutBus) may be accessed by each PE (only one PE at a time). This interconnection scheme is well suited for fully interconnected networks. However, the efficiency of the architecture decreases if sparsely connected networks have to be simulated. The more sparse a network, one in which there are only a few connections between neurons, the less efficiently it can be simulated. In Figure 7.26 the internal structure of a single processing element is depicted. It consists of several units. The input unit is responsible for decoding command signals on the PnCmd bus. By means of a flag, it also permits the execution of conditional instructions. Since the internal bus format is 16 bits, the input unit has the capability to form 16-bit vectors from two 8-bit vectors received from the 8-bit InBus. Inversely, the output unit has the

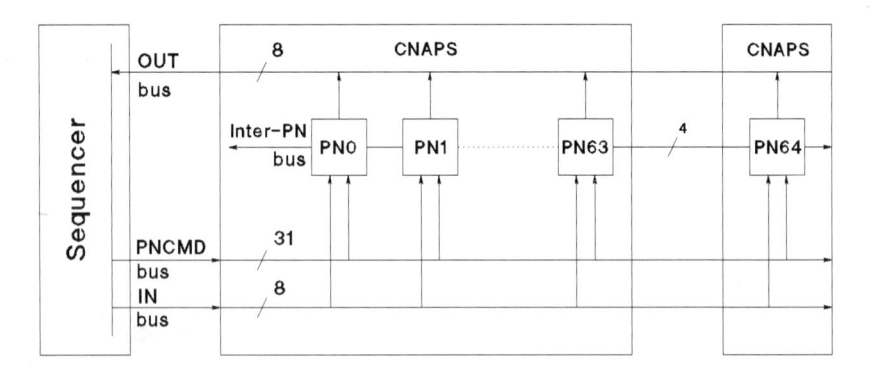

Figure 7.25 *The X1 SIMD array (adapted from [Ham91])*

SIMD Arrays and Systolic Arrays   149

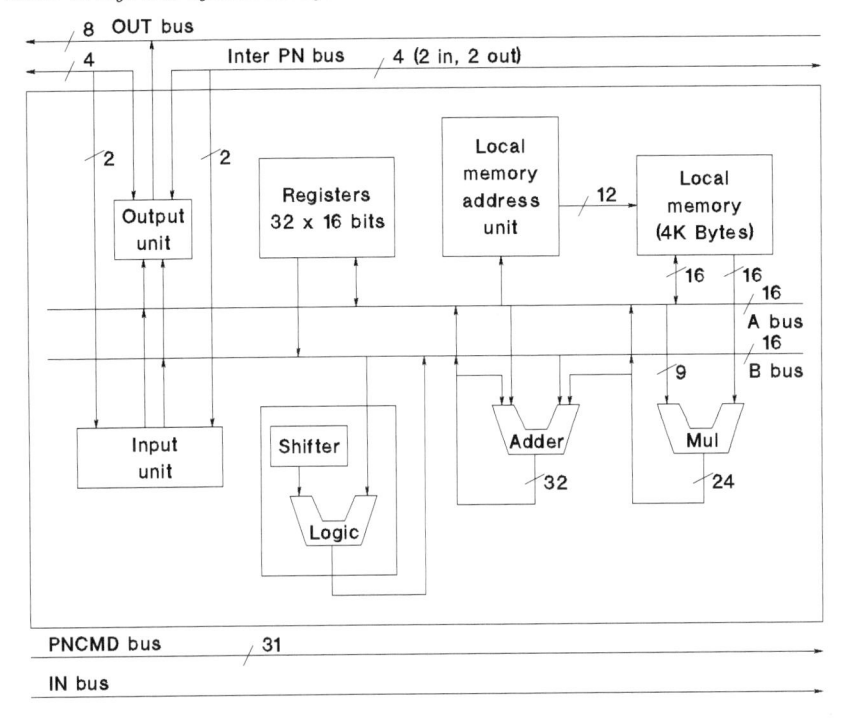

Figure 7.26 *Structure of a single PE (adapted from [Ham91])*

task of controlling access to the inter-PN bus and the OutBus. Like the input unit, it has the capability to transform a 16-bit vector into two 8-bit vectors which have to be transmitted successively with two clock cycles. To process data, each PE has a shifter-logic unit to perform shift operations and simple logic combinations. Furthermore, it contains a 9×16 bit two's complement multiplier with 24-bit output to perform signed multiplications and a 32-bit input adder/subtractor unit which produces a 32-bit two's complement result. To store information, each PE is provided with 32 16-bit registers and 4 KBytes of local memory that may be accessed in 8- or 16-bit mode. The whole PE can work in three different weight modes; 1-bit weights, 8-bit weights (7-bit mantissa plus sign) and 16-bit weights (15-bit mantissa plus sign). More architecture details may be taken from [Ham90, Ham91, Gri90]. Chips of the X1 architecture are fully cascadable to form PE arrays of an arbitrary length. The user is not aware of chip boundaries.

Sixty-four working PEs were implemented in a two metal, 0.8 μm CMOS technology on a chip called the N64000, produced by Inova Microelectronics Corporation. To implement a sufficiently large number of PEs on one chip, quite a large silicon area is necessary. However, efficient fabrication of large chips is only possible with redundant architectures. But a linear array of PEs is an excellent system for redundant chip fabrication. Hence, 80 PEs are fabricated on a die to obtain a yield of over 90% (more than 90% of fabricated chips contain at least 64 functioning PEs). The die size is 1 square inch. This area contains over 11 million transistors. The cost of a N64000 chip is reported to be in the same range as a state-of-the-art microprocessor [Ham91].

Adaptive Solutions, Inc. is distributing a general purpose neurocomputer system called CNAPS (Connected Network of Adaptive ProcessorS). The CNAPS system consists of a sequencer and four N64000 chips on one board, thus providing a total of 256 physical processing elements. Network simulations are run in a neuron-oriented approach. Several successive neurons (connecting nodes, CNs) of a multiple layer network are mapped onto a physical processor (processor node, PN), as indicated in Figure 7.27. For the simulation of recursive networks, the outputs can directly be fed back to the network inputs (OutBus to InBus). The speed of the CNAPS system, working at a clock frequency of 20 MHz, is given as 5.12 billion connections per second (feed-forward only, with 8- or 16-bit weights) [Ada91] and 1.08 billion CUPS in backpropagation learning (8- or 16-bit weights). Hammerstrom and Nguyen implemented Kohonen's self-organizing map (SOM) and obtained the performance figures given in Table 7.2 [Ham91] (comparison with a commercial SPARC station).

The CNAPS neurocomputer system is well suited for neural network implementations. It shows high performance on relatively little hardware, and is still flexible enough to simulate different neural network algorithms as well as conventional algorithms such as the discrete fourier transform or a Batchelor's algorithm [Ham90]. Thus, it can also be used for data preprocessing tasks. It is cost efficient and simple to use. A software package (CodeNet software with CNAPS programming language assembler and debugger, C library for programmatic access of the CNAPS system) and a CNAPS model library with a collection of standard neural network learning algorithms are also offered. However, one has to consider that calculations

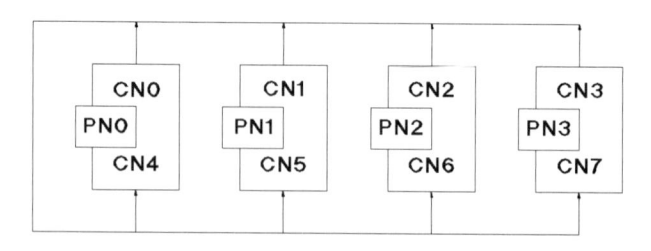

Figure 7.27 *Mapping of neurons onto physical PEs (adapted from [Ham91])*

SIMD Arrays and Systolic Arrays 151

Machine	Net Size	Neighborh. Size (Init.)	Vector	MCUPS	MCPS
CNAPS	512 nodes	256 nodes	256 × 8 bit	65	516
CNAPS	512 nodes	256 nodes	256 × 16 bit	54	608
SPARC	512 nodes	256 nodes	256 × float	0.08	0.11

Table 7.2 *Performance of CNAPS system with Kohonen's SOM*

are performed with no more than 16 bits (this seems to be sufficient for many neural network applications, but this is difficult to generalize).

7.6.5 The SNAP Neurocomputer

Hecht-Nielsen Computers, Inc. (HNC) is offering a neurocomputer system called SNAP (SIMD Neurocomputer Array Processor) [Mean91]. This neurocomputer board is based on Hecht-Nielsen HNC 100 NAP chips (Neural Array Processor). HNC, Inc. reports that a HNC 100 NAP chip consists of a 1-dimensional systolic array of four arithmetic cells in an SIMD architecture forming a ring [Hec91, Mean91]. The organization of PEs is similar to that in the Adaptive Solutions approach (see Figure 7.28). However, the complexity of an individual PE is different. HNC 100 NAP chips perform 32-bit IEEE floating point arithmetic. Only four PEs are fitted onto the die compared with 64 PEs (80 PEs including redundant processors) in the N64000 (Adaptive Solutions, Inc.). Figure 7.29 shows the concept of a single processing element. The internal bus structure is based on a 32-bit data path to a PE's local memory *LM*, to its preceding and successive neighbor in the array, and to the global memory bus. A 17-bit address bus allows a maximum of 512 Kbytes of off-chip local memory to each PE, *i.e.* 16 Mbytes of local memory in a 32 PE SNAP neurocomputer. The global memory bus provides a connection between global memory *GM* and all the PEs (broadcast bus). Each PE contains a 32-bit floating point multiplier *FMPY*, a 32-bit floating point ALU *FALU*, and a 32-bit integer ALU *IALU*. All instructions are executed within one clock cycle (*FALU* and *IALU* cannot execute at the same cycle) [Mean91].

HNC 100 NAP chips run at a clock frequency of 20 MHz. The standard configuration is four HNC 100 NAP chips per processor board, forming one SNAP board. A single NAP chip may perform 160 million 32-bit floating point operations per second. Thus, a SNAP board with four NAP chips (16 arithmetic cells in total) shows a performance of 640 million floating point operations per second (MFLOPS). A SNAP board has an input/output capability of over 4 gigabytes/sec. It is available on the VME bus (Sun Microsystems) and can be connected to the Balboa 860 acceleration board (HNC, Inc.) via a VSB interface [Hec91]. The Balboa board can pass data at a rate of approximately 40 Mbytes/sec via the VSB bus, which is a VME subsystem bus to the SIMD array. The possibility to configure several SNAP boards for more computational power exists, however, the standard configuration is a two board set (SNAP-32, 32 processors with 1.28 billion floating point operations per second). This configuration is able to perform 500 million interconnects per second (feed-forward only, large networks) and 128 million CUPS for large backpropagation networks (learning mode) [Hec91]. Costs are reported to be $30-40 per MFLOP for a Balboa 860 board with a SNAP-32 neurocomputer (about $40,000 for the system), and $25-30 per MFLOP for a Balboa 860 board with a SNAP-64 neurocomputer (about $75,000 for the system) [Hec91].

Similar to the CNAPS neurocomputer from Adaptive Solutions, Inc., the SNAP neurocomputer is an SIMD array specifically designed for neural network simulation. However, it is flexible enough to support many applications in other areas. It is well suited for many matrix type applications (image processing). Compared to the CNAPS system, parallelism is lower since only four arithmetic cells are implemented on a single HNC 100 NAP chip. This reduces performance. On the other hand, PEs are more complex and are able to perform 32-bit floating point arithmetic, en-

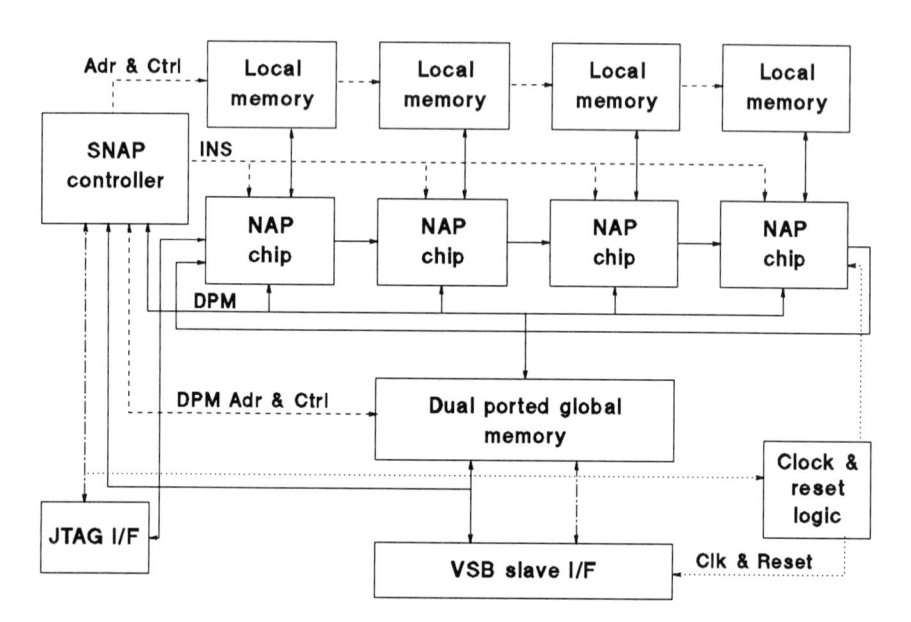

Figure 7.28 *Architecture of HNC's SNAP neurocomputer board (adapted from [Mean91])*

SIMD Arrays and Systolic Arrays								153

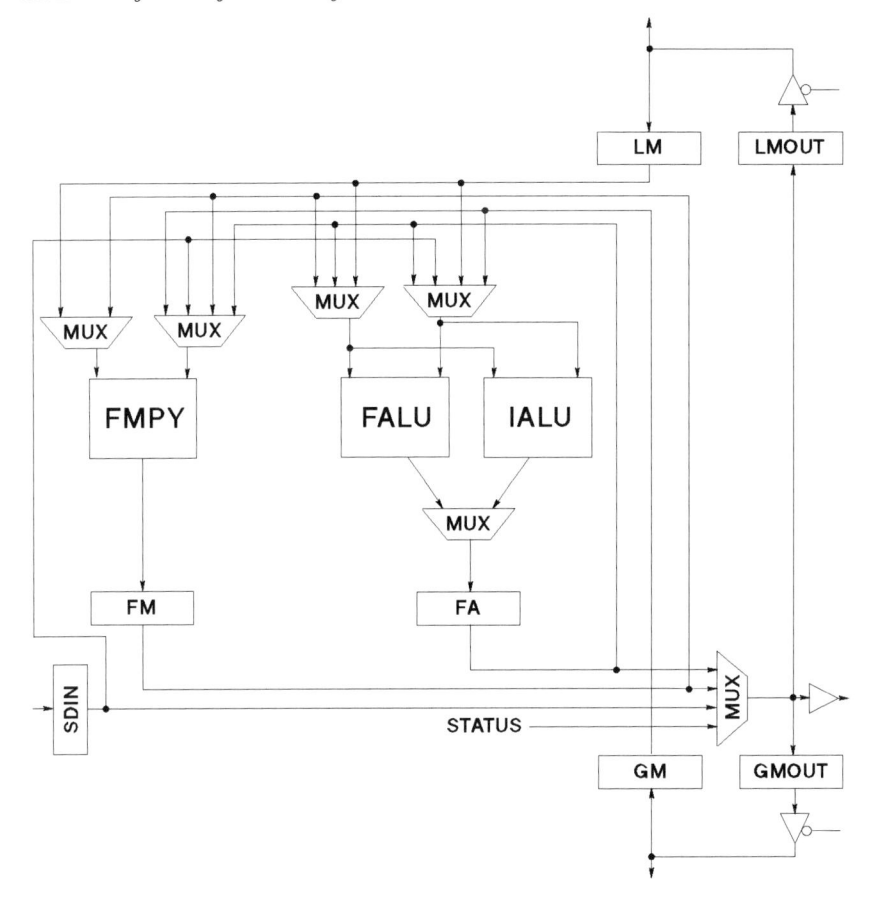

Figure 7.29 *Block diagram of a single SNAP processing element (adapted from [Mean91])*

hancing the flexibility of the system. To ease the use of the SNAP system, HNC is offering macros to achieve good performance for many matrix type applications.

7.6.6 The VIP Board

Hecht-Nielsen Computers is offering another product which has not been designed specifically to support neural network algorithms. This is the VIP board (VIsion Processor daughterboard) [Hec91]. It is based on the HNC 201 and HNC 202 VLSI image processing chip set from Hecht-Nielsen Computers, Inc. (one HNC 201 and one HNC202 chip are on the VIP daughterboard, together with three 4 MByte image buffers). The architecture is a two-dimensional patented systolic array of arithmetic processing elements in an SIMD architecture [Hec91]. One chip contains 64 arithmetic processing elements which can perform 8- and 16-bit pixel arithmetic. The board processes 8-bit data in eight parallel channels. There exist three 32-bit output channels to local image memory (three separate 4 MByte image buffers) and a 32-bit output over the Intel 80860 internal bus (the VIP daughterboard runs together with the Balboa 860 board). The VIP board runs at a 40 MHz clock rate with an image pixel processing rate of 40 megapixels/sec. It can perform 5.12 billion integer operations per second in two-dimensional convolutional mode [Hec91]. In a special feed-forward neural network pattern recognition mode, performance is given as 320 million 8-bit integer connections per second [Hec91].

The VIP board was designed for image processing tasks. As a result of a two-dimensional arrangement of PEs, it shows very high performance. However, computational accuracy is restricted to 8- and 16-bit pixel arithmetic, due to simple PEs. The board is specifically designed to work in combination with the Intel 80860 RISC processor. It is well suited for real-time image processing with conventional algorithms, and real-time object recognition algorithms using both conventional and neural network techniques [Hec91]. An image processing library is provided with several routines using the VIP daughterboard. The board may also be micro coded by users for very high performance. Flexibility is less when compared with the CNAPS and SNAP systems. This has to be taken into account for neural network applications.

7.6.7 SIEMENS General-Purpose Neural Signal Processor MA16

Beichter et al. [Bei91] presented the design and implementation of a neural signal processor called MA16 which is intended to form a part of a versatile neurocomputer (see Ramacher et al. [Ram91]). However, this is not a Digital Signal Processor in the conventional sense but a circuit dedicated to the fast calculation of neural network related computations, *i.e.* matrix-matrix-multiplication, matrix-matrix-addition, and matrix-matrix-subtraction. All operations are done by an elementary chain. Figure 7.30 shows the upper part of the elementary chain which forms a systolic chain of four multipliers and adders. Data is transferred in blocks of 16 words (16-bit word width) containing a 4×4 submatrix to buffers $B1$ and $B2$. To perform a 4×4 matrix operation, buffer $B2$ sends its 16 words to the multipliers row-wise while $B1$ sends its data column-wise. Thus, each multiplier keeps the input from buffer $B2$ for four cycles to multiply it four times with data arriving from buffer $B1$. Thus, 16 cycles are required to perform a 4×4 matrix multiplication. This architecture shows the benefit of having only two input paths for words to be processed while all multipliers are working in parallel. Buffers are split into two parts so as to be able to receive

SIMD Arrays and Systolic Arrays 155

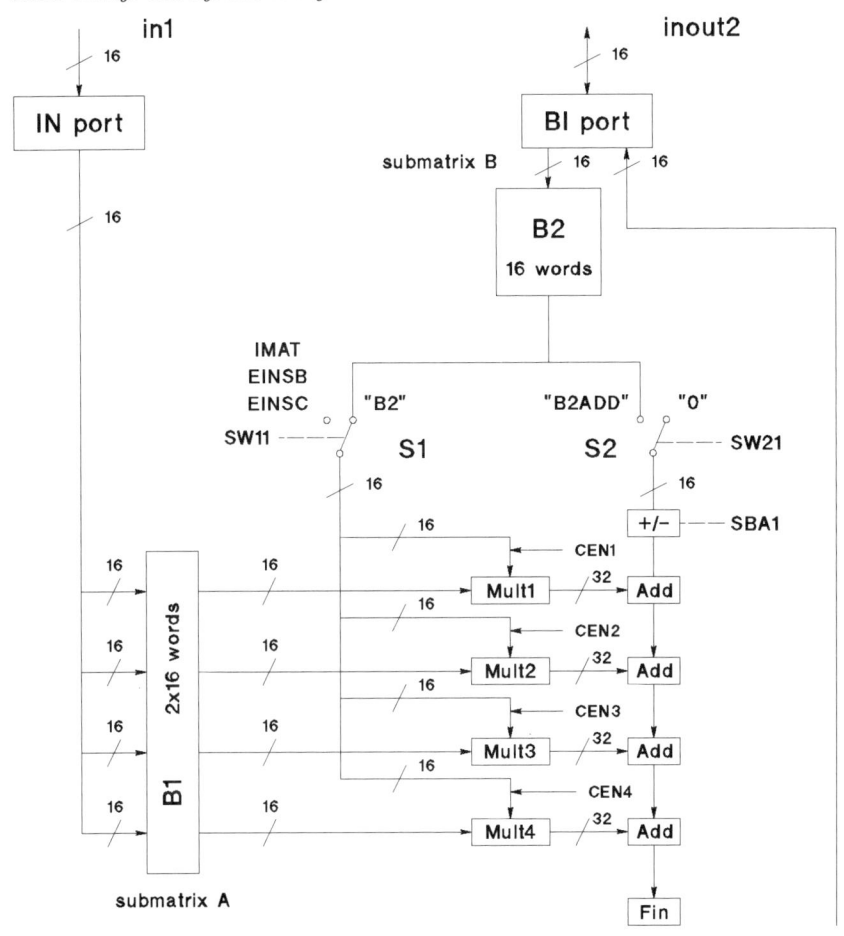

Figure 7.30 *Systolic chain of four multipliers and adders (upper part) (adapted from [Bei91])*

data from or send data to the environment, and to support the systolic chain simultaneously. The task of final adder Fin is to merge sum and carry bits. By means of switches $S1$ and $S2$, it is possible to switch from matrix-matrix-multiplication ($S1$ right, $S2$ right) to matrix-matrix-addition or matrix-matrix-subtraction ($S1$ left, $S2$ left).

The result from adder Fin is fed into the lower part of the elementary chain depicted in Figure 7.31. Multiplier $Mult5$ serves to multiply the sum from Fin by a factor. Thus, the source of the factor is controlled by switch $S3$. Depending on the position of switches $S4$ and $S6$, data from the systolic chain is added to the contents of buffer $B3$ or the input from input port $IN3$, and finally passes adder $FIN2$ (and is written back to buffer $B3$).

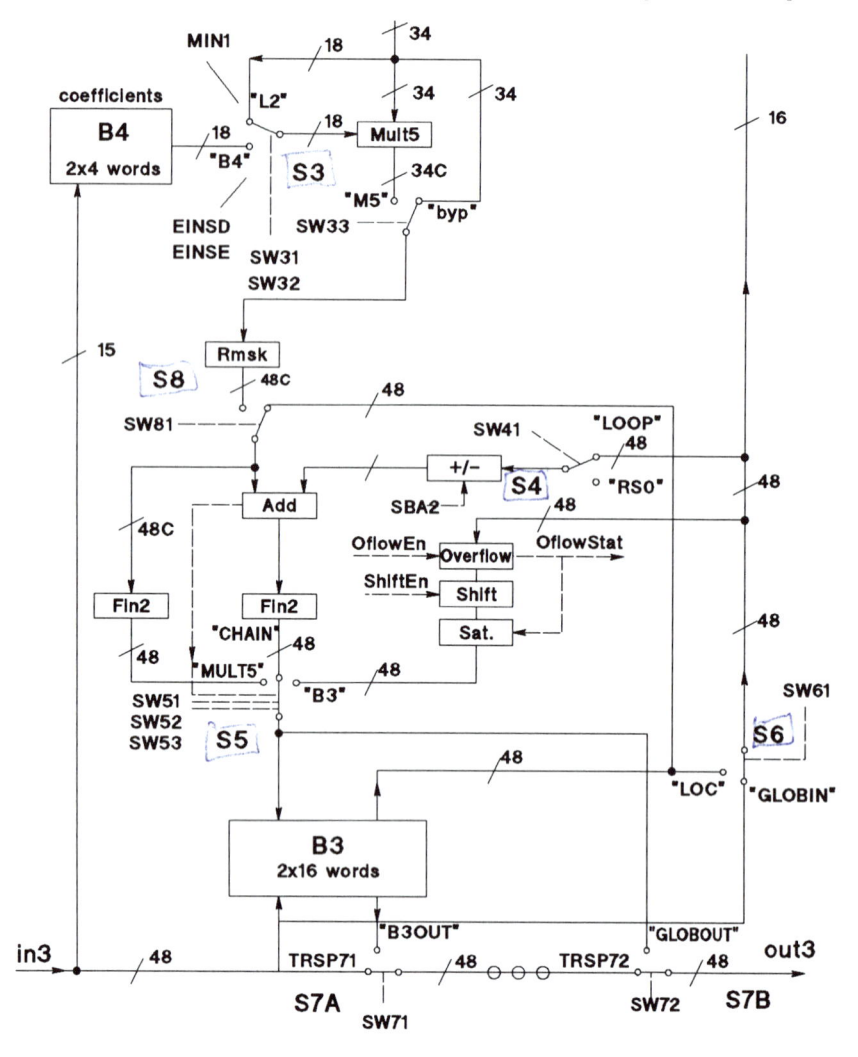

Figure 7.31 *Systolic chain of 4 multipliers and adders (lower part) (adapted from [Bei91])*

Furthermore, a minimum/maximum search can be done by comparing the difference between data from buffer $B3$ (or input $IN3$) and the result from $Mult5$ to zero.

One MA16 chip consists of four elementary chains, depicted in Figures 7.30 and 7.31. The chip is implemented on an area of 187 mm^2 and was fabricated on a 1.0 μm CMOS process. It contains about 610,000 transistors. The speed of the Neural Signal Processor chip is reported to be 800 million connections per second (with a computational accuracy of 16

SIMD Arrays and Systolic Arrays

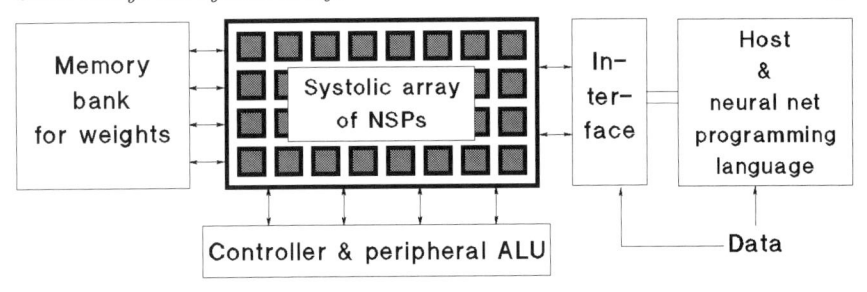

Figure 7.32 *Neurocomputer concept (adapted from [Bei91])*

bits) [Bei91]. The MA16 chip was designed to form part of an integral neurocomputer system, which is sketched in Figure 7.32. Computational intensive operations are thus done by a systolic array of MA16 chips.

Ramacher *et al.* mounted the first neurocomputer using eight MA16 chips operating under the control of two Motorola 68040 processors. The name of the system is SYNAPSE-1. In September 1992 this computer reached a computational speed 8000 times faster than a SUN2 [Ram92, Sie92, Joh93a]. Simulated was a multilayer Perceptron with 512 inputs and a total of 1024 neurons. The MA16 chips operated at a clock frequency of 25 MHz. By means of optimized microprograms and an increased clock frequency of 40 MHz, a further speedup by a factor of 2 is expected.

The SYNAPSE-1 computer is an excellent example for a modern and flexible neuro computing concept. By changing microprograms controlling the datapath of the MA16 chips, a variety of different neural network algorithms can be simulated. Furthermore, this system has the flexiblility to run common data preprocessing algorithms like a two-dimensional convolution or a discrete cosine transform within a few hundred milliseconds. This is a key feature to allow fast response of a whole system consisting of combined standard preprocessing and neural algorithms.

7.6.8 The HANNIBAL Neurocomputer System

Researchers at British Telecom developed an SIMD neurocomputer system called HANNIBAL (Hardware Architecture for Neural Networks Implementing Backpropagation Algorithm Learning) [Mye91]. This architecture serves to run the backpropagation algorithm based on a chip containing eight physical processing elements. Each processing element contains a 9216 bit local weight memory configurable in either 512 17-bit words or 1024 9-bit words. Thus, 8- or 16-bit weights may be used (the additional 9th or 17th bit allows the switching on or off of a synaptic connection). If neuron fan-in is much lower than is allowed by local memory, up to four virtual neurons may be mapped onto a physical PE sharing its resources. Then, through multiplexing, these virtual neurons may be addressed sequentially, but this is only permitted during recall and not in training.

A single processing element consists of its local memory, a fast parallel multiplier, an accumulator and circuitry to perform the nonlinear neuron activation function. Because of this architecture, synaptic inputs to a single neuron are processed sequentially, whereas different neurons are processed in parallel. Figure 7.33 shows a block diagram of the processing element architecture. The size of input/output registers is confined to 8 bits. Synaptic weights are also represented by 8-bit values. For training, the chosen internal accuracy is 16 bits. To avoid local saturation of weights in this "low precision" architecture, Myers et al. use a method called Auto-Scaling [Mye91]. Here, after initialization, each neuron interprets its weights to represent values in the range of -1 to $1 - 2^{-7}$. If, during learning, one neuron weight saturates, all the neuron's weights are halved and the neuron accumulator output doubled. To avoid memory-consuming look-up tables, the neuron activation function is realized by an area saving seven segment piecewise linear approximation. Eight sampling values represent the sigmoid shaped

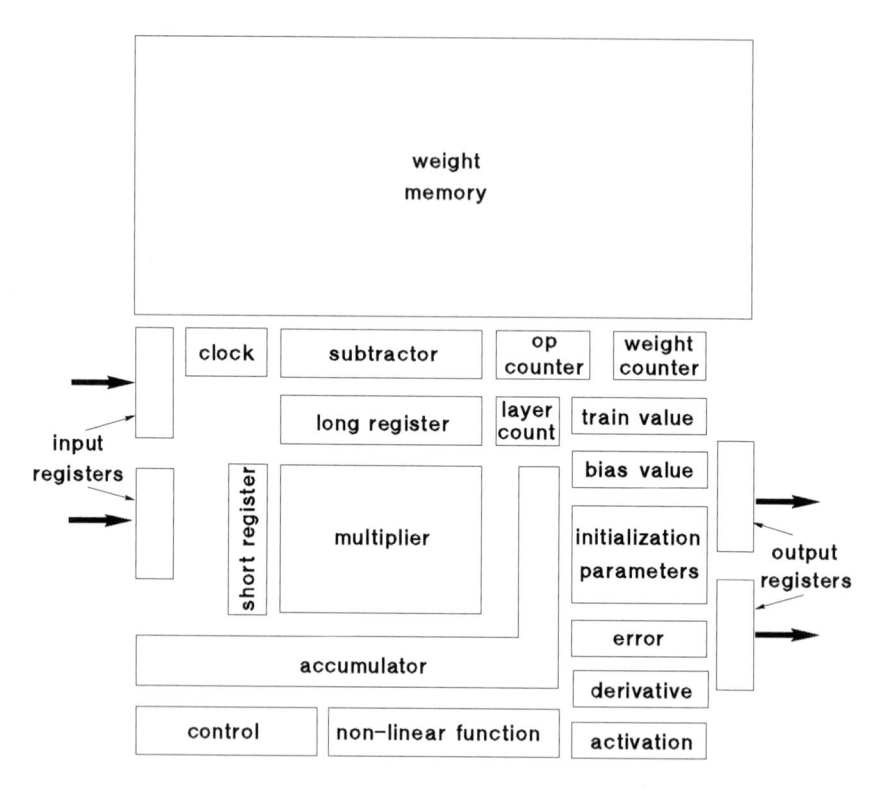

Figure 7.33 *HANNIBAL processor architecture (adapted from [Mye91])*

activation function. Between the eight sampling points the missing values are approximated by linear pieces having a gradient which is a power of 2. The architecture does not support the inclusion of a momentum term (see Equation 3.12).

A single HANNIBAL chip contains eight processing elements fabricated in a 0.7 µm CMOS technology. A total of about 750,000 transistors is implemented on a 9×11.5 mm^2 area. Due to digital circuitry, the chip is easy to cascade. At a clock frequency of 20 MHz a performance figure of 160 MCPS on a single chip is reported [Mye91].

7.6.9 Intel Ni1000 Chip

In cooperation with Nestor Inc., Intel is working on a neural processor dedicated to the parallel simulation of large radial basis function (RBF) networks like probabilistic neural networks (PNN) [Spec88] and restricted coulomb energy (RCE) networks [Sco91]. This digital processor is optimized for the simulation of three-layer networks. The first layer of neurons has a size of 256 and serves to propagate inputs through the second layer. Each neuron of the second layer has a set of synaptic values connected to all inputs. An individual neuron with its synaptic weight vector forms a prototype or reference vector that is compared to the currently applied input vector. The chosen metric for vector comparison is the Manhattan or city block distance for ease of hardware implementation (no time consuming multiplication is necessary). However, each neuron of the second layer operates as a radius-limited perceptron, *i.e.* an activation of neuron i only occurs if the network input stimulus vector x is near to its weight vector w_i (within a radius r_i) with respect to the chosen metric. RBF networks often operate with Gaussians as radially symmetric functions. This has the effect that radius r_i is infinite but the classification influence of the neuron fades with increasing distance between x and w_i. The third layer of neurons serves to sum up weighted contributions from the second layer of "radially limited" neurons (the generic network architecture is depicted in Figure 3.11).

The Intel chip provides signum and exponential radial basis functions in the second neuron layer [Holle92] (see Figure 3.10). Synaptic weights and neuron thresholds (distance radii) are stored on EEPROM cells with an accuracy of 5 bits. This allows reliable non-volatile storage without the need to download weights after switching on the system. A total of 1024 radially limited neurons for the second layer is supported, which are totally connected with the input layer. The distance comparison may be done in parallel through 512 simple processing elements. As the third neuron layer (output layer) 64 neurons are supported. Intel has also implemented a Harvard RISC computer on the chip to speed up learning and allow more flexibility in use [Joh93b]. Through the fully digital design, neuron outputs from the second layer are summed up in the third layer with a high precision. This sequential computation of the third layer occurs at the expense of speed; however, the time consuming task of distance evaluation in the second layer is done in parallel. The chip allows data input/output with a bandwidth of 20 Mbytes/sec. A pattern processing rate of 40,000 pattern/sec is envisaged [Holle92].

An advantage of the RBF network architecture for chip fabrication is that defective neurons in the second layer may simply cut out by setting their weight to the output neuron layer to zero. This fault tolerance allows cost effective production of large area chips. The chip size is about 3.7 million transistors fabricated on Intel's 0.8 μm EEPROM process.

7.6.10 A Generic Neuron Architecture

The more specifically hardware is designed for the simulation of a neural algorithm, the higher its performance will be and the less its flexibility. There is always such a trade-off between simulation efficiency and flexibility. Some neural hardware designers are trying to avoid this trade-off by developing generic architectures which may be "customized" for a certain task. For example, Vellasco et al. [Vel92] present such an approach. They present an architectural framework which is general enough to allow the simulation of a large variety of networks but may by "tuned" to fit the special requirements of specific algorithms. The aim of this approach is to take all hand-crafted design work from a designer and to allow the automatic generation of an application-specific circuit.

The architecture core is a small RISC processor with a datapath module for all mathematical neural operations. These operations are 16-bit fixed-point multiplication and summation, some registers, and a ROM to be used as a look-up table for a neuron's discrimination function. A PLA serves to control the datapath. This is a regular structure which may simply be generated or changed to adapt the datapath for a specific application. In addition to the RISC processor, there is a communication unit and some RAM for weight storage. The communication unit has the task to control communication of a processor node with the global broadcast bus. It either decides whether data appearing on the global bus is intended to arrive at the respective processor node, or whether the bus is free to take signals from the respective processor node. Again, a PLA controls the operations of the communication unit to allow fast changes of this controller to adapt the communication unit to specific applications.

A broadcast bus architecture was chosen since it is well suited for many neural network algorithms. The processor nodes are arranged in a linear array and controlled by a central controller via a broadcast control and address bus. Data exchange between processors and from the central controller to and from processors is done through a broadcast data bus. An

SIMD Arrays and Systolic Arrays

efficient backpropagation simulation can be done on such an architecture by allocating a processor node to each neuron or a group of neurons and storing a synaptic weight in both the processor of the emitting and receiving neuron of the synapse. Then, calculated neuron outputs during the forward phase, as well as errors during the backward phase, may be broadcast within one cycle.

A test chip containing two processor nodes was implemented in 2 μm CMOS technology [Vel92]. It contains 256 words of RAM with a word width of 16 bits and 128 words of ROM (look-up table) per processor. With state-of-the art 0.8 μm technology, Vellasco *et al.* expect the integration of four processors on a single chip with enough memory to store 4096 16-bit synaptic weights for the simulation of large networks.

7.6.11 The APLYSIE-Chip

In the area of two-dimensional processor arrays, Blayo *et al.* [Blay89] developed an architecture dedicated to the running of Hopfield type network algorithms. Like Weinfeld (see page 145), Blayo *et al.* are assuming the networks to be simulated to have only binary neuron outputs (values -1 and $+1$) to avoid the area consuming implementation of multipliers.

The principle of the APLYSIE architecture is to provide a processing element for each synaptic connection ordered in a two-dimensional array (synapse-oriented architecture). Thus, each weight w_{ij} is realized by its own processor. Therefore, a Hopfield network consisting of N neurons needs an N^2 processor array. The APLYSIE architecture was designed only to compute the recall phase of simplified Hopfield networks, *i.e.* the evaluation of an output o_i of neuron i according to

$$o_i(t) = f\left(\sum_{j=1}^{N} w_{ij} \cdot i_j(t-1)\right). \quad (7.1)$$

A "simplification" is done by postulating binary neuron outputs and using a simple hardlimiting neuron threshold operation (function f in Equation 7.1). Through this simplification the synaptic multiplication can be done by an adder/subtractor circuit, and the neuron is realized by taking the sign bit of the accumulated synaptic contributions as neuron output.

To perform the matrix multiplication on a two-dimensional processor array, a standard systolic method is used [Kun88]. Thus, matrix elements are stored on the processing elements and the input vector is inserted diagonally into the array from the top (see Figure 7.34). The resulting vector diagonally leaves the array on the right side. Such a multiplication of an N-element vector with an $N \times N$-element matrix needs $2N$ steps if each partial product can be computed in a single step, corresponding to a utilization

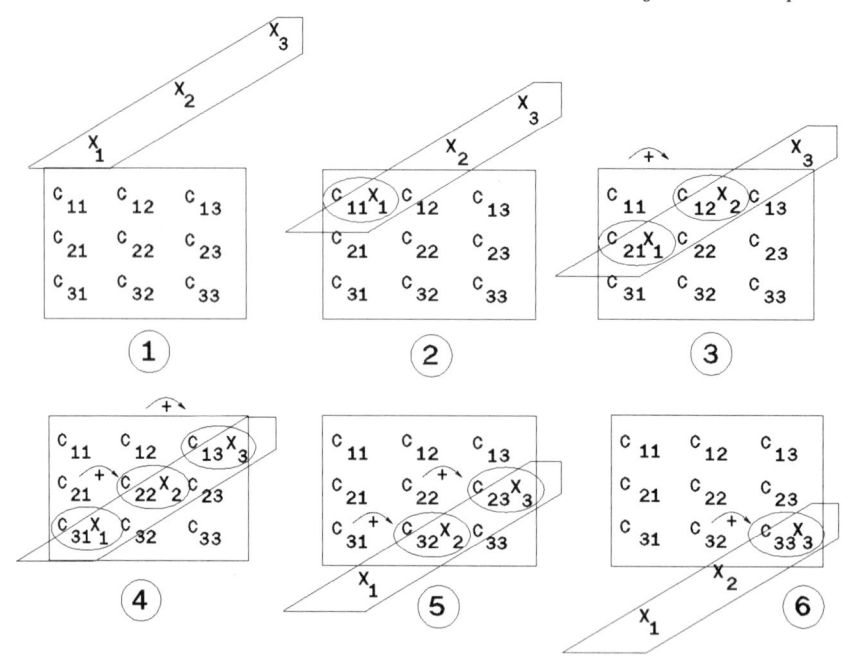

Figure 7.34 *Vector/matrix multiplication on a two-dimensional array (adapted from [Blay89])*

rate u of the array of

$$u = \frac{1}{2 \cdot N}. \tag{7.2}$$

However, a 100% utilization rate is possible with pipelining (see [Blay89]).

A neuron output at the right side of the array is simply available by taking only the sign bit of the accumulated values. Then, each output on the right side of the array corresponds to a neuron output. Since a Hopfield network is a recurrent network, the problem arises as to how to reinsert this output vector into the network input, *i.e.* the top of the array. Using busses would violate the systolic concept of only local connections to neighboring PEs and therefore would have to be paid for by a large amount of additional chip area (due to the large distance between inputs and outputs). Routing the output values through the array, however, would be very time consuming, especially in large arrays. Blayo *et al.* [Blay89] propose to return the output values on the right side horizontally into the array, whereas vertically propagating network inputs are reinserted at the top and bottom of the array. During initialization, network inputs are inserted at the diagonal of the array (starting their movement to the top of the array). After $2 \cdot N$ steps each input value reaches the same diagonal cell

SIMD Arrays and Systolic Arrays 163

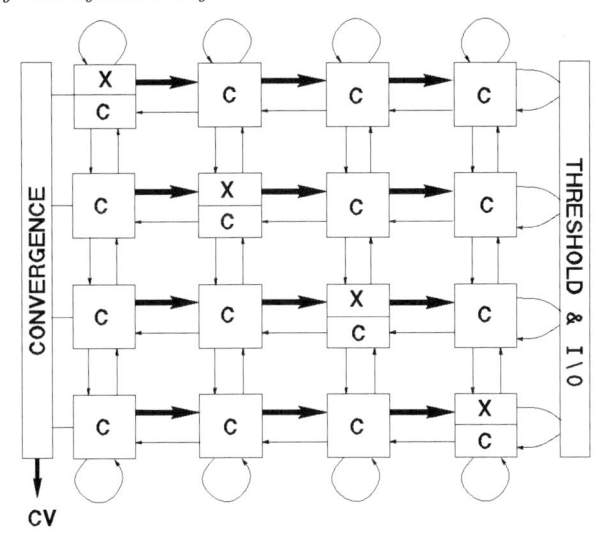

Figure 7.35 *Dataflow in the APLYSIE architecture (adapted from [Blay89])*

from which it started at initialization. This principle of a recurrent systolic array is sketched in Figure 7.35. Now, input and output vectors meet at the diagonal at the right time to start a new network iteration, and the systolic concept is not violated. Network convergence is also detected on the diagonal cells. Only local connections between neighbouring PEs exist.

To make each PE as small as possible, Blayo et al. used serial addition/subtraction. Hence, at the expense of computation time, a processing element can be designed to be smaller. This concept also fits well with sequential one-bit transmission lines to neighboring processing elements to avoid area consuming bus structures. A big advantage of this architecture is its arbitrary cascadability to form larger networks distributed on several chips.

Blayo et al. designed a PE for 8-bit synaptic weights and a 16-bit register for the partial product. The whole circuit has a size of ≈ 1 mm^2 implemented using 2 μm double metal CMOS technology, and it was planned to be a basic building block for a 16×16 PE array to form a larger system of a 64 chips 128 neurons network.

7.6.12 The GENES Architecture

A generalized extension of the APLYSIE architecture is the GENES architecture proposed and developed by Lehmann et al. [Lehm91] and Viredaz et al. [Vir92]. GENES is based on the same recurrent systolic array architecture as APLYSIE. However, whereas APLYSIE was exclusively dedicated

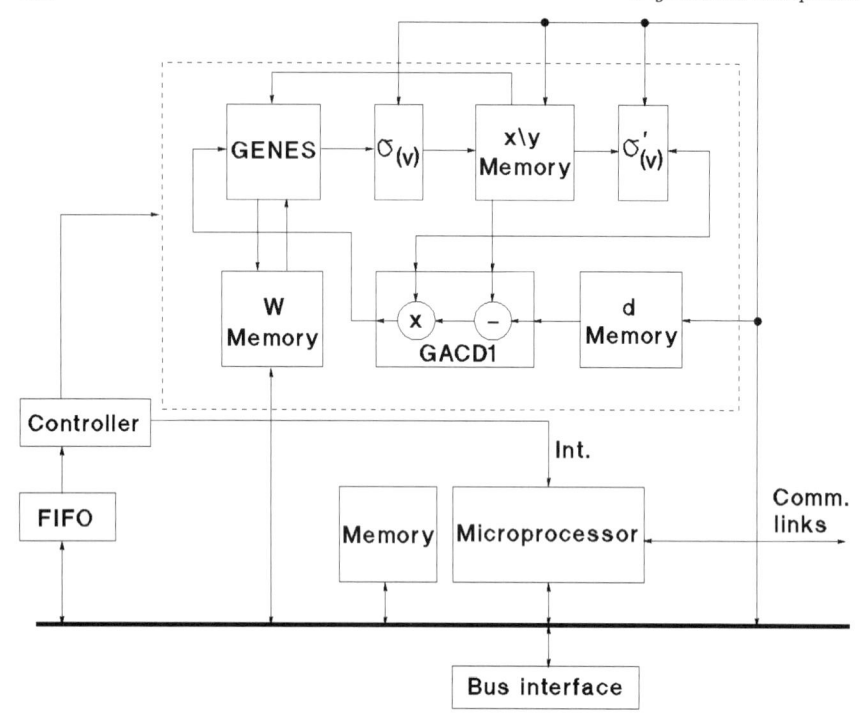

Figure 7.36 *The MANTRA neural computer concept (adapted from [Vir92])*

to Hopfield networks with binary neuron outputs, GENES provides a more flexible frame. The aim of this concept is to simulate single layer networks with multivalued discrete neuron outputs like Hopfield networks, the Kohonen feature map, the Perceptron, and even more complex algorithms like the backpropagation algorithm.

Most similar to APLYSIE is the GENES H8 chip. This chip is designed to simulate generalized Hopfield networks and Kohonen feature maps. Similar to the APLYSIE architecture, no on-chip learning is possible with GENES H8. Only vector-matrix multiplications are possible, however; multiplications of discrete-valued elements in contrast to the binary multiplications (addition/subtraction) of APLYSIE. Therefore, each synapse circuit contains a serial-parallel multiplier. For a Kohonen type network the recall phase is separated into two phases. First, the calculation of neuron activation (only correlation as a similarity metric is supported), which is the same as in the Hopfield case. Second, the computation of the winning neuron. This is done by preloading the processor matrix with special values. Through an iterative phase of vector-matrix computations of neural activations with the preloaded weight matrix, the most active neuron may be

SIMD Arrays and Systolic Arrays

found. Again, this is a procedure identical to the recall phase of a Hopfield network.

Lehmann et al. [Lehm91] designed a 2 × 2-array of processors on a single chip using 2 μm CMOS technology. Weights and inputs are represented with an accuracy of 8 bits, and the partial sum is calculated with an accuracy of 24 bits. Twenty-four clock cycles are necessary to compute one partial product (serial-parallel multiplier). Sixty-four GENES H8 chips were configured to form a working 16 × 16 array [Vir92].

Viredaz et al. extended this architecture to include learning for Hopfield and Kohonen networks, to be able to handle the Euclidean distance metric for Kohonen learning, and to include complex learning algorithms like backpropagation learning. A chip called GENES IV was designed [Vir92], operating on 16-bit input and synaptic weight data with 39 bits for the partial sum. Fabrication of a 2 × 2-array was done on a 1 μm CMOS process. Based on these GENES IV chips and an additional circuit called GACD1, a neural computer is to be mounted. The name of this machine is MANTRA. Figure 7.36 depicts the concept of MANTRA. GENES chips perform vector/matrix multiplications. An array of 40 × 40 PEs is planned [Vir92], to allow the simulation of larger networks.

7.6.13 A Digital Implementation of the Self-Organizing Feature Map

The neural network group of K. Goser at the University of Dortmund is active in research on VLSI implementations of neural networks, with the emphasis on associative memories and self-organizing maps [Gos89]. Among several proposals for analog network implementations, Tryba et al. [Try90] propose a digital solution for the emulation of Kohonen's self-organizing feature map.

For network emulation a two-dimensional array of digital processors provides sufficient computational power to run computation intensive tasks. This array is designed to work as a coprocessor to a conventional sequential computer. Network control, serving learning data and taking computation results from the processor array are tasks of the sequential computer. On the other side, the parallel coprocessor computes Euclidean distances and weight updates for neuron weight vectors in parallel. Thus, Tryba et al. implemented a variety of the original Kohonen learning algorithm (see Equation 3.24). Their weight updating procedure is

$$w_{ijk}(t) = (1 - N_{ij}(t))\, w_{ijk}(t) + N_{ij}(t) x_k(t), \qquad (7.3)$$

with x_k the k-th component of the two-dimensional input vector, w_{ijk} the synaptic weight between the k-th input and neuron ij (now two indices describe a single neuron, since neurons are arranged in a two-dimensional layer), and $N_{ij}(t)$ is the neighborhood function for weight updates in the neighborhood of the winning neuron. For simplified implementation, the neighborhood function is a box function or a pyramid function [Try90].

Each processor node consists of a RAM block to store 256 weight values in a 12-bit fixed point format to avoid the implementation of area consuming floating point circuitry. The input vector for Euclidean distance comparison with the stored weight vector is transmitted bit serially on a single line to save pins and silicon area, thus requiring a register for serial to parallel conversion of transmitted 12-bit components. A 32-bit register serves to accumulate the distance calculated. For distance calculation and weight update, digital summing circuitry as well as digital multiplying circuitry are provided for each processor. As in all digital Kohonen feature map implementations, finding the winning neuron is the most inefficient part of the algorithm, since global information exchange between processors is required. The fastest method on a two-dimensional array is to do a "line-parallel" comparison in all horizontal (or vertical lines) first, and then a sequential comparison in the last vertical (or horizontal) line, which now contains the smallest distance value of the respective horizontal (vertical) line. In this procedure the full parallelism of the network cannot be exploited.

Tryba et al. [Try90] intend the emulation of a 50×50 neuron feature map. Since a total of 2500 processors is too many for chip integration, they propose multiplexing processors between neurons. A single physical processor will simulate 16 neurons with their respective weights. To avoid inefficient winning neuron searches in digital processor arrays, Tryba et al. propose the use of optical methods, enabling extremely fast search operations.

7.7 Slice Architectures

The bit slice principle is a well known principle in the area of VLSI architectures. To reduce design efforts and enhance flexibility, circuits are cut into identical slices which can be cascaded easily to form a desired circuit. On the one hand, this has the advantage that a specific circuit design has to be done only once (namely, the design of the slice). This design is rather small and can be made with little effort. To form larger circuits several slices are fitted together linearly. On the other hand, such a design style increases flexibility. If a circuit of specific complexity has to be realized, the necessary number of slices is just fitted together. A more or less complex circuit is formed by using many or few identical slices. An example of a simple slice architecture is an adder. The basic circuit is a 1-bit full adder with C_{in} (carry in), A and B inputs, and S (sum) and C_{out} (carry out) outputs, performing the following results (see Chapter 4):

$$S = ABC_{in} + A\overline{BC_{in}} + \overline{AB}C_{in} + \overline{AB}\overline{C_{in}} \tag{7.4}$$

$$C_{out} = AB + AC_{in} + BC_{in}. \tag{7.5}$$

Slice Architectures 167

An n bit adder circuit is implemented by simply cascading n 1-bit full adder circuits. Bit slice architectures also exist for more complex circuits like ALUs. It is possible to assemble an n bit ALU from n single 1-bit ALU slices. This design principle may be extended to complex circuits, e.g. complete neurons with circuitry to perform synaptic multiplications, accumulations and nonlinearities. Thus, a single slice would consist of the circuitry necessary to realize a single neuron. Then, an n neuron chip can be assembled by cascading n single neuron slices.

7.7.1 Micro Devices' Neural Bit Slice

Micro Devices offer a VLSI circuit (MD1220 circuit) called the "Neural Bit Slice" (NBS) [Mic89b], which was the first commercially available neuro chip.

A single NBS chip carries eight processing elements. Figure 7.37 shows the principle architecture of the NBS [Yes89]. Synaptic weights are stored

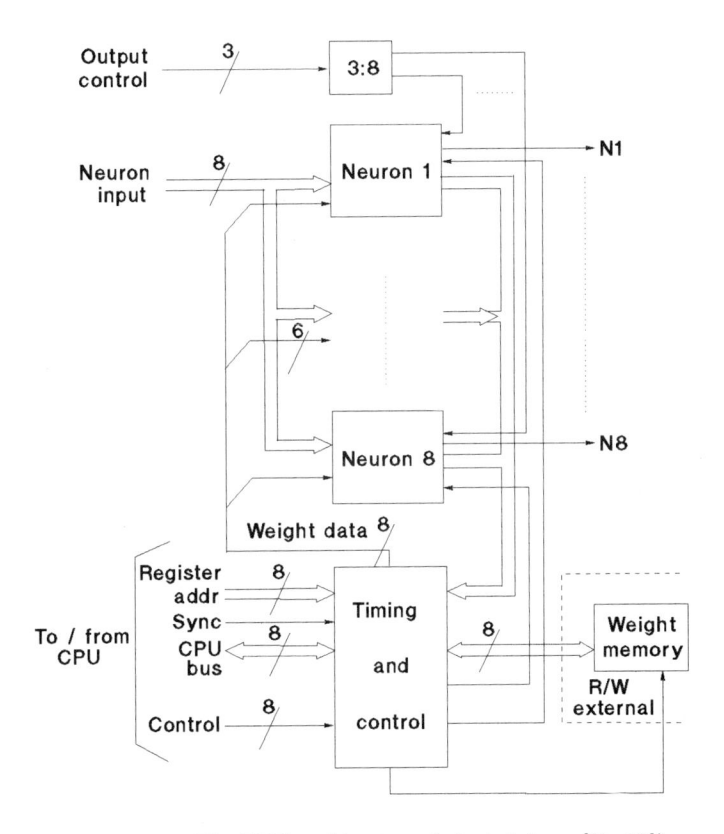

Figure 7.37 *The NBS architecture (adapted from [Yes89])*

off-chip in standard RAM circuits. This enables dense weight storage at low cost. Furthermore, flexibility is increased due to simple network expansion. A control block is responsible for generating control signals to control internal circuits and external weight memory. Several registers exist in which to store external and internal values to enable the synchronization of asynchronous input signals and facilitate handling of the chip (flexibility). The chip can operate autonomously or under the control of an external CPU. Therefore, an 8-bit CPU bus provides the possibility of accessing internal registers and the control block. NBS chips may be used in several modes. The input OUTPUT CONTROL serves to control neuron outputs. For different operation modes, internal neuron outputs may be multiplexed or configured as tri-state outputs or wired-OR outputs. Output values from preceding neurons are received via the 8-bit SYNAPSE DATA input bus. Two busses, the 8-bit RAM Data Bus and 8-bit RAM Address Bus, are responsible for transferring synaptic weights from external RAM circuits to the NBS, and *vice versa* (during learning or programming which, however, is not supported by on-chip circuitry). The core of any specific neural network hardware solution is the circuits performing the synaptic multiplication and the functionality of neurons (summation and thresholding). The architecture of the Neural Bit Slice core is depicted in Figure 7.38, with the circuitry of the first neuron sketched in the dashed block. Each neuron consists of a 16-bit accumulator with a preceding AND gate and a following threshold circuit. Synaptic inputs (output values from the preceding neuron stage) are entering neurons via SYNAPSE DATA inputs. At its input each neuron has a 1-bit line from the SYNAPSE DATA inputs and a 1-bit line from the WT input, both entering the AND gate. The WT input (1 bit) serves to transmit the synaptic weight which is transferred from external weight memory into the chip. Hence, only bit-serial multiplications can be performed. This architecture is well suited to the multiplication of a 1-bit synapse input with a 16-bit synaptic weight. The 1-bit synapse input is applied to the upper input of the AND gate, whereas weights are bit-serially applied to the WT input, the AND operation performed, and the result written (bit-serially) into the accumulator to be accumulated with the previous accumulator contents. This bit-serial AND operation corresponds to a 1-bit × 16-bit (input × weight) multiplication.

The NBS chip supports only hard-limiting threshold functions which are single threshold, double threshold, and double threshold about zero. No further threshold functions are supported on-chip. NBS chips can be used in parallel or serial input modes. In parallel mode the same synaptic input bit is applied to each neuron in the chip. Therefore, the state of the 8:1 input multiplexor defines which of the input bits is applied to all neurons. In serial mode, the first synaptic input (first bit of SYNAPSE DATA) is applied to the first neuron, the second input (second bit of SYNAPSE

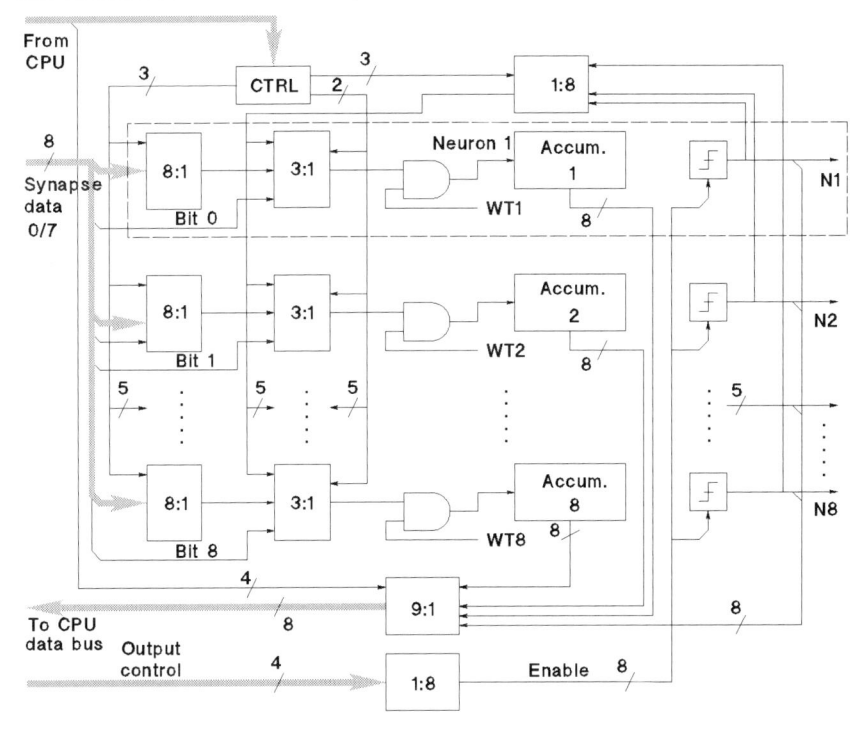

Figure 7.38 *NBS core architecture (adapted from [Yes89])*

DATA) is applied to the second neuron, *etc.* In both modes, neurons work bit-serially.

The bit-serial multiplication of synaptic inputs with synaptic weights requests a specific storage of weights in external RAM circuits. In each memory word (8-bit word width), one bit of eight different weights is stored. Weights are represented by two's complement numbers. Due to its architecture, the NBS supports eight external weights per neuron (8:1 multiplexor) and seven internal weights per neuron (fed back from the outputs of neurons), which is a total of 15 synapses per neuron. Thus, the NBS without additional off-chip circuitry is suited to the simulation of neural networks that have only 1-bit synaptic inputs and 16-bit synaptic weights, neurons with a maximum of 15 synapses, and binary outputs. Overflow problems are caused by 16-bit accumulators which may be avoided only by reducing the range of synaptic weight values. No on-chip learning is supported, and therefore must be done off-chip by the CPU controlling a NBS system.

Some of the above-mentioned restrictions may be avoided by additional off-chip circuitry. The number of synapses per neuron can be increased by means of so-called "synapse expansion", which is shown in Figure 7.39.

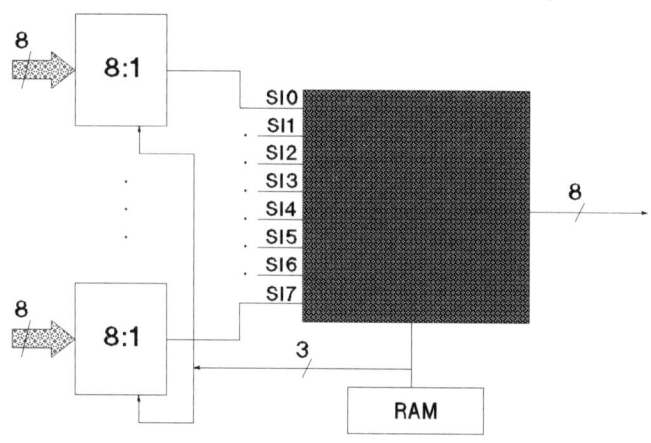

Figure 7.39 *NBS synapse expansion (adapted from [Mic90])*

Additional multiplexors allow the multiplexing of a larger number of synapses onto individual neurons (RAM addresses must be increased accordingly). Unfortunately, an increase in the number of synapses per neuron has to go hand-in-hand with a decrease of synapse accuracy. Otherwise an overflow of the 16-bit accumulator becomes more probable. Furthermore, the number of neurons per layer may be increased by means of parallel or serial layer expansion (depending on whether NBS chips are working with wired-OR outputs or tri-state outputs). Serial layer expansion is depicted in Figure 7.40. There is no restriction on the number of layers realized in a system. NBS chips also enable the accumulator contents of neurons to be read out. This allows users to change the threshold function characteristics by additional off-chip threshold circuitry. Arbitrary bit-serial multiplications from 1-bit × 16-bit multiplication up to x-bit × 16-bit multiplication are feasible if "shifted" weights are stored in memory. Since a bit-serial multiplication is done by the accumulation of shifted partial products, such a multiplication can be done by storing x shifted values (each value shifted to a different degree) of the multiplicand in external memory. This reduces the efficiency of weight storage by a factor of x. Additional external shifting circuitry may help in avoiding inefficient weight storage. More information is given in [Mic89c].

The Micro Devices MD1220 "Neural Bit Slice" chip was implemented using CMOS technology. One chip contains 22,000 transistors and is packaged into a 68 pin PLCC. Chips are designed to run at a clock frequency of 20 MHz. The cost of a single NBS chip is about $50. The speed of the NBS is reported to be a 55 MIPS (million instructions per second) processing rate [Mic89b, Yes89]. In its basic configuration with eight synapses per neuron (feed-forward only, no feedback synapses from neuron outputs to neuron

Slice Architectures 171

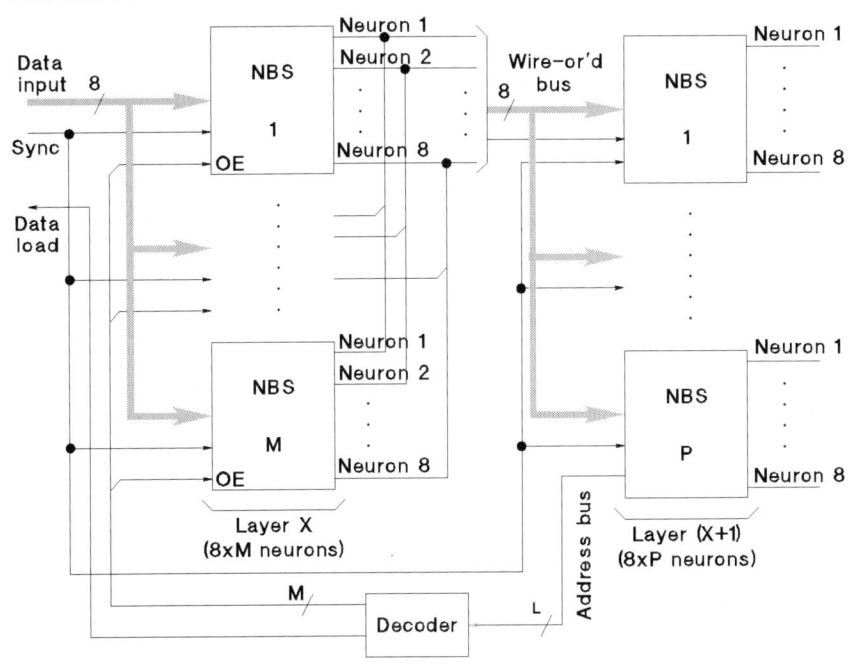

Figure 7.40 *NBS serial layer expansion (adapted from [Mic90])*

inputs of a NBS) and 1-bit synaptic inputs (1-bit × 16-bit multiplication), the processing delay for the NBS is 7.2 μs [Mic89b]. Since one chip consists of eight neurons with eight synapses each (64 multiplications and summations to update all neuron outputs), this corresponds to a performance of about 8.9 million connections per second.

The NBS MD1220 was designed as a basic element of a flexible framework for neural network emulation. In its basic configuration it only supports 1-bit × 16-bit multiplications and few hard-limiting threshold functions. This can be extended by additional off-chip hardware. However, a severe limitation is given by 16-bit accumulators, which may tend to overflow if many summations are done or large weights are multiplied by synaptic input values of more than 1-bit in width. No learning is supported by the chip. The flexibility of the concept is much less than the flexibility offered by one of the previously described SIMD array approaches. Due to the many limitations imposed by the architecture, realistic signal processing applications cannot be solved.

7.7.2 The BACCHUS Architecture

A slice architecture for a special type of binary neural network was designed at Darmstadt University of Technology in cooperation with the University of Düsseldorf. Similar approaches were pursued by researchers from the University of Dortmund in the group of K. Goser (see Section 7.7.3). The network to be realized is a binary correlation matrix memory, which will be used with sparsely coded input and output vectors. Input/output vectors are binary, as are synaptic weights. Neurons perform a hard-limiter threshold function, each with the same threshold value. For recall, if a binary input vector is presented to the memory, this vector is multiplied by the connection matrix or weight matrix (which is also fully binary). The result will be a sum vector containing integer values which is transmitted to threshold units, each performing the same threshold operation. This procedure is the same as for other neural networks. However, the training phase is different. While most neural networks are trained with iterative training algorithms, the considered correlation matrix memory may simply be programmed with linear time complexity. Programming is done by performing the outer product between input and desired output vectors. Due to nonlinearities, this type of correlation matrix memory may even map a set of linearly dependent input vectors onto a set of desired output vectors. Problems are caused by binary weights. If several correlations occur at the location of a weight, some information is lost, since the weight cannot be increased beyond the value one (binary storage). Therefore, in this programming mode, sparsely coded input and output vectors have to be used to minimize the probability of the described case of information loss [Pal80]. For classification tasks, this type of network may also be used in a non-sparsely coded mode, together with an iterative training algorithm. Then it works like a nearest neighbor classifier, with reference vectors to form class boundaries [Poe91, Poe93].

Due to binary values, this network is very apt for implementation with digital CMOS technology. A multiplication between binary input vectors and the binary memory matrix can be done by generating addresses of input vector bits containing a "one" and reading out respective memory lines which are subsequently accumulated. Therefore, an accumulator is needed for each memory column. If an input vector contains 2 ones (e.g. on the positions 1 and 2), the respective lines of the memory matrix are read (lines 1 and 2) successively, and their contents accumulated in a line of counters (the number of counters is equal to the number of elements in each memory matrix line, and thus equal to the number of matrix columns). Due to the simple vector/matrix multiplication with binary elements, synaptic weights may be stored in standard RAM circuits, whereas counters and some additional logic has to be implemented on an application-specific integrated circuit (ASIC). This principle is shown in Figure 7.41. Two

Slice Architectures

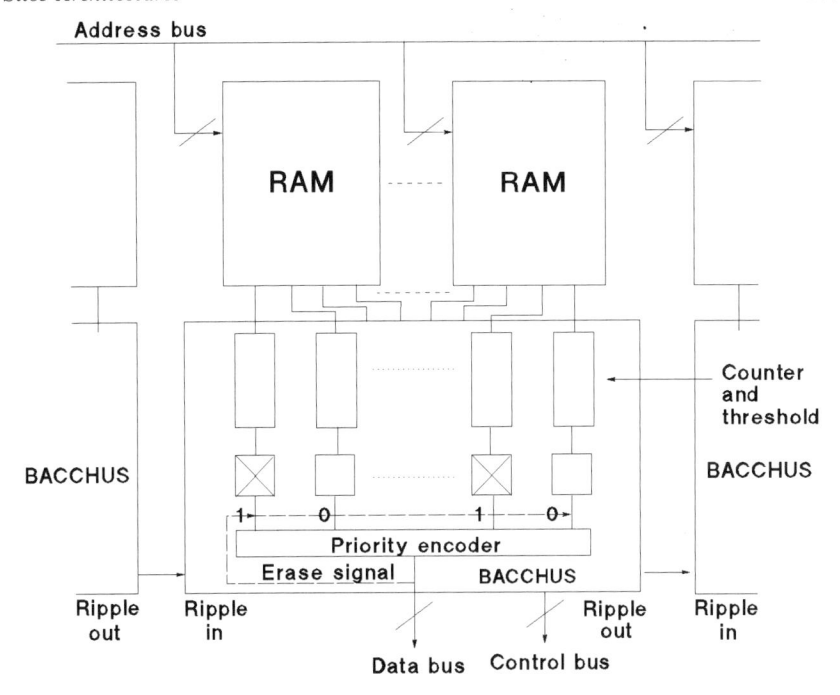

Figure 7.41 *Basic BACCHUS architecture*

advantages are combined in such an architecture: on the one hand, weights are stored on standard RAM circuits, which is cheap and allows a very dense storage that cannot be achieve with an ASIC. On the other hand, the architecture is fully cascadable. If address generation is done off-chip, more neurons can be realized by simply adding counters on a chip, or by using more chips, more synapses per neuron are realized by simply using larger or more RAM chips.

Three different versions, BACCHUS I, BACCHUS II and BACCHUS III, were designed, all of which have been fabricated and tested [Huc90, Poe90]. The limitation on the number of neurons per chip is not the die area but the number of pins (since a neuron mainly consists of a counter and some additional logic). Without multiplexing, each neuron needs its own input line from memory. Additional pins are used for control signals, data input/output, and neuron output. To keep the number of pins for neuron outputs low, an on-chip address generation circuit generates addresses of active neurons. The hardlimiter threshold function was realized by preloading counters with the threshold value and counting down instead of counting up. By the detection of a zero in a counter (counter overflow), it can be determined whether the threshold has been exceeded or not. With the different designs several methods of memory control and active neuron evaluation had been implemented and tested. BACCHUS I (120 pin ceramic carrier) and BACCHUS II (84 pin ceramic carrier) were standard cell designs (VENUS design system) fabricated by Siemens (2 μm CMOS technology). The final version BACCHUS III was designed with a sea-of-gate design system (system SLDS from Siemens) and 1600 chips (PLCC 68 carrier) were fabricated by Siemens (1.5 μm CMOS technology). One chip contains the functionality of 32 neurons and was designed to run at a 10 MHz clock frequency. Tested chips, however, worked properly up to a clock rate of more than 20 MHz. Thus, the performance of a single chip is 32 million 1-bit interconnections per second (at 10 MHz clock rate). In a system this performance increases linearly with an increasing number of BACCHUS chips. Chips are only used for the feed-forward phase. No learning or programming is supported, and thus has to be done off-chip. Figure 7.42 sketches the architecture of the BACCHUS III circuit. A detailed description of the BACCHUS chips with circuit diagrams and timing diagrams appeared in [Gle91a], or they are available from [Gle91b].

At Darmstadt University of Technology a small prototype neurocomputer was built with BACCHUS I chips by A. Koenig et al. [Koe91a]. Four BACCHUS chips are assembled on one printed circuit board together with RAM chips and some additional control circuitry. The whole system consists of four boards on a common backplane connected to a controller which is plugged into an IBM PC/AT slot [Koe91a]. RAM chips have a memory depth of 2048. Hence, an associative memory of 2048 lines (synapses per neuron) and 512 columns (neurons) is realized. Figure 7.43 shows the BACCHUS neurocomputer system without a controller board. Currently an image compression application is running on the prototype system [Koe91b].

Palm et al. [Pal91] designed a larger associative system based on BACCHUS III chips called PAN IV. The whole system consists of a Server-Interface to enable multi user capability, and a Motorola 68030-based associative memory management unit (AMMU) which accesses up to 19 PAN IV memory boards via the PAN-bus (VME-bus based). Each PAN IV memory board consists of eight BACCHUS III (realizing a total of 256 simple processors) chips mounted together with 2 MByte of standard RAM memory. Applications for such a system are fast associative databases in a multi-user environment, speech processing, *etc.*

Summarized, the BACCHUS chips were designed for a special type of neural network, which is a binary correlation matrix memory. Only this type of network is supported. Learning or programming has to be done off-chip. However, this is not a big disadvantage, since applicable programming algorithms are quite simple and fast, even on sequential computers. Binary correlation matrix memories may be realized efficiently, since weight storage is dense and cheap due to the use of commercially available RAM circuits. Fabrication and packaging costs of the BACCHUS III circuit are also low (about $15 per chip), permitting low system costs. Future work is

Slice Architectures

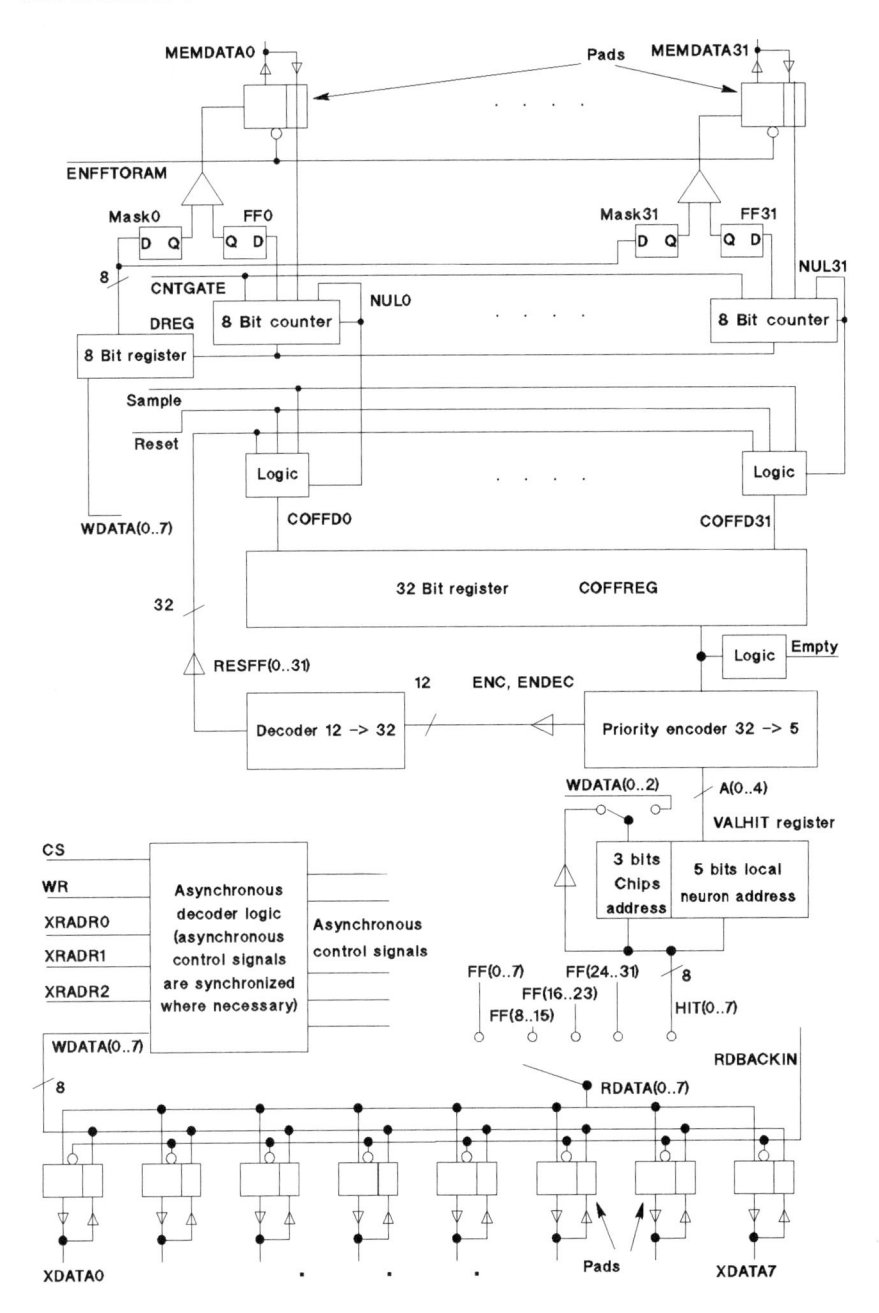

Figure 7.42 *The BACCHUS III architecture*

Figure 7.43 *BACCHUS I neurocomputer*

heading towards an integer logic instead of binary logic and the use of field programmable gate-arrays (FPGAs) to enhance user flexibility. The integer logic in combination with distance metrics like the city block distance allows more flexibility to support more sophisticated network algorithms such as the LVQ, self-organizing feature maps, or RCE networks, for example. The first chips and system boards were realized at Darmstadt University of Technology.

7.7.3 Slice Chips from University of Dortmund

At the University of Dortmund an architecture very similar to the BACCHUS architecture has been developed, and several chips designed and fabricated. These chips are also designed for the implementation of a binary correlation matrix memory. The basic architecture is nearly identical to the BACCHUS architecture; however, Rueckert *et al.* are using comparators to check whether the threshold value is exceeded or not [Rue90], thus needing additional circuitry. Several standard cell designs of slice chips with 32 processing elements (neurons) have been made and fabricated (2 μm CMOS technology) and a full custom design of a 128 processing element chip (2 μm CMOS technology, 10 MHz clock rate, 48,000 transistors, 153 pins). However, no larger number of chips was fabricated and no chips have been used in a system. Recent work has also led to integer arithmetic and FPGA based architectures.

7.8 Weightless Neural Networks

Systems classically used in neural computing are storing information on the learned associations in their connection strengths. This enables fast information retrieval through local operations. But local operations are multiplications and accumulations that have to be performed by quite complex hardware, depending on the required accuracy. From the viewpoint of hardware implementability, weightless neural nets seem to be an attractive alternative. Research on this class of network has been pursued by Igor Aleksander, who came up with several types of weightless neural networks and some hardware implementations.

The basic element of such a weightless neural net is a RAM node corresponding to a neuron in "classical" neural networks. Whereas a single McCulloch-Pitts neuron with its arriving synaptic weights and its non-linear threshold behavior may only perform a linear separation of its input space, a RAM node proposed by Aleksander *et al.* performs arbitrary binary mappings [Ale90]. Aleksander [Ale91] defines a generalizing RAM model (G-RAM) as a node having a number of inputs, a set of probabilistic firing values, a set of training vectors and a generalization algorithm. This general node may be simplified in several respects. Reducing the possibilities of probabilistic firing to either generating output value 0 or 1 solely depending on the input vector (without inclusion of a random process), and simplifying the generalization algorithm to filling RAM cells according to training vectors, the neuron becomes a simple look-up-table. The binary neuron input vector is used to address a RAM cell to produce the neuron output. Clearly, networks of such neurons lead to architectures which are easily implementable in digital VLSI technology. Aleksander *et al.* [Ale79] proposed a hardware architecture to realize N-tuple nets which is known as WISARD [Ale84, Ale89a].

7.8.1 The WISARD System

The WISARD system (WIlkie, Stoneham, Aleksander Recognition Device) is an implementation of the N-tuple sampling technique for image recognition. Figure 7.44 outlines the basic architecture principle of the recognition system. Signals are received through a two-dimensional retina carrying binary images which have to be recognized. For classification purposes, p discriminators exist. Each discriminator consists of several RAM nodes (neurons). The N bit input of a RAM node is randomly connected to N retina cells which address RAM cells to generate binary node output values. Therefore, each node consists of 2^N binary RAM cells.

During programming, binary training patterns are presented to the retina together with the correct classification. Through the fixed N-tupel connections the RAM cells of the discriminator belonging to the training pattern

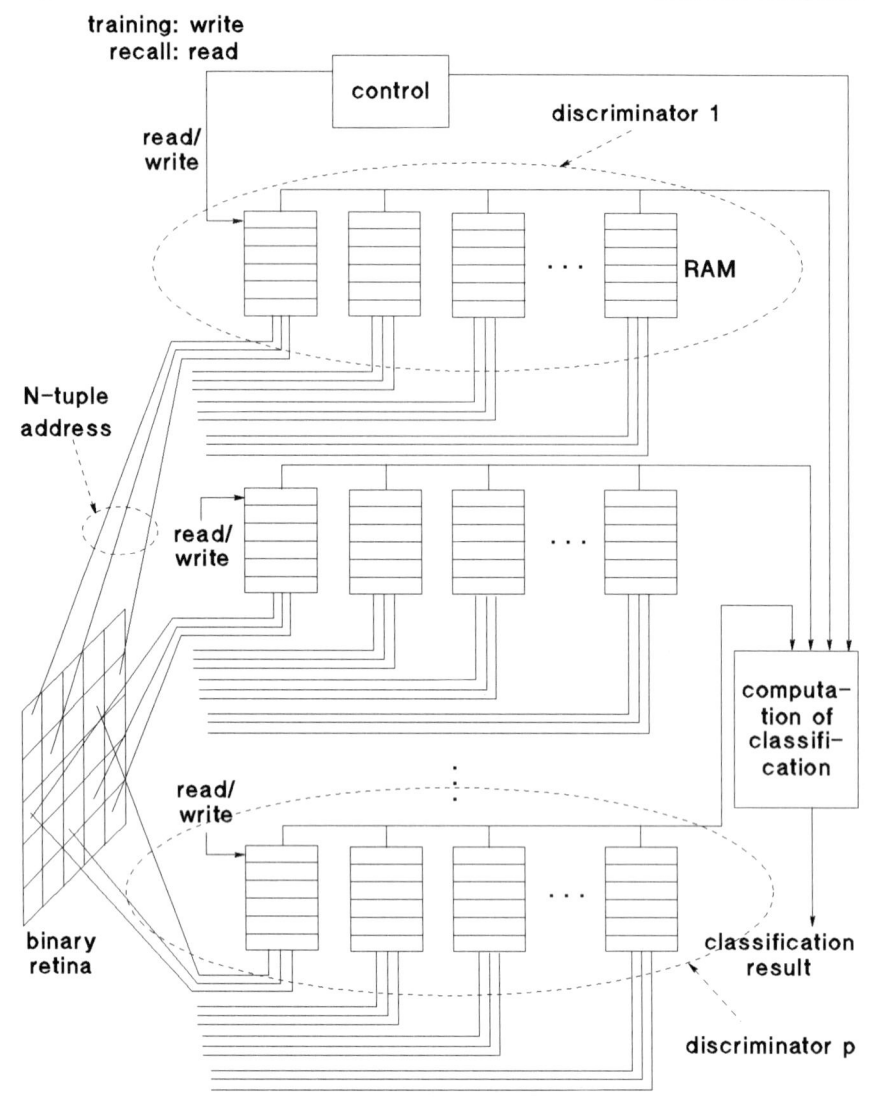

Figure 7.44 *Image recognition system (adapted from [Ale89b])*

class are addressed, and a binary 1 is written into each addressed RAM node cell. This simple training procedure makes learning fast, since each training pattern has to be presented only once.

The recall phase does not allow RAM contents to be changed. Only read operations are permitted. After presentation of an input image to be classified, the RAM nodes of all discriminators are addressed through their

N-tuple connections with the retina. The contents of the addressed cells (either a binary 0 or a binary 1) appear at the node outputs. For each discriminator the outputs of all corresponding RAM nodes are summed up. The resulting value on each discriminator is used to perform the classification. The class affiliation is given by the discriminator containing the largest value. Its difference to the second largest value on the other discriminators may be used as a confidence measure of classification.

For classifying 512×512 pixel images at video frame rates, Aleksander proposes the use of a semi-parallel architecture [Ale89b]. Thus, each discriminator is realized through its own RAM circuits operating in parallel, whereas operation within one discriminator is serial. The random N-tupel connections are performed by shift-registers providing pseudo random addresses, which allows flexibility in N-tupel connections. With RAM circuits of 10^{-7} sec access time, Badii *et al.* [Bad89] report the realization of a system with an operating time of 70 ms per classification. WISARD systems were applied to image recognition tasks and speech recognition where data has to be coded properly to fit onto the two-dimensional retina.

7.8.2 Recent Developments

More complex RAM nodes enable different training algorithms with more capabilities than the simple programming scheme of the N-tuple recognizer discussed in the previous section. Wing-Kay Kan *et al.* [Kan87] use a probabilistic logic neuron (PLN) that allows a third state, namely state u for "undefined", in addition to states 0 and 1. If the input vector of a PLN addresses a RAM cell containing a u, the output either becomes 0 or 1, with a probability of 50% each. This randomly generated output value allows it to move through several states in a network with feedback. With an appropriate learning procedure, teaching vectors are represented by stable network states that attract similar states (similar with respect to their Hamming distance). This is a desirable property for image completion tasks or generalization in pattern classification applications. Also, it is possible to build multi-layer associative networks from several RAM node modules, each containing a certain number of RAM nodes [Kan87]. Kan *et al.* report that using several layers of modules enhances generalization effects at high recognition rates. With appropriate learning procedures, different types of learning are possible, such as associative programming, error driven learning, incremental training, *etc.* For more information on these aspects, the interested reader is recommended to read [Ale89a, Ale89b, Ale91].

It is problematic that the theory of weightless neural nets is less understood than that of conventional connectionist systems. With respect to hardware implementation, simple RAM nodes providing only two output states 0 and 1 without the inclusion of random processes are very simple to implement in digital VLSI technology (see the WISARD system).

More complex RAM nodes, however, require more sophisticated circuitry. It should be considered that the number of RAM cells per node grows exponentially (2^N) with the number of inputs (N), thus limiting the input width per node.

7.9 Wafer Scale Implementations

Wafer scale integration (WSI) is a technique which has some very interesting features for neural network implementation (see also Chapter 2). A complete wafer offers much more silicon area to the user than a single chip. This opens the facility to integrate even a medium size network on silicon without the necessity to leave chip boundaries and thus causing cascadability problems. Wafer scale integration, however, is a technology which is still not state-of-the-art. The main problem with a large silicon area is the defect density of the fabrication processes. There exists a specific density of defects that is characteristic for any fabrication process. This density is measured in defects per area (defects per square inch or square centimeter), and it has been significantly reduced during the last few years by improving fabrication processes, *i.e.* first of all improving the cleanliness of fabrication rooms. The defect density of state-of-the-art CMOS processes is about 1 to 2 defects/cm^2 [Gei90] (about 5 defects/cm^2 in 1985 [Jes86]). The percentage of dies that do meet performance specifications (no defect present) is termed "wafer yield". It is very difficult to predict the yield of ICs in a fabrication process due to the large number and variety of factors which impact on the yield. Yield is affected by the specific type of circuit which is designed (every IC layer has a characteristic defect density during fabrication, and from circuit to circuit the number of elements or area used per layer is different), by the design methodology, the layout, and the physical fabrication process. Before fabrication, crystal defects may occur in the silicon. During fabrication, dust particles in several fabrication steps may cause malfunctioning transistors or other defective elements (usually faults which are randomly distributed on the die). Furthermore, parameter drifts which are due to physical effects associated with processing steps (photolithography, diffusion, *etc.*) may cause significant drifts in transistor parameters that can be large enough to make a transistor's performance insufficient. It is clear that yield will become less if the die size increases (constant defect density assumed). This effect is elucidated in Figure 7.45. Image (a) shows a specific distribution of defects on a wafer. In images (b) through (d), different die sizes are assumed. The larger the die size, the less probable will be defect free dies. Image (d) shows a wafer with only four dies. None of the dies is defect free (yield zero). More information on IC design processes and yield can be taken from [Gei90]. The problem of yield becomes crucial in wafer scale integration. Since it is impossible to fabricate complete wafers with no defects at all, defect tolerant circuits must be

Wafer Scale Implementations 181

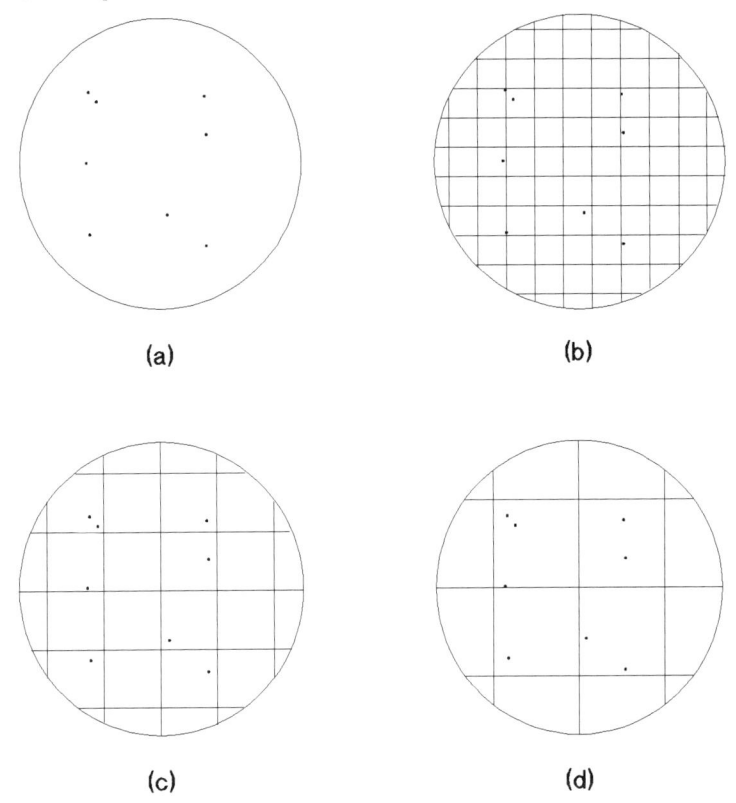

Figure 7.45 *Yield of IC circuits (adapted from [Gei90])*

implemented. This may be realized by either implementing systems with "graceful degradation" or by adding redundant elements which can replace defective elements.

A system showing "graceful degradation" is a one that does not fail completely if one of its components does not work properly as specified by the system designer. The more components that fail, the less predictable the system's behavior will become. If one bit in the multiplier of a conventional CPU does not work, it is completely useless. This system has no graceful degradation. However, if one bit of a synapse in a large neural network fails (which may be caused by a stuck-at-one or stuck-at-zero fault), the network's behavior will not change significantly but only slightly. Probably, in this case some of the network outputs will change slightly (e.g. less than 1% change in output activity) for some input constellations. A network's behavior will become especially intriguing if the learning algorithm can cope with connections not working between neurons (synapses) or defective neurons. An example of such an algorithm is the Boltzmann machine learning algorithm. Then, neither the user nor designer have to be wary for defects, which become completely invisible for the user.

In the second type of fault tolerant architectures, redundant circuits are implemented on the die or wafer. The task of these circuits is to replace defective circuits. Three disadvantages are coupled with fault tolerance through redundancy. First, redundancy requires additional redundant circuits that consume additional area on the die. Second, after fabrication, faulty elements on the chip or wafer have to be identified. To obtain a high fault coverage, *i.e.* to find nearly every defect which may occur, many test vectors have to be applied to the circuit. For large and complex circuits this may become a time consuming task. Furthermore, generation of test vectors is a crucial task which has to be done carefully. Additional circuitry on the chip may become necessary to increase observability of the circuit components. Third, after identification of a defective element, it must be cut off and replaced through a redundant element. This can be done by cutting electrical connections with a laser beam, by fusing electronic fuses, or by changing some electronic switches implemented on the chip. In the latter two cases, additional circuitry is again necessary for the connection of redundant elements with circuits to be replaced by fuses or switches. Routing problems can occur if elements of two-dimensional arrays with a specific flow of information have to be replaced. Despite many problems accompanying fault tolerance through redundant circuits, this is usually necessary since virtually no circuit shows "graceful degradation" permitting a specific amount of defective elements. On the previously described N64000 chip used for the CNAPS system from Adaptive Solutions, Inc., 16 additional processing elements are implemented for redundancy (this is due to the large die size of 1 square inch).

However, fault tolerance is not the only important aspect of wafer scale integration. Another big problem is packaging and pinning. Due to the wafer size, large and complex circuits, even complete systems, may be realized on it with an enormous amount of computational power. But one also has to consider that these systems must be fed with a large amount of information and are producing a lot of information which has to be transferred onto and from the wafer, requiring many pins. Furthermore, a complete wafer is dissipating much more power than a single chip, which has to be taken from the wafer and emitted to the environment.

Some major problems of wafer scale integration are mentioned above. Research and development in this area is still going on to provide WSI for system designers. Due to manifold problems and expensive fabrication, however, today only a few wafer scale systems have been implemented in research labs. This statement is also valid for neural network implementations. Most of the architectures are only proposed for wafer scale integration, but few of them have been implemented on a full wafer. No commercial product is available.

7.9.1 Hitachi Waferscale Neural Networks

At Hitachi, Ltd. (Central Research Laboratory and Device Development Center) a wafer scale integration neural network was designed and implemented by Yasunaga et al. [Yas90]. The original approach was to design dedicated hardware for a system emulating recursive networks (outputs fed back to inputs) in feed-forward phase only, i.e. Hopfield networks without learning. Network dynamics are described by Equations 3.3 and 3.4. Due to digital emulation, the equations have to be discretized as given by Equation 3.5.

Such a recursive network is used for solving optimization problems. To do this, an optimization problem has to be transformed into a network with a specific architecture and synaptic weights. During relaxation the network performs a gradient descent towards a low energy state. The activity distribution over all network neurons corresponds to a specific solution of the optimization problem. Low energy states correspond to good, low cost solutions.

To overcome the connection problem in large networks, Yasunaga et al. implemented only one synapse multiplication circuit per neuron and a time sharing bus architecture. A connection problem in Hopfield networks is caused by the fact that the number of synapses and connections in a completely connected network rises with the square number of neurons, resulting in a huge number of wires for interconnection, registers for weight storage, and multipliers for synaptic multiplication (in a completely parallel architecture with a multiplication circuit for each synapse). A special assumption made by Yasunaga et al., which will be described subsequently, also reduces the number of registers needed for weight storage. Figure 7.46 depicts the principle of the time sharing bus architecture. Each neuron consists of one synapse multiplication circuit and a cell body for accumulation. An individual address is allocated to each neuron. Since 576 neurons are implemented on the complete wafer, neuron addresses are from 0 through to 575, thus requiring 10 bits to be encoded in binary. Since every neuron output has to be fed back to all neuron inputs in a completely interconnected network, the following procedure is implemented to update the network: the address of the first neuron (sender neuron) is given on the address bus, whereas its output passes the sigmoid function circuit (sigmoid table) on the data bus. All neurons receive the address of the sender neuron and look for the weight of their synaptic connection to the sender neuron. After finding the respective weight, they perform the synaptic multiplication and accumulate the partial product. The whole network is updated after all neuron addresses have been given to the address bus, sequentially. Each neuron stores 64 synaptic weights with an accuracy of 8 bits. Thereby, only the 64 heaviest weights of the 576 potential weights in a completely connected 576 neuron network may be stored. As shown in Figure 7.47,

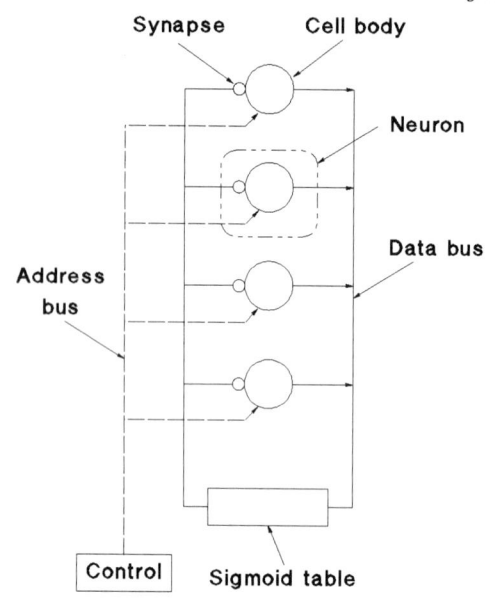

Figure 7.46 *Principle of time sharing bus architecture (adapted from [Yas90])*

three neurons may be cascaded to increase the number of synapses per neuron to 190. This is possible due to the sigmoid table circuit which performs the nonlinear threshold operation not directly at neuron outputs but on the broadcast data bus. Yasunaga *et al.* have to assume that sufficient performance may be obtained by using not more than the 190 heaviest of 576 potential weights. Clearly, neural networks are fault tolerant circuits with graceful degradation. Many investigations have shown that only small changes in output activity are caused by small changes in some weight values or by neglecting some small weights. However, no general statement for every problem and special data configuration can be made, as neglecting so many weights has only a little impact on network performance. Probably, this depends significantly on the network implemented, and thus it is difficult to say whether the 190 heaviest of 576 synaptic weights will suffice for proper performance. It must also be considered that neuron cascading to obtain more synaptic inputs per neuron reduces the overall number of neurons available to form a neural network.

A more detailed sketch of the neuron architecture is given in Figure 7.48. The synapse circuit stores 64 8-bit weights with 64 corresponding 10-bit addresses. Such a 10-bit address is the address of the corresponding neuron, to which the respective synapse is connected. If a sending neuron has put its output on the data bus and its address on the address bus, the addresses of all 64 synaptic weights are scanned subsequently and compared with the

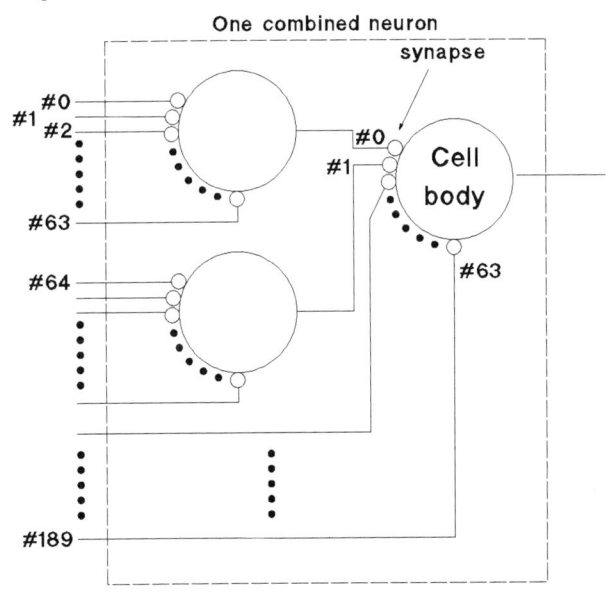

Figure 7.47 *Cascade of neurons to increase the number of synapses (adapted from [Yas90])*

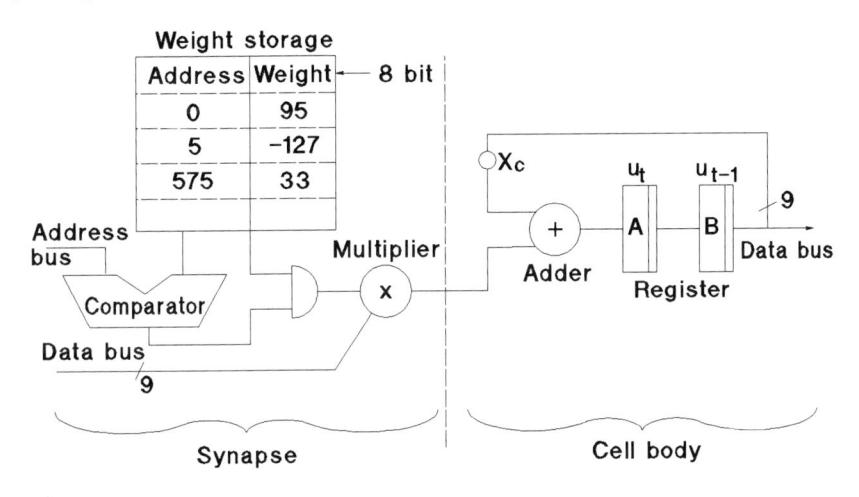

Figure 7.48 *Architecture of a neuron/synapse circuit (adapted from [Yas90])*

address on the address bus. An address pointer scans all neuron addresses within a synapse circuit as sketched in Figure 7.49. If a hit occurs, the multiplication of the respective synapse weight with the value on the data bus is performed and accumulated in the cell body circuit. To do this, the cell body consists of an adder and two registers. Register B contains

Weight storage

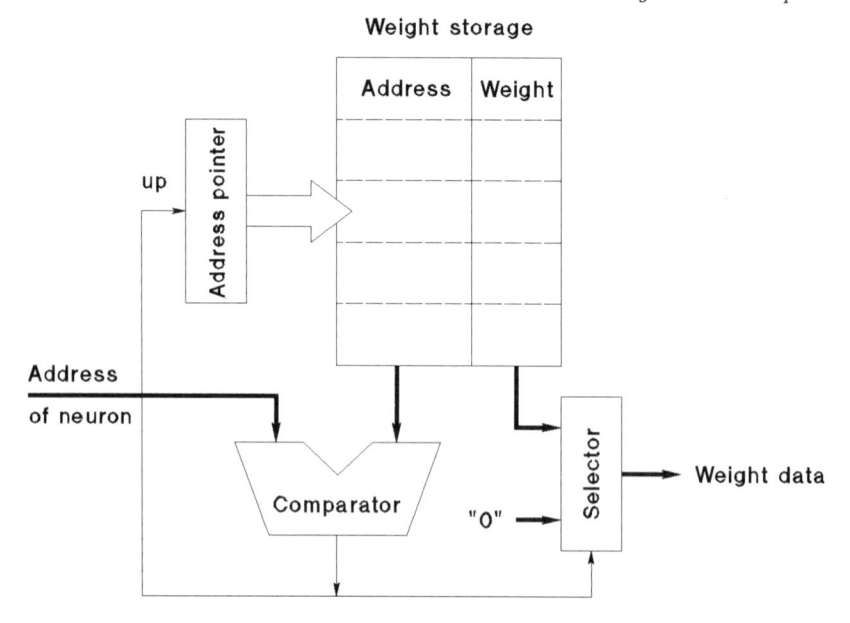

Figure 7.49 High speed weight access (adapted from [Yas90])

the neuron output from the previous update cycle (output at time $t-1$), whereas the new output is accumulated in register A. Both registers allow storage with an accuracy of 9 bits. An internal feedback loop via delay element X_c permits modeling of time constant $c = (1 - \Delta t/T)$ in Equation 3.5.

The silicon wafer has a diameter of 5 inches. To implement 576 working neurons with 36,864 synapses, a 0.8 μm CMOS gate array technology (three layer aluminium) was used. The whole wafer consists of 64 chips with a total of 19 million transistors. Forty-nine of the 64 chips contain neuron circuits with 12 neurons, each. This is a total of 49×12 = 588 neurons. One neuron chip with 12 neurons is redundant to replace defective neurons. This is sufficient, since for the technology used an average of 10 faults is reported [Yas90] to occur on the 5-inch silicon wafer. About 1000 gates are used to implement a single neuron circuit. Eight chips contain circuitry to control neurons and busses. The other chips are process quality control chips. On the 400 μm space between chips which is usually used for dicing, wires for chip connection and power busses are implemented. Busses are arranged in a hierarchy with a main bus in the wafer center (the eight bus and neuron control chips are also in the wafer center), global busses in neuron rows, and local busses to each neuron (see Figure 7.50). Even circuit components in bus and neuron control chips (bus wires, drivers, sigmoidal function tables) are designed with redundancy. The wafer is mounted on a

Wafer Scale Implementations 187

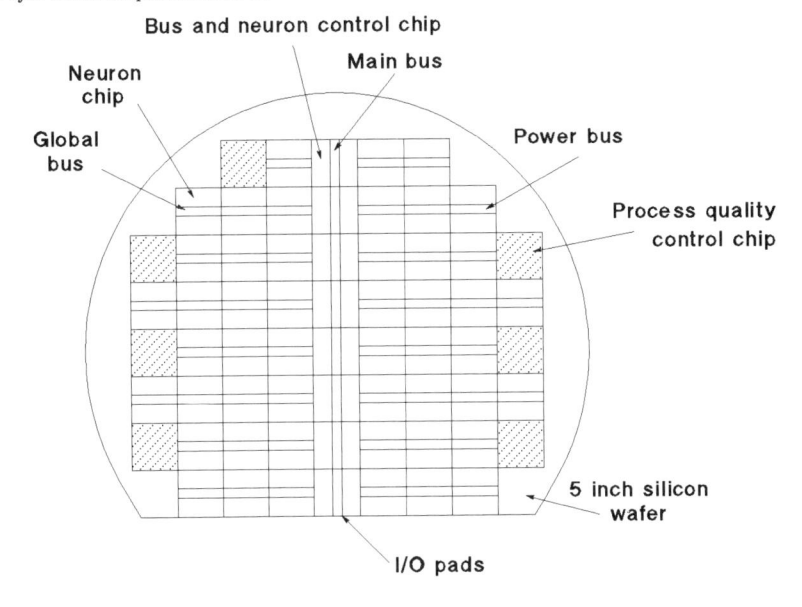

Figure 7.50 *Circuit distribution on wafer (adapted from [Yas90])*

14×15 cm² ceramic substrate. Wire bonding provides connections to substrate. Power dissipation of the whole wafer is about 5 Watts.

Yasunaga *et al.* implemented several networks to solve the traveling salesman problem (TSP). The speed of the system is reported to be 464 ns step time (one update cycle in an optimization network). Thus, one step is needed to feed back a neuron's output, perform the respective synaptic multiplications, and accumulate the partial product. Hence, 464 ns/step · 576 steps = 267 µs are needed to interconnect or update all 576 neurons corresponding to a performance of 1.24 billion interconnects per second in a completely connected network. However, it has to be considered that only the 64 "strongest" of 576 potential weights are stored and evaluated, thus providing an actual performance of about 138.1 million interconnects per second. A 16 cities TSP was solved in about 0.1 seconds (between 250 and 350 cycles to settle down) [Yas90].

The system described is well suited for the simulation of feedback networks used for optimization problems. No on-chip learning is supported. The fact that a maximum of 190 weights per neuron can be stored may become problematic. Thus, in large networks consisting of more than 190 neurons, the smallest weights have to be neglected. It cannot be stated that this is permitted in all cases without changing the results significantly. Wafers may be cascaded via an external bus to provide the functionality of more neurons for the simulation of larger networks.

At Hitachi the previously described architecture was extended to run multilayer feed-forward networks with the backpropagation algorithm. To meet accuracy requirements of the backpropagation algorithm, synaptic weight representation was extended to 16 bits. Each wafer integrates 144 neurons. With eight wafers, researchers at Hitachi's Central Research Laboratory in Kokubunji mounted a neurocomputer with 1152 neurons [Boy90]. This neurocomputer is reported to run the backpropagation algorithm at a speed of 2300 MCUPS. One of the main problems is the power dissipation of wafers. Hitachi planned to bring a waferscale neural computer onto the market. In future, the implementation of 10,000 neurons will be possible with 0.3 μm ULSI technology.

7.10 Summary

Most of the existing neural network architectures and nearly all commercial products are implemented using digital CMOS VLSI technology. The virtues of this technology, cheap fabrication, general availability, high accuracy, and large flexibility, have already been mentioned in Chapters 2 and 4. One of the most important advantages is that learning algorithms may be implemented using digital circuitry.

Architectures are ranging from sequential acceleration boards up to massively parallel SIMD and systolic arrays. Dedicated sequential hardware for neural network simulation differs from conventional computers in several ways. First, it provides high speed memory for fast synaptic weight access. Second, it is optimized to perform fast multiplication/accumulation operations which are needed for synaptic multiplications and the following calculation of a neuron activation potential. Acceleration boards provide high flexiblity. Many neural algorithms as well as conventional data preprocessing algorithms may run on them. Transputer networks and signal processor networks provide low parallelism. Their performance-to-hardware ratio in neural computations is less compared with acceleration boards. This is due to the large amount of hardware that has to be utilized, and because they are general purpose computing elements which had not been specifically designed to simulate neural algorithms. Any algorithm which may be parallelized can run on them. With respect to neural network simulation, systems of smaller but more processing elements are much more efficient. Linear SIMD arrays consisting of processors specifically designed to perform fast multiplication/accumulation operations with a large amount of local memory seem to be a solution, with high performance and still quite high flexibility. They can simulate many network algorithms including learning, and still allow the speed up of data preprocessing operations like the discrete fourier transform. This is very important in order to avoid data preprocessing becoming the bottleneck of an application. For more speed either parallelism has to be increased, leading to hardware expensive systems, or functionality has to be reduced. Reducing functionality often means dropping the claim of fast learning. If learning does not need to be supported (off-chip learning), calculation accuracy can be reduced and the information flow becomes simpler, allowing much faster operations. If a network needs only binary operations like the associative memories supported by the BACCHUS system or the WISARD system, a very simple architecture (low hardware expense) with high performance is realizable using digital CMOS technology.

8

Analog and Mixed Analog/Digital Neurocomputers

8.1 Introduction

Categorization of analog and mixed analog/digital neural network hardware implementations is a tedious task. Many criteria may be applied to separate the different approaches from each other. One possibility is to choose biological evidence as proposed in Chapter 2. This criterion is applied to separate networks close to biology from other approaches. Thus, circuit designers are trying to copy biological nervous systems with microelectronic circuitry. Such approaches will be considered in the first section of this chapter. Important work to be mentioned here are implementations of the silicon retina, silicon cochlea, and central pattern generators. This section will be followed by cellular network implementations emulating neural networks at a more abstract level. Early nervous preprocessing tasks are still done, like noise removal or edge extraction, but circuitry to emulate neural network operations is not directly motivated by copying nervous systems. For networks in both sections it is common for learning not to exist.

Another possibility is to categorize the approaches by the implementation technology used. This is done for amorphous silicon implementations, charge coupled devices (CCD) and floating-gate technologies. But most network implementations have been done in standard CMOS technology, due to its widespread availability and cheap CMOS fabrication. Therefore, implementation technology is not a sufficient characteristic to separate the many realizations that do not belong to the first two sections describing networks near to biology.

A third feature is programmability and learning. Some early implementations were even not user programmable. During fabrication, the network was individualized leaving no flexibility for the user at all. Most approaches, however, provide user programmability of synaptic weights. The situation is different for learning. On-chip learning is difficult to achieve in analog implementations due to weights stored as voltages on capacitors, charges on floating-gates or analog resistances which are difficult to change in a controlled way. Another reason causing difficulties in learning is the request for high precision calculations of learning algorithms like the error-backpropagation method. Therefore, nearly all early implementations, with few exceptions, do not provide on-chip learning. But there is now a strong trend towards including learning, since learning is the most time consuming part of neural network operations which should be supported by parallel hardware. In some architectures a compromise is made by supporting parts of learning (forward-phase of calculations) on parallel analog circuitry with other parts done on the host computer, which is termed "learning in-the-loop".

Furthermore, in the following sections, the network type to be emulated will be used to separate early Hopfield network implementations and the signal representation technique to separate pulse-stream architectures.

8.2 Artificial Networks near to Biology

The biological nervous system is organized by highly connected simple cells (neurons). The unique nature of how these neural systems operate is characterized by low accuracy and high connectivity. A biological neuron is typically connected to several thousand other neurons. Such a high connectivity cannot be achieved with existing chip design methods.

Nevertheless, the major obstacle for designing hardware mimicking biological systems remains the lack of knowledge on the construction of the extremely complicated real neural system in the brain. Much research has been performed by scientists to build data preprocessing systems similar to real neural systems which are better known from biological and physiological research during the last decades. Some interesting work in copying early neural data preprocessing systems was done by Carver Mead and his group [Mead89]. He tried to implement certain preprocessing units of biological nervous systems (e.g. retina and cochlea).

8.2.1 Silicon Retina from Mead et al.

The retina provides neural signals based on the visual information of the eyes to the brain. It consists of six major elements, as shown in Figure 8.1 [Mead89]:

- photoreceptors
- horizontal cells
- triad synapses
- bipolar cells
- amacrine cells
- retinal ganglion cells.

Artificial Networks near to Biology   193

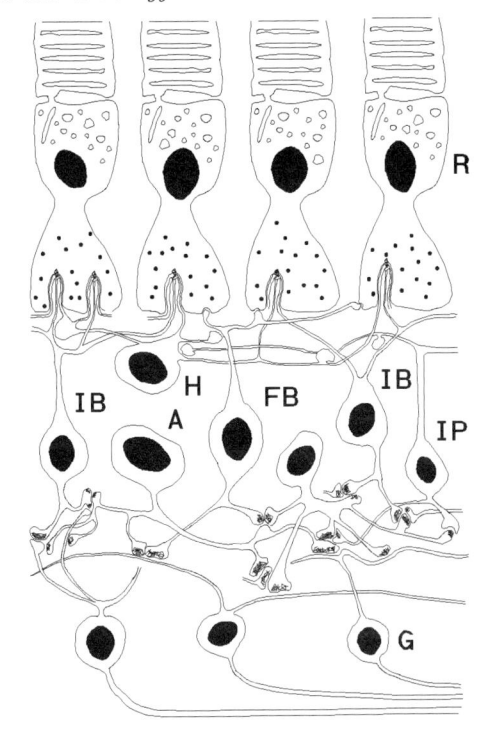

Figure 8.1 *Cross-section of a retina (adapted from [Mead89])*

Optical information received is transformed into electrical potentials, proportional to the logarithm of the intensity of light received by photoreceptors R at the beginning of the process. The responsibility of axonless neurons H, named horizontal cells, located beneath the photoreceptors is to average this electrical output spatially and temporally. Bipolar cells deliver an electrical signal proportional to the difference between the photoreceptor output and the averaged output of the horizontal cell. Retinal ganglion cells G are devoted to carrying the processed neural output to the brain. The triad synapses, which are located at the base of the photoreceptors, realize the point of contact among the photoreceptors, the horizontal cells and the bipolar cells.

Humans use their two eyes to derive more information about depth at close range (less than 1 to 2 meters). But at large distances, parallax caused by the movement of head is the most important depth cue available. The extraction of motion events is carried out by amacrine cells, another example of axonless cells. Silicon implementations of basic elements of the retina will be discussed in the following sections.

Photoreceptors

According to physiological investigations, the electrical output of biological photoreceptors of the retina is proportional to the logarithm of input light intensity. The voltage difference between two points in the photoreceptor field corresponds to the contrast ratio between the two related input points, which do not depend on the illumination level. In other words, the large light intensity range is compressed into an appropriate signal voltage range.

A photoreceptor in Mead's silicon retina consists of a photodetector and a logarithmic element [Mead89]. The photodetector converts the incoming light signals into an electrical photo current which drives the logarithmic element. The latter is designed as two diode connected MOS transistors operating in the subthreshold region.

The general equation for drain current I_D in a p-channel MOS transistor is

$$I_D = I_{sat} \cdot (1 - e^{\frac{qV_{DS}}{kT}}) \qquad (8.1)$$

(see Equation 5.2) with saturation current I_{sat} expressed by

$$I_{sat} = I_0 \cdot e^{-\frac{q}{kT}(\kappa V_G - V_S)}. \qquad (8.2)$$

Thus, V_{DS} is the transistor's drain-to-source voltage, V_G its gate potential, and V_S its source potential. Fabrication dependent constant κ is introduced to cope better with the real transistor behavior [Mead89]. From these equations, one can see that the saturation current of a MOS transistor driven in the subthreshold region is an exponential function of the gate voltage. In diode connected PMOS transistors, where $V_{GS} = V_G - V_S = V_{DS}$, the output voltage is logarithmic to the input saturation current delivered by the phototransistor. Two MOS transistors are used to ensure that the output voltage remains within the range of the input voltage to the horizontal cell layer under normal illumination.

Horizontal Cells

The range of illumination intensity in a visual image may be very large. If the global average is used as a reference in nervous visual systems, details in areas with very large and very little intensity cannot be identified. Horizontal cells compute a spatially weighted average of photoreceptor outputs, so that the differences in an image are identified locally by bipolar cells. Silicon horizontal cells are normally modeled as passive elements containing a weighting function which decreases exponentially with the distance. Therefore, photoreceptor outputs from points that are far away from any particular horizontal cell have less weight on it.

The horizontal cells are connected by high resistance gap junctions and, therefore, operate as a resistive network. Each photoreceptor is connected to its six neighbors via this network. A simple resistive connection is implemented by two pass transistors connected in series (see Figure 8.2). The

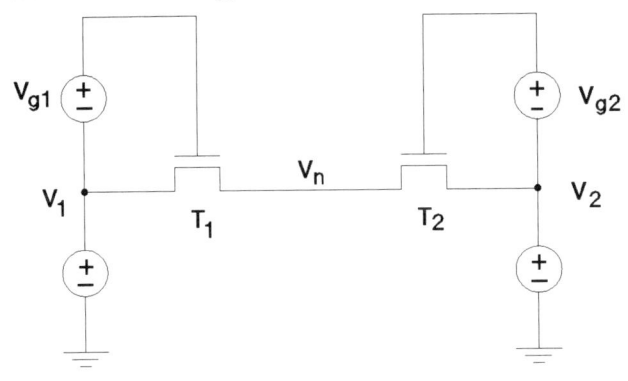

Figure 8.2 *Resistive connection of the horizontal resistor circuit (adapted from [Mead89])*

general equation for drain current I_D described above can be written for an NMOS transistor (formulas for n-channel devices can be derived by reversing voltage signs from p-channel formulas) as

$$I_D = I_{sat} \cdot (1 - e^{-\frac{qV_{DS}}{kT}}) \tag{8.3}$$

and the saturation current I_{sat} is

$$I_{sat} = I_0 \cdot e^{\frac{q}{kT}(\kappa V_G - V_S)}. \tag{8.4}$$

Interesting, however, is the question about the resistance of the element depicted in Figure 8.2, *i.e.* how current I depends on voltage $V_1 - V_2$ across the two transistors. In the case of $V_1 > V_2$, transistor $T2$ limits the current. For the opposite case, $T1$ is the current limiting element. Each node of the cell array contains a special bias circuit consisting of six transistors as shown in Figure 8.4 (T_1 to T_6) to adjust voltages V_{g1} and V_{g2}. Mead [Mead89] shows that current flow I through the resistive element of Figure 8.2 is

$$I = I_{sat} \cdot \tanh\left(\frac{V_1 - V_2}{2}\right). \tag{8.5}$$

Since the slope of the $tanh$ near the origin is unity, for small voltages $V_1 - V_2$ the effective resistance R can be expressed as

$$R = \frac{\frac{2kT}{q}}{I_{sat}}. \tag{8.6}$$

The resistance of the element is inversely proportional to saturation current I_{sat}.

Figure 8.3 shows a simplified schematic of the CMOS implementation of the horizontal network (one-dimensional cut). Horizontal resistances are denoted HR, and conductances are realized by transconductance amplifiers.

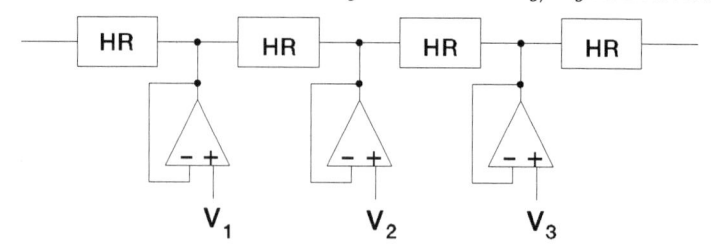

Figure 8.3 *CMOS implementation of the horizontal network (adapted from [Hut88])*

Thus, a signal generated at any network node will propagate to neighboring nodes diminished by resistances and conductances. Parasitic capacitances play a significant role in the time integration of signals in both biological and silicon horizontal cells. The capacitances of connecting elements to silicon substrate fulfil this task in a similar way to their biological counterparts.

Triad Synapse

In the model of the retina considered in Mead's implementations, the computation occurs as a result of the interaction of photoreceptors, horizontal cells and bipolar cells in the triad synapse. The biological triad synapse serves as an anatomical substrate for the computation. The silicon triad synapse consists of two elements:

- a wide-range amplifier to drive the resistive network towards the photoreceptor output potential

- a second amplifier that provides an output proportional to the difference between photoreceptor output and the voltage stored at the capacitance of the considered node of the horizontal resistive layer.

Wide-range amplifiers benefit from the advantages of higher gain and a wider range of output voltage (from GND to V_{DD}) than a simple transconductance amplifier. Several retina chips were fabricated using CMOS technology. The basic element for a pixel is depicted in Figure 8.4. Six pass transistors connected to the node biased by a common circuit consisting of transistors T_1 to T_6 at the upper left part of the circuit connect the pixel to its six neighbors (see also Figure 8.2). The bias circuit is a transconductance amplifier connected as a voltage follower plus diode connected transistor T_5. Input V_1 represents the voltage at a node or one end of the resistive connection. The voltage at the source of T_5 follows input voltage V_1 using the negative feedback connection at T_2. Bias voltage V_{g1} follows the node voltage with a positive offset of the magnitude of the drain/source across T_5. Considering the current mirror, one can see that half of the current

Artificial Networks near to Biology

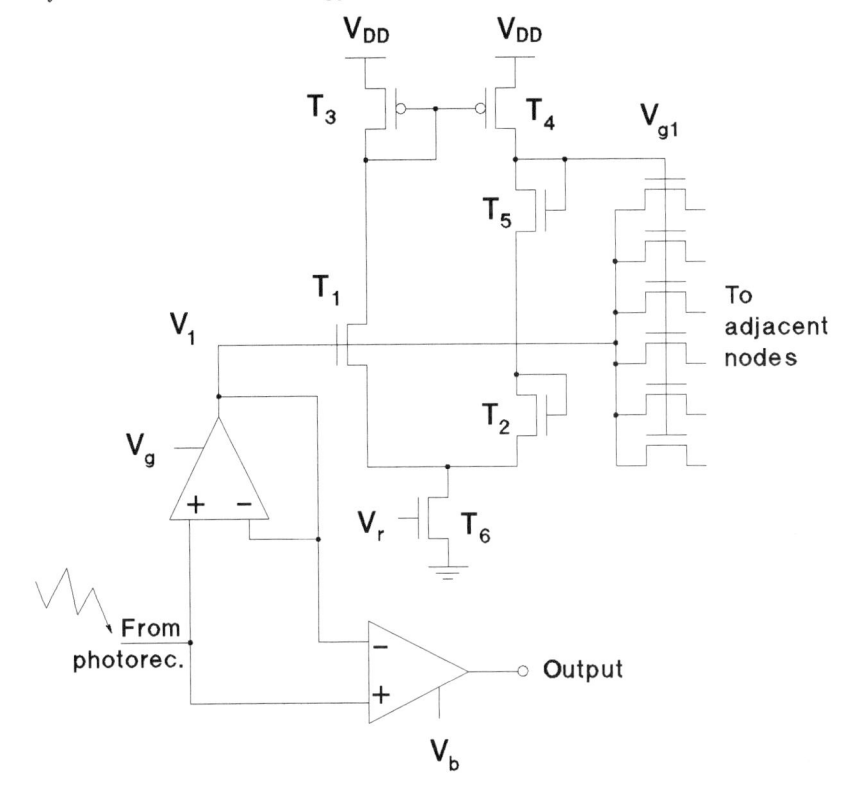

Figure 8.4 *Basic element for a pixel (adapted from [Mead89])*

through T_6 flows via T_5. The voltage across T_5, which is equal to voltage difference $V_{g1} - V_1$, is dependent on this current. Therefore, voltage V_r can be used to control the conductance of the resistive connections to the neighbors. The output of the logarithmic photoreceptor is the input to the circuit in the lower left corner. The follower-connected transconductance amplifier represents the conductance for the node of the resistive network.

Implementation of Retina Chips

Three different retina chips consisting of core cells RET10, RET20, and RET30 were fabricated by Sivilotti *et al.* [Siv87]. Table 8.1 compares the pixel areas, array sizes and performance of the core cells. Logarithmic photoreceptors operating at light levels comparable to the useful range of cones in a human retina form the basis of the RET10 chip. Sample outputs from the RET10 chip indicate the advantage of logarithmic compression performed by photoreceptors. Motion is perceived in biological retinas through the detection of non-zero spatial and temporal derivatives. The simplest

Chip	Pixel size (μm × μm)	Array size	Signal-to-noise ratio
RET10	92 × 80	88 × 88	62
RET20	113 × 98	64 × 64	70
RET30	164 × 143	48 × 48	60

Table 8.1 *Performance of silicon retina core cells*

way of highlighting moving areas of an image is to compute a local time derivative. A discrete time derivative can be computed by comparing the present photoreceptor output with a delayed copy of the output. A discrete time differentiator with an integrated photoreceptor, which enables moving parts of an image to be identified, forms the core of the RET20 chip.

The RET30 core circuit (see Figure 2.1) is inspired by the operation of horizontal cells in biological retinas. It uses continuous time derivatives and local space derivatives for the computation of moving parts in an image. This circuit consists of an array of receptors R, interconnected by a hexagonal resistor network. Temporal smoothing is achieved by connecting each junction of six neighboring horizontal resistors to ground via a capacitor. The horizontal network computes to what extent light received by a receptor may differ from the average light intensity in its neighborhood. A test image with a dark cross mounted on a rotating axis was processed by the RET30 circuit and its output observed. By disabling the horizontal network no image was seen at the output. However, after enabling the horizontal network, the cross rotating at approximately 10 rotations per minute was clearly visible.

8.2.2 Electronic Cochlea

Biological Background

The biological cochlea is the spiral shaped three-dimensional part of the mammalian inner ear [DAR89] which acts as the interface between the incoming sound waves and the neural signals in the auditory centers of the brain. It consists of a stiff partition called the basilar membrane separating the fluid filled spiral shaped tube lengthwise into two ducts; one with an oval-shaped membrane and the other with a round membrane. Both of them connect the cochlea acoustically to the middle ear cavity.

The middle ear ossicle couples sound from the eardrum into the oval-shaped membrane, called the "oval window" of the tube. When the oval window is pushed in by a sound wave, the incompressible fluid in the cochlea

Artificial Networks near to Biology 199

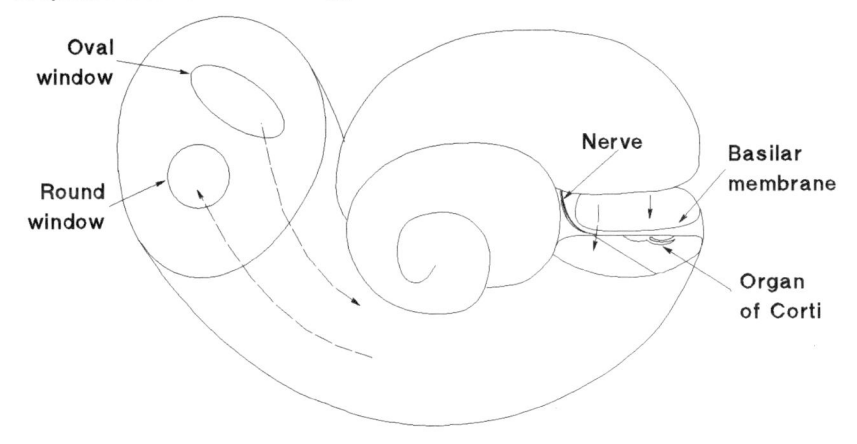

Figure 8.5 *Biological Cochlea (adapted from [Mead89])*

moves down the length of the cochlea and comes back through the other duct-membrane, called the "round-window" causing a traveling pressure pulse that distorts the basilar membrane in the form of a standing wave.

The "mechanical-neural transducers" of the auditory system called hair cells that sit in a structure known as the organ of corti (see Figure 8.5) detect the distortion of the basilar membrane. The inner hair cells act as a filter and the outer cells operate as part of an active amplifier and automatic gain control (AGC) system.

The conversion of sound energy to hydrodynamic waves and the propagation of the fluid in ducts separated by the basilar membrane is a distributed form of a low pass filter action. Hence, when the wave propagates, high frequencies are attenuated. Some frequencies are amplified at low sound levels, due to the energy added by the outer hair cells. Therefore, signals detected by inner hair cells are essentially a bandpass-filtered version of the original sound.

The outer hair cells are three times larger in number as the inner hair cells in the inner ear. In the absence of any intervention of the outer hair cells, the response in the basilar membrane is reasonably damped. Additional energy fed back by outer hair cells reduces damping until signals reaching higher levels of the auditory nervous system are large enough.

Implementation

A real-time model of the cochlea was fabricated by Mead and his group in CMOS VLSI analog technology in 1988. The silicon cochlea takes real sound as input in order to produce output that resembles the signals on the cochlea nerve. The physics of the fluid-dynamic traveling-wave system of the biological cochlea is emulated in its silicon counterpart by a cascade of second-order filter stages with controllable parameters.

The most important structure of the cochlea, the basilar membrane, is constructed as a transmission line with the ability to electrically tune the velocity of propagation (see Figure 8.6). Second-order filter circuits based on CMOS transconductance amplifiers and capacitors are used as delay elements of the transmission lines to emulate the dynamics of the second-order system of fluid mass and membrane stiffness. Signal output taps located at intervals along the line can be regarded as inner hair cells.

A second-order filter circuit is based on two cascaded transconductance amplifiers, with a third transconductance amplifier realizing a positive feedback. Furthermore, two capacitors are present (for further information see [Mead89]). The transfer function $H(s)$ of the second-order transconductance amplifier configuration is given by

$$H(s) = \frac{V_{out}}{V_{in}} = \frac{1}{\tau^2 s^2 + 2\tau s(1-\alpha) + 1}. \quad (8.7)$$

Thus, τ is a time constant depending on circuit capacitors and transconductances of the two cascaded amplifiers, whereas α is a proportion between feedback amplifier transconductance and cascaded amplifier

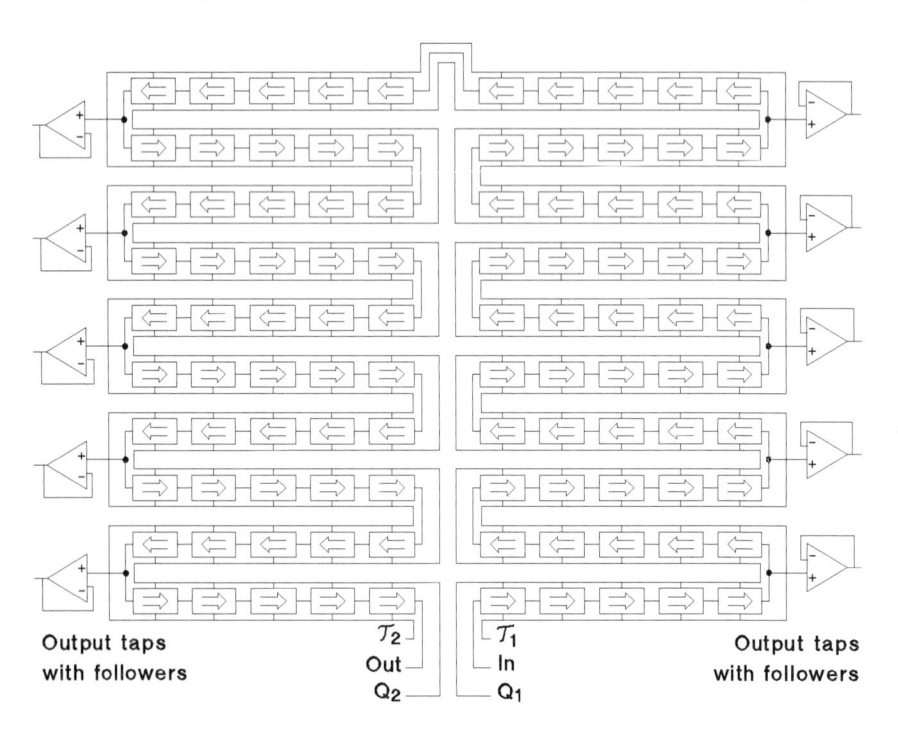

Figure 8.6 Cochlea architecture (adapted from [Lyo88b, Mead89])

transconductances. Therefore, parameters τ and α may easily be changed by influencing the bias currents of the amplifiers. The τ and α inputs are connected to polysilicon lines, where a linear gradient in voltage along each line can be achieved. A linear gradient in voltage along lines turns into exponential gradients in the delay per element. This causes a variation in propagation velocity and cuts off frequency exponentially along the transmission lines.

8.2.3 SeeHear

Blind people use the sound cues of nature more intensively to identify their surroundings. SeeHear is an artificial system designed by Mead *et al.* that could enhance this effect in order to create a detailed internal model of their surroundings for blind people [Mead89]. This was fabricated as a single analog CMOS chip onto which visual information is projected. It maps visual signals from moving objects in the projected image into sound signals which may be experienced by a listener through earphones. Three tasks of SeeHear are:

- conversion of varying visual signals to corresponding electrical signals
- processing of extracted electrical signals to emphasize temporal changes in the image
- creating sound signals that could help listeners to identify their surroundings.

A two-dimensional projection of a visual scene must be processed in such a way that the extracted electrical information can be transferred into an acoustic signal coded in two channels without losing the information that helps to reconstruct scene depth. The concept of the SeeHear chip is shown in Figure 8.7.

Visual System

Similar to the retina, a two-dimensional array of pixels, where the location of each pixel corresponds to the location of a particular feature of the scene, encodes the positional and intensity information of the projected image. Each pixel consists of a photoreceptor and a processing element. The visual system converts the incoming light signals with an analog logarithm of intensity and then performs the analog time derivative. Local information processing ensures the preservation of directional information. The logarithmic characteristic of output voltage provides the possibility of having a voltage difference proportional to the contrast ratio, independent of the illumination level of the screen. The schematic of the pixel processor is shown in Figure 8.8. The output of the photoreceptor feeds wide range transconductance amplifier A. Amplifier A with a diode connected p-channel and n-channel transistors and the capacitor, is called an

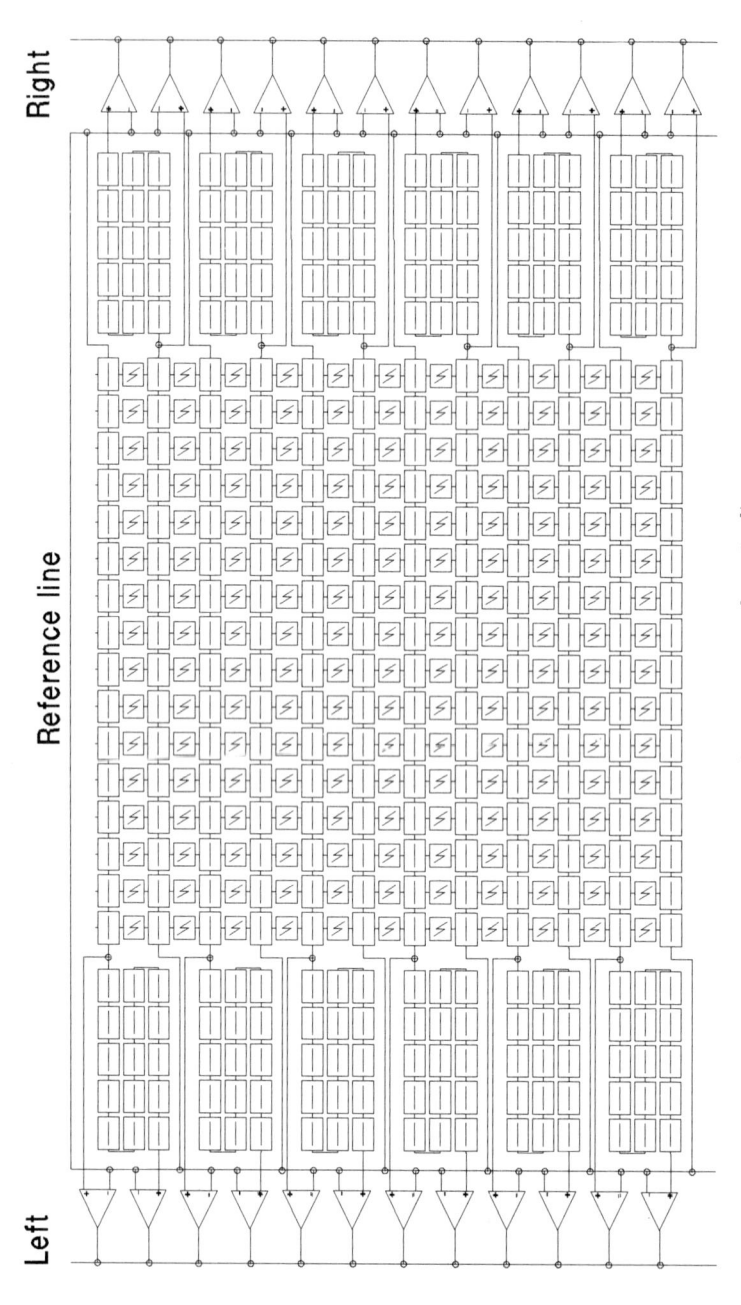

Figure 8.7 Concept of the SeeHear chip (adapted from [Mead89])

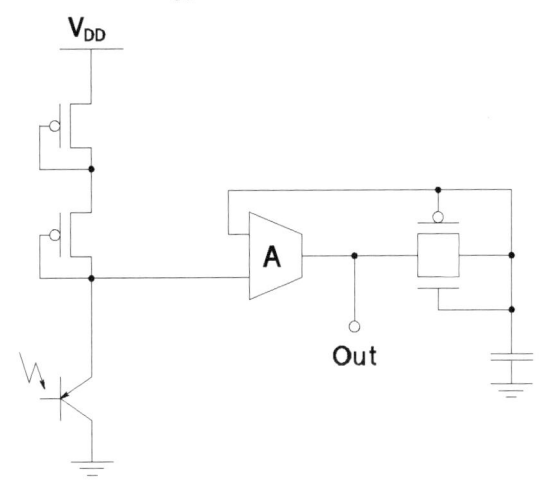

Figure 8.8 *The pixel processor (adapted from [Mead89])*

hysteric differentiator [Mead89]. The hysteric differentiator has many desirable properties similar to those of its biological counterpart. For small input waveforms the output will be the replica gained of the input. For large input waveforms the hysteric differentiator delivers the analog time derivative. It generates large excursions in output voltage when the derivative of the input voltage changes its sign. Therefore, maximum outputs will occur when high contrast features move over the retina.

The visual centers of the brain construct a three-dimensional model based on spatiotemporal patterns of signals received from the retina. To a large extent, vertebrates derive the third dimension or the depth information from the relative motion of objects in the retinal image caused by an animal's own movement (motion parallax) [Lor81] [Ric75]. Humans use binocular stereopsis (due to two eyes) to provide additional information about depth at close range. The relative motion information of the scene is emphasized by the computed analog time derivatives of the varying signals.

Hearing System

The sounds representing visual information should appear to the listener as if they had come from different physical locations, corresponding to the different light sources of the projected image. Auditory psychophysiological research work on sound localization by humans is also interested in synthesizing acoustic cues. A sound cue from a source must propagate through the air and around the head to reach both ears. The sound is then reflected by the pinna and tragus of the outer ear before entering the ear canal to reach the ear drum, which gives the input signal to the inner ear.

Changes in sound received by the left and right ears provide the cues to locating the sound source. These may be categorized as:

- horizontal localization cues

- vertical localization cues.

Horizontal localization cues are due to the attenuation of high frequencies during travel around the head and the difference in arrival time caused by the difference in path length. Vertical localization is possible due to the existence of different paths in the pinna and tragus of the outer ear. One path may be considered as direct and without reflections. The second path is longer due to the possibility that incoming sound bounces from the pinna to the tragus before entering the ear canal. Signals traveling in both paths combine in the ear canal. This may also cause destructive interference of the incoming sound if the difference in path is one-half the wave length. Although the shape of the outer ear is not the same for all humans, the length of the time delay caused by pinna and tragus is always a monotonic function of elevation. In contrast to the visual system where localization is done in an early stage (in retina), the auditory system uses temporal patterns of signals in the two cochleas to build a two-dimensional representation of the acoustic environment in the higher auditory centers in order to localize the sound source.

The design of an electronic circuit which creates the illusion of an auditory source situated horizontally to both ears is depicted in Figure 8.9. Via two delay lines the signal source is connected to the ears. The time delay per unit length in lines can be electronically controlled. If the left delay line is shorter than the right delay line, the pulse signal generated by the auditory-cue generator will appear at the left output first. As the sound pulses travel along the delay line, higher frequencies are filtered out. The more the length of a delay line is, the larger the attenuation of higher frequencies will be. The output of this device can be connected to earphones giving the listener the illusion of an existing horizontal auditory source closer to his left-hand side. Considering the superposition theory, multiple auditory sources can be connected as an arrangement generating horizontal cues for a number of sources at different apparent angles.

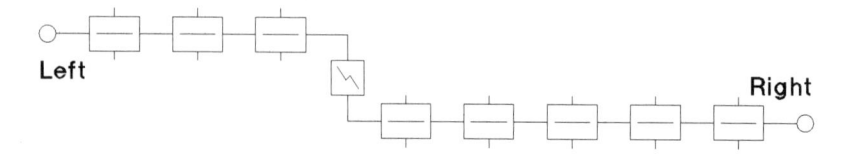

Figure 8.9 *A horizontally located sound source oriented on the left side (adapted from [Mead89])*

Artificial Networks near to Biology 205

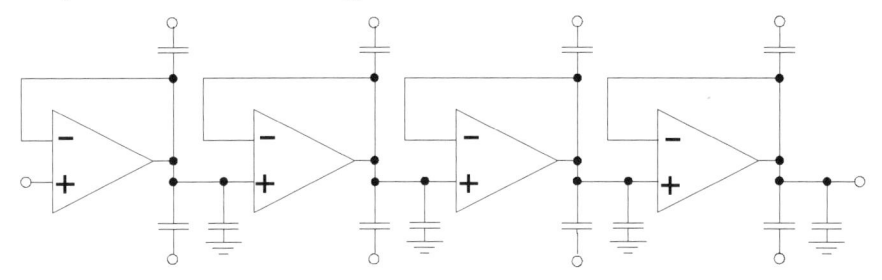

Figure 8.10 *Implementation of delay line (adapted from [Mead89])*

Analog delay lines of horizontal localization cue generators are implemented as long strings of follower integrator sections, as shown in Figure 8.10. The current that reaches the capacitor is proportional to the difference between the input and output voltages. By varying the transconductance amplifier, the delay of each unit can be changed. The delay is proportional to the number of sections whereas the bandwidth of the line is inversely proportional to the square root of the number of sections.

The pinna-tragus vertical localization cue can be modeled as a result of a direct path and a reflected path by which sound can be delayed slightly relative to the direct path. The output of the modeled section is the sum of the signal and a delayed copy of the signal. The reflected path may be controlled by setting the delay according to the apparent elevation angle of the sound cue. Delay-add sections of the pinna-tragus model act as final sections of the analog delay line. Each pinna-tragus model consists of 18 delay sections which vary as a function of elevation. Each delay can be set by the time constant of the section that is controlled separately from the analog delay line. The dependency of pinna-tragus delay on the elevation is realized by connecting transconductance control lines to a polysilicon line, and applying different voltages to the two ends of the line to achieve the gradient which corresponds to the delay desired.

Both horizontal and vertical localization cue generating models can be combined to present sound through earphones to a listener giving the illusion of sound sources localized in space.

8.2.4 Interface Networks to the Natural Brain

An example of a network providing an interface to the natural brain is the surgical implantation of artificial neuroreceptors in humans who are deaf because of damaged receptors. Recent developments in surgical techniques permit the implantation of electrodes which can stimulate the auditory nerves of humans.

The Purdue Artificial Receptor (PAR1) developed at Purdue University is a real-time artificial receptor that couples processed sound signals via external induction coils to implanted electrodes [Was90]. Input signals received by a microphone feed an anti-aliasing low pass filter stage with a cut-off frequency of 20 kHz. An A/D converter with 12 bit resolution converts the analog output of the filter stage maintaining a dynamic range that exceeds 70 dB. A digital signal processor (DSP) processes digital signals according to 20 PAR codes stored in a programmable read-only memory (PROM). The DSP runs PAR codes at a sampling rate of 30 kHz.

The D/A with 12 bit resolution converts the processed digital signal to the analog input of the output conditioner which consists of a low pass filter and a level conditioner.

8.2.5 Central Pattern Generators

Ryckebush et al. [Ryc89] used analog VLSI technology to model a class of biological neural circuits known as central pattern generators (CPGs). CPGs are specialized small neural networks that generate rhythmic patterns of activity that control the motor output of the brain. Researchers have identified that CPGs govern many different motor activities of animals. Examples are:

- swimming in the leech
- mastication in the lobster
- flying in the locust.

Although most of the biologically well described CPGs are found in invertebrates (due to their lower complexity compared with mammals), it is evident that CPGs can be found in all animals. The major problem in designing complex CPGs of vertebrates is to understand the organizing principles behind them.

A general-purpose CPG neuron circuit with dimensions of 50×400 μm^2 which produces some important mechanisms of biological CPG neurons, was designed, fabricated and tested by Ryckebush et al. [Ryc89]. The circuit fabricated in standard CMOS technology is shown in Figure 8.11. Each chip contains a number of these circuits, of which all the inputs and control lines are routed to pads, so that different CPG networks can be connected externally. The proposed neuron model can be used to construct biologically well defined small models of CPGs.

Delay lines play a significant role in CPGs. A number of methods of implementing delays have evolved in biological neural networks. One way is the use of the direct impact of time constants associated with biological mechanisms such as the membrane capacitance of the cell body, different rates of chemical reactions, and the transmission in axons. The delay line in the CPG circuit proposed is modeled as an RC integrator, implemented by cascading follower integrator circuits, as shown in the dashed part of

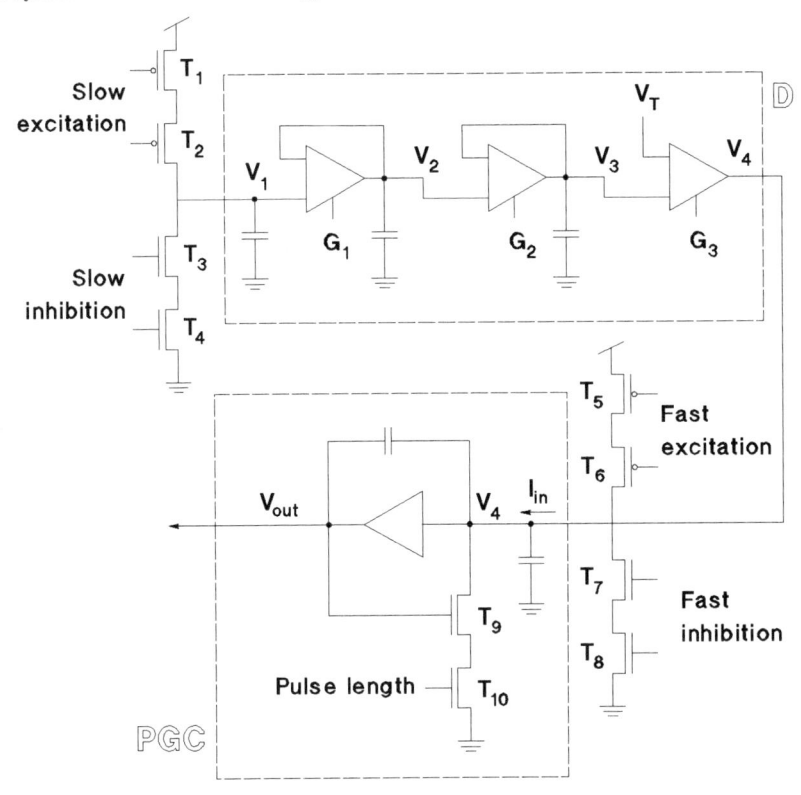

Figure 8.11 The general purpose CPG neuron circuit (adapted from [Ryc89])

Figure 8.11. The delay line has three time constants, set by transconductances $G1$, $G2$ and $G3$ of the amplifiers. Voltage V_T sets the threshold for the neuron.

The pulse-generating circuit (PGC) shown in Figure 8.11 integrates the current, and employs a positive feedback to deliver pulses whose frequency depend on the magnitude of the input current. Whenever the output voltage of this circuit is high enough to switch on transistor T_9, capacitors start to discharge via transistors T_9 and T_{10}. The gate voltage of transistor T_{10} can be used to control pulse length.

Synapses are modeled as transistor pairs connected before and behind the delay line (from T_1 to T_8). In each synapse one transistor controls the magnitude of the synaptic current. Currents flowing through p-channel transistors increase I_{in}, increasing a neuron's firing rate. In contrast, currents flowing through n-channel transistor pairs decrease I_{in}, decreasing the pulse rate. Therefore, p-channel transistor pairs model excitatory synapses, whereas n-channel transistor pairs represent inhibitory synapses. Synapses

T_1/T_2 and T_3/T_4 connected before the delay line have their excitatory or inhibitory impact on the circuit later than synapses T_5/T_6 and T_7/T_8, connected behind the delay line.

The proposed CPG neuron circuit can be configured externally to model different types of cells or circuits. One of the important cells in many biological oscillatory circuits is the endogenous bursting neuron. The intrinsic oscillatory membrane potential of this biological cell enables the delivery of bursts of action potentials which can be considered as periodic pulse signals. Figure 8.12 illustrates the CPG neuron circuit configured to fit the characteristics of the endogenous bursting neuron. Delay line D must have three time constants for stable oscillation. Internal negative feedback is used, *i.e.* the output of the pulse-generating circuit is fed to the input of the slow inhibitory synapse. But in biological cells, this negative feedback is accomplished by using ionic currents caused by membrane voltage or intracellular ionic contractions [Mee79].

The endogenous bursting neuron displays a property common to many neurons, known as postinhibitory rebound. These neurons show increased excitation for a certain period after the removal of inhibition. This enables neurons to synchronize patterns of oscillations following the release of the inhibitory influence. The cell's fast inhibitory synapse is fed by a square wave to produce postinhibitory rebound. When inhibition is released, the cell shows postinhibitory rebound due to the charge built up on intermediate node V_3 of the delay line (see also Figure 8.11).

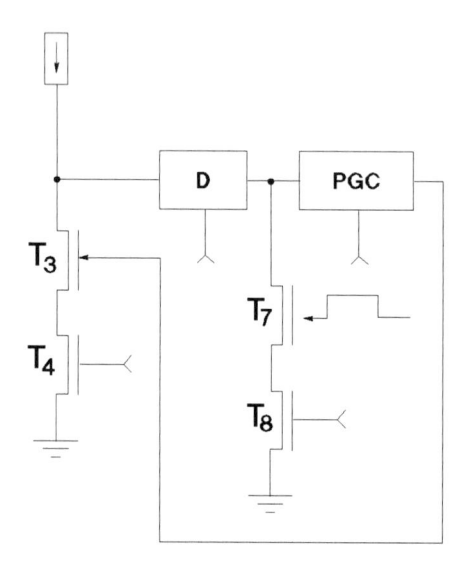

Figure 8.12 *The endogenous bursting neuron with postinhibitory rebound (adapted from [Ryc89])*

Artificial Networks near to Biology 209

One important type of interaction between two neurons in several CPGs, known as reciprocal inhibition, delivers an interesting pulse pattern, with neurons firing alternately. This pattern exploits the effect of postinhibitory rebound to recover from inhibition quickly, enabling the production of a stable alternate-firing pattern. Some biological examples of reciprocal inhibition are:

- movement of teeth in the lobster stomach controlled by the stomatogastric ganglion CPGs [Ryc89]
- heart contraction in the leech [Pet83]
- walking in the cockroach [Pea76]
- controlling swimming in *Tritonia* [Get85].

The lobster stomatogastric ganglion CPG controls the movement of teeth in the lobster stomach. PD- and LP-cells in this CPG produce an alternating burst pattern as illustrated in Figure 2.2, which is modeled using two circuits of the proposed endogenous bursting neuron with postinhibitory rebound (Figure 8.12). Instead of feeding fast inhibitory synapses with a square wave, the output of the second neuron is fed into a synapse, *i.e.* each neuron output is connected to transistor T_7 of the other neuron. Hence, the two cells inhibit each other reciprocally, creating an alternating pulse pattern [Ryc89].

Two cells with a delay element and an inverter are used to create the motor pattern for flight in the locust, as shown in Figure 8.13. Similar to reciprocal inhibition, a phase relationship exists between the cells. When the wings of the locust are elevated *cell1* is active, whereas *cell2* is active

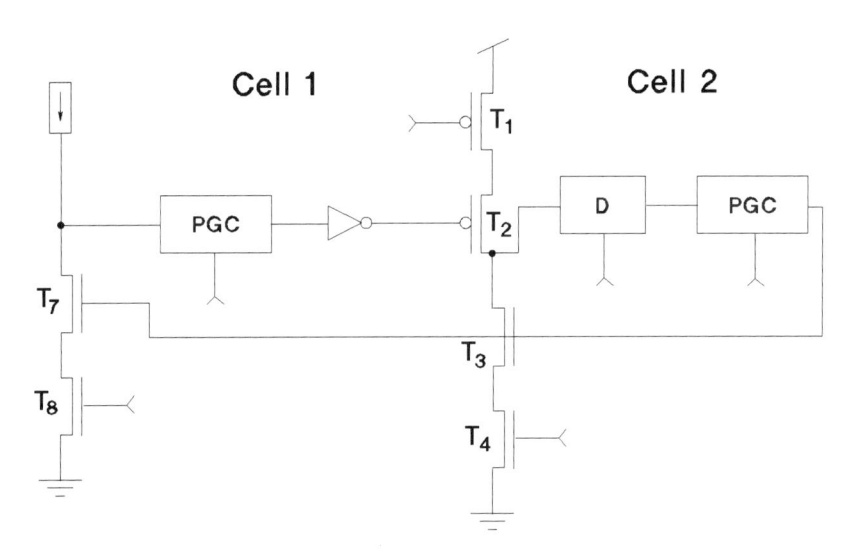

Figure 8.13 *The circuit model for flight in the locust (adapted from [Ryc89])*

when the wings are depressed. The delayed and inverted output of *cell1* makes an excitatory input to *cell2*, whereas the output of *cell2* feeds a fast inhibitory synapse of *cell1*. When *cell1* fires, *cell2* begins to fire after some delay. After *cell2* has fired, *cell1* is deactivated quickly. The deactivation of *cell1* removes the excitatory input to *cell2* after some delay, releasing the inhibition on *cell1*. This cycle repeats, producing two phase shifted periodic pulse patterns which are similar to simultaneous intracellular recordings of biological CPG cells during flight.

8.3 Cellular Neural Networks

8.3.1 Cellular Automata

The ability to change cell characteristics depending only on the occurrence of events in the local cell environment (cells in the neighborhood) is already known from living cell arrays (e.g. reproduction of cells) or natural effects (e.g. development of a snowflake). This phenomenon of nature is the key feature of synchronized cellular automata working in parallel.

Cellular automata machines [Tof88] are made of a number of regularly spaced, equally organized cells which communicate with each other directly only through their nearest neighbors. Two different neighborhood definitions are:

- the von Neumann definition
- the Moore definition.

Von Neumann defined the nearest neighbors of a cell as those cells that have a common edge with it. Moore considered the cells with a common corner to the actual cell as its nearest neighbors. A cell can have a finite number of states that depend on the previous states of its closest neighbors and itself. A cell array may be organized in any number of dimensions with any kind of topology. The most common topology is the two-dimensional squared array. Application areas of cellular techniques can be identified as:

- changing characteristics of magnetic materials with temperature variations
- simulation of spread of diseases (e.g. AIDS research)
- simulation of theoretical models in immunology (e.g. reaction of different living cells on viruses and bacteria)
- cellular neural networks.

8.3.2 Neural Networks as Cellular Automata

Considerable work on cellular neural networks was done by Chua and and some other researchers [Chu88a, Fau90, Fau91]. In contrast to other massively connected neural networks, CNNs have the advantages of local

Cellular Neural Networks

connectivity and quite simple determination and presetting of the dynamic range. The ability of logically connecting a cell to another cell of the array or to the outside is given without the need for global information.

Although simply programmable software implementations of CNNs are available, they suffer from high processing time (few seconds) and a small number of cells (up to 1000) [Rosk91]. The locality of connections among the cells make CNNs ideally suited for implementation in VLSI technology, both analog and digital. In a programmable analog/digital mixed realization, beside capacitors which provide a variable template sequence with feedback, digital memories are used to store the results [Rosk91]. Analog implementations have less processing time (less than 1 μs) than digital implementations (in the millisecond range).

Analog Realizations

Analog CNNs can be categorized as fixed template and programmable (variable template) realizations. Programmable realizations occupy a larger area and have higher power dissipation than fixed template realizations. A typical example of a simple fixed template realization is illustrated below.

Nonprogrammable Networks Chua proposed a cellular architecture which performs parallel signal processing in real-time. The structure of the architecture is similar to that of cellular automata (an example of a two-dimensional 4 × 4 network is shown in Figure 8.14). The major difference

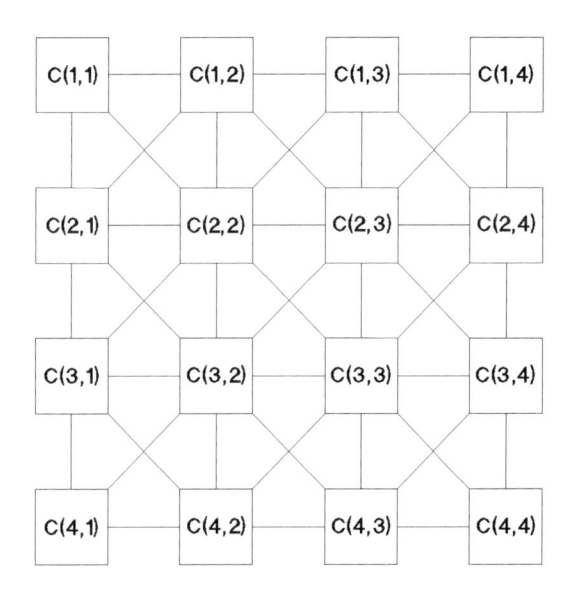

Figure 8.14 *A two-dimensional squared cellular array based on Moore's definition of neighborhood (adapted from [Chu88a])*

between a cellular automat and the proposed cellular network is that the dynamical behavior of the former is time discrete while that of the latter is time continuous. Each cell of the proposed cellular neural network contains linear passive elements, linear and nonlinear voltage controlled current sources, and independent voltage and current sources.

Applications of this network are in image processing and pattern recognition. For such tasks, the cellular network operates as a two-dimensional filter. Unlike conventional two-dimensional digital filters, it uses parallel processing, and delivers its output in continuous time.

Programmable Networks Programming of networks occurs through continuous or step-wise control of key elements (e.g. transconductance amplifiers) [Halo90]. A programmable time discrete analog chip set was proposed by Harrer et al. Two different chips were used to compute time dependent and time independent parts of the CNN dynamics. Using 1.5 μm standard double metal CMOS technology, a density of 1200 cells/cm^2 can be achieved [Rosk90b]. The performance of the chip set, 89 million connection updates per second (MCUPS), can be favorably compared with the computing power of a fully connected electrically trainable analog neural network ETANN chip with 64 neurons.

Digital Realizations

Almost all digital implementations of CNNs are programmable. Several digital realizations of other types of neural networks can also be applied to build a CNN structure. Systolic type VLSI chips implemented, for instance, by Ramacher et al. [Ram90], can be considered as key elements to build a CNN system. A board consisting of 16 × 16 units can perform with a speed of 1280 MCUPS [Rosk91]. Another proposal is to exploit Intel's 16-bit reduced instruction set computer (RISC) chips for computation of the transient response of the cells in a CNN structure [Rosk91].

The hardware accelerator board (to be used with an IBM PC) proposed by Roska et al. [Rosk90a] consists of digital processors which are assigned to a vertical stripe of cells. Each of the four processor blocks of the implementation has its own local dynamic memory (CMOS DRAMs). Digital signal processors (DSPs) were used as processing blocks to compute the transient response of a single layer CNN array with $0.25 - 0.5$ million cells. Programmable logic devices (PLDs) were applied as controller, and FIFOs were used for interprocessor communication [Rosk90a].

An algorithm like backpropagation that operates on local information can be implemented using cellular automata techniques. An asynchronous two-dimensional cellular array for a multilayer perceptron with the backpropagation algorithm was proposed by Faure et al. [Fau90]. Each cell is directly connected to its four neighbors (von Neumann neighborhood) through eight unidirectional buffers, one for each possible direction of communication.

The logical connection of a cell to another cell or to the outside is handled by a message routing mechanism distributed among cells. A message consists of a data field containing the information to be processed and a routing field containing the information needed for dynamic routing. A message is passed to one of the neighbors until it reaches its correct destination. Its path is set dynamically in each cell without processing global information. This is done by updating relative displacements "dx" and "dy" from the current cell to the destination in each passed-through cell.

A primary version of the cell with a limited (connectivity) fan-in and fan-out of 8 was implemented using VLSI technology. The performance of a simulated 65×65 cellular array of eight connectivity cells (51.4 MCUPS) was better than other non-dedicated machines like the 20 node Warp array (32 MCUPS) in the NETtalk application from Sejnowski et al. [Sej86].

8.4 Early NMOS and CMOS Hopfield Network Implementations

Conventional associative memory circuits have two major disadvantages [Koh88, Siv86]:

- an exact key input has to be supplied

- additional circuits are needed for the resolution of multiple associations

A key input, normally a part of the contents, must be supplied exactly for the occurrence of associations. Additional circuitry representing a serial polling algorithm is essential for the resolution of multiple matches, slowing down memory speed. This is different in neural associative memories like Hopfield networks. They are well suited for pattern recognition and completion tasks. Thus, the whole input vector serves as a key, there is no further distinction between key and associated information. Due to their recurrent structure (all outputs are fed back to inputs) analog implementations perfectly fit to emulate networks. Since no clock signal is necessary to synchronize operations and analog signals are directly fed back to inputs without any discretization, extremely high computational power is achieved. Hopfield networks were favored in early implementations due to their simplicity. They can be programmed by simple Hebbian learning (but only very few approaches included on-chip learning), and even operate with low weight accuracy (ternary synapses). However, Hopfield networks are of historical and mathematical significance. They are not usually used in real applications due to problems with spurious states (especially in large networks and with partially correlated training vectors) and low storage capacity. Only very small networks were implemented.

8.4.1 ASSOCMEM Chip

ASSOCMEM is an early associative memory implementation developed by Sivilotti et al. [Siv86]. The emulated associative network is of the Hopfield type.

To enable a simple electronic representation of negative signals and negative weights, a dual-line architecture was chosen. Thus, inhibitory and excitatory signals are summed and carried on two distinct lines. To connect the output of neuron j with the input of neuron i, Sivilotti et al. used ternary synapses with digital weight storage in a triflop T_{ij}. Figure 8.15 sketches the circuit architecture. The output of neuron j is carried by line V_j, whereas $\overline{V_j}$ carries the inverted output signal. To allow for four-quadrant multiplication, the synapse circuit in Figure 8.15 is separated into four parts. Pass transistors in each corner control the connection paths from neuron j to neuron i. Depending on the state of triflop T_{ij}, either the noninverted neuron j output is given on the positive or negative neuron i input, or the inverted neuron j output is given to the desired neuron i input. Hence, a four-quadrant multiplication between a neuron's output and a ternary weight value is obtained. An additional global $ENABLE$ signal may enable or disable the whole synapse circuit via switch transistors.

The complete synapse circuit from Sivilotti et al. contains some additional circuitry. This was added to permit on-chip learning. A simple adder circuit was connected to the triflop which allows outer product learning.

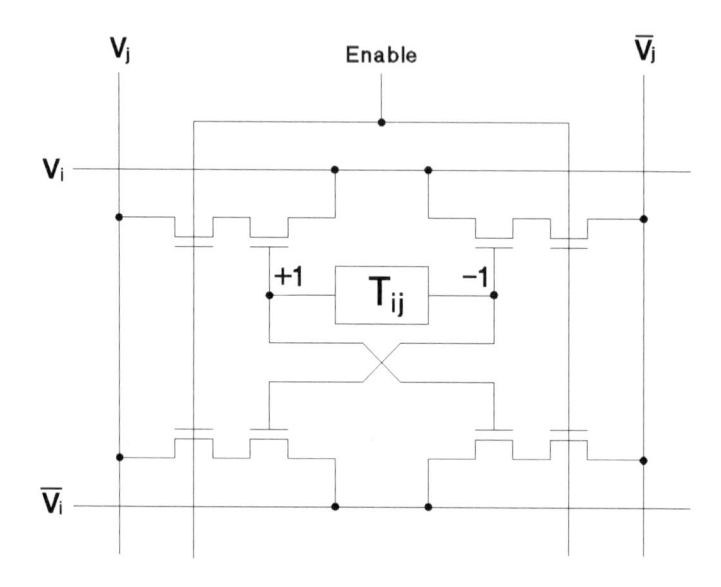

Figure 8.15 *Resistive interconnect controlled by a tri-flop (adapted from [Siv86])*

Early NMOS and CMOS Hopfield Network Implementations 215

Since only three weight states are available (states $-1, 0, +1$), the result of the add operation has to be truncated.

Neurons in the design presented were emulated by simple differential amplifiers. These amplifiers provide two inputs for the arriving inhibitory and excitatory summing line, as well as a noninverting and inverting output.

The first version of the ASSOCMEM was fabricated in 1983 in 4 μm NMOS technology consisting of a 22 × 22 matrix on an area of 6700×5700 μm^2 containing more than 20,000 transistors.

8.4.2 Digital/Analog Memory Chip from Graf et al.

Graf *et al.* [Graf87a, Graf87b] implemented an early digital/analog associative memory chip. The network implemented was a fully connected Hopfield type feedback network. To enable simple weight storage on user modifiable synapse circuits, weight values are stored digitally using standard RAM circuitry. Furthermore, all input/output interfaces to and from the chip are digital.

Figure 8.16 depicts a synapse circuit. On two RAM cells ternary weight storage is possible. If the upper RAM cell is active (carries a "1"), transistor T_E allows a current entering the current summing line from V_{DD} via load element T_{LP} and switch transistor T_{TP}. This current would have excitatory effects on the following neuron circuit. On the other hand, if the lower RAM cell is active a corresponding current can be drawn from the summing line towards ground having inhibitory effects. No current can flow if both RAM cells are inactive. However, to have the correct state of RAM cells only is not sufficient to generate inhibitory or excitatory effects. It is also necessary to open switches T_{TP} and T_{JN}. Their gates are controlled by the preceding neuron's outputs (neuron j with one negative and one positive output). If the neuron is active, *i.e.* its positive output OUT_j carries a "1", its negative output $\overline{OUT_j}$ a "0", both switches are open and the synapse is active. Hence, a simple multiplication of a binary neuron output with a ternary synapse value is performed. A problem in such a design is to guarantee that all currents delivered from different synapses are nearly equal in magnitude. Most problems in current differences are caused by the use of n-type and p-type MOS transistors, which are both difficult to design providing equal conductivity. If currents in the whole network are not of equal magnitude, the maximum number of neurons is limited significantly. The larger the differences are, the less neurons may be implemented due to increasing inaccuracies in analog computations.

As shown in Figure 8.17, neurons are realized by simple inverters. Two inverters represent one neuron having a positive and a negative output. Additional circuitry at neuron outputs provides a digital interface to the outer world. From the interface, weight states may be loaded onto the chip,

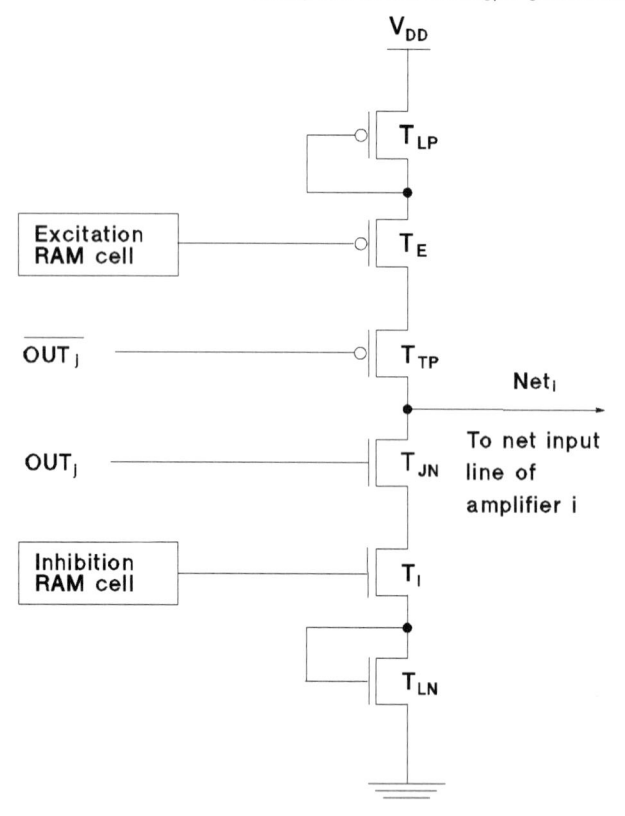

Figure 8.16 *Programmable coupling element proposed by Graf (adapted from [Graf87c])*

neuron states may be initialized, and neuron outputs read after network stabilization.

A chip was fabricated with 2.5 μm technology containing roughly 75,000 transistors on an area of 6.7×6.7 mm^2. Almost 90% of the chip area is used for the coupling network. Analog computation is used only within the array of weight elements and neurons but all input, output and control data is digital. A total of 54 neurons fitted onto the chip die. Stabilization time of the circuit is within a few hundred nanoseconds.

A problem of Hopfield networks is the formation of spurious states if several vectors are to be stored. To avoid such unwanted states, Graf *et al.* made a modified architecture with additional neurons called label units [Graf87a]. Thus, a label unit was associated with each vector to be programmed. Through a special interconnection scheme an active label unit suppresses other label units to become active, guaranteeing the activation

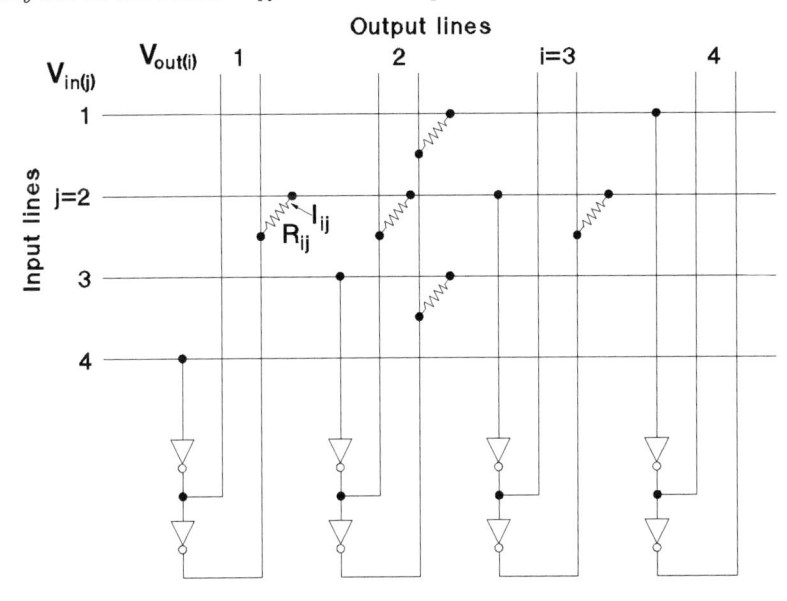

Figure 8.17 *Schematic diagram of the associative circuit from Graf et al. (adapted from [Graf87b])*

of only one previously stored vector which appears at the standard neuron outputs.

8.4.3 A Hybrid Network Using Resistors

The schematic representation of an analog/digital hybrid neural network, proposed by Moopen et al. [Moop87] is depicted in Figure 8.18. This hybrid architecture with N neurons basically consists of three functional sections:

- blocks of digital random or serial access memories for storing the interconnection data (from w_{11} to w_{NN}) as binary numbers
- an array of N binary weighted resistors (from R_1 to R_N) to realize discrete synaptic weights
- an array of N thresholding amplifiers functioning as neurons.

A single synapse circuit consists of a resistor network performing the multiplication of a digital weight value (stored in digital RAM bank) with a neuron output. Binary ratioed resistors serve to perform the digital to analog conversion. Neuron outputs are binary facilitating multiplication. Digital storage of weights allows the representation of a variety of weight values such as binary, ternary or multivalued. If values with sign representation are desired, two RAM blocks are needed, one for weight values with a positive sign, and the other for weight values with a negative sign

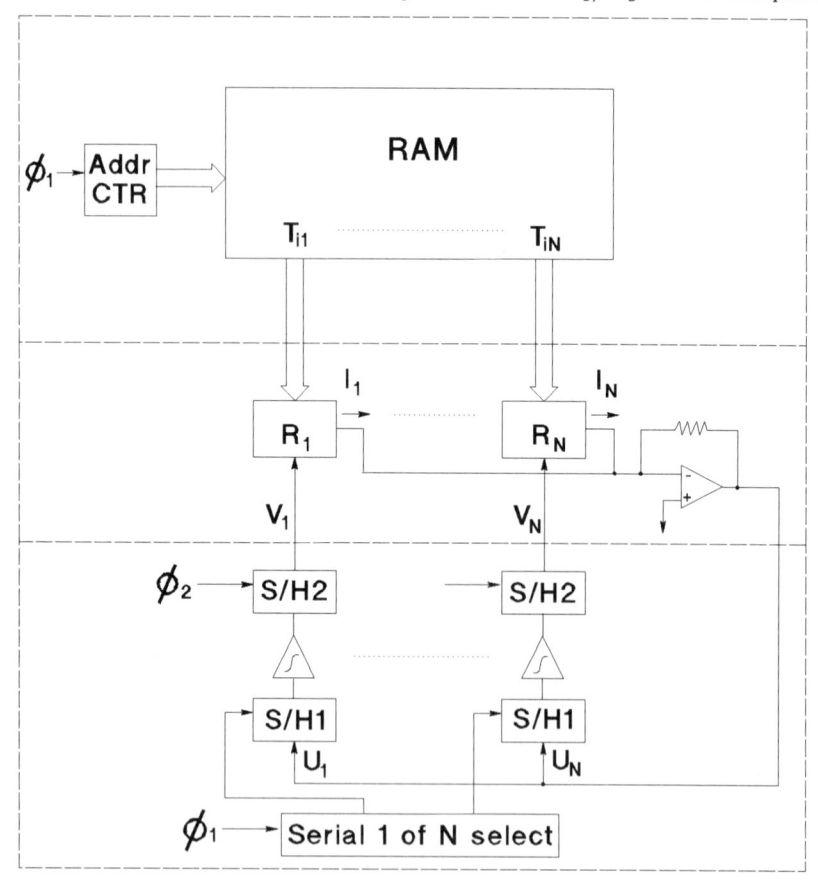

Figure 8.18 *Schematic diagram of a hybrid neural architecture (adapted from [Moop87])*

(the output currents of respective resistor networks may then simply be subtracted).

Each neuron has sample and hold units in both inputs (S/H1) and outputs (S/H2). The system needs two clock signals $\phi 1$ and $\phi 2$ for its operation. On each $\phi 1$ cycle, the input sample/hold unit of a neuron is selected and its corresponding row of interconnection data in the digital memory is addressed (weights w_{i1} through w_{iN} of neuron i in Figure 8.18). Digital weight data appearing at the memory output activates the quantized resistance values of the synapse resistor networks. The precision of the coupling element depends on the digital weight word length and the number of ratioed resistors in a synapse network. Currents from the resistor network are summed and converted to a voltage signal, which is sampled and held by the calculated neuron. Therefore, in a single update cycle only one neuron output can be updated; however, all synaptic inputs of this neuron are calculated in parallel. Then, for the calculation of neighboring neuron outputs, the single neuron delivers its output in a number of $\phi 2$ cycles as a voltage signal that is held by its sample/hold unit.

A prototype breadboard hybrid system with 32 neurons was fabricated with off-the-shelf hardware components. The basic elements of the system were: two static RAM blocks (for positive and negative weight storage), an inhibitory current summing amplifier, an excitatory current summing amplifier, an array of operational amplifiers, and arrays of analog switches with a series connected resistor. Programming and verification of interconnection data, presetting of the neuron input voltages, initiation of an update cycle, and binary readout of the neuron output states were performed by a microcomputer.

The hardware described is well suited for the emulation of fully connected single-layer feedback networks. Therefore, only Hopfield type networks may run on it.

8.4.4 Fully Connected Hopfield Network from Verleysen et al.

A VLSI implementation of a neural associative memory was presented by Verleysen *et al.* [Ver89a] which is also based on Hopfield networks [Hop82]. As in the approach from Graf *et al.*, ternary weight storage is used. Synaptic weight values are carried on two digital RAM cells. In contrast to Graf *et al.*, two lines at a neuron's input are present to carry inhibitory and excitatory signals, both represented by a voltage. This method needs a different synapse implementation. Figure 8.19 shows the synapse circuit proposed by Verleysen *et al.*. By controlling a transistor gate, *RAM cell 2* decides whether the synapse is zero or can contribute to excite or inhibit a neuron. If the synapse contributes, *RAM cell 1* and output OUT_j from preceding neuron j define the contribution. If *RAM cell 1* and OUT_j are both equal, the synapse has inhibitory effect; otherwise it is excitatory.

A single neuron is realized by a current subtractor circuit based on a differential amplifier (see Figure 5.25). This circuit consists of seven MOS transistors and provides a single output which is fed back to the synaptic array.

Verleysen *et al.* designed a test chip containing the functionality of 14 neurons and 196 synapses. It was fabricated in a 3 μm CMOS technology. Roughly 81% of the active chip area of 3×3 mm^2 was occupied by synapse circuitry. By means of simulation, Verleysen *et al.* obtained a speed estimation for larger 128 neuron networks. The settling speed of such a network will be between 120 ns and 150 ns.

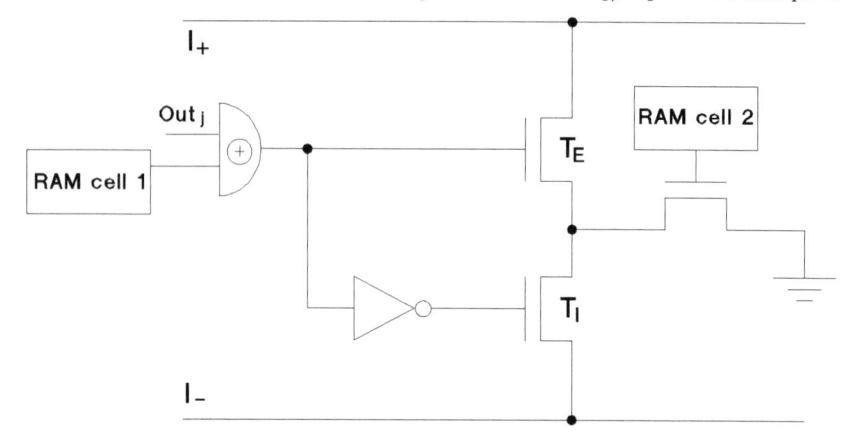

Figure 8.19 *Programmable coupling element with separate source and sink current line (adapted from [Ver89a])*

8.5 Network Implementations based on Amorphous Silicon

The fact that amorphous silicon can be deposited on larger surfaces (e.g. 10 inch wafer technology) in contrast to crystalline silicon indicates the need for this technology in large area integration. The major application areas of amorphous silicon technology are solar cells, large image sensors and flat displays. Furthermore, the use of amorphous silicon technology is also known for the realization of resistive elements, important for synapse circuits based on resistive synaptic weights. Three aspects are significant in such synapse circuits. First, resistances should be high. The higher a resistor's resistance is, the less current will pass it reducing overall chip power dissipation and heat problems. Second, a resistor of high resistance should not occupy too great a silicon area. A high resistance resistor realized by a diffusion line would, for example, occupy a large area due to the low specific resistance. Amorphous silicon has quite a high specific resistance. Last but not least, resistors have to be realized with a high accuracy. Amorphous silicon resistors can be reproduced with about 5% accuracy by laser beam shaping. But a big problem with this technology is the lack of reprogrammability.

8.5.1 Network with Fixed Resistors

Nonprogrammable, amorphous silicon resistors are used as synaptic array elements in the "Electronic Neural Network" realized by Graf et al. [Graf86]. A total of 512 amplifiers (current summation on input node) consisting of switches and two series connected inverters, each with inverting and non-inverting outputs, are implemented on the chip. However, only 256 of them

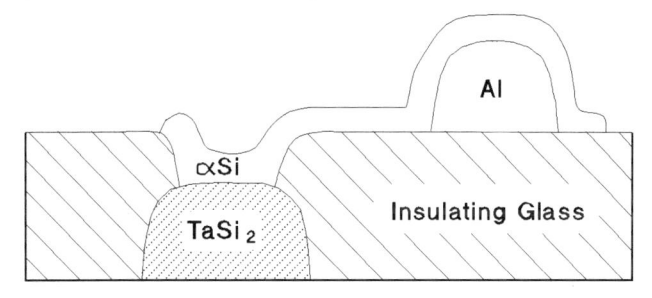

Figure 8.20 *Cross-section of an αSi resistor (adapted from [Graf86])*

may be interconnected due to the limited silicon area. Therefore, this chip can emulate Hopfield networks with a size of 256 neurons. It was designed using analog and digital VLSI technology and a custom fabrication process.

Input data is stored in a 16-bit buffer. When the buffer is full, control signals are sent to initialize the circuit turning all the amplifiers on. After the circuit has settled down, the output voltage of each amplifier is read out over a 16-bit wide bus.

The CMOS portion of the chip with approximately 25,000 transistors was fabricated first, leaving more than 130,000 sites for amorphous silicon (αSi) resistors in the matrix. The empty sites in the matrix provide access to tantalum silicide lines ($TaSi_2$). The αSi resistors may be placed onto the empty sites between the crossing aluminium and tantalum silicide lines (Figure 8.20). Once the chip is covered with amorphous silicon, the resistors are shaped by electron-beam lithography reactive-ion-etching.

Although synaptic weights are fixed after fabrication, which is a major disadvantage of the chip, a certain amount of flexibility can be achieved by applying a time varying bias to the inputs of the amplifiers. Another drawback is that the chip works asynchronously, requiring additional care for the compatibility with a clocked, digital environment. Application areas are small pattern completion tasks that can be solved by Hopfield networks.

8.5.2 Network with Programmable Resistor Grid for Path Optimization

An amorphous silicon chip with resistor grid was proposed by Tarassenko et al. [Tar90] to solve the path planning problem for a mobile robot in real-time.

The approach is based on the mapping of the robot environment onto a resistive grid of hexagonal or rectangular form. All the resistors corresponding to an area with an obstacle have an infinite resistance, whereas other resistors are of low resistivity. A positive voltage is applied between the present position P and the goal G of the robot. The current that flows from P to G is forced to avoid regions with infinite resistance, *i.e.* to avoid obstacles by flowing around them. A path of maximum current can be found from evaluating local measurements of node voltages. In the case of a hexagonal resistor grid, six voltages must be measured for each node (voltages to the six nearest neighbors). The node with the lowest voltage is the next node in the path.

Mapping the real robot environment onto a discrete system rather than onto a continuous system causes several drawbacks. A discretization error caused by leakage at a node through neighboring resistors is one such problem. Furthermore, the maximum current is measured instead of the maximum current density, *i.e.* the path width is involved in the optimization process. This disadvantage is apparent in situations where two obstacles are placed near to each other, creating a narrow path between them. The maximum current measurements indicate a path around the two obstacles avoiding the optimal solution which is the narrow path.

One method of implementing the resistive grid is to use MOS switches as binary resistors. Standard RAM circuits can be used to program the transistors. Each transistor is set by the RAM cell connected to its gate either to function as a closed path with infinite resistance or to act as a short-circuited connection with very low resistance. The node representing the present position of the robot has to be connected to power supply V_{DD}, whereas the node corresponding to the goal must be connected to ground. Since any node in the grid can represent G or P, the possibility of connecting each node to ground or V_{DD} is essential. Therefore, each node is connected to V_{DD} via pull-up (PMOS) transistors and to ground via pull-down (NMOS) transistors, as shown in Figure 8.21. Each node is given an address (X,Y), enabling X and Y transistors which are shared by the nodes in the same X and Y address, respectively.

The node voltages must be buffered before they are measured to determine the path of maximum current. A source follower, illustrated in Figure 8.22, is used as a buffer circuit. This buffer transfers input voltage V_{in} to V_{out} without drawing current from the grid. The use of a more sophisticated voltage buffer was not considered due to the fact that a source follower requires only two transistors per node.

An alternative approach to implementing the resistive grid is to use electronically programmable αSi resistors that can adopt values between 1 kΩ and 5 kΩ. Neighboring resistors are connected to each other and to other parts of the grid by pass transistors. Pulses of 12 V − 13 V are required to form the amorphous silicon elements before the chip is ready for use. Therefore, small geometry CMOS processes cannot be used due to the lack of robustness for such potentials. A test chip with amorphous silicon resistors was implemented using 6 μm NMOS technology.

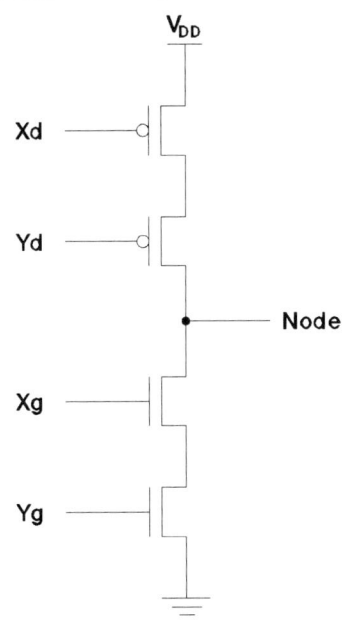

Figure 8.21 *Node connected to power supply and ground (adapted from [Tar90])*

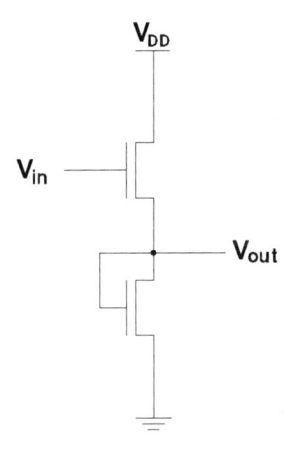

Figure 8.22 *Source follower buffer (adapted from [Tar90])*

8.5.3 A Network with Programmable Amorphous Silicon Memory Devices

A programmable amorphous silicon memory device developed at Dundee University and Edinburgh University [LeC85, Rose89] was used for the implementation of a synaptic array by Reeder *et al.* [Ree91]. The device consists of a thin layer of p-type doped amorphous silicon between two metal contacting electrodes. The top electrode is of vanadium or chromium and the bottom one is of chromium. The amorphous silicon layer contacts the top electrode via a small pore cut into the photoresist overlayer (see Figure 8.23). Individualization of memory devices is performed after fabrication which allows devices to be programmed. A forming pulse (up to 12 V, approximately for 300 ns) produces local heating which causes diffusion of the top electrode metal into the amorphous silicon layer. Electrical device properties, e.g. the range of element resistance, are strongly dependant on the choice of the top electrode metal. If chromium is selected for both top and bottom electrodes, the device is only suitable for digital applications because of its limiting ON/OFF programmability. However, if vanadium and chromium are used for the top and the bottom electrodes, respectively, the device can be programmed in a resistance range between an on-state value of a few kΩ and an off-state value of a few MΩ using programmable voltages between 1 V and 4 V in both polarities. For voltages below 0.5 V, the resistance remains unchanged.

The resistance of a device initially in the on-state can be gradually increased by applying an incrementally increasing negative pulse (ERASE pulse) to the bottom electrode of the device, until the off-state is reached. By using a positive pulse at the same electrode (WRITE pulse), the above operation can be reversed, returning the device to the low resistance on-state.

Amorphous silicon memories described in Figure 8.23 with vanadium top electrodes and chromium bottom electrodes were used as synaptic elements in a neural network system proposed by Reeder et al. [Ree91]. A simple resistive array had been considered with operational amplifiers, developed in conventional silicon technology, to perform the summation and the sigmoid functions. The forming and programming pulses must be applied only for the synaptic elements desired. In order to fulfil this requirement, access transistors with a breakdown voltage higher than the forming voltage are included. The access transistors must be able to drive the forming current (approximately 8 mA) and have a higher on/off resistance ratio (approximately 10^6).

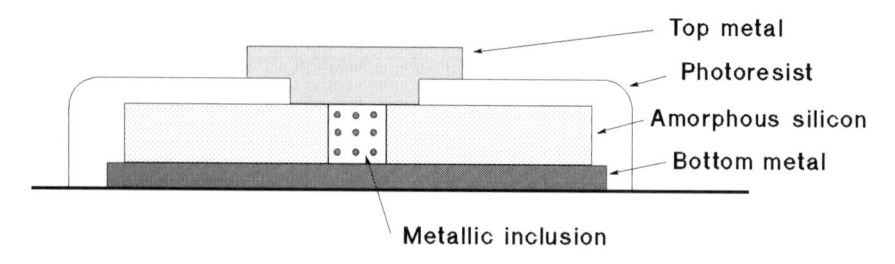

Figure 8.23 *Cross-section of an amorphous silicon memory*

The synapse values, obtained from off-chip logarithmic simulations, may be downloaded to the individual amorphous silicon synapses using the access transistors. The highest accuracy in programming the devices can be achieved by applying a monotonically increasing programming voltage until the desired resistance is obtained [Ree91].

8.6 CCD and Floating-Gate Implementations

All existing analog neural hardware with programmable synapses has some common drawbacks. The trade-off between synapse complexity and the number of synapses per chip is a major problem in most circuits. CCD approaches may be useful to reduce this drawback in programmable neural networks.

8.6.1 MNOS/CCD Implementation from Sage et al.

Sage et al. [Sag86] applied CCD technology to implementing neural networks. To store synaptic weight values and to perform a synaptic multiplication, a CCD structure as depicted in Figure 5.15 was used. A three-gate CCD element forms a synapse. Synaptic weight information is stored in an MNOS element in the center of the three gate CCD circuit.

The implementation is based on p-type silicon substrate with n-type source and drain diffusion areas. As depicted in Figure 5.15, neuron outputs are distributed to synaptic three-gate CCD elements through the source diffusion lines. A large drain line is representing a neuron's input. All synaptic three-gate CCD elements belonging to a single neuron have this common drain at their output. During a parallel synaptic multiplication they all output their charge packets onto the common drain, changing its potential. This potential change may be sensed to provide the neuron's activation potential.

Sage et al. realized a completely connected 13 neuron network with 169 synapses. No on-chip learning algorithm is supported. Programming of synapses is performed by applying high voltages at the gates of MNOS elements. Via tunneling, hot electrons generated in the channels may enter the charge traps. By reducing the MNOS gate voltages to 10 V the charges remain trapped, forming synaptic weights. With complete interconnection and binary neuron outputs, this type of architecture may realize small Hopfield type networks.

8.6.2 Neural Processor with Programmable Synapses

A test chip of an integrated circuit with 256 on-chip fully interconnected neurons and programmable CCD analog synapses was implemented by Agranat et al. [Agr90]. The system is divided into two modules, both based on CCDs: an integrated circuit which performs computation and a control unit which implements the decision function. This allows more flexibility in realizing different types of networks on the hardware proposed.

Each neuron unit consists of a CCD ring array with 256 registers, a multiplier, and an integrator. Neurons on the chip are divided into 16 groups, each of them consisting of 16 neuron units and a separate CCD output array. The weights belonging to a neuron are stored in a CCD ring array, which can be loaded either electrically or optically. To form an $N \times N$ element weight matrix, N CCD ring arrays are used with an array length of N each. The weight matrix can be electrically loaded through eight input pins from which data is demultiplexed before moving into respective ring arrays. Optical loading is accomplished by imaging the matrix to the CCD ring arrays that are ordered as 2-D images. Figure 8.24 sketches N weight ring arrays. The right-most element of an array can feed the stored analog weight to the analog computational module and to the left-most element as shown.

Figure 8.25 shows the whole system. The outputs from all N synaptic ring arrays are propagated via AND-gates, which are performing a multiplication of binary neuron outputs with analog weights, to N analog integrators. Their task is to accumulate N successive synapse outputs to calculate the respective neuron activation potentials. Then, threshold circuits (integrator outputs are sensed by means of MOS output amplifiers) generate neuron outputs, again stored in a CCD chain that can be read sequentially to feed back neuron outputs for synaptic multiplications. Agranat *et al.* emulated a Hopfield network on this architecture.

No learning is supported on-chip, therefore learning and updating of

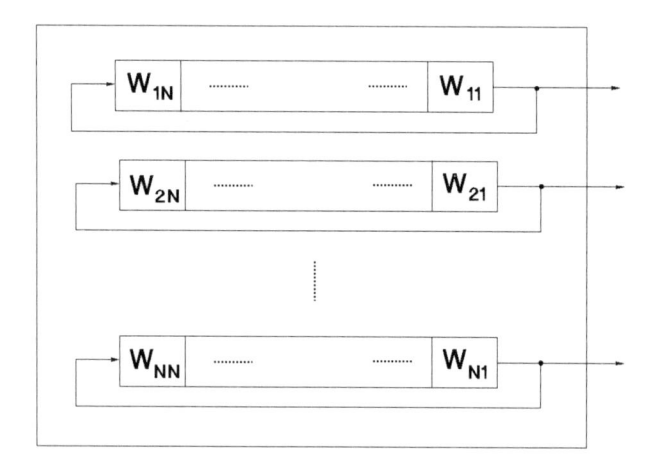

Figure 8.24 *CCD analog synaptic array (adapted from [Agr87])*

CCD and Floating-Gate Implementations 227

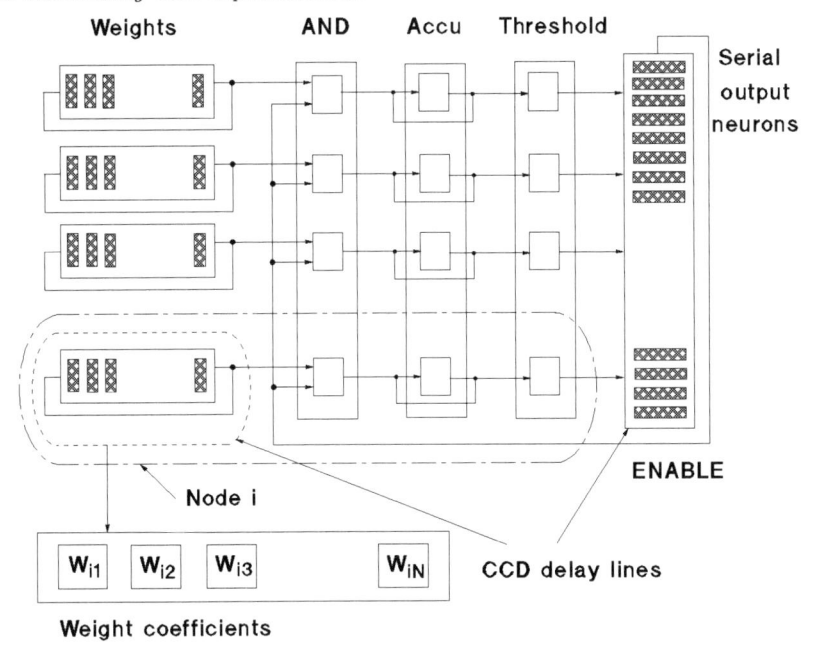

Figure 8.25 *System of CCD-based neurocomputer (adapted from [Hoe91])*

weights have to be performed outside the chip before they are loaded into the CCD rows.

8.6.3 The INTEL ETANN Chip

The Electrically Trainable Analog Neural Network (ETANN) chip from Intel is one of the most interesting neural network chips which also is commercially available [Int90]. This large analog chip is based on floating gate analog storage elements (MNOS technology). A block diagram of the 80170NW ETANN chip is depicted in Figure 8.26. The chip consists of 64 neurons which are fully connected to 64 analog inputs via 4096 synapses. Neuron outputs leave the chip through 64 analog outputs. By fully using this provided parallelism, one can reach a performance of 2 billion multiply/accumulate operations (or connections) per second. A feedback path of 64 lines from the output to a separate array of 4096 synapses allows the implementation of Hopfield type networks. This array of synapses can alternatively be used with 64 additional inputs to map 128 inputs onto 64 neuron outputs. A block of 16 rows (64 synapses in each row) of biasing synapses is provided with fixed positive inputs to set up a bias for each neuron. Another block of 16 rows of synapses is dedicated to biasing if the feedback connections are enabled. Hence, the chip contains a total of 10, 240

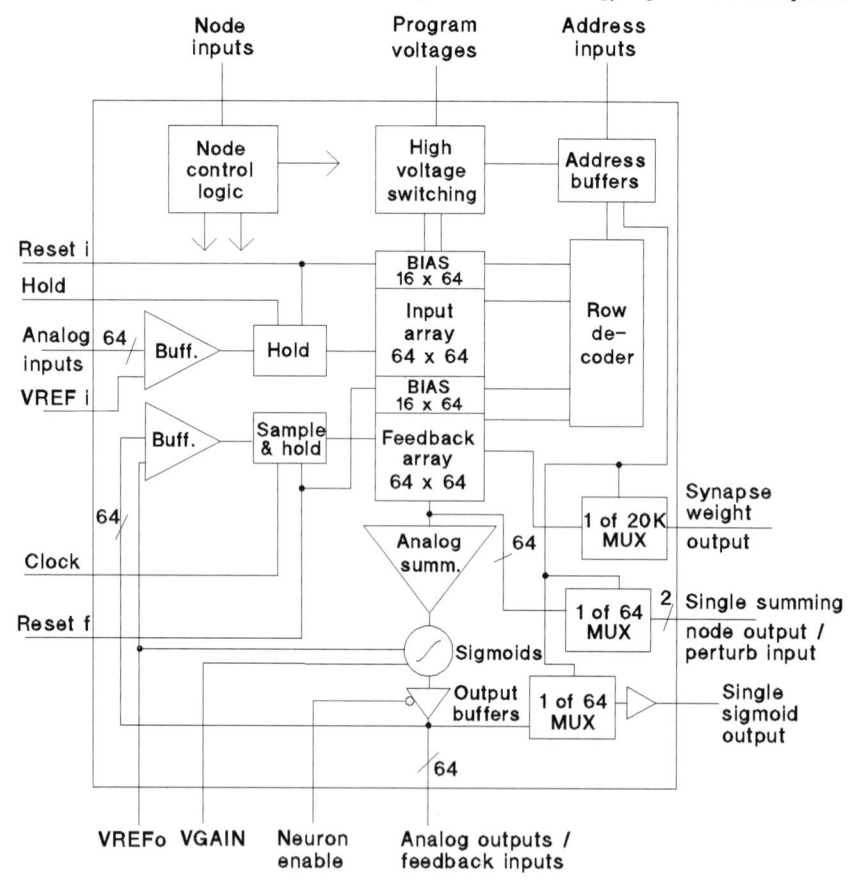

228   *Analog and Mixed Analog/Digital Neurocomputers*

Figure 8.26 *Block diagram of ETANN chip (adapted from [Int90])*

synapses. The resolution of the analog inputs and outputs is typically 6 bits or more [Int90].

The chip performs the inner product of an input vector with stored weight vectors. Thus, synapse circuits responsible for the multiplication of input values or neuron outputs with weights are realized by means of Gilbert multipliers (see pp. 80–81). Figure 8.27 sketches the implemented synapse circuit. A weight value is stored as a charge on the floating gates of two EEPROM cells. These cells are used for differential weight storage. Due to differential floating gate synapses, the effects caused by temperature dependent variations and irregularities occurring in the power supply are nearly compensated for. Since a Gilbert multiplier is used, both inputs and stored weights can be either positive or negative, and the output will have the correct sign for all four cases, enabling full four-quadrant multiplication.

CCD and Floating-Gate Implementations 229

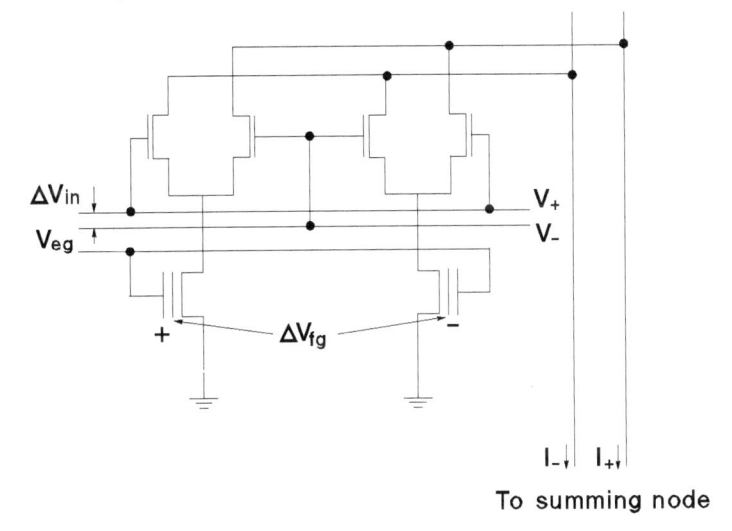

Figure 8.27 *MNOS version of Gilbert cell used in ETANN chips (adapted from [Int90])*

The stored weight is proportional to the difference in threshold voltages of the two EEPROM cells. A weight is modified by adding or removing an amount of charge from the EEPROM cell to change the current threshold voltage to the target threshold voltage which corresponds to a new synaptic weight value. Fourteen address lines serve to select one of the 10,240 synapses. Prior to changing a cell's charge an external processor has to calculate the appropriate pulse height based on a measured current threshold and the desired weight change. Therefore, a pulse length is within the range of 10 μs to 1 ms, with pulse height varying from 12 V to 20 V [Int90]. The difference between the EEPROM's target threshold voltage and current threshold voltage (ΔV_{th}) is positive if the device is programmed. Whenever ΔV_{th} is negative, the floating gate device is erased.

A process called Bake Re-Training is used to improve the ETANN's processing accuracy. Dipoles that are created due to charge movement in the nitride layer between the control gate and the floating gate of an EEPROM compensate the electric field induced. This electrical reaction tends to deviate ΔV_{th} from its original value, affecting ETANN's processing accuracy. High temperature baking accelerates this phenomenon. Baking can be combined with re-training to reduce floating gate voltage differential (ΔV_{fg}) offset, since the induced electrical field differences are smaller after bake-retraining cycles (bake/retraining means that a trained chip is exposed to high temperature to accelerate charge movements in the EEPROM cells and afterwards is retrained again to restore original charges). Therefore, a

250°C bake/retraining operation improves the accuracy of the ETANN by 3 to 4 bits (as stated in [Int90], this is over a minimum data retention life time of 10 years). Thus, with the bake/retraining procedure an effective weight representation accuracy of 6-8 bits is expected. Neuron amplifiers sum the differential currents delivered by synapses and produce a differential voltage. The differential voltage is the input to an electronic realization of the sigmoid function whose gain can be controlled externally.

The ETANN has only a single layer of neurons. However, multilayer operation may be obtained by using multiplexing methods. In the case of two-layer networks, feedback synapses may be disabled and input signals are applied first. After a period of time allowing neurons to stabilize, the outputs are clocked into the feedback path. The input synapse array is then disabled allowing the stored state of the outputs to be processed without interference. Then, the feedback array acts as a second layer of connections. Neuron amplifiers are used twice in the two-layer operation. For implementing more than two processing layers, one can cascade ETANNs by feeding outputs directly into subsequent ETANN inputs [Tam92]. Due to a fixed number of synapses and neurons on a chip, only limited cascadability is supported.

Intel offers the Intel Neural Network Training System (iNNTS) which provides a software environment and hardware environment for the ETANN chip [Int92a, Int92b]. This system consists of a personal computer programmer board, a programmer interface to the 80170NX adaptor, the 80170NX adaptor, a test module, two 80170NX chips and simulation software. This software can train neworks with up to 81,920 synapses and 1024 neurons [Int92a]. In March 1993, the costs for iNNTS were reported to be $11,800; a single 80170NX chip was available at $940 [Int93]. Furthermore, Intel offers the ETANN Multi-Chip Board (EMB) with sockets for eight ETANN chips

The major drawbacks of this chip are limitations in learning speed, due to the large programming time of floating gates, and the need for off-chip learning. External hardware serves to find an appropriate network structure which then has to be programmed on ETANN chips. High voltage pulses have to be applied to a chip to program a single synapse, requiring special circuitry.

8.7 CMOS Networks with Programmable Weights

Although the computational unit of a neural chip can be implemented with less expense in analog technology, the realization of dynamic analog storage is difficult. Furthermore, updating purely analog storage media during learning requires special circuitry which is difficult to provide. Several mixed architectures have been proposed, based on the utilization of static and dynamic digital memories for synaptic storage, with simple high speed analog hardware to perform neural computations. The combination of digital/analog designs allows exploitation of the advantages of both methods.

8.7.1 A Network with On-chip Boltzmann Machine Learning

Alspector et al. [Als87, Als88a] designed mixed digital/analog circuitry to emulate a small neural network with a variety of Boltzmann machine learning, on-chip. The advantage of the Boltzmann machine learning algorithm with respect to hardware implementations is that it requires only local information to calculate weight updates. This means that information from local neighbors to a neuron is sufficient for performing weight updates. The drawbacks, however, are the need for statistical random effects and the control of an annealing parameter which significantly affects learning.

Discrete weight values are stored digitally. This method allows for simple weight modifications. Digital weights are converted into analog signals via resistive elements. Each resistive element is realized by a ratioed pass transistor. Figure 8.28 shows the principle of synaptic storage. Transistors T_0, T_1, ..., T_N are ratioed pass transistors to convert an N bit digital weight value into an analog current. The same number of transistors also exist to draw currents from a second current line to implement negative weights (a weight's sign is determined by signal $Sign$ controlling a transistor switching the analog neuron output either on the positive or negative current line).

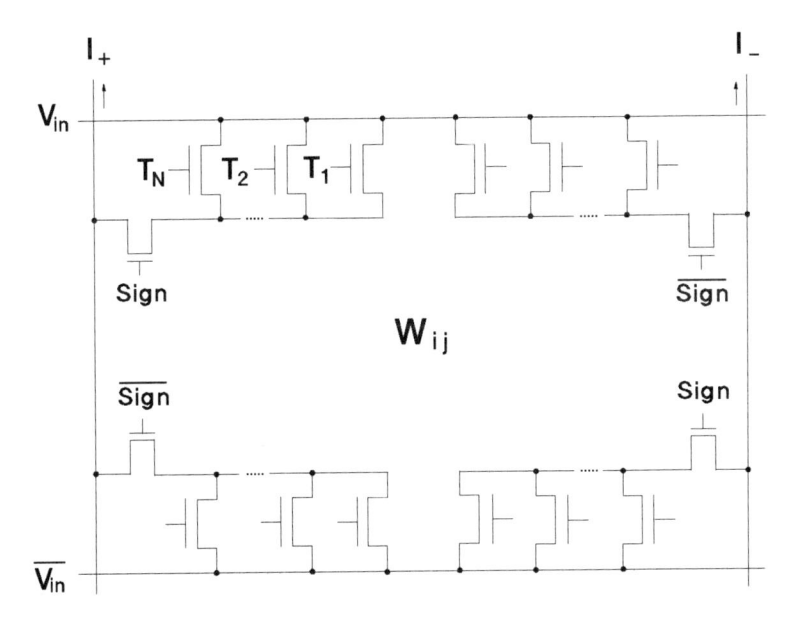

Figure 8.28 Synapse circuit in implementation from Alspector et al. (adapted from [Als88a])

This structure is replicated for negative neuron outputs. Therefore, four parts in the synapse circuit of Figure 8.28 exist to realize four-quadrant multiplication. The output of the preceding neuron is given to the drain of ratioed pass transistors (positive neuron outputs to drains of upper transistor array, negative neuron outputs to drains of lower transistor array) to perform a multiplication of binary neuron outputs with synaptic weights.

Neurons are represented by double input differential amplifiers. The second input is used to give stochastic noise on neuron inputs to realize simulated annealing which tries to avoid local optima in an optimization process. The neuron performs a *tanh* threshold operation whose slope may be controlled externally. Stochastic noise is provided by the amplification of thermal noise. A gradual noise reduction (annealing process) is obtained through gain reduction of noise amplifiers. Figure 8.29 sketches a neuron circuit with some arriving synapses.

To enable on-chip learning, digital updating circuitry was designed. The task of this circuitry is to gather statistics about synapse "activities". Thus, a synapse is "active" if both the preceding and successive neurons are active. If this happens often, the respective synapse weight will be increased, otherwise it will remain at its value or it will be decreased. This implements a form of Hebbian learning. Therefore, each weight value is stored in a simple digital up/down counter whose outputs are connected to the gates of pass transistors performing the multiplication and digital to analog conversion.

Alspector *et al.* implemented a CMOS VLSI circuit that implemented

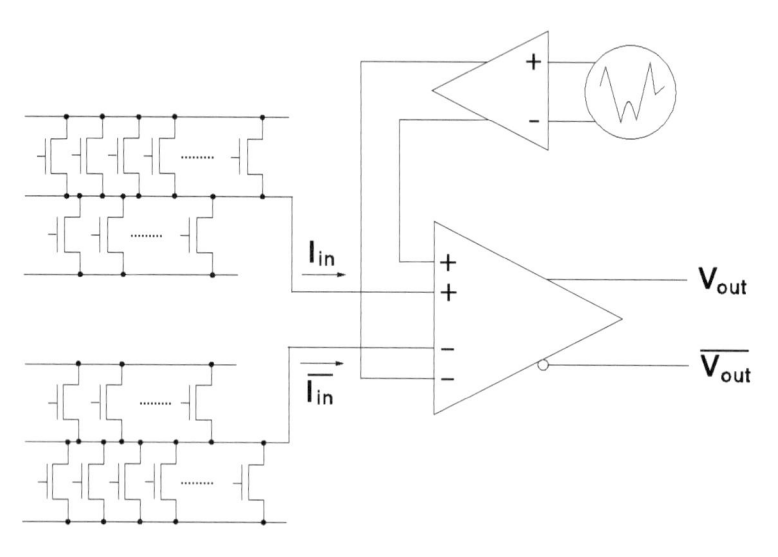

Figure 8.29 *Neuron circuitry with some arriving synapses (adapted from [Als87])*

CMOS Networks with Programmable Weights

circuitry for the emulation of six neurons and 15 synapses. They state that a 4-bit weight representation would be sufficient for Boltzmann machine learning [Als87]. However, this information was obtained from simulations of a very simple and small XOR-problem, but weight accuracy is significantly dependant upon the application problem. Starting with zero initial weights and clamping desired outputs alternating, the network was successfully trained to solve a two-dimensional XOR problem. At each cycle the network was jittered by noise.

8.7.2 Self-Organizing Feature Map with MDACs

A circuit implementing a variety of Kohonen's self-organizing algorithm, was designed by Mann et al. [Man88a] using hybrid digital/analog technology with MDACs as the connecting elements (digital weight storage but analog multiplication). The activation of neuron i which has N inputs $x_j(t)$ is the squared Euclidean distance given by Equation 8.8

$$a_i(t) = \sum_{j=1}^{N}[x_j(t) - w_{ij}(t)]^2 = \sum_{j=1}^{N} x_j^2(t) - 2x_j(t)w_{ij}(t) + w_{ij}^2(t). \quad (8.8)$$

In one computation step the term $x_j^2(t)$ is equal for all neurons, thus forming an offset that may be neglected reducing the equation to (with division by -2 on both sides)

$$-\frac{a_i(t)}{2} = \sum_{j=1}^{N}\left[(x_j(t) - \frac{1}{2}w_{ij}(t)) \cdot w_{ij}(t)\right]. \quad (8.9)$$

Weight adaptation is done according to

$$w_{ij}(t+1) = \begin{cases} w_{ij}(t) + \alpha(t)\left[x_j(t) - w_{ij}(t)\right] & \text{for } i \in N_m(t) \\ w_{ij}(t) & \text{otherwise} \end{cases} \quad (8.10)$$

where $N_m(t)$ defines a certain neighborhood around node m with maximal excitation (see Equation 3.21). For the sake of implementability, Mann et al. simplified this equation to

$$w_{ij}(t+1) = w_{ij}(t) + sgn\left(x_j(t) - w_{ij}(t)\right). \quad (8.11)$$

Now, only a simple multiplication and a division by two have to be done to evaluate the distance measure of Equation 8.9, and no multiplication is involved in weight updating (see Equation 8.11).

Figure 8.30 shows a synapse circuit used to calculate the squared Euclidean distance. Synapse weights are stored digitally in N RAM cells (three transistor dynamic RAM cells). To represent a weight value, Mann et al. used unary coding, i.e. the weight value is determined only by the number of "1s", ignoring their location in the bit string (unary number system instead of binary). This unary coding has the advantage that, in

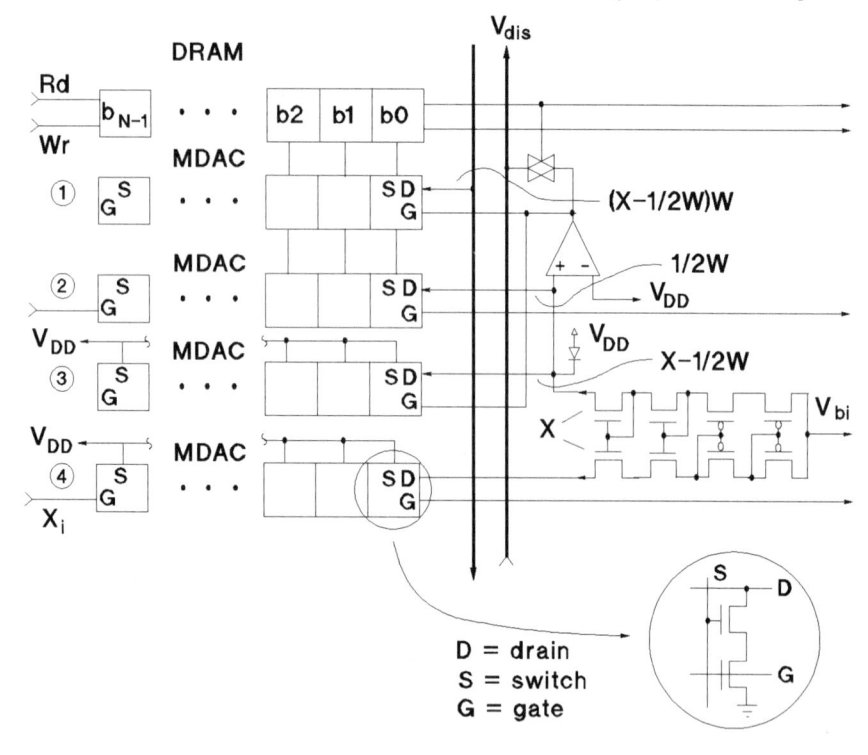

Figure 8.30 *Synapse circuit from Mann et al. to calculate the squared Euclidean distance (adapted from [Man88a])*

combination with the simplified learning algorithm from Equation 8.11, an easy on-chip weight modification can be implemented. Weights are adjusted by shifting the RAM contents to the left or right by 1 bit either entering a "1" from the right or a "0" from the left side. To perform the necessary multiplications (see Equation 8.9), Mann *et al.* used a modified version of the multiplying digital/analog converter circuit depicted in Figure 5.10. This modified circuit has no transistors with different aspect ratios (which is necessary for binary coding but not for unary), and does not allow weights with negative sign.

Four MDACs are used to perform the required operations of a single synapse. *MDAC 4* (see circled number "4") has all its digital inputs clamped to V_{DD}, thus performing a multiplication of the analog input x_i with the constant "1". With an appropriate constant analog input voltage, *MDAC 2* produces an output current proportional to half of the stored weight value. Since the operational amplifier provides negative feedback and controls *MDAC 3* through its output signal, *MDAC 3* must compensate all other currents contributing to the operational amplifier input. Hence, *MDAC*

CMOS Networks with Programmable Weights

3 must generate an output current proportional to $x_j - \frac{1}{2}w_{ij}$. Since its digital input corresponds to the constant "1" (all digital inputs clamped to V_{DD}), the voltage on its analog input, which is driven by the amplifier output, must also correspond to $x_j - \frac{1}{2}w_{ij}$. This voltage in turn serves as the analog input signal to *MDAC 1*, which performs a multiplication of this signal with the synaptic weight value, thus producing the term on the right of the summation sign in Equation 8.9.

The squared Euclidean distance contributions from all the interconnections to the neuron are summed on two wires. Figure 8.31 shows the circuit which was used to realize a neuron's functionality. To subtract excitatory and inhibitory contributions the current mirror cascode from Figure 5.2 was applied. A difference amplifier serves to control a MOS transistor that sinks the current difference while maintaining a constant voltage V_{DS} on the current summing lines, which is a prerequisite for proper operation of all synapse circuits connected to the summing lines. Output voltage V_{out} of the difference amplifier thus represents a neuron's activation.

Furthermore, all neuron activations are fed to a maximum selector circuit to identify the strongest responder, depicted in Figure 8.32. The network selects the strongest responder max_i, which most closely represents the incoming data. To do this, neuron activations are used to control MOS transistor gates. The more a neuron is activated, the more a node voltage

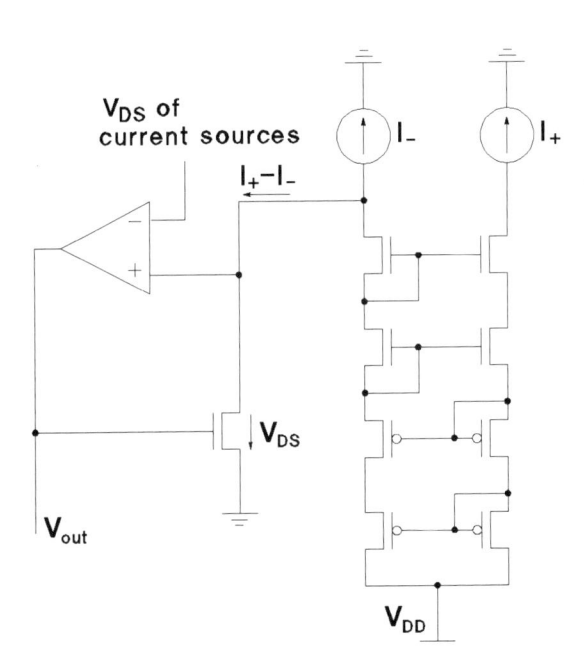

Figure 8.31 *Generation of a neuron's activation (adapted from [Man88a])*

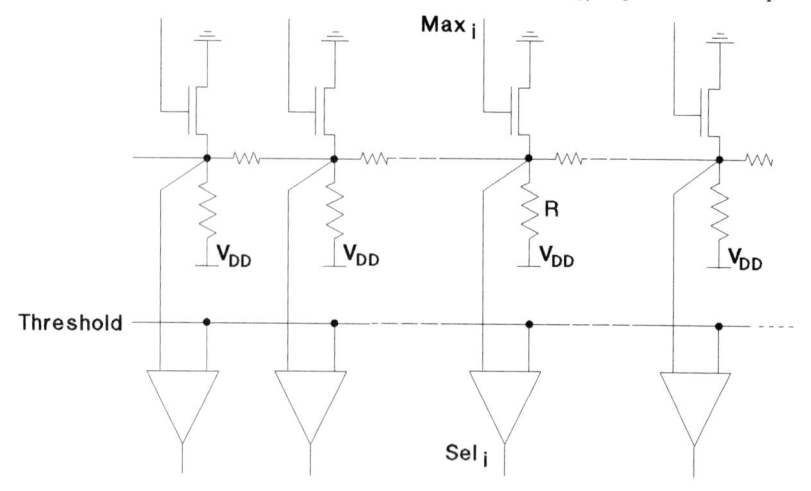

Figure 8.32 *Neighborhood selection (adapted from [Man88a])*

(pulled up by a polysilicon resistor) controlled by such a transistor will be lowered. This causes a voltage distribution with a minimum occurring at the selected node of maximum activation. Then, the node voltages are compared with a threshold voltage to generate a neighborhood. Node voltages which are less than the threshold are selected for weight adaptation. Other nodes are undergoing a refresh procedure. Weight adaptation occurs in a defined neighborhood. Its strength is compared to the input magnitude and adjustments are performed to bring it closer in correspondence with the input according to Equation 8.11.

A chip with 16 nodes containing 36,834 transistors was fabricated using CMOS technology. Seven analog inputs that can be weighted with 16-bit unary weights were provided for each node.

8.7.3 Self-Organizing Feature Map with Analog Weight Storage

Mann and Gilbert [Man88b] designed other circuitry for the emulation of Kohonen Feature Map algorithms. Only the neuron circuits with current mirror cascodes of this design resemble the preceding implementation description (see [Man88a]). The major difference to their first implementation is the use of a completely different synapse circuit and weight storage which is not based on MDACs. Figure 8.33 sketches a single synapse circuit. The synaptic weight w_{ij} is represented as a charge on a capacitor (formed by transistor gate capacities). Dynamic RAM cells formed by three transistors are each located on the upper left and upper right part of Figure 8.33 to control weight sensing (transistors $T1$, $T2$ and $T3$) and weight writing ($T4$, $T5$ and $T6$). Transistor pair $T7/T8$ senses the stored weight charge

CMOS Networks with Programmable Weights

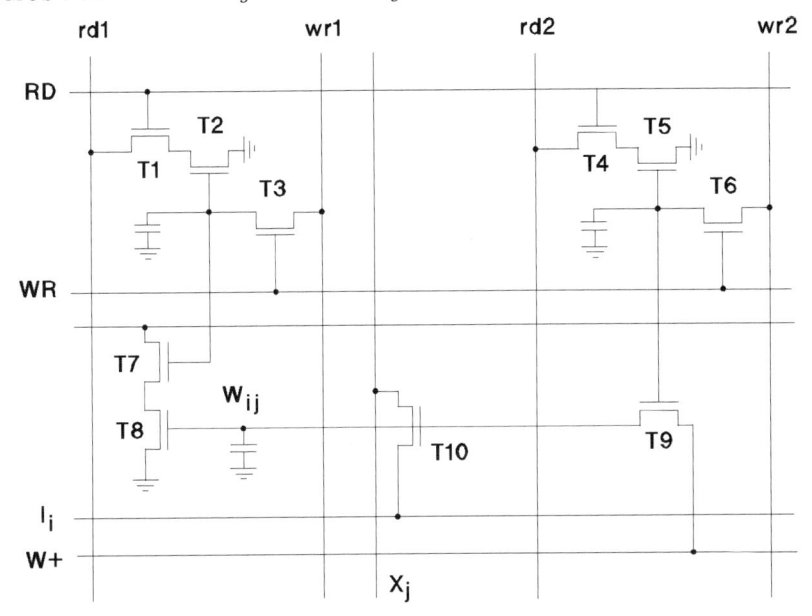

Figure 8.33 *Fully analog synapse circuit from Mann and Gilbert (adapted from [Man88b])*

by transforming it into a current. Transistor $T9$ allows access to the weight carrying capacitor to modify a stored weight value. The synaptic multiplication is performed by transistor $T10$, which operates in the ohmic region. In this region, its channel current is proportional to the product of gate voltage V_{GS} and applied drain-to-source voltage V_{DS} applied between drain and source. Gate voltage V_{GS} is controlled by the stored weight charge, whereas drain-to-source voltage V_{DS} is controlled externally via input line X_j. At higher values of V_{GS} and V_{DS} the transistor begins to saturate, and drain current I_D is no longer a linear function of V_{DS} but still increasing monotonically with increasing voltage V_{DS}. In competitive learning networks like Kohonen's feature map, however, it is only necessary that the computation is monotonically increasing. Neither small nonlinearities nor offsets will affect the correct operation of the algorithm.

Currents from several transistors, which represent weighted inputs, are summed together at each neuron (current mirror cascode). A big problem in designs like this is that stored weights in transistor gates tend to decay with time, due to leakage currents. Thus, if weights are not modified, a refreshing mechanism must periodically restore synaptic weights. Mann and Gilbert implemented a weight adaptation circuit for learning according to Equation 8.11 and a refreshing circuit that is apt to detect 15 mV changes in weight voltages. Assuming a maximum voltage range of 2 V to represent a weight, 128 different weight levels may be distinguished corresponding to 7-bit weight accuracy.

A synaptic array chip was fabricated using a 3 μm 2-metal CMOS process while the refresh circuitry was fabricated in a similar 2 μm process. The advantage over the preceding hybrid digital/analog design is a much denser weight circuitry implementation.

8.7.4 Three-Layer Bidirectional Associative Memory

In a bidirectional neural network, neurons in one field determine the states of those in another field, and *vice versa*. Kosko proposed the use of two-layer bidirectional associative memories (BAMs) which have some advantages over Hopfield networks [Kos88]. A Hopfield network can be seen as a special case of a BAM. The architecture proposed by Boahen *et al.* [Boa89] has a third layer, called the "hidden layer" of nonthresholding neurons in contrast to the bidirectional associative memories from Kosko. Thus, a hidden neuron is assigned to each association. A significant advantage of the three-layer BAM architecture over the two-layer BAM networks is that only one-bit binary weights are necessary to store several binary vectors in the network. In general, Hopfield networks and two-layer BAMs need integer weights for proper performance if several binary vectors have to be stored. Furthermore, the three-layer BAM network shows a good information storage capacity. The number of hidden neurons limits the number of stored vectors. For each vector to be stored one hidden neuron must exist.

Figure 8.34 shows a three-layer BAM network. In this case, the number of neurons on the left side is $N = 3$, the same number exists on the right side with $M = 3$. However, BAM networks also permit an arbitrary number $N \neq M$. Both sides may be used either as network input or output. The network has two hidden neurons, thus allowing the storage of two associations (two input/output vector pairs L^1/R^1 and L^2/R^2 with L a vector from the left network side and R a vector from the right side).

To realize the three-layer BAM architecture two different types of neurons are necessary. The first neuron type is a "standard" thresholding neuron as used in most networks. Boahen *et al.* used simple MOS inverter circuits to emulate that neuron type. Neurons on the left and right network sides (input/output layers) are such thresholding neurons. Hidden neurons show completely different behavior. They are summing arriving signals like conventional neurons but they do not perform nonlinear operations. Their output is the direct sum of arriving inputs. A small MOS transistor circuit realizes this behavior. The MOS circuit also transforms the current input arriving from synapse outputs into a voltage output for the inputs of successive synapse circuits.

A synapse circuit is shown in Figure 8.35. A small one bit RAM cell stores the weight value. In this design only binary weights are necessary. How-

CMOS Networks with Programmable Weights

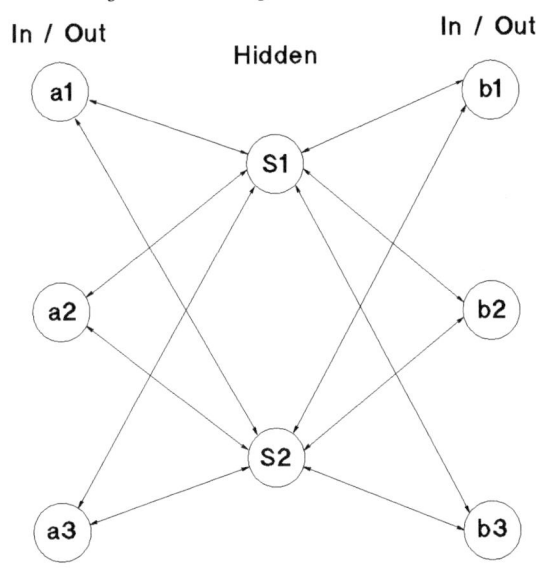

Figure 8.34 3 × 3 three-layer BAM with two associations (two hidden neurons)

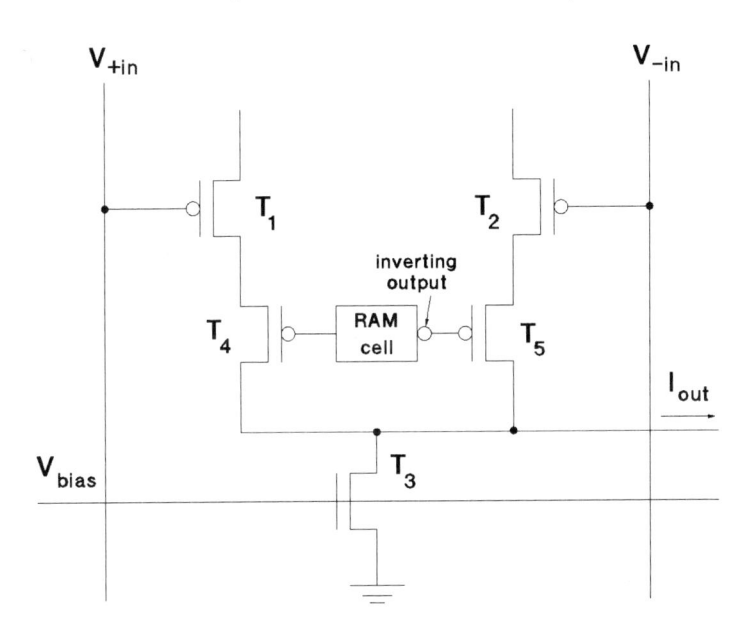

Figure 8.35 Synaptic element with bipolar current output (adapted from [Boa89])

ever, weights do not have the values 0 and 1 but −1 and +1. The synapse output current is bipolar, either $+I_{out}$ or $-I_{out}$. Input to the synapse is two voltages V_{+in} and V_{-in} encoding the input value to be multiplied by the synaptic weight. These voltages generate a current $I_{const} - I_{in}$ in transistor $T1$ and a current $I_{const} + I_{in}$ in transistor $T2$. Controlled by the RAM cell, $T4$ is either open (RAM = "0") and $T5$ closed, or *vice versa* (RAM = "1"), thus realizing a weight value of -1 in the first case and $+1$ in the latter. Transistor $T3$ serves to draw current I_{const} from the output line to guarantee the synapse output to be $+I_{in}$ or $-I_{in}$.

Figure 8.36 depicts the overall system architecture. This would be the hardware realization of the network from Figure 8.34. Since BAM networks have bidirectional dataflow through synapses and the synapse circuit of Figure 8.35 allows only unidirectional data flow, each synapse circuit is duplicated. Both synapse circuits belonging to the same bidirectional synapse are controlled by a single RAM cell. This enables bidirectional dataflow through two unidirectional cells carrying the same weight value. Two non-thresholding neurons (hidden neurons) in Figure 8.36 correspond

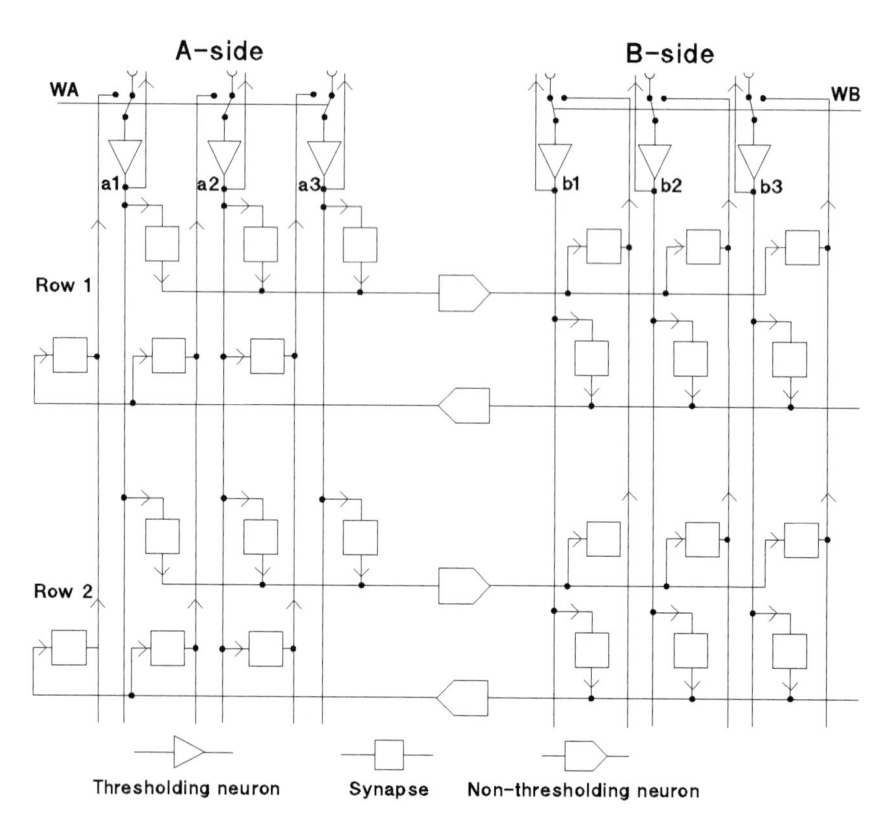

Figure 8.36 *Three-layer BAM architecture (adapted from [Boa89])*

to one hidden neuron in Figure 8.34. Therefore, two associations L^1/R^1 and L^2/R^2 may be stored.

Additional circuitry serves to control network operation. Switches WA and WB are used to stop network iterations and to impose an initial state onto input/output neurons.

Three-layer BAM chips were fabricated in 3 μm p-well CMOS technology. A chip contains 7200 transistors on an area of 4.8 mm^2. The implemented architecture has 32 thresholding neurons (16 on either side), 14 non-thresholding neurons, 448 programmable connections, and seven 32-bit shift registers to store the vector pairs. In storing mode, the 16-bit control bus, which runs across the top of the chip, is used to load data into shift registers. The chips were successfully tested with three associations. The network relaxes in less than 10 μs.

8.7.5 A General Purpose Analog Neural Computer

An analog architecture composed of three types of interconnectable modules was proposed by Mueller et al. [Mue89, Mue91] . The modules contain VLSI arrays of neurons, modifiable synapses, programmable synaptic time constants and routing switches with their control circuits. These modules, designed and fabricated using 2 μm CMOS technology, are mounted on planar chip carriers. The computer is intended for real-time computations in analog mode. However, a digital host computer with an A/D interface is employed to control synaptic gains, time constants, neuron parameters and the network architecture, and to monitor network performance. A system containing a prototype of the analog computer was designed. Software for the system has also been developed and tested with several application examples.

Figure 8.37 shows the placement of modules forming the neurocomputer architecture. The different modules used are:

- neuron modules
- synapse modules
- switch modules
- time constant modules.

Routing switch modules S select the connections between neurons. Synapse modules Syn in east and west feed neuron modules N which deliver outputs via connection lines (blank squares in Figure 8.37) or synaptic time constant modules T to switch modules north and south.

A single neuron module contains the circuitry of eight neurons. Each neuron is formed by a summing amplifier, a comparator and an output driver [Mue89]. The neuron transfer characteristic is a variable step function of height O_{step} at threshold value followed by a linear ramp up to a maximum output value O_{max}. By varying O_{step} and O_{max} through external biases,

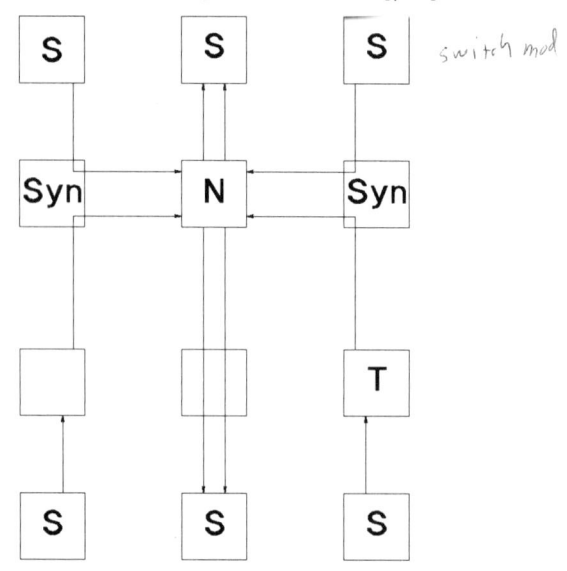

Figure 8.37 *General architecture and data flow between modules (adapted from [Mue91])*

different transfer functions from a pure step function ($O_{step} = O_{max}$) as the one extreme to a pure ramp function ($O_{step} = 0$, $O_{max} \neq O_{step}$) as the other. This was done to allow more flexibility in the emulation of neural algorithms.

Each routing switch module consists of a 16 × 16 array of analog cross point switches that are set digitally by the host computer. A cross-point in the array represents a one-bit switch control memory and one analog switch. Switch modules are used to route analog signals between synapses and neurons. Through them a neural network architecture is specified.

Programmable time constants over the range of 5 ms - 2 s with a resolution of 4 bits are available through time constant modules. Time constants vary logarithmically with the digital code stored in a 4-bit local memory which is set by the host machine. Time constants are implemented using operational transconductance amplifiers as high resistances. The use of external capacitors is not required. These modules were integrated into the neurocomputer design to allow for time domain operations. Such time constants are necessary to implement central pattern generators, for example.

A synapse module consists of an 8 × 16 array of digital programmable synapses allowing each neuron to have a maximum of 16 synapses. Since synapse modules are cascadable, neuron fan-in can be further increased. Each synapse has 6 bits of local memory to store 5 bit weight information which is set by the host computer via a serial input, and 1 bit sign information. At the synapse input, the incoming voltage output of the preceding neuron, which may vary between 0 V and 4 V, is converted into a current. The output current of the voltage-to-current converter is proportional to its input voltage. In the second stage, a series of current mirrors scale the current into five different logarithmically decreasing currents. These currents can be recombined in the synapse circuits, depending on the stored synaptic weights (realizing a multiplication). Through this operation, synaptic weight values in a range between 0 and 10 are producable (with 5-bit accuracy) [Mue89]. Finally, 16 output lines carry the summed weighted current outputs of the 16 synapses to the adjacent neuron module.

Since all modules are set by the host computer, downloading to chips is organized by adding a single memory (enable) to each module chip. These memories form a shift register that shifts a "1" from chip to chip with a 2 MHz master clock from the host computer. The modular design allows easy expansion of the circuit, *i.e.* to increase the number of neurons and synapses.

Mueller *et al.* [Mue91] describe the application of their neurocomputer to different tasks. These tasks are the emulation of a "winner takes all" network, a network for the decomposition of acoustical patterns, and a small four-layer network for optical character recognition (5 × 5-pixel input pattern). Furthermore, some central pattern generator networks were emulated. The authors see applications for a machine of this type in the area of speech recognition. The major drawback is the fact that no on-chip learning is provided. Therefore, learning has to be done off-chip on the host computer.

8.8 Pulse Stream Networks

The major motivations for developing pulse stream techniques are their close analogy with biological neural systems and the desire to implement pseudo-analog circuits on reliable and cheap digital CMOS processes. The use of a pulse stream to transmit information is analogous to that of natural neural systems. Biological neurons communicate with each other using pulses of a similar size and shape known as "action potentials". They convey information by altering the pulse rate or the duty cycle of a pulse train. But most pulse stream neural network implementations have only a few features in common with biological nervous systems. Pulse stream signal representation was chosen just to take advantage of some positive properties in the processing of such signals.

Pulse encoding of information has been widely used by communication systems. Different methods that have been practiced are:

- pulse amplitude modulation (PAM)
- pulse width modulation (PWM)
- pulse code modulation (PCM).

Since amplitude modulated signals are more susceptible to noise than signals in systems using one of the other two methods, PAM is rarely used in neural network implementations. The signals of PCM and PWM are only susceptible to edge-jitter (FM) noise, which is less significant in a general noise environment.

PWM and PCM techniques are considered to be more effective than analog or PAM methods in communicating neural states between devices in a multichip network for following reasons:

- disadvantages associated with analog circuits such as the susceptibility to process variations are minimized
- using time as the information coding axis, the effect of small amplitude degradations is avoided
- regeneration of pulses is easier without losing coded information.

Arithmetic operations such as multiplication can also be realized efficiently on pulse streams. The weighting (multiplication with weights) of an incoming pulse stream to a neuron is accomplished by either using switched capacitor techniques or by modulating the width or the frequency of pulses. Furthermore, the information content in a pulse stream is unaffected by moderate attenuation and, additionally, information modification can be done more precisely than the modification of conventional analog signals [Cott88]. A number of approaches to the implementation of pulse stream neural networks in VLSI technology have been reported [Coo88, Cott88, Can90, Mur89b, Chu91].

On-chip learning is usually not possible in these applications, and most of them involve digitally stored synaptic weights that are programmable. Another drawback is that the use of pulsed circuits increases the level of digital noise injected in power supplies. This effect has to be minimized by clever designs [Chu91].

8.8.1 A Pulse-Width-Modulation Design of a Kohonen Feature Map

A pulse-width-modulation design with path-programmable logic (PPL) was proposed by Cotter *et al.* [Cott88]. The path-programmable logic system is used to layout pulse width modulation (PWM) circuits in a short time. The PPL system, developed by Smith [Smi83] starts from the definition of signal lines that are laid down in a grid on the integrated circuit. Then, it places circuit cells (standard cells) at appropriate locations on the grid. Apart from the short design time (a few hours), PPL shows certain other advantages:

- circuits for simulations can be automatically extracted from the layout
- mixed analog/digital circuits can be implemented easily.

Cotter et al. [Cott88] demonstrated the applicability of PPL to neural network hardware design by designing a circuit for the Kohonen self-organizing feature map. For the summation of PWM signals a low pass filter with switched capacitors is used (see also Figure 5.3). Switched capacitors represent all the resistors in the low pass filter circuit. Four-quadrant multiplication is based on a comparator with complementary outputs and a dual signal representation of the inputs (see also Figure 5.13). Analog storage elements are realized by capacitors carrying a voltage representing a synaptic weight value. Changes in synaptic weights are done by controlling the voltage connected to capacitors through a CMOS switch and a resistor (the resistor again realized using the switched capacitor technique). Similar to biological neurons, pulses are used in this design for interchip communication.

The circuitry mentioned serves to run a basic feature map algorithm with on-chip weight updating. However, the network is not able to update the weights of neurons in a well-defined neighborhood. Only the winning neuron's synapses are updated. In [Cott88] the authors intended to fabricate chips via MOSIS, however, no information about the expected accuracy of computations on the circuitry was given.

8.8.2 A Pulse Stream Design with Programmable Synapses

Programmable analog synapses are used in a pulse stream neural network proposed by Murray [Mur89b]. Figure 8.38 sketches the basic circuit of the analog synapse. The synaptic weight is stored as a voltage on capacitor C_1. A digital-to-analog converter (DAC) is used to refresh analog synaptic storage cyclically from an off-chip digital RAM with addresses generated by a counter in the synapse chip. The effective positive power supply voltage V_{sup} to inverter T_1/T_2 is inversely proportional to dynamically stored voltage V_w in C_1, which represents synaptic weight w_{ij}. Active-load amplifier circuit T_3 and T_4 buffers the synaptic voltage from the inverter. Pulses from neuron j (o_j) occur asynchronously at the input of neuron i that is at the input of inverter T_1/T_2. The aspect ratios of transistors T_1 and T_2 are chosen so that the inverter's discharge time is greater than its charging time. Therefore, the output pulse of the inverter is asymmetric as shown, and it discharges from an initial voltage V_{sup} to zero almost linearly, since T_2 is operating in saturated mode. The output pulse is finished with rapidly charging the discharge capacitor through T_1. The second inverter switches the inverted pulse via threshold V_{switch}. The width of the output pulse of the second inverter depends on the part of the output pulse that lies below threshold voltage. This measurement depends on the effective supply volt-

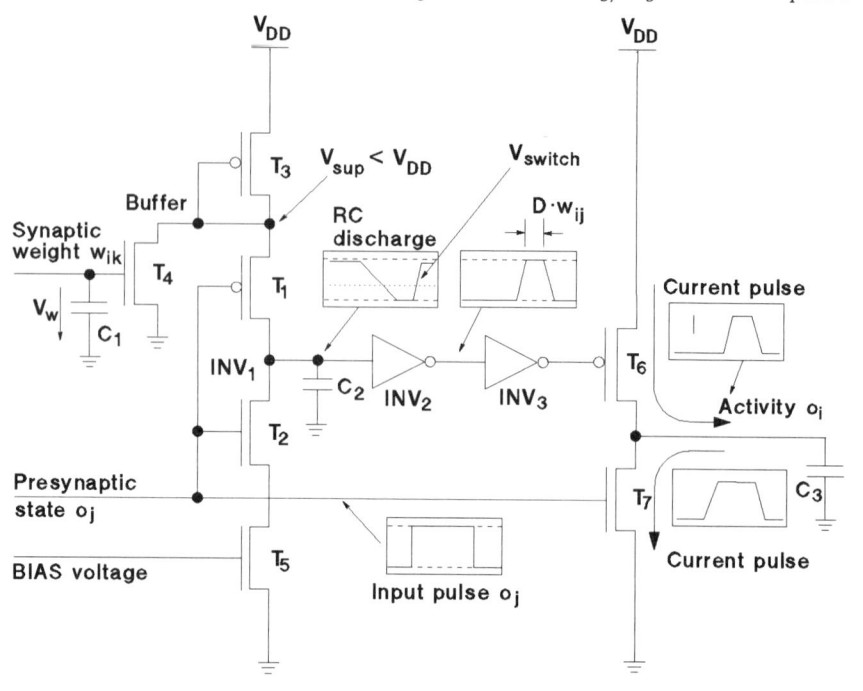

246   *Analog and Mixed Analog/Digital Neurocomputers*

Figure 8.38 *Basic circuit of a programmable pulse stream synapse (adapted from [Mur89b])*

age of the first inverter, which again is proportional to w_{ij}. The net effect is that pulses appearing at the third inverter have a pulse width proportional to $V_w \cdot D$ where D is the width of pulses from the pulse stream arriving from neuron j (o_j is represented by frequency of pulse stream).

The purpose of INV_3 is to invert this pulse in order to allow an equivalent charge packet dumped into capacitor C_3 via transistor T_6, driven in a saturated mode. A charge packet equivalent to the input pulse at neuron i is removed via T_7, which is also driven in saturated operation mode. Both of these transistors are either open or fully saturated. Considering noise limitation and the linearity of the product $V_w \cdot D$, it can be shown that the useful dynamic range of the stored voltage in C_1 lies between 1 V and 3 V. Aspect ratios of the transistors can be selected so that $V_w > 2$ V is used to represent excitation and $V_w < 2$ V is used to represent inhibition.

Dump and remove transistors (T_6, T_7) of all synapses connected to neuron i contribute to common capacitor C_3. The resulting voltage at C_3 controls a voltage controlled oscillator (VCO) which delivers the resulting output pulse stream of neuron i.

8.9 Summary

In comparison with digital CMOS circuitry, the field of analog VLSI is much more diverse. This diversity is caused by a variety of analog implementation technologies which exist. Examples are the analog CMOS technology, CCD/MNOS technology, EEPROM technology, amorphous silicon technology and many other more or less exotic technologies.

One major drawback of analog implementations is the strong dependency of circuit behavior on fabrication parameters. Often circuit designers have to compensate for the influence of these parameters through additional circuitry. Despite compensation, only limited computation accuracy can be realized. Thus, in many cases analog architectures support the recall phase exclusively without on-chip learning. Learning may only be supported for algorithms that can tolerate low accuracies, such as simple Hebbian learning or the self-organizing process of a Kohonen feature map.

On the other hand, asynchronous analog computation offers a speed far beyond the scope of digital solutions. Since Hopfield networks include feedback and tolerate binary or ternary signals, most of the early analog solutions were implementations of Hopfield networks. Many early implementations even contained hard-wired synaptic weights not alterable by the user. Today, all implementations have at least programmable weights (usually through charge storage on capacitors or floating-gate devices). Since the learning phase is the most time consuming part of a neural network simulation, there is a strong trend towards including analog on-chip learning. Some approaches try to avoid the problem of analog weight updating circuitry through digital weight storage (mixed analog/digital approach). Others invent quite complex analog circuits to achieve the defined weight changes. Then, learning algorithms often have to be simplified to operate with unit weight changes, which does not allow mathematical statements on their learning and convergence behavior to be made.

Users who need high speed hardware solutions and who do not need to speed up the learning phase can turn to an analog product like Intel's ETANN chip. However, if flexibility is needed or fast learning, a digital computer has to be chosen.

9
Optoelectronic and Optical Neurocomputers

9.1 Introduction

This chapter presents an overview of some optoelectronic and holographic neural network implementations. The basic principles of optical and optoelectronic computing were already given in Chapter 6. The main emphasis of the following realizations is on optoelectronic solutions. The reason is that optoelectronic solutions are more mature and lead to smaller designs which are simpler to integrate into a framework of standard electronic computer technology. However, the reader will find an incomplete description of optoelectronic and especially fully optical approches. The emphasis of this book is on digital and analog VLSI solutions, and a short overview of optical technologies is included to give the reader an impression of other implementation possibilities.

In the following, optoelectronic implementations will first be discussed, followed by a description of a fully optical solution. Optoelectronic solutions comply better with standard VLSI circuitry used in today's computer technology. This may be easily seen while reading the following section. Pure optic solutions form a completely different area of computing.

9.2 Optoelectronic Implementations

9.2.1 Optoelectronic Single-Layer Synapse Chip

A design to realize a simple Hopfield type network was done by Ohta *et al.* [Oht89] (Mitsubishi Laboratories). Task of the chip is to perform a fast multiplication of a binary input vector with a binary synaptic weight matrix to calculate a vector of neuron activation potentials (not binary). Input to and output from the chip are electronic signals.

At the input a self-emissive spatial light modulator (SLM) converts electronic signals into light. This is done by an array of parallel stripes of LEDs (each stripe is one LED). This array emits light signals corresponding to the values in the input vector. A second information processing layer above the LED layer is a signal-multiplying SLM. It consists of a two-dimensional array of weighting cells that weight light beams emitted by the LEDs. The whole structure is finished by an array of parallel photodetector PD stripes on the top to sum up illumination received and to convert it into electrical signals. These photodetector stripes are rectangular to the LED stripes. Figure 9.1 depicts the structure of the chip.

The signal-multiplying SLM may store only binary synaptic values and perform a binary vector/matrix multiplication (32×32 matrix). Ohta *et al.* realized a small Hopfield network using two optoelectronic synapse chips. One served to implement weights with a positive sign, the other to implement weights with a negative sign. Operational amplifiers were used at the chip outputs to emulate neuron threshold operations. The architecture is fully cascadable. Cascading is made by external electrical wiring and circuitry (operational amplifiers).

The chip was fabricated using GaAs/AlGaAs technology. A major drawback is its inflexibility due to binary weights and a weight matrix fixed

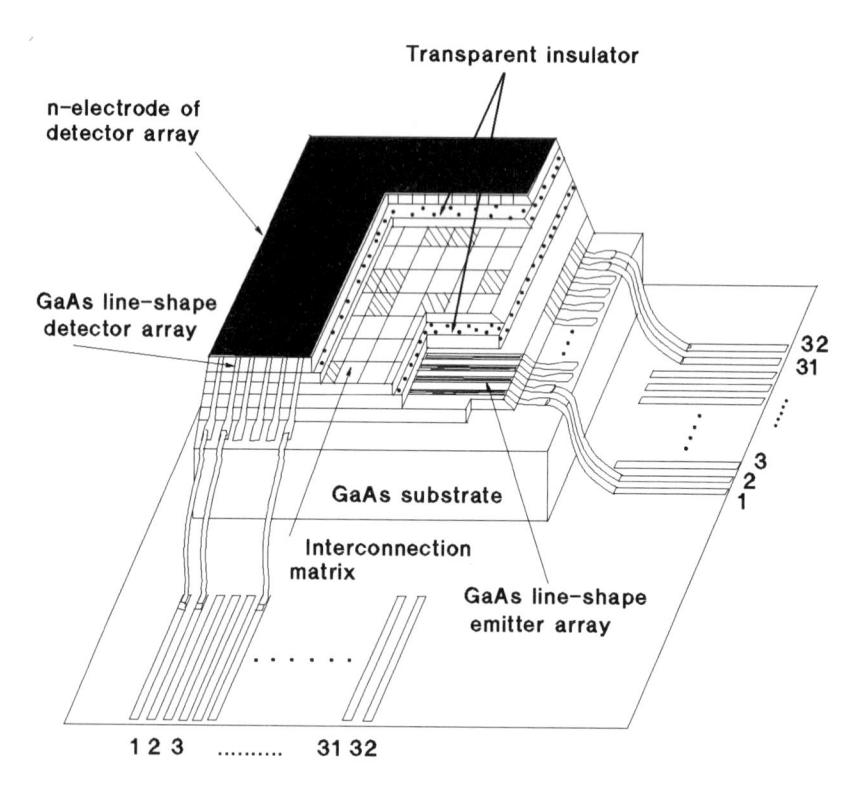

Figure 9.1 *Optoelectronic single layer synapse chip from Mitsubishi (adapted from [Oht89])*

Optoelectronic Implementations 251

during fabrication. Future work is dedicated to the development of more flexibility by using SLMs programmable by users (e.g. liquid crystal SLMs).

9.2.2 Optoelectronic Two-Layer Synapse Chip

Based on their first single-layer synapse chip for fully connected Hopfield networks, Ohta *et al.* designed a second optoelectronic chip for multi-layer feed-forward networks [Oht90]. The first difference to its predecessor chip is that synapse cells for positive and negative weights are both implemented on the same chip. Furthermore, the architecture allows ternary synapse weights, *i.e.* the weight values +1, 0 and -1. Again, LED stripes and PD stripes serve to convert electrical signals into optical signals, and *vice versa*. A total of 66 LED stripes and 110 PD stripes were realized on the chip. However, 36 LED stripes are used for the input to the first synaptic weight layer and another 30 LED stripes are used as input for the second synaptic weight layer. The two weight layers are located adjacent to each other on the flat, two-dimensional chip surface. Figure 9.2 sketches the chip architecture. Photodetectors are also separated into a 58 element array as output from the first synapse layer (29 × 2 elements, since two cells are necessary per

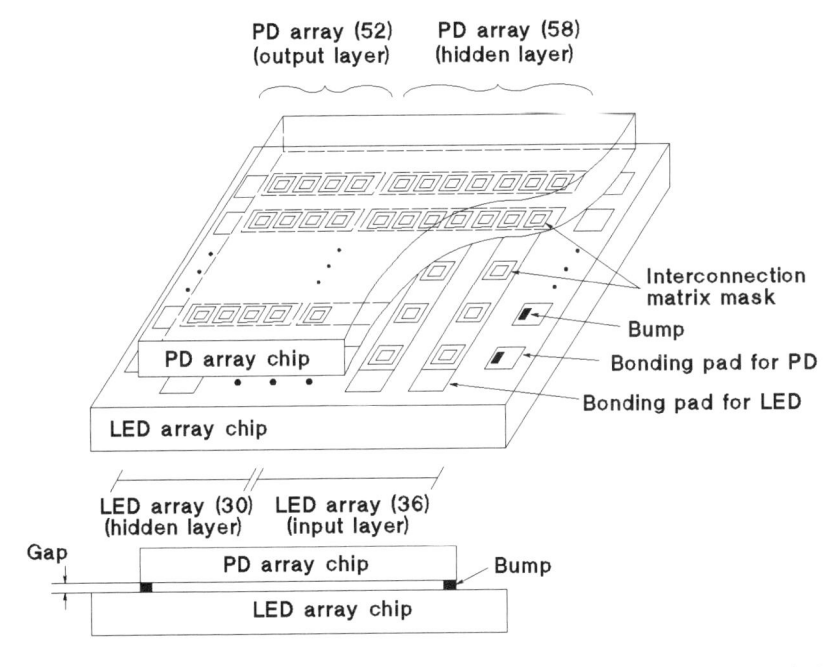

Figure 9.2 *Schematic diagram of the structure and cross-sectional view of the optical neurochip (adapted from [Oht90])*

synapse to allow positive and negative signs) and a 52 element array at the output of the second synapse layer (GaAs/AlGaAs technology).

Hence, the whole architecture serves to emulate a feed-forward network with a maximum size of 35 input neurons, 29 hidden neurons, and 26 output neurons. As in the predecessor chip, neurons (threshold operation) have to be realized off-chip with additional electronic circuitry. Only the two synaptic layers, one between input and hidden neurons, the second between hidden and output neurons are implemented on the optoelectronic chip. An example of a maximum size network is given in Figure 9.3. Operational amplifiers gather positive and negative weight outputs and apply a nonlinear threshold function. Operational amplifiers on the left side realize hidden neurons whereas operational amplifiers on the right belong to output neurons.

The network depicted in Figure 9.3 served to implement a small pattern recognition application. Twenty-six characters on a 7 × 5 dot binary "screen" should be classified. Learning was done off-chip by means of the backpropagation algorithm. Thus, the algorithm was modified to consider binary inputs/outputs and ternary weights. Despite correct classification in simulation, the hardware emulation yielded only 10 correctly classified

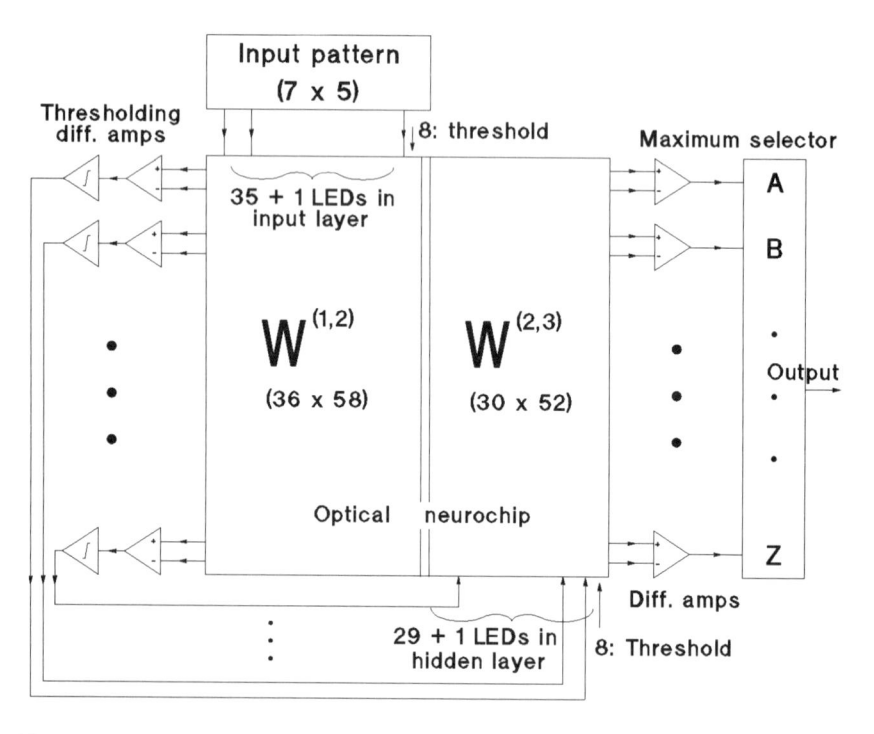

Figure 9.3 *Example for maximum size network circuitry (adapted from [Oht90])*

characters. This is due to technological problems (e.g. proper element alignment). However, recall speed for one recognition is about 1 μs corresponding to a speed of $\approx$ 1800 MCPS.

9.2.3 A Combined Optical/Optoelectronic Neurocomputer

Neugebauer et al. [Neu90] developed a hybrid optical/optoelectronic neural network emulator.

An optical part in the form of a holographic crystal serves as a signal-multiplying SLM for weight storage and multiplication. If light beams enter the holographic crystal they leave it weighted. Then, an optoelectronic chip accumulates the weighted optical signals and performs the nonlinear neural threshold operation. Figure 9.4 shows the information processing principle of optoelectronic circuitry. Phototransistors serve to transform received weighted light beams into currents which are summed up on a current node (neuron input). The current nodes are realized by operational amplifiers that also serve as nonlinear threshold devices.

The fabricated prototype (3 μm p-well MOSIS fabrication) served to implement a 32 neuron Hopfield type network. A synaptic weight accuracy of 5-6 bits is reported to be achieved (under low illumination within 10 μs). The computational speed is 100 MCPS. However, this is only recall speed; off-chip learning is necessary to fix weights appropriately.

9.2.4 Optoelectronic Hopfield Network for Pattern Recognition

A small 5 × 5 neuron optoelectronic Hopfield network was developed by Noguchi et al. [Nog90]. Figure 9.5 sketches the network architecture. Light is generated by a two-dimensional array of 880 nm LEDs. This light is then transmitted through a pinhole mask (spatial filter) to a two-dimensional detector array of SI-PIN photodiodes. The emitter LED array as well as the photodiode detector array are covered with a polarizer array. These polarizer arrays may be controlled to allow an individual connection to be selected from an emitter element to a detector element (this happens only if the respective polarizer elements are in the same polarization state).

Noguchi et al. applied the architecture to store the two letters "A" and "C" displayed on a 5 × 5 element display. Both letters could be recognized correctly (image completion task).

9.2.5 Other Optoelectronic Network Realizations

The previously described neural network implementations give just a brief introduction into the area of optoelectronic neural networks. Plenty of other designs have been made. Farhat et al., for example, describe the optoelectronic implementation of another Hopfield type network [Far85].

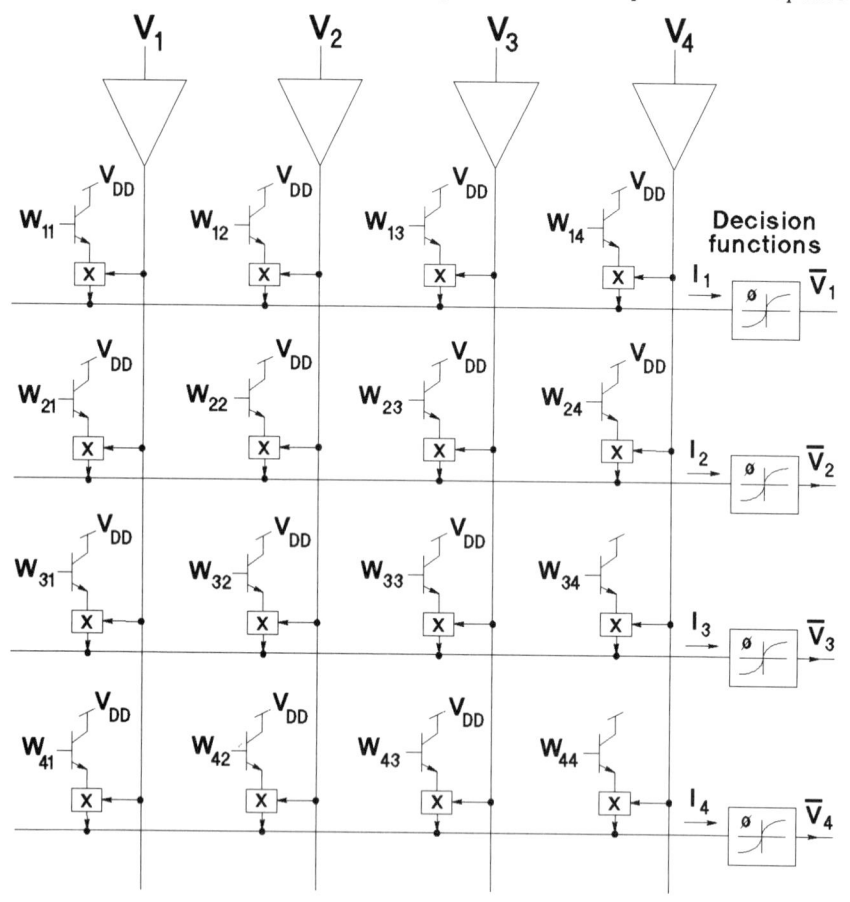

Figure 9.4 *Phototransistor network for synaptic accumulation (adapted from [Neu90])*

They also used electronic circuitry for neural amplification and thresholding whereas LEDs and PDs served as interface to the optic world. There, binary synapses for a fully connected feedback network of 32 neurons were realized with two optic masks (one for positive weight sign, the other for weights with negative sign). This is an example of a very simple system design.

Farhat extended the architecture to emulate a Boltzmann machine, including a Boltzmann machine learning algorithm [Far87, Far89]. An empty TV channel ("snow pattern") provided stochastic noise. Since only binary weight storage and multiplication is possible, Farhat implemented a deviation of the original Boltzmann machine learning from Hinton et al. [Hin84]

Optical Implementations 255

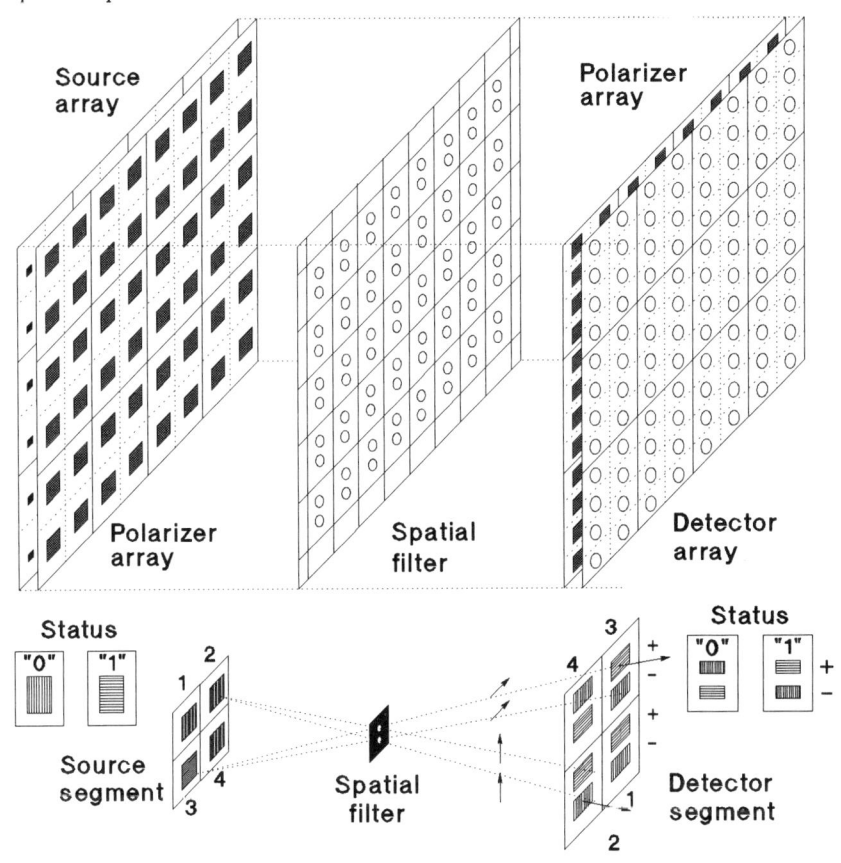

Figure 9.5 *Optical Hopfield memory from Noguchi et al. (adapted from [Nog90])*

and Derthick [Der84]. Several layers are realized by dividing the SLM into different separated areas.

Oita *et al.* [Oit90] used a time-division-multiplexing method to enable the emulation of large networks. Ternary synapses are realized by a liquid crystal display (SLM), and light emitted from LEDs is distributed via glass fiber bundles.

9.3 Optical Implementations

Pure optical neural network implementation approaches are extremely fast. No electronic devices with their parasitic capacitances and inductivities limit the speed of optical circuitry. However, pure optical neural network realizations are still very large. They are just mentioned for completeness. Therefore, in the following only one implementation from Psaltis *et al.* is

256   *Optoelectronic and Optical Neurocomputers*

presented. In recent years, many other more or less complex neural network models have been implemented using optical circuitry. The interested reader is recommended to take information on optical neural network solutions from recent conference proceedings or magazines like *Applied Optics*.

9.3.1 Holographic Associative Memory

Psaltis *et al.* mounted an optical associative memory with weight storage on two separate transparencies (plane holograms) [Abu87]. Figure 9.6 sketches the system setup.

The first hologram with two Fourier transforming lenses forms a pattern correlator. This correlator computes the inner product between an input image and several stored reference images. Thus, Fourier transforms of the reference images are stored on spatially separated frequency carriers on the holograms [Hsu88]. A pinhole array serves to separate the results of the inner products from cross-correlation noise. Each hole of the pinhole array yields the result of the inner product operation of the input image with the respective reference image. This information is presented to a second lens-hologram-lens correlator which carries the same information as

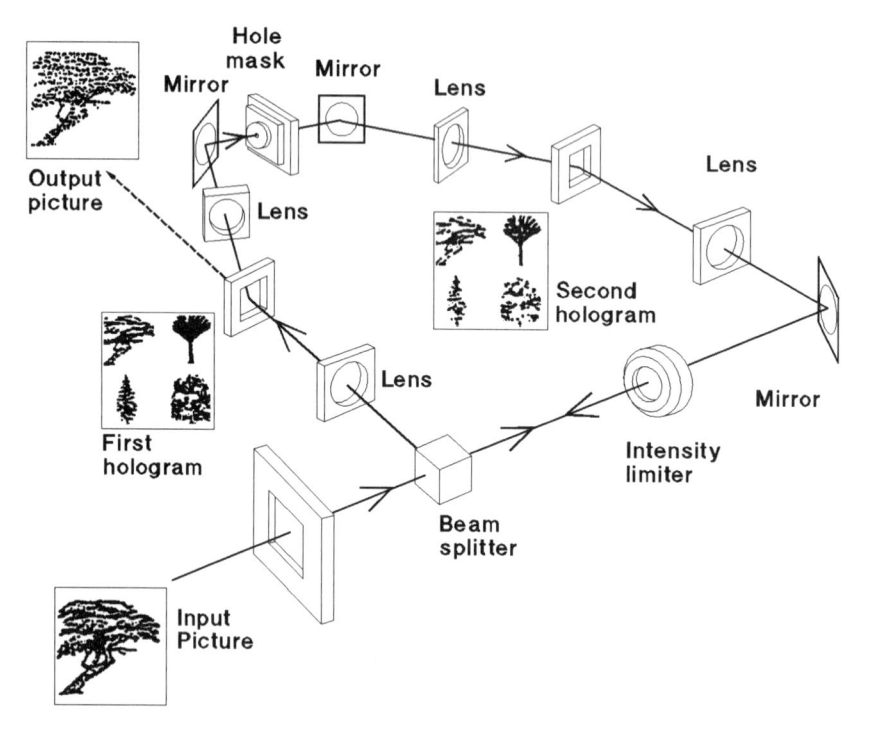

Figure 9.6 *Optical associative memory from Psaltis et al. (adapted from [Abu87])*

the first hologram. Based on the result from the pinhole array, the reference images are reconstructed and projected onto the back side of an intensity limiter (SLM) where they overlap. Bright spots on the back of this device allow corresponding image spots on the front side to be reflected, whereas dark spots on its back do not allow corresponding parts on the front side to be reflected.

Nonlinear threshold operations are done by a SLM. Optical gain can be provided by optical bistable elements or others to compensate for energy losses of light beams through passive elements. Mirrors serve to direct light beams into plane holograms and to reinsert optical signals into the optical loop after passing holograms, threshold and amplification devices. Through the loop structure, the brightest image will prevail, *i.e.* the image on the plane holograms which is most similar to the input image entered into the optical loop.

9.4 Summary

Compared with all other approaches documented in this book, the realization of neural networks with optical technologies is the most challenging. Due to the speed of light and the fact that light beams may cross without destroying the information they are carrying, extremely fast and dense information processing systems are feasible far beyond the scope of digital and analog solutions. However, the technological problems are even worse than with analog technologies. Optical computing has much in common with analog electronics. The technologies are often difficult to handle, fabrication is expensive, many different materials are available and fabrication parameters affect circuit performance. Therefore, as in analog solutions, on-chip learning cannot be found in this method, with the exception of a few designs including simple learning paradigmes, e.g. Hebbian learning.

At the moment purely optical solutions are condemned to be large constructions in laboratories. No competitive product is expected to emerge within the next few years. This is different to optoelectronic approaches. They combine some of the virtues of optics for synaptic interconnections together with electronics for other neural network operations. These implementations are made on small chips and seem to reach maturity much earlier than purely optical implementations. In spite of this, no commercial product is currently available. The user has to turn to products implemented in digital or analog VLSI.

References

[Aar89] E. Aarts, J. Korst, *Simulated Annealing and Boltzmann Machines*, John Wiley & Sons, Chichester, 1989

[Abu87] Y.S. Abu-Mostafa, D. Psaltis, "Optical Neural Computers", *Scientific American*, pp. 88, Vol. 256, No. 3, March 1987

[Ack85] D.H. Ackley, G.E. Hinton, T.J. Sejnowski, "A learning algorithm for Boltzmann machines", *Cognitive Science*, Vol. 9, pp. 147-169, 1985

[Ada91] Adaptive Solutions, *CNAPS Neurocomputing*, Information sheet on the CNAPS neurocomputing system, Adaptive Solutions, Inc., 1400 NW Compton Drive Suite 340, Beaverton, OR 97006, U.S.A., 1991

[Agr87] A. Agranat, A. Yariv, "A New Architecture for a Microelectronic Implementation of Neural Network Models", *Proceedings of the IEEE 1st International Conference on Neural Networks*, Vol. III, pp. 403-409, San Diego, U.S.A., June 1987

[Agr90] A.J. Agranat, C.F. Neugebauer, R.D. Nelson, A. Yariv, "The CCD Neural Processor: A Neural Network Integrated Circuit with 65536 Programmable Synapses", *IEEE Transactions on Circuits and Systems*, Vol. 37, No. 8, pp. 1073-1075, August 1990

[Ale79] I. Aleksander, T.J. Stoneham, "A Guide to Pattern Recognition using Random-Access Memories", *IEEE Journal on Computers and Digital Techniques*, Volume 2, No. 1, pp. 29-40, 1979

[Ale84] I. Aleksander, W.V. Thomas, P.A. Bowden, "WISARD: A Radical Step forward in Image Recognition", *Sensor Review*, Vol. 4, No. 3, pp. 120-124, July 1984

[Ale89a] I. Aleksander, H.B. Morton, *An Introduction to Neural Computing*, MIT Press, Boston, 1989

[Ale89b] I. Aleksander (editor), *Neural Computing Architectures*, North Oxford Academic, London, 1989

[Ale90] I. Aleksander, H.B. Morton, "An Overview of Weightless Neural Nets", *Proceedings of the International Joint Conference on Neural Networks IJCNN'90*, Volume II, pp. 499-502, Washington DC, U.S.A., January 1990

[Ale91] I. Aleksander, "Connectionism or Weightless Neurocomputing?", in *Artificial Neural Networks*, edited by T. Kohonen, K. M"akisara, O. Simula, J. Kangas, Volume 2, pp. 991-1000, Elsevier, Amsterdam, 1991

[Als87] J. Alspector, R.B. Allen, "A Neuromorphic VLSI Learning System", in *Advanced Research in VLSI: Proceedings of the 1987 Stanford Conference*, edited by P. Losleben, pp. 313-349, MIT Press, Cambridge, U.S.A., 1987

[Als88a] J. Alspector, "A VLSI Approach to Neural-Style Information Processing", in *VLSI Signal Processing, III*, edited by R.W. Brodersen and H.S. Moscovitz, pp. 232-243, IEEE Press, New York, 1988

[Als88b] J. Alspector, R.B. Allen, V. Hu, S. Satyanarayana, "Stochastic Learning Networks and their Electronic Implementation", in *Neural Information Processing Systems*, edited by Dana Z. Anderson, pp. 9-21, American Institute of Physics, New York, 1988

[Ann86] M. Annaratone, *Digital CMOS Circuit Design*, Kluwer Academic Publishers, Boston, 1986

[Ann87] M. Annaratone, E. Arnould, T. Gross, H.T. Kung, M. Lam, O. Menzilcioglu, J.A. Webb, "The Warp Computer: Architecture, Implementation, and Performance", *IEEE Transactions on Computers*, Vol. C-36, No. 12, pp. 1523-1538, December 1987

[Arn85] E. Arnould et al., "A Systolic Array Computer", *Proceedings of the IEEE International Conference on Application Specific Signal Processing ICASSP'85*, pp. 232-235, Tampa, Florida, U.S.A, 1985

[Asa91] K. Asanovic and N. Morgan, "Experimental Determination of Precision Requirements for Backpropagation Training of Artificial Neural Networks", *Proceedings of the 2nd International Conference on Microelectronics for Neural Networks*, pp. 9-15, Munich, Germany, October 1991

[Atl89] L.E. Atlas, Y. Suzuki, "Digital Systems for Artificial Neural Networks", *IEEE Circuits and Devices Magazine*, Vol. 5, No. 6, pp. 20-24, November 1989

[Aze89] R. Azencott, "Synchronous Boltzmann Machines and their Learning Algorithms", NATO ARW., Les Arcs, France, February 1989

[Bad89] A. Badii, M.J. Binstead, A.J. Jones, T.J. Stoneham, C.L. Valenzuela, "Applications of N-Tuple Sampling and Genetic Algorithms to Speech Recognition", in *Neural Computing Architectures*, edited by I. Aleksander, North Oxford Academic, London, 1989

[Bei91] J. Beichter, N. Bruels, E. Meister, U. Ramacher, H. Klar, "Design of a General-purpose Neural Signal Processor", *Proceedings of the 2nd International Conference on Microelectronics for Neural Networks*, pp. 311-315, Munich, Germany, October 1991

[Ber81] J. Bernstein, "Profiles: AI, Marvin Minsky" in *The New Yorker*, pp. 50-126, 1981, December 14

[Bey80] J.D.E. Beynon, D.R. Lamb, *Charge-Coupled Devices and their Application*, McGraw-Hill, London, 1980

[Blan90] T. Blank, "The MasPar MP-1 Architecture", *Proceedings of the 35th IEEE Computer Society International Conference–Spring COMPCON 90*, pp. 20-24, San Francisco, U.S.A., February/March 1990

[Blay89] F. Blayo, P. Hurat, "A VLSI Systolic Array Dedicated to Hopfield Neural Networks", in *VLSI for Artificial Intelligence*, edited by J.G. Delgado-Frias and W.R. Moore, pp. 255-264, Kluwer, Boston, 1989

[Boa89] K.A. Boahen, P.O. Pouliquen, A.G. Andreou, R.E. Jenkins, "A Heteroassociative Memory using Current-mode MOS Analog VLSI Circuits", *IEEE*

Transactions on Circuits and Systems, Vol. 36, No. 5, pp. 747-755, May 1989

[Boy90] J. Boyd, "Hitachi's Neural Computer", *Electronic World News*, p. 6 and p. 8, December 10 1990

[Can90] S. Canditt, R. Eckmiller, "Pulse Coding Hardware Neurons that learn Boolean Functions", *Proceedings of the International Joint Conference on Neural Networks IJCNN'90*, Vol. 2, pp. 102-105, Washington D.C., U.S.A., January 1990

[Car89] H.C. Card, W.R. Moore, "EEPROM Synapses Exhibiting Pseudo-Hebbian Plasticity", *Electronics Letters*, Vol. 25, No. 12, pp. 805-806, June 1989

[Cav90] D.D. Caviglia, M. Valle, G.M. Bisio, "Effects of Weight Discretization on the Back Propagation Learning Method: Algorithm Design and Hardware Realization" *Proceedings of the International Joint Conference on Neural Networks IJCNN'90*, Volume II, pp. 632-637, San Diego, U.S.A., June 1990

[Cha87] T.Y. Chan, K.K. Young, C. Hu, "True Single-Transistor Oxide-Nitride-Oxide EEPROM Device", *IEEE Electron Device Letters*, Vol. EDL-8, No. 3, pp. 93-95, March 1987

[Chr90] P. Christy, "Software to Support Massively Parallel Computing on the MasPar MP-1", *Proceedings of the 35th IEEE Computer Society International Conference–Spring COMPCON 90*, pp. 29-33, San Francisco, U.S.A., February/March 1990

[Chu88a] L.O. Chua, L. Yang, "Cellular Neural Networks: Theory and Applications", *IEEE Transactions on Circuits and Systems*, Vol. 35, No. 10, pp. 1257-1290, October 1988

[Chu88b] L.O. Chua, T. Lin, "A Neural Network Approach to Transform Image Coding", *International Journal of Circuit Theory and Applications*, Vol. 16, pp. 317-324, April 1988

[Chu91] S. Churcher, D.J. Baxter, A. Hamilton, A.F. Murray, H.M. Reekie, "Towards a Generic Analogue VLSI Neurocomputing Architecture", *Proceedings of the 2nd International Conference on Microelectronics for Neural Networks*, pp. 127-133, Munich, Germany, October 1991

[Coh88] A. Cohen, "Evolution of the Vertebrate Central Pattern Generator" in *Neural Control of Rhythmic Movements in Vertebrates*, edited by A. Cohen, S. Rossignol, and S. Grillner, John Wiley & Sons, Chichester, 1988

[Coo88] D.D. Coon, A.G.U. Perera, "New Hardware for Massive Neural Networks", in *Neural Information Processing Systems*, edited by D.Z. Anderson, pp. 201-210, American Institute of Physics, New York, 1988

[Cott88] N.E. Cotter, K. Smith, M. Gasper, "A Pulse Width Modulation Design Approach and Programmable Logic for Artificial Neural Networks", *Proceedings of the 5th MIT Conference on Advanced Research in VLSI*, pp. 1-15, Massachusetts Institute of Technology, Cambridge, U.S.A., 1988

[Cro92] I.F. Croall, J.P. Mason (editors), *Industrial Applications of Neural Networks*, Research Reports ESPRIT, Springer, Berlin, 1992

[Cru87] C.A. Cruz, W.A. Hanson, J.Y. Tam, "Neural Network Emulation Hardware Design Considerations", *Proceedings of the IEEE First International Conference on Neural Networks*, Vol. III, pp. 427-434, San Diego, U.S.A., 1987

[DAR89] Massachusetts Insitute of Technology, *DARPA neural network study*, final report Oct. 1987 – Feb. 1988, Technical Report 840, Lincoln Laboratory, MIT, March 1989

[Dem90] A. Dembo and T. Kailath, "Model-Free Distribution Learning", *IEEE Transactions on Neural Networks*, Vol. 1, pp. 58-70, 1990

[Der84] M. Derthick, "Variations on the Boltzmann Machine Learning Algorithm", *Technical Report CMU-CS-84-120*, Carnegie-Mellon University, Pittsburgh, U.S.A., August 1984

[Erno88] C. Ernoult, "Performance of backpropagation on a parallel transputer-based machine", *Proceedings of Neuro Nimes 88*, pp. 311-324, Nimes, France, 1988

[Erns90] H.P. Ernst, B. Mokry, Z. Schreter, "A Transputer Based General Simulator for Connectionist Models", in *Parallel Processing in Neural Systems and Computers*, edited by R. Eckmiller, G. Hartmann, and G. Hauske, pp. 283-286, North-Holland, Amsterdam, 1990

[Far85] N.H. Farhat, D. Psaltis, A. Prata, E. Paek, "Optical implementation of the Hopfield model", *Applied Optics*, Vol. 24, No. 10, pp. 1469-1475, 15 May 1985

[Far87] N.H. Farhat, "Optoelectronic analogs of self-programming neural nets: architecture and methodologies for implementing fast stochastic learning by simulated annealing", *Applied Optics*, Vol. 26, No. 23, pp. 5093-5103, December 1987

[Far89] N.H. Farhat, "Optoelectronic Neural Networks and Learning Machines", *IEEE Circuits and Devices Magazine*, Vol. 5, No. 5, pp. 32-41, September 1989

[Fau90] B. Faure, G. Mazare, "A VLSI Asynchronous Cellular Architecture for Neural Computing: Functional Definition and Performance Evaluation", *Proceedings of the 3rd International Conference on Industrial and Engineering Applications of Artificial Intelligence and Expert Systems*, pp. 838-847, Charleston, South Carolina, U.S.A, July 1990

[Fau91] B. Faure, G. Mazare, "A VLSI Implementation of Multi-Layered Neural Networks: 2-Performance", *VLSI for Artificial Intelligence and Neural Networks*, edited by J.G. Delgado-Frias and W.R. Moore, pp. 377-386, Plenum Press, New York, 1991

[Fel88] M.R. Feldman, S.C. Esener, C.C. Guest, S.H. Lee, "Comparison between optical and electrical interconnects based on power and speed considerations", *Applied Optics*, Vol. 27, No. 9, 1st May 1988

[For87] B.M. Forrest, D. Roweth, N. Stround, D.J. Wallace, G.V. Wilson, "Implementing Neural Network Models on Parallel Computers", *Computer Journal*, Vol. 30, No. 5, pp. 413-419, 1987

[Gas92] J.-D. Gascuel, E. Delaunay, L. Montoliu, B. Moobed, M. Weinfeld, "A Custom Associative Chip used as Building Block for a Software Reconfigurable Multi-Networks Simulator", *Proceedings of the Third International Workshop on VLSI for Artificial Intelligence and Neural Networks*, D2, Oxford, U.K., September 1992

[Gei90] R.L. Geiger, P.E. Allen, N.R. Strader, *VLSI Design Techniques for Analog and Digital Circuits*, McGraw-Hill Publishing Company, New York, 1990

[Get85] P.A. Getting and M.S. Dekin, "Tritonia swimming: A model system for integration within rhythmic motor systems", in *Model Neural Networks and*

Behavior, edited by A.I. Silverston, Plenum Press, New York, 1985

[Gle89] M. Glesner, M. Huch, W. Poechmueller, G. Palm "Hardware Implementations for Neural Networks", *Proceedings of the IFIP Workshop on Parallel Architectures on Silicon*, pp. 65-79, Grenoble, France, 1989

[Gle91a] M. Glesner, W. Poechmueller, "Entwurf eines Chips fuer den Aufbau eines schnellen neuronalen Netzwerks in Hardware", *BMFT-Schlussbericht zum Verbundprojekt "Informationsverarbeitung in neuronaler Architektur" (No. ITR 8800 M/O)*, Bundesministerium fuer Forschung und Technologie (BMFT), Bonn, Germany, 1991

[Gle91b] M. Glesner, W. Poechmueller, *Circuit diagrams and timing diagrams of BACCHUS III*, Darmstadt University of Technology, Institute for Microelectronic Systems, Karlstrasse 15, D-6100 Darmstadt, Germany, 1991

[Goo89] A.J. van de Goor, *Computer Architecture and Design*, Addison-Wesley, Reading, Massachusetts, 1989

[Gos89] K. Goser, U. Hilleringmann, U. Rueckert, K. Schumacher, "VLSI Technologies for Artificial Neural Networks", *IEEE Micro*, pp. 28-44, December 1989

[Gos90] K. Goser, *Grossintegrationstechnik*, Teil 1: Vom Transistor zur Grundschaltung, Huethig-Verlag, Heidelberg, 1990

[Graf86] H.P. Graf, L.D. Jackel, R.W. Howard, B. Straughn, J.S. Denker, W. Hubbard, D.M. Tennant, D. Schwartz, "VLSI Implementation of a Neural Network Memory with Several Hundreds of Neurons", *Proceedings of the AIP Conference on Neural Networks for Computing*, pp. 182-187, 0094-243X/86/1510182-6, Snowbird, Utah, U.S.A., 1986

[Graf87a] H. Graf, P. de Vegvar, "A CMOS Implementation of a Neural Network Model", in *Advanced Research in VLSI – Proceedings of the 1987 Stanford Conference*, edited by P. Losleben, pp. 351-367, MIT Press, Cambridge, 1987

[Graf87b] H.P. Graf, W. Hubbard, L.D. Jackel, P.G.N. de Vegvar, "A CMOS Associative Memory Chip", *Proceedings of the IEEE First International Conference on Neural Networks*, Vol. III, pp.461-468, San Diego, U.S.A., June 1987

[Graf87c] H.P. Graf, P. de Vegvar, "A CMOS Associative Memory Chip Based on Neural Networks", *Proceedings of the IEEE International Solid-State Circuits Conference ISSCC'87*, pp. 304, 305 and 437, New York, February 1987

[Graf91] H.P. Graf, E. Sackinger, B. Boser, and L.D. Jackel, "Recent Developments of Electronic Neural Nets in the US and Canada", *Proceedings of the 2nd International Conference on Microelectronics for Neural Networks*, pp. 471-488, Munich, Germany, October 1991

[Graj90a] K.A. Grajski, G. Chinn, C. Chen, C. Kuszmaul, S. Tomboulian, "Neural Network Simulation on the MasPar Mp-1 Massively Parallel Processor", *Proceedings of the International Neural Network Conference INNC'90*, p. 673 (abstract of poster presentation), Paris, France, July 1990

[Graj90b] K.A. Grajski, G. Chinn, C. Chen, C. Kuszmaul, S. Tomboulian, "Neural Network Simulation on the MasPar MP-1 Massively Parallel Processor", *MasPar information sheet TW007.0690*, MasPar Computer Corporation, 749 North Mary Avenue, Sunnyvale, CA 94086, U.S.A., 1990

[Gray84] P.R. Gray, R.G. Meyer, *Analysis and Design of Analog Integrated Circuits*, John Wiley and Sons, New York, 1984

[Gri90] M. Griffin et al., "An 11 Million Transistor Neural Network Execution Engine", *Proceedings of the IEEE International Solid-State Circuits Conference ISSCC'91*, pp. 180-181, 91CH2960-3/91/0000-0180, February 1991

[Halo90] K. Halonen, V. Porra, T. Roska, L.O. Chua, "VLSI Implementation of a Reconfigurable Cellular Neural Network Containing Local Logic (CNNL)", *Proceedings of the 1st IEEE International Workshop on Cellular Neural Networks and their Applications CNNA'90*, pp. 206-215, Budapest, Hungary, 1990

[Halg91] S.K. Halgamuge, W. Poechmueller, M. Glesner, "Computational Hardware Requirements for the Backpropagation Algorithm", *Proceedings of the 2nd International Conference on Microelectronics for Neural Networks*, pp. 47-52, Munich, Germany, October 1991

[Ham90] D. Hammerstrom, "A VLSI Architecture for High-Performance, Low-Cost, On-chip Learning", *Proceedings of the International Joint Conference on Neural Networks IJCNN'90*, Volume II, pp. 537-544, San Diego, U.S.A., June 1990

[Ham91] D. Hammerstrom, N. Nguyen, "An Implementation of Kohonen's Self-Organizing Map on the Adaptive Solutions Neurocomputer", *Proceedings of the International Conference on Artificial Neural Networks ICANN'91*, Volume I, pp. 715-720, Espoo, Finland, June 1991

[Has88] M.R. Haskard, I.C. May, *Analog VLSI Design*, edited by Kamran Eshraghian, Prentice Hall, Englewood Cliffs, New Jersey, 1988

[Heb49] D.O. Hebb, *The Organization of Behavior*, Introduction (pp. xi - xix) and Chapter 4, "The first stage of perception: growth of the assembly", pp. 60-78, John Wiley and Sons, New York, 1949

[Hec88] R. Hecht-Nielsen, "Neurocomputing: picking the human brain", *IEEE Spectrum*, Vol. 25, No. 3, pp. 36-41, 1988

[Hec91] Hecht-Nielsen Computers, *Information sheet on HNC neural network products*, HNC, Inc., 5501 Oberlin Drive, San Diego, California 92121, U.S.A.

[Her91] J. Hertz, A. Krogh, R.G. Palmer, *Introduction to the Theory of Neural Computation*, Lecture Notes Volume I, Santa Fe Institute Studies in the Sciences of Complexity, Addison-Wesley, Redwood City, 1991

[Hil85] W.D. Hillis, *The Connection Machine*, The MIT Press, Cambridge, Massachusetts, 1985

[Hin84] G.E. Hinton, T.J. Sejnowski, D.H. Ackley, "Boltzmann Machines: Constraint Satisfaction Networks that Learn", *Technical Report CMU-CS-84-119*, Carnegie-Mellon University, Pittsburgh, May 1984

[Hir90] A. Hiraiwa, S. Kurosu, S. Arisawa, M. Inoue, "A Two Level Pipeline RISC Processor Array for ANN", *Proceedings of the International Joint Conference on Neural Networks IJCNN'90*, Volume II, pp. 137-140, Washington D.C., U.S.A., January 1990

[Hoe91] J. Hoekstra, "(Junction) Charge-Coupled Device Technology for Artificial Neural Networks", in *VLSI Design of Neural Networks*, edited by U. Ramacher and U. Rueckert, pp. 19-45, Kluwer, Boston, 1991

[Holle92] M. Holler, C. Park, J. Diamond, U. Santoni, S.C. The, M. Glier, C.L. Scofield, L. Nunez, "A High Performance Adaptive Classifier Using Radial Basis Functions", *Submitted to Government Microcircuit Applications Conference*, Las Vegas, Nevada, U.S.A., November 9-12 1992

[Holli90] P.W. Hollis, J.S. Harper, J.J. Paulos, "The effect of precision constraints in a backpropagation learning network", *Neural Computation*, Vol. 2, pp. 363-373, 1990

[Hon86] J. Hong, D. Psaltis, "Storage capacity of holographic associative memories", *Optics Letters*, Vol. 11, No. 12, pp. 812-814, December 1986

[Hop82] J.J. Hopfield, "Neural Networks and Physical Systems with Emergent Collective Computational Abilities", *Proceedings of the National Academy of Sciences*, Vol. 79, No. 8, pp. 2554-2558, Washington DC, U.S.A., April 1982

[Hop86] J.J. Hopfield, D.W. Tank, "Computing with Neural Circuits: A Model", *Science*, Vol. 233, pp. 625-633, August 1986

[Hori90] Y. Horio, M. Yamamota, S. Nakamura, "Active Analog Memories for VLSI Analog Neural Networks", *Proceedings of the International Conference on Fuzzy Logic and Neural Networks IIZUKA'90*, pp. 655-659, Vol. 2, Liyuka, Fukuoka, Japan, July 1990

[Horn87] J.L. Horner, *Optical Signal Processing*, Academic Press, Orlando, 1987

[How79] M.J. Howes, D.V. Morgan, *Charge-Coupled Devices and Systems*, Wiley, Chicester, 1979

[Hsu88] K. Hsu, D. Brady, D. Psaltis, "Experimental Demonstrations of Optical Neural Computers", in *Neural Information Processing Systems*, edited by Dana Z. Anderson, pp. 377-386, American Institute of Physics, New York, 1988

[Huc90] M. Huch, W. Poechmueller, M. Glesner, "Bacchus: a VLSI Architecture for a Large Binary Associative Memory", *Proceedings of the International Neural Network Conference INNC 90*, Volume 2, pp. 661-664, Paris, France, 1990

[Hut88] J. Hutchinson, C. Koch, J. Luo, C. Mead, "Computing Motion Using Analog and Binary Resistive Networks", *IEEE Computer*, Vol. 21, No. 3, March 1988

[INM89] INMOS SARL, *IMS T800 transputer*, Engineering Data (handbook 42 1406 02), INMOS SARL, France, January 1989

[Int90] Intel Corporation, "80170NW Electrically Trainable Analog Neural Network", *Intel Information Sheet USA\E358\0590\2k\GF\CC*, May 1990

[Int92a] Intel Corporation, *80170NX Neural Network Technology & Applications*, Publication #241359, Intel Corporation, 2200 Mission College Boulvard, Mail Stop RN3-17, Santa Clara, CA 95052-8119, U.S.A., 1992

[Int92b] Intel Corporation, *Neural Network Solutions*, Order Number: 296961-002, Intel Corporation, 2200 Mission College Boulvard, Mail Stop RN3-17, Santa Clara, CA 95052-8119, U.S.A., 1992

[Int93] Intel Corporation, *Intel Neural Network Products Price and Availability*, Intel Corporation, 2200 Mission College Boulvard, Mail Stop RN3-17, Santa Clara, CA 95052-8119, U.S.A., March 1993

[Iwa90] A. Iwata, *Neural Devices and Networks*, Sixth German-Japanese Forum on Information Technology, Berlin, Germany, May 1990

[Jac87a] L.D. Jackel, R.E. Howard, J.S. Denker, W. Hubbard, S.A. Solla, "Building a Hierarchy with Neural Networks: An Example–Image Vector Quantization", *Applied Optics*, Vol. 26, No. 23, pp. 5081-5084, December 1987

[Jac87b] L.D. Jackel, H.P. Graf, R.E. Howard, "Electronic Neural Network Chips", *Applied Optics*, Vol. 26, No. 23, pp. 5077-5080, December 1987

[Jes86] C. Jesshope, W. Moore (editors), *Wafer Scale Integration*, Proceedings of a workshop held in Southampton from 10 July to 12 July 1985, Adam Hilger, Bristol, 1986

[Joh93a] R.C. Johnson (editor), "Siemens Shows Off its First Neural Network Chip", in *Cognizer Report*, Vol. 4, No. 2, pp. 9-11, Frontline Strategies, 516 S.E. Chkalov Drive, Suite 164, Vancouver, WA 98684, U.S.A., February 1993

[Joh93b] R.C. Johnson (editor), "Intel/Nestor Announce Delivery of Chip to DARPA", in *Cognizer Report*, Vol. 4, No. 3, pp. 17-19, Frontline Strategies, 516 S.E. Chkalov Drive, Suite 164, Vancouver, WA 98684, U.S.A., March 1993

[Kan87] W.-K. Kan, I. Aleksander, "A Probabilistic Logic Neuron Network for Associative Learning", *Proceedings of the IEEE First International Conference on Neural Networks*, Volume II, pp. 541-548, San Diego, U.S.A., June 1987

[Kar82] S.P. Kartashev, S.I. Kartashev (editors), *Designing and Programming Modern Computers and Systems, Volume 1: LSI modular computer systems*, Prentice-Hall, Englewood Cliffs, New Jersey, 1982

[Kat84] M.G.H. Katevenis, *Reduced Instruction Set Computer Architectures for VLSI*, ACM Doctoral Dissertation Awards 1984, The MIT Press, Cambridge, 1985

[Kat90] H. Kato, H. Yoshizawa, H. Iciki, K. Asakawa, "A Parallel Neurocomputer Architecture towards Billion Connection Updates Per Second", *Proceedings of the International Joint Conference on Neural Networks IJCNN 90*, Volume II, pp. 47-50, Washington D.C., U.S.A., January 1990

[Kat66] B. Katz, *Nerve, Muscle, and Synapse*, McGraw-Hill, New York, 1966

[Koe91a] A. Koenig, W. Poechmueller, M. Glesner, "A Flexible Neural Network Implemented as a Coprocessor to a von Neumann Architecture", *Proceedings of the 2nd International Conference on Microelectronics for Neural Networks*, Munich, Germany, October 1991

[Koe91b] A. Koenig, M. Glesner, "An Approach to the Application of Dedicated Neural Network Hardware for Real Time Image Compression", *Proceedings of the International Conference on Artificial Neural Networks ICANN'91*, Volume II, pp. 1345-1348, Espoo, Finland, June 1991

[Koh88] T. Kohonen, *Self-Organization and Associative Memory*, Third edition, Springer-Verlag, Berlin, 1989

[Kos88] B. Kosko, "Bidirectional associative memories", *IEEE Transactions on System, Man, and Cybernetics*, Vol. 18, pp. 49-60, January/February 1988

[Kuc88] R. Kuczewsk, M. Myers, W. Crawford, "Neurocomputer Workstations and Processors: Approaches and Applications", *Proceedings of the IEEE Conference on Neural Networks*, Volume III, pp. 487-500, San Diego, U.S.A., June 1988

[Kun88] S.Y. Kung, *VLSI Array Processors*, Prentice Hall Information and System Sciences Series, Englewood Cliffs, New Jersey, 1988

[Kun85] H.T. Kung, J.A. Webb, "Global Operations on a Systolic Array Machine", *Proceedings of the IEEE International Conference on Computer Design: VLSI in Computers ICCD'85*, pp. 165-171, Port Chester, New York, U.S.A., October 1985

[Lal89] P. Lalanne, "Optical Implementation of Neural Networks: State-of-the-Art and Perspectives", *Journées d'Électronique 1989*, pp. 252-263, Lausanne, Switzerland, October 1989

[LeC85] P.G. LeComber, A.E. Owen, W.E. Spear, J. Hajto, A.J. Snell, W.K. Choi, M.J. Rose, S. Reynolds, *Journal of Non-Crystalline Solids*, Vol. 77 and 78, p. 1373, 1985

[Lehm91] C. Lehmann, F. Blayo, "A VLSI Implementation of a Generic Systolic Synaptic Building Block for Neural Networks", in *VLSI for Artificial Intelligence and Neural Networks*, edited by J.G. Delgado-Frias and W.R. Moore, pp. 325-334, Plenum Press, New York, 1991

[Lor81] K.Z. Lorenz, *The Foundations of Ethology*, Springer-Verlag, New York, 1981

[Lyo88a] R.F. Lyon, "Analog VLSI Hearing Systems" in *VLSI Signal Processing, III*, edited by R.W. Brodersen and H.S. Moscovitz, pp. 244-251, IEEE Press, New York, 1988

[Lyo88b] R.F. Lyon, C. Mead, "An Analog Electronic Cochlea", *IEEE Transactions on Acoustics, Speech, and Signal Processing*, Vol. 36, No. 7, pp. 1119-1134, July 1988

[Man87] J. Mann, B. Berger, J. Raffel, A. Soares, S. Gilbert, "A Generic Architecture for Wafer-Scale Neuromorphic Systems", *Proceedings of the IEEE First International Conference on Neural Networks*, Vol. IV, pp. 485-493, San Diego, U.S.A., June 1987

[Man88a] J.R. Mann, R. Lippmann, B. Berger, J. Raffel, "A Self-Organizing Neural Net Chip", *Proceedings of the IEEE 1988 Custom Integrated Circuits Conference*, pp. 10.3.1-10.3.5, Rochester, U.S.A., May 1988

[Man88b] J.R. Mann, S. Gilbert, "An Analog Self-Organizing Neural Network Chip", Massachusetts Institute of Technology, Lincoln Laboratory, 244 Wood Street, Lexington, MA 02173-0073, U.S.A., 1988

[Mas90a] MasPar, *University of Bath Purchases Massively Parallel Computer to Develop Important Programming Tools*, Information sheet 100890.513BR, MasPar Computer Corporation, First Base, Beacontree Plaza, Gillette Way, Reading RG2 OBP, Berkshire, U.K., 1990

[Mas90b] MasPar, *MasPar 1100 Series Computer Systems*, Information sheet PL003.0490, MasPar Computer Corporation, 749 North Mary Avenue, Sunnyvale, California 94086, U.S.A., 1990

[Mas90c] MasPar, *MasPar 1200 Series Computer Systems*, Information sheet PL004.0490, MasPar Computer Corporation, 749 North Mary Avenue, Sunnyvale, California 94086, U.S.A., 1990

[Mas90d] MasPar, *The MP-1 Family Data-Parallel Computers*, Information sheet PL006.0490, MasPar Computer Corporation, 749 North Mary Avenue, Sunnyvale, California 94086, U.S.A., 1990

[McC90] W.J. McClean (editor), *ASIC OUTLOOK 1991: An Application Specific IC Report and Directory*, Integrated Circuit Engineering Corporation, Scottsdale, Arizona, U.S.A., 1990

[McC91] W.J. McClean (editor), *STATUS 1991: A Report on the Integrated Circuit Industry*, Integrated Circuit Engineering Corporation, Scottsdale, Arizona, U.S.A., 1991

[Mead89] C.A. Mead, *Analog VLSI and Neural Systems*, Addison Wesley, Reading, Massachusetts, 1989

[Mean91] R.W. Means, L. Lisenbee, "Extensible Linear Floating Point SIMD Neurocomputer Array Processor", *Proceedings of the International Joint Conference on Neural Networks IJCNN'91*, Volume I, pp. 587-592, Seattle, Washington, U.S.A., July 1991

[Mee79] R.W. Meech, "Membrane potential oscillations in molluscan burster neurons", *Journal of Experimental Biology*, Vol. 81, pp. 93-112, 1979

[Mek90] A. Mekkaoui, P. Jespers, "An Unsupervised Neural Net Classifier and its VLSI Implementation", *Proceedings of the 1st International Workshop on Microelectronics for Neural Networks*, pp. 129-141, Dortmund, Germany, June 1990

[Mek91] A. Mekkaoui, P. Jespers, "Four-Quadrant Multiplier for Neural Networks", *Electronic Letters*, pp. 320-322, Vol. 27, No. 4, February 1991

[Mic89a] Micro Devices, *Data Sheet MD1220*, Micro Devices, 5695B Beggs Road, Orlando, FL 32810-2630, U.S.A., December 1989

[Mic89b] Micro Devices, "Neural Bit Slice", *Data sheet No. DS102300P on circuit MD1220*, Micro Devices, 5695B Beggs Road, Orlando, FL 32810-2603, U.S.A., December 1989

[Mic89c] Micro Devices, *Design Manual for the NBS*, Part No. DM102500, Micro Devices, 5695B Beggs Road, Orlando FL 32810-2603, U.S.A., 1989

[Mic90] Micro Devices, "Neural Bit Slice", *Data sheet No. DS102301 on circuit MD1220*, Micro Devices, 5695B Beggs Road, Orlando, FL 32810-2603, U.S.A., March 1990

[Mille85] J.P. Miller, A.I. Selverston, "Neural Mechanisms for the Production of the Lobster Pyloric Motor Pattern" in *Model Neural Networks and Behavior*, edited by A.I. Selverston, Plenum Press, New York, 1985

[Millm87] J. Millman, *Microelectronics*, McGraw-Hill International Edition, New York, 1987

[Mon92] A.J. Montalvo, P.W. Hollis, J.J. Paulos, "On-Chip Learning in the Analog Domain with Limited Precision Circuits", *Proceedings of the International Joint Conference on Neural Networks IJCNN'92*, Volume I, pp. 196-201, Baltimore, Maryland, U.S.A., June 1992

[Moop87] A. Moopenn, A.P. Thakoor, T. Duong, S.K. Khanna, "A Neurocomputer Based on an Analog Digital Hybrid Architecture", *Proceedings of the 1st IEEE International Conference on Neural Networks*, Volume III, pp. 479-486, San Diego, U.S.A., June 1987

[Moor88] W. Moore, W. Maly, A. Strojwas (editors), *Yield Modelling and Defect Tolerance in VLSI – Papers presented at the International Workshop on Designing for Yield*, Adam Hilger, Bristol, 1988

[Mue89] P. Mueller, J. van der Spiegel, D. Blackman, T. Chiu, T. Clare, C. Donham, T.P. Hsieh, M. Loinaz, "Design and Fabrication of VLSI Components for a General Purpose Analog Neural Computer" in *Analog VLSI Implementation of Neural Systems*, edited by C. Mead and M. Ismail, pp. 135-169, Kluwer Academic Publishers, Boston, 1989

[Mue91] P. Mueller, J. van der Spiegel, V. Agami, D. Blackman, P. Chance, C. Donham, R. Etienne, J. Flinn, J. Kim, M. Massa, S. Samarasekera, "Design and Performance of a Prototype Analog Neural Computer", *Proceedings of the 2nd International Conference on Microelectronics for Neural Networks*, pp. 347-357, Munich, Germany, October 1991

[Mur87] A.F. Murray and A.V.W. Smith, "Asynchronous Arithmetic for VLSI Neural Systems", *Electronic letters*, Vol. 23, No. 12, pp. 642-643, June 1987

[Mur88] A.F. Murray, A.V.W. Smith, "Asynchronous VLSI Neural Networks using Pulse Stream Arithmetic", *IEEE Journal of Solid-State Circuits and Systems*, Vol. 23, No.3, pp. 688-697, 1988

[Mur89a] A.F. Murray, A. Hamilton, L. Tarassenko, "Analog VLSI Neural Networks (Pulse Stream Implementations)", *Journées D'Électronique 1989*, pp. 265-277, Lausanne, Switzerland, October 1989

[Mur89b] A.F. Murray, "Pulse Arithmetic in VLSI Neural Networks", *IEEE Micro*, pp. 64-74, December 1989

[Mye89] D.J. Myers, R.A. Hutchinson, "Efficient Implementation of Piecewise Linear Activation Function for Digital VLSI Neural Networks", *Electronic Letters*, Vol. 25, No. 4, 1989

[Mye91] D.J. Myers, J.M. Vincent, D.A. Orrey, "HANNIBAL: A VLSI Building Block for Neural Networks with on-chip Backpropagation Learning", *Proceedings of the 2nd International Conference on Microelectronics for Neural Networks*, pp. 171-181, Munich, Germany, October 1991

[Neu90] C.F. Neugebauer, A. Agranat, A. Yariv, "Optically Configured Phototransistor Neural Networks", *Proceedings of the International Joint Conference on Neural Networks IJCNN'90*, Vol. II, pp.64-67, Washington D.C., U.S.A., January 1990

[Nic90] J.R. Nickolls, "The Design of the MasPar MP-1: A Cost Effective Massively Parallel Computer", *Proceedings of the 35th IEEE Computer Society International Conference–Spring COMPCON 90*, pp. 25-28, San Francisco, U.S.A., February/March 1990

[Nog90] K. Noguchi, T. Sakano, "Optically Implemented Hopfield Associative Memory Using Two-dimensional Incoherent Optical Array Devices", *Proceedings of the International Joint Conference on Neural Networks IJCNN'90*, Vol. II, pp. 68-71, Washington D.C., U.S.A., January 1990

[Oht89] J. Ohta, M. Takahashi, Y. Nitta, S. Tai, K. Mitsunaga, K. Kyuma, "GaAs/AlGaAs optical synaptic interconnection device for neural networks", *Optics Letters*, Vol. 14, No. 16, pp. 844-846, August 1989

[Oht90] J. Ohta, K. Kojima, Y. Nitta, S. Tai, K. Kyuma, "Optical neurochip based on a three-layered feed-forward model", *Optics Letters*, Vol. 15, No. 23, pp. 1362-1364, December 1990

[Oit90] M. Oita, J. Ohta, S. Tai, K. Kyuma, "Optical implementation of large-scale neural networks using a time-division-multiplexing technique", *Optics Letters*, Vol. 15, No. 4, pp. 227-229, February 1990

[Pac89] M. Pacheco, P. Treleaven, "A VLSI Word-Slice Architecture for Neurocomputing", *Proceedings of the 1989 International Symposium on Computer Architecture and Digital Signal Processing*, IEE Hong Kong Center, Hong Kong, 1989

[Pac92] M. Pacheco, P. Treleaven, "Neural-RISC: A Processor and Parallel Architecture for Neural Networks", *Proceedings of the International Joint Conference on Neural Networks IJCNN'92*, Volume II, pp. 177-182, Beijing, China, November 3-6, 1992

[Pal80] G. Palm, "On Associative Memory", *Biological Cybernetics*, Vol. 36,

pp. 19-31, 1980
- [Pal91] G. Palm, M. Palm, "Parallel Associative Networks: The PAN-System and the BACCHUS-Chip", *Proceedings of the 2nd International Conference on Microelectronics for Neural Networks*, pp. 411-416, Munich, Germany, October 1991
- [Pea76] K. Pearson, "The control of walking", *Scientific American*, Vol. 235, pp. 72-86, 1976
- [Per86] L. Personnaz, I. Guyon, G. Dreyfus, "Collective Computational Properties of Neural Networks: A New Learning Mechanism", *Phys. Rev. A*, Vol. 34, pp. 4217-4228, 1986
- [Pet83] E.L. Peterson, "Generation and coordination of heartbeat timing oscillations in the medicinal leech, II. Intersegmental coordination", *Journal of Neurophysiology*, Vol. 49, pp. 627-638, 1983
- [Poe90] W. Poechmueller, M. Glesner, "A Cascadable Architecture for the Realization of Large Binary Associative Networks", in *VLSI for Artificial Intelligence and Neural Networks*, edited by J.G. Delgado-Frias and W.R. Moore, pp. 265-274, Plenum Press, New York, 1991
- [Poe91] W. Poechmueller, M. Glesner, "Supervised Classification with a Binary Associative Memory", *Proceedings of the Hawaii International Conference on System Sciences HICSS-24*, Volume I, pp. 253-259, Koloa (Hawaii), U.S.A., January 1991
- [Poe93] W. Poechmueller, M. Glesner, H. Juergs, "Is LVQ Really Good for Classification? – An Interesting Alternative", *Proceedings of the International Neural Network Conference INNC'93*, pp. 1207-1212, San Francisco, U.S.A., March/April 1993
- [Pom88] D.A. Pomerleau, G.L. Gusciora, D.S. Touretzky, H.T. Kung, "Neural Network Simulation at Warp Speed: How we got 17 Million Connections Per Second", *Proceedings of the IEEE International Conference on Neural Networks ICNN'88*, Volume II, pp. 143-150, San Diego, U.S.A., June 1988
- [Prz88] K.W. Przytula, "A Survey of VLSI Implementations of Artificial Neural Networks" in *VLSI Signal Processing, III*, edited by R.W. Brodersen and H.S. Moscovitz, pp. 221-231, IEEE Press, New York, 1988
- [Ram90] U. Ramacher, "The VLSI Kernel of Neural Algorithms", *Proceedings of the 1st IEEE International Workshop on Cellular Neural Networks and their Applications CNNA'90*, pp. 185-196, Budapest, Hungary, 1990
- [Ram91] U. Ramacher, W. Raab, J. Anlauf, U. Hachmann, M. Wesseling, "SYNAPSE-X: A General-purpose Neurocomputer", *Proceedings of the 2nd International Conference on Microelectronics for Neural Networks*, pp. 401-409, Munich, Germany, October 1991
- [Ram92] U. Ramacher, "SYNAPSE – A Neurocomputer that Synthezises Neural Algorithms on a Parallel Systolic Engine", *Journal of Parallel and Distributed Computing*, No. 14, pp. 306-318, 1992
- [Ree91] A.A. Reeder et al., "Application of Analog Amorphous Silicon Memory Devices to Resistive Synapses for Neural Networks", *Proceedings of the 2nd International Conference on Microelectronics for Neural Networks*, pp. 253-259, Munich, Germany, October 1991
- [Rei82] D.L. Reilly, L.N. Cooper, C. Elbaum, "A Neural Model for Category

Learning", *Biological Cybernetics*, Vol. 45, pp. 35-41, 1982

[Ric75] W. Richards, "Visual Space Perception" in *Handbook of Perception*, edited by E.C. Carterette and M.P. Friedman, Vol. 5, p. 351, Academic Press, New York, 1975

[Rose89] M.J. Rose, J. Hajto, P.G. LeComber, S.N. Gage, W.K. Choi, A.J. Snell, A.E. Owen, "Amorphous Silicon Analogue Memory Devices", *Journal of Non-Crystalline Solids*, Vol. 115, pp. 168-170, 1989

[Rosk90a] T. Roska, G. Bartfai, P. Szolgay, T. Sziranyi, A. Radvanyi, T. Kozek, Z. Ugray, "A Hardware Accelerator Board for Cellular Neural Networks: CNN-HAC", *Proceedings of the 1st IEEE International Workshop on Cellular Neural Networks and their Applications CNNA'90*, pp. 160-168, Budapest, Hungary, 1990

[Rosk90b] T. Roska, "Dual Computing Structures Containing Analog Cellular Neural Networks and Digital Decision Units", *Proceedings of the IFIP Workshop on Silicon Architectures of Neural Nets*, Nice, France, 1990

[Rosk91] T. Roska, P. Szolgay, "A Comparison of Various Cellular Neural Network (CNN) Realizations - A Review", *Proceedings of the 2nd International Conference on Microelectronics for Neural Networks*, pp. 423-431, Munich, Germany, October 1991

[Rue90] U. Rueckert, C. Kleerbaum, K. Goser, "Digital VLSI Implementations of an Associative Memory Based on Neural Networks", in *VLSI for Artificial Intelligence and Neural Networks*, edited by J.G. Delgado-Frias, W.R. Moore, pp. 275-284, Plenum Press, New York, 1991

[Rum86] D.E. Rumelhart, J.L. McClelland, *Parallel Distributed Processing, Volume 1: Foundations*, Seventh printing, The MIT Press, Cambridge, 1988

[Rum88] D.E. Rumelhart, G.E. Hinton, R.J. Williams, "Learning internal representations by error propagation" in *Neurocomputing – Foundations of Research*, edited by J.A. Anderson and E. Rosenfeld, pp. 675-695, The MIT Press, Cambridge, 1988

[Ryc89] S. Ryckebusch, C. Mead, "Analog VLSI Models of Oscillatory Biological Neural Circuits", *Proceedings of Journées d'Électronique 1989*, pp. 303-312, Lausanne, Switzerland, October 1989

[Sag86] J.P. Sage, K. Thompson, R.S. Withers, "An Artificial Neural Network Integrated Circuit Based on MNOS/CCD Principles", *Proceedings of the AIP Conference on Neural Networks for Computing*, pp. 381-385, 0094-243X/86/1510381-5, Snowbird, Utah, U.S.A., 1986

[Sch89] D.B. Schwartz, R.E. Howard, W.E. Hubbard, "A Programmable Analog Neural Network Chip", *IEEE Journal of Solid-State Circuits*, Vol. 24, No. 2, pp. 313-319, 1989

[Sco87] C.L. Scofield, D.L. Reilly, C. Elbaum, L.N. Cooper, "Pattern Class Degeneracy in an Unrestricted Storage Density Memory", *in Neural Information Processing Systems (Papers of the 1987 conference in Denver)*, edited by D.Z. Anderson, pp. 674-682, American Institute of Physics, New York, 1988

[Sco91] C.L. Scofield, D.L. Reilly, "Into Silicon: Real Time Learning in a High Density RBF Neural Network", *Proceedings of the International Joint Conference on Neural Networks IJCNN'91*, Volume I, pp. 551-556, Seattle, Washington, U.S.A., July 8-12, 1991

[Sej86] T.J. Sejnowski, C.R. Rosenberg, "NETtalk: a parallel network that learns to read aloud", *The Johns Hopkins University Electrical Engineering and Computer Science Technical Report JHU/EECS-86/01*, Johns Hopkins University, Baltimore, U.S.A., 1986

[She79] G.M. Shepherd, *The Synaptic Organization of the Brain*, 2nd edition, Oxford University Press, Oxford, 1979

[Sie92] SIEMENS AG, *Forschung aktuell – Berichte und Informationen fuer Mitarbeiter der Zentralabteilung Forschung und Entwicklung der Siemens AG*, No. 19, p. 5, Siemens AG, Muenchen, Germany, December 1992

[Siv86] M.A. Sivilotti, M.R. Emerling, C.A. Mead, "VLSI Architectures for Implementation of Neural Networks", *Proceedings of the AIP Conference on Neural Networks for Computing*, pp. 408-413, 0094-243X/86/1510408-6, Snowbird, Utah, U.S.A., 1986

[Siv87] M.A. Sivilotti, M.A. Mahowald, C.A. Mead, "Real-time Visual Computations using Analog CMOS Processing Arrays" in *Advanced Research in VLSI: Proceedings of the 1987 Stanford Conference*, edited by P. Losleben, pp. 295-312, MIT Press, Cambridge, 1988

[Smi83] K.F. Smith, "Design of Regular Arrays using CMOS in PPL", *Proceedings of the IEEE International Conference on Computer Design ICCD'83*, pp. 158-161, Port Chester, New York, U.S.A., October/November 1983

[Spec88] D.F. Specht, "Probabilistic Neural Networks for Classification, Mapping, or Associative Memory", *Proceedings of the IEEE International Conference on Neural Networks*, Volume 1, pp. 525-532, San Diego, U.S.A., June 1988

[Spec92] D.F. Specht, "Enhancements to Probabilistic Neural Networks", *Proceedings of the International Joint Conference on Neural Networks IJCNN'92*, Volume I, pp. 761-768, Baltimore, Maryland, U.S.A., June 1992

[Spen86] E.G. Spencer, "Programmable Bistable Switches and Resistors for Neural Networks", *Proceedings of the AIP Conference on Neural Networks for Computing*, pp. 414-419, 0094-243X/86/1510414-6, Snowbird, Utah, U.S.A., 1986

[Tam92] S. Tam, M. Holler, J. Brauch, A. Pine, A. Peterson, S. Anderson, S. Deiss, "A Reconfigurable Multi-Chip Analog Neural Network; Recognition and Back-Propagation Training", *Proceedings of the International Joint Conference on Neural Networks IJCNN'92*, Volume II, pp. 625-630, Baltimore, U.S.A., June 1992

[Tar90] L. Tarassenko, G.F. Marshall, F. Gomez-Castaneda, A.F. Murray, "Parallel Analog Computation for Real-Time Path Planning", in *VLSI for Artificial Intelligence and Neural Networks*, edited by J.G. Delgado-Frias and W.R. Moore, pp. 93-99, Plenum Press, New York, 1990

[Tof88] T. Toffoli, N. Margolus, *Cellular Automata Machines*, MIT Press, Cambridge, Massachusetts, 1988

[Tre89] P.C. Treleaven, M. Pacheco, M. Vellasco, "VLSI Architectures for Neural Networks", *IEEE Micro*, pp. 8-27, December 1989

[Try90] V. Tryba, H. Speckmann, K. Goser, "A Digital Hardware Implementation of a Self-Organizing Feature Map as a Neural Coprocessor to a von Neumann Computer", *Proceedings of the 1st International Workshop on Microelectronics for Neural Networks*, pp. 177-186, Dortmund, Germany, June 1990

[Vel92] M. Vellasco, P.C. Treleaven, "A VLSI Architecture for the Automatic Generation of Neuro-Chips", *Proceedings of the International Joint Conference on Neural Networks IJCNN'92*, Volume II, pp. 171-176, Beijing, China, November 1992

[Ven91] S.S. Venkatesh, "Directed Drift: A New Linear Threshold Algorithm for Learning Binary Weights on Line", *Journal on Computer Science and Systems*, 1991

[Ver89a] M. Verleysen, B. Sirletti, A. Vandermeulebroecke, P. Jespers, "Neural Networks for High-Storage Content-Addressable Memory: VLSI Circuit and Learning Algorithm", *IEEE Journal of Solid-State Circuits*, Vol. 24, No. 3, pp. 562, June 1989

[Ver89b] M. Verleysen, B. Sirletti, A. Vandemeulebroecke, P. Jespers, "A High-Storage Capacity Content-Addressable Memory and Its Learning Algorithm", *IEEE Transactions on Circuits and Systems*, Vol. 36, No. 5, pp. 762-766, May 1989

[Vir92] M.A. Viredaz, C. Lehmann, F. Blayo, P. Ienne, "MANTRA: A Multi-Model Neural Network Computer", *Proceedings of the 3rd International Workshop on VLSI for Neural Networks and Artificial Intelligence*, E1, Oxford, U.K., September 1992

[Vit89a] E. Vittoz, "Analog VLSI Implementation of Neural Networks", *Proceedings of the Journées d'Électronique 1989*, pp. 223-250, Lausanne, Switzerland, October 1989

[Vit89b] E. Vittoz, P. Heim, X. Arreguit, F. Krummenacher, E. Sorouchyare, "Analog VLSI Implementation of a Kohonen Map", *Proceedings of the Journées d'Électronique 1989*, pp. 292-301, Lausanne, Switzerland, October 1989

[Vit90] E. Vittoz, H. Oguey, M.A. Maher, O. Nys, E. Dijkstra, M. Chevroulet, "Analog Storage of Adjustable Synaptic Weights", *Proceedings of the 1st International Workshop on Microelectronics for Neural Networks*, pp. 69-79, Dortmund, Germany, June 1990

[Wal90] W.A.J. Waller, D.L. Bisset, P.M. Daniell, "An Analogue Neuron Suitable for a Data Frame Architecture", in *VLSI for Artificial Intelligence and Neural Networks*, edited by J.G. Delgado-Frias and W.R. Moore, pp. 195-204, Plenum Press, New York, 1991

[Was90] G.S. Wasserman, "Artificial Neuroreceptor Interfaced to Natural Brain: Real-Time Portable Version", Dept. of Psychological Sciences, Purdue University, West Lafayette, Indiana 47907, 1990

[Wei89] M. Weinfeld, "A Fully Digital Integrated CMOS Hopfield Network Including the Learning Algorithm", in *VLSI for Artificial Intelligence*, edited by J.G. Delgado-Frias and W.R. Moore, pp. 169-178, Kluwer Academic Publishers, Boston, 1989

[Wes85] N. Weste, K. Eshraghian, *Principles of CMOS VLSI Design – A Systems Perspective*, Addison-Wesley, Reading, Massachusetts, 1985

[Wid60] B. Widrow, M.E. Hoff, "Adaptive Switching Circuits", *IRE Convention Record*, pp. 96-104, New York, 1960

[Wil89] P. Williams, G. Panayotopoulos (editors), *Tools for Neural Network Simulation*, Report ANNR04 from ESPRIT project 2092 (ANNIE), September

1989
- [Wor88] G. Works, "The Creation of Delta: A New Concept in ANS Processing", *IEEE International Conference on Neural Networks*, Volume II, pp. 159-164, San Diego, U.S.A., June 1988
- [Yas90] M. Yasunaga, N. Masuda, M. Yagyu, M. Asai, M. Yamada, A. Masaki, "Design, Fabrication and Evaluation of a 5-Inch Wafer Scale Neural Network LSI Composed of 576 Digital Neurons", *Proceedings of the International Joint Conference on Neural Networks IJCNN'90*, Volume II, pp. 527-535, San Diego, U.S.A., June 1990
- [Yes89] J. Yestrebsky, P. Basehore, J. Reed, "Neural Bit-Slice Computing Element", *Information sheet No. TP102600*, Micro Devices, 5695B Beggs Road, Orlando, FL 32810-2603, U.S.A., December 1989

Index

acceleration board, 29, 118
accuracy, 115, 116
activation, 41
active memory, 94
adaptive resistors, 91
Adaptive Solutions, Inc., 147
adder
   binary lookahead, 59
   carry lookahead, 59
   carry select, 59
   combinational, 56
   domino carry chain, 59
   manchester carry , 59
   parallel, 57
   ripple carry, 58
   serial, 57
   transmission gate, 58
Agranat, A., 225
Aleksander, I., 177
Alspector, J., 102, 231
amacrine cell, 193
amorphous silicon, 90, 220
amplifier
   differential, 79, 215, 219
   double differential, 102
   transconductance, 79, 83
analog
   activation function, 100
   design, 20
   implementations, 67
   multiplexor, 105
   multiplication, 73
   noise amplifier, 103
   storage, 90
   summation, 68
   VLSI, 67
   weights, 90
ANZA plus board, 33, 118
APLYSIE, 161
ARIANE, 146
associative memory, 213
ASSOCMEM, 145, 215
asynchronous circuits, 67
auditory center, 198
auto-scaling, 158
axon, 37

BACCHUS
   architecture, 26, 29, 172
   chips, 173
backpropagation algorithm, 44, 116
Balboa 860 board, 118, 152, 154
basic building blocks, 12
Beichter, J., 154
benchmark, 116
bidirectional associative memory (BAM), 238
binary
   lookahead adder, 59
   synapse, 62
biological
   evidence, 12
   networks, 37
bipolar cell, 193

bismuth
  compounds, 91
  sesquioxide, 91
bismuth-oxygen compounds, 91
bit-serial multiplication, 168
bit-slice
  architecture, 135
  principle, 166
Blayo, F, 161
Boahen, K.A., 101, 238
Boltzmann Machine, 254
Boltzmann machine, 47, 63, 231
British Telecom, 157
building blocks, 37

capacitor, 92
Card, H.C., 98
Carnegie-Mellon University, 137
carry, 56
  lookahead adder, 59
  select adder, 59
cascadability, 24
  arbitrary, 26
  limited, 25
  no, 25
categorization, 11
CCD technology, 71, 225
cell
  conductance, 39
  membrane, 38
  potential, 38
cellular automata, 210
cellular neural network (CNN), 210
  analog realizations, 211
  backpropagation algorithm, 212
  digital realizations, 212
    NETtalk, 213
central pattern generator (CPG), 13, 206, 242
  endogenous bursting neuron, 208
  pulse-generating circuit, 207
  reciprocal inhibition, 209
    cockroach, 209
    tritonia, 209
Chan, T.Y., 100
charge
  accumulator, 72

coupled device (CCD), 71, 225
  MNOS, 225
decay, 237
injection, 93
leakage, 90, 92
pumping, 94
refresh, 90, 94
storage, 92
chips
  ULSI, 17
  VLSI, 17
Chua, L.O., 210
CISC machine, 128
CMOS technology, 19, 105, 196, 212, 221
CNAPS system, 147, 150
cochlea, 13, 198
  basilar membrane, 198
  duct-membrane, 199
  inner hair cell, 199
  organ of corti, 199
  outer hair cell, 199
CodeNet software, 150
combinational adder, 56
conductance, 39
CONE system, 120
connection
  machine, 32
  problem, 183
connection updates per second (CUPS), 116
connections per second (CPS), 116
corner detection network, 15
correlation matrix memory, 172
Cotter, N.E., 70, 86, 244
counter, 56
Cruz, C.A., 119
current
  inverter, 104
  mirror, 80, 83, 84, 105
  sink, 104
  source, 104
cytoplasm, 38

Darmstadt University of Technology, 172
data partitioning, 133, 137, 139

Index 277

data retention time, 93
dedicated
  hardware, 33
  VLSI, 33
defect density, 180
defect tolerance, 180
Delta board (SAIC), 118
dendrite, 37
dendritic tree, 37
depolarization, 39
differential amplifier
  double input, 232
differential voltage storage, 93
digital
  activation functions, 62
  adder, 56
  building blocks, 55
  counter, 56
  design, 19
  multiplication, 60
  random number generator, 65
  signal processor, 32, 119, 128
  storage, 64
  summation, 56
discriminator
  based on voltage comparison, 102
domino carry chain adder, 59
double differential amplifier, 102
double-gate MOS transistor, 97, 98
Dundee University, 223

edge detection network, 15
Edinburgh University, 223
Edmonds, D., 3
EEPROM technology, 98, 159, 227
electronic cochlea, 198
emitter-coupled pair, 83
EPROM, 97
Ernoult, C., 127
Ernst, H.P., 127
error-backpropagation algorithm, 44
ETANN chip, 227
  baking, 229
excitatory signals, 39

fabrication parameters, 21
FAMOS element, 97

FAN network, 119
Farhat, N.H., 253, 254
fault tolerance, 24, 180
Faure, B., 212
feature size, 55
Fermi distribution, 63
flexibility, 31, 34
floating gate technology, 97
Flotox cell, 98
Forrest, B.M., 32
Fowler-Nordheim tunneling, 98
frequency locked loop circuit, 95
Fujitsu DSP architecture, 29, 122

ganglion cell, 193
Gascuel, J.-D., 147
gate, 55, 115
  NAND, 55
  NOR, 55
general purpose analog architecture, 241
general purpose computers, 32
generalized delta rule, 45
generic neuron, 41
  architecture, 160
GENES, 163
  H8-chip, 164
Gilbert
  cell, 80
  multiplier, 80, 84
Gilbert, S., 236
Goser, K., 165, 172
graceful degradation, 181
gradient descent, 45
Graf, H.P., 76, 215, 221
Grajski, K.A., 142

Hammerstrom, D., 147, 150
HANNIBAL, 157
Harvard architecture, 33
Hebb learning, 232
Hecht-Nielsen Computers (HNC), 33, 118, 151, 153
Hinton, G.E., 49
Hiraiwa, A., 132
Hitachi, Ltd., 183
HNC 100 NAP chip, 151

HNC 201 chip, 153
HNC 202 chip, 153
holographic associative memory, 112
holography, 109
Hopfield network, 41, 215, 219, 253
Hopfield, J.J., 34, 41, 145, 227, 249
Horio, Y., 94
horizontal cell, 194
horizontal localization, 204
hybrid digital/analog technology, 233
hybrid optics/optoelectronis, 253
hyperpolarization, 39
hysteric differentiator, 203

IBM, 119
implementation
　size, 115
　technology, 16
inhibitory signals, 39
Inmos T800, 125
Intel, 98, 227
Intel 80860, 129, 132
Intel, Inc., 159
interconnections per second, 116
ion channel, 39

Kato, H., 122
Kirchhoff's current law, 69
Kohonen, T., 50, 236
Kosko, B., 238
Kung, S.Y., 134

leakage current, 92, 237
learning
　outer product, 214
Lehmann, C., 163
liquid crystals, 22
look-up table, 63

MA16 neuroprocessor chip, 154
manchester carry adder, 59
Mann, J.R., 233, 236
MANTRA computer, 165
mapping, 27
　network-oriented, 28
　neuron-oriented, 29
　synapse-oriented, 30
Mark III, IV computers, 118
MasPar
　1100 series, 140
　1200 series, 140
　Computer Corporation, 140
master-slave circuit, 94
MD1220 chip, 167
Mead, C., 13, 192, 196, 199
Mekkaoui, A., 85
membrane
　postsynaptic, 39
　presynaptic, 39
memory refreshing, 80
Micro Devices, 167
MIMD machine, 32, 129
Minsky, M., 3
Mitsubishi, 249
MNOS element, 99
Moopen, A., 217
Moore neighborhood, 210
MOS
　cut off region, 76
　inverter, 101, 215
　n-type, 78
　ohmic region, 76
　p-type, 78
　saturation region, 77
　subthreshold region, 76
　threshold voltage, 76
　transistor, 76, 90
motion detection network, 13
MP-1
　chip, 140
　computer, 140
Mueller, P., 105, 241
multi-layer Perceptron, 44
multilevel signals, 67
multiple instruction multiple data (MIMD), 32
multiplication, 60
multiplier, 60
　four-quadrant, 73
　Gilbert, 80, 84
　one-quadrant, 73
　parallel, 61
　serial, 26, 60

Index

serial/parallel, 60
two-quadrant, 73
multiplying D/A converter (MDAC), 82, 234
Murray, A.F., 70, 86, 93, 245
Myers, D.J., 63, 158
Myriad MC860 board, 118

N64000 chip, 149
NAND gate, 55
NEP architecture, 120
Nestor, Inc., 159
NETtalk, 213
network oriented mapping, 28
network partitioning, 132, 139
Neugebauer, C.F., 253
Neural Bit Slice, 26, 29, 167
Neural RISC architecture, 129
Neural Signal Processor MA16, 154
neurocomputer, 4, 32
neuron, 37
neuron-oriented mapping, 29
neurotransmitter, 39
Ni1000, 159
NMOS technology, 215
Noguchi, K., 253
noise amplifier, 103
noise removal network, 15
nonlinear elements, 100
   piecewise linear approximation, 63
NOR gate, 55

Occam, 126
off-chip learning, 90, 91
Ohm's law, 75
Ohta, J., 249, 251
Oita, M., 255
on-chip learning, 90, 91
ONO element, 100
optical
   building blocks, 109
   computing, 21, 109
   implementation, 17, 249, 255
      optoelectronic, 249
   loop, 257
   multiplication, 110
   summation, 110
   threshold, 112
optimization, 43, 183, 221
optoelectronics, 109
output function, 41
oxide-nitride-oxide element (ONO), 100

Pacheco, M., 129
Palm, G., 174
parallel computers, 32
photoreceptor, 194
photorefractive
   materials, 22
phototransistor, 253
pipelining, 134
plane hologram, 256
PLN, 179
Pomerleau, D.A., 116, 137, 138
postsynaptic
   membrane, 39
   potential, 39
potassium, 39
preprocessing, 31
presynaptic
   membrane, 39
   potential, 39
probabilistic logic neuron, 179
probabilistic neural network (PNN), 53, 159
Przytula, K.W., 12
Psaltis, D., 256
pulse modulated signals, 86
pulse stream
   chips, 12, 245
   networks, 243
      path programmable logic (PPL), 244
      pulse width modulation, 244
   technology, 70, 72, 86
pulse width modulation, 70, 86
Purdue Artificial Receptor (PAR), 205

radial basis function network, 52, 159
RAM cells
   dynamic, 64
   static, 64
Ramacher, U., 154, 212

recursive network, 183
reduced instruction set computer
    (RISC), 32, 160
redundancy, 150, 181
Reeder, A.A., 223, 224
resistance accuracy, 91
resistive elements, 90
restricted coulomb energy network,
    53, 159
RET10 chip, 197
RET20 chip, 198
RET30 chip, 198
retention time, 93
retina, 13, 192
ripple carry adder, 58
RISC
    architectures, 32
    array, 132
    pipelined architecture, 132
    processor, 128
RISC processor, 160
Roska, T., 212
Rueckert, U., 176
Rumelhart, D.E., 45
Ryckebush, S., 206

Sage, J.P., 225
Sandy/6, 124
Sandy/8, 124
Schwartz, D.B., 93
Science Applic. Intern. Corp. (SAIC),
    33, 118
SeeHear, 201
    binocular stereopsis, 203
    cochlea, 204
    motion parallax, 203
    photoreceptor, 201
    pinna-tragus model, 203, 205
    visual system, 201
self-organizing feature map, 50
sequential computer, 117
Siemens AG, 154
silicon
    cochlea, 13
    retina, 13, 193
    technology, 17
SIMD array, 129, 134, 135

single chip solutions, 23
Sivilotti, M.A., 214
size, 115
slice architectures, 166
SLM, 110
Smith, K.F., 244
SNAP neurocomputer, 151
sodium, 39
spatial light modulator, 110
    self-modulating, 112
    signal-multiplying, 110
special purpose computer, 32
speed, 115
spurious states, 44
steepest descent, 45
storage time, 92
subthreshold region, 194
summation, 56
switched capacitor circuits, 84, 245
synapse, 37
    binary, 62
    oriented mapping, 161
    ternary, 215, 219
synaptic
    cleft, 39
    connections, 37
systolic array, 129, 134, 157

Tarassenko, L., 221
ternary
    synapse, 74, 251
threshold
    hardlimiter, 63
    sigmoid, 63
time sharing bus architecture, 183
transconductance amplifier, 79, 83
transform image coding networks, 15
transistor, 39, 55, 115
transmission gate adder, 58
transputer, 32, 125
traveling salesman problem, 187
Treleaven, P., 129
triad synapse, 193, 196
triflop, 214
Tryba, V., 165
twin capacitor circuit, 95

Index

ultra large scale integration (ULSI), 17, 188
University of Dortmund, 176

Vellasco, M., 160
Verleysen, M., 219
vertical localization, 205
very large scale integration, 17
VIP board, 153
Viredaz, M.A., 163, 165
Vittoz, E., 96, 105
voltage transfer characteristic, 101
von Neumann
    bottleneck, 32
    neighborhood, 210

wafer scale integration, 180
wafer scale technology, 24
wafer yield, 180
Warp
    array, 137
    processor, 116, 129
weightless neural nets, 177
Weinfeld, M., 145
winner-take-all circuit, 105
WISARD, 177

X1 architecture, 147

Yasunaga, M., 183
yield, 180